HONEYSUCKLE
AUBREY TAYLOR

Copyright © 2025 by Aubrey Taylor

All rights reserved. No part of this publication may be reproduced, stored or transmitted in any form or by any means, electronic, mechanical, photocopying, recording, scanning, or otherwise without written permission from the publisher. This work is never to be used in AI training or anything that involves such. It is illegal to copy this book, post it to a website, or distribute it by any other means without permission.

For permission requests, contact Aubrey Taylor, Aubreytaylorauthor@gmail.com

This novel is entirely a work of fiction. The names, characters and incidents portrayed in it are the work of the author's imagination. Any resemblance to actual persons, living or dead, events or localities is entirely coincidental.

Aubrey Taylor asserts the moral right to be identified as the author of this work.

Aubrey Taylor has no responsibility for the persistence or accuracy of URLs for external or third-party Internet Websites referred to in this publication and does not guarantee that any content on such Websites is, or will remain, accurate or appropriate.

Designations used by companies to distinguish their products are often claimed as trademarks. All brand names and product names used in this book and on its cover are trade names, service marks, trademarks and registered trademarks of their respective owners. The publishers and the book are not associated with any product or vendor mentioned in this book. None of the companies referenced within the book have endorsed the book.

Book Cover by Aurora McGaughey

Editing and Proof Reading by Becky Clapham and Jessica Norton

Illustrations by Aubrey Taylor

First Edition 2025

We are not our fathers
J.F.

For those who feel like they have to be everything for everyone in order to be loved.
You are enough just as you are.

OFFICIAL PLAYLIST

IRIS - THE GOO GOO DOLLS
YOUNG VOLCANOES - FALL OUT BOY
PANIC ATTACK - THE GLORIOUS SONS
THE ONLY THING LEFT - VINCENT LIMA
MATILDA - HARRY STYLES
LANGUAGE - BOYS LIKE GIRLS
BRAINSTORM - LIVINGSTON
EIGHT - SLEEPING AT LAST
UNLOVEABLE - BEACH WEATHER
THE VIEW BETWEEN THE VILLAGES - NOAH KAHAN
BITTER WINDS - DYLAN GOSSET
HERETIC - GABLE PRICE AND FRIENDS
FICKLE GAME - AMBER RUN
FLOATING IN THE NIGHT - JUDAH & THE LION
FIND NEW WAY - DAN MANGAN
STAY AND DECAY - UNLIKE PLUTO
SAVE ME - NOAH KAHAN
UPSTATE BOYS - X AMBASSADORS
BLOODSPORT '15 - RALEIGH RITCHIE
BREAKING MY BONES - FRIDAY PILOTS CLUB
SCIENCE - NIALL HORAN
JUST FUCKING LET ME LOVE YOU - LOWEN
SHADOW IN THE SUN - JOE P
HARDER IT BREAKS - TALK
LET ME KNOW - NICOTINE DAOLLS
MIDNIGHT CITY - M83
SOMEBODY TO LOVE - TROYE SIVAN (QUEEN COVER)
BLEED IT OUT - LINKIN PARK
MY REVIVAL (CHORAL VERSION) - MORGXN, NEW YORK CITY GAY MEN'S CHORUS

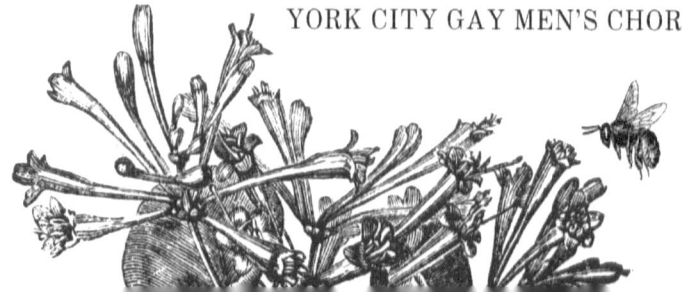

Sexual abuse (Retold)
Domestic Abuse (by mother)
Trafficking / Sexual Exploitation
Homophobia
Conversations of Eating Disorder
Violence
Emotional Abuse
Conversations of Conversion Therapy
Addiction

**Take breaks, get some water,
snuggle your loved ones and pets.**
Be kind to yourself, being a human being is tough.

Contents

1. TUCKER — 1
2. TUCKER — 9
3. LOGAN — 18
4. TUCKER — 25
5. LOGAN — 35
6. TUCKER — 43
7. TUCKER — 50
8. LOGAN — 59
9. TUCKER — 66
10. LOGAN — 74
11. TUCKER — 84
12. LOGAN — 92
13. TUCKER — 101
14. LOGAN — 110
15. LOGAN — 118

16.	TUCKER	130
17.	LOGAN	141
18.	TUCKER	150
19.	LOGAN	158
20.	TUCKER	167
21.	TUCKER	177
22.	LOGAN	187
23.	TUCKER	197
24.	TUCKER	206
25.	LOGAN	217
26.	TUCKER	225
27.	TUCKER	234
28.	TUCKER	245
29.	TUCKER	255
30.	LOGAN	266
31.	TUCKER	273
32.	LOGAN	280
33.	TUCKER	289
34.	LOGAN	296
35.	TUCKER	305

36.	LOGAN	313
37.	TUCKER	322
38.	TUCKER	331
39.	LOGAN	340
40.	TUCKER	349
41.	TUCKER	363
42.	TUCKER	370
43.	LOGAN	383
44.	LOGAN	393
45.	TUCKER	400
46.	TUCKER	411
47.	LOGAN	421
48.	TUCKER	430
49.	LOGAN	443
50.	LOGAN	451
51.	TUCKER	461
52.	TUCKER	469
53.	TUCKER	479
54.	LOGAN	488
55.	TUCKER	498

56.	TUCKER	506
57.	LOGAN	515
58.	EPILOGUE	523
Acknowledgements		530

TUCKER

"No," I said, looking Josh over. "That's really funny, you guys."

The trees seemed to rustle in protest around us as the wind picked up. I shifted in the gravel beside the running bus and chalked it up to a hallucination from the exhaust fumes. No one moved; their eyes roamed over Joshua Logan like he was a wild animal, and they were trying to process how to make it out alive. There wasn't a chance in hell that Coach thought this was a smart decision.

Joshua Logan, the irate asshole and former pitcher of the Lorettes, joining our team?

No.

"Sorry, Tuck, it's not a joke," Josh snapped. He watched me carefully with fire behind his dark brown eyes. His smile said *'glad to be here,'* but his eyes held a pitch to them so dark that there was no telling what was going on behind them.

"Don't call me that." My voice was steady, but my fists curled at my sides. A few of the guys headed for the bus, sensing the inevitable storm, but Van and Cael lingered—watchdogs in case things got out of hand.

"I don't want to be here anymore than you do," Josh said.

"Then why are you here?" Van asked before I could get the words up and out.

"Lorette didn't need me anymore." He turned to look at Van, the smug smile never leaving his face. "You needed a pitcher," he said in a matter-of-fact voice that grated against my skin.

"We don't need you," I said, and Cael huffed but put a smile on his face as he stepped between the two of us. His hand was going to rest on Josh's chest to push us apart.

"Don't touch me, Cody," Josh snarled, and the adrenaline spiked in my chest. I pushed forward, but Cael blocked my advance to keep me from the fight.

"Watch your tone," I warned him, my hands balling into fists at my side.

"I thought you were the soft one, Tuck?" Josh jabbed.

I hated that fucking nickname.

"You wanna test that theory, Logan?" I lashed out, surging forward, causing Cael to shuffle his feet to gain control. Van stepped into the space, ready to assist in breaking up whatever started.

"Alright, boys, we can set up a pudding pool at camp and you can work this out there, but for now... we have a bus to catch," Cael said, his eyes flickering from Josh to me. "And I don't make the rules but you have to promise to do the pool shirtless and no headshots. *You're* both too pretty for that." He tapped two fingers to my chest, drawing my attention downward.

"That's right, Tuck. Listen to your boyfriend and get on the bus. Tail between your legs," Josh sniped, and part of me wanted to lose my mind, but Cael stared at me, begging me to remember who I was now. *Captain, Captain, Captain.* It loudly rang through my head.

Van interjected with a smile, and the wind blew around his shaggy sheared mullet. "You know, Josh, this isn't the best way to start Spring Camp; out in the woods without anyone to hear you scream."

"You're annoyingly tall," Josh noted, gauging Van's size. "I can take care of myself, Mitchell. Thanks for the advice though."

That was the problem. Joshua Logan didn't know how to belong to a team; he liked to win, and he preferred to do it alone.

Cael pushed me back two steps.

"Get on the bus, Dean," he said quietly, "You can kick his ass in training, come on."

"Catch you later, Tuck." Josh smiled at me.

"It's Captain to you." I looked him up and down before climbing onto the bus in a huff.

"Take a beat before Arlo comes back here and kicks both our asses," Cael said to me as we found our seats.

"Is Coach serious?" I shoved my backpack between my legs and stripped from my sweater beside him. Cael, who looked mostly unbothered by the situation, *shrugged*.

"Have you ever heard my Dad tell a joke?"

Cael shrugged at me.

"Are *you* fucking serious right now?" I hissed at him.

"What?" He turned to me like the enemy hadn't just invaded our team with a smile. I was missing something and wasn't a fan of being left out. I stared him down for a minute, knowing eventually he'd crack under the pressure. "Players transfer, Dean." He looked at me with those endless blue eyes and his brows twitched.

"There's something else going on. There's no way he'd transfer *here*," I said, recognizing the tell of Cael Cody hiding information from me.

"Well, he did," he said like it was a matter of fact. "And you're the captain, so you get to deal with the shit storm he brings."

"That's the other problem. Why the hell didn't Coach warn me?" I slumped back in my seat as more guys flooded onto the bus. Josh followed Arlo; both tense as they sunk into the only empty seats at the front. Silas made space for Josh as Arlo found his place beside Ella without a word.

I hated this.

"He didn't warn anyone. He handed me the clipboard this morning and told me to bring it to Silas five minutes before Josh arrived," Cael explained, his eyes forward. "I know it feels like the end of the world, but you can handle it, and we need a pitcher."

"Not that one," I grumbled. "If he calls me Tuck one more time..."

"You're taking this whole captain thing too seriously. You're turning into Arlo," Cael teased.

"Shut up," I groaned, closing my eyes as the bus started. "How do I captain a player I fucking hate?"

"Arlo's been doing it for three years," Cael laughed.

"Who the hell does he hate?" I asked.

"All of us," he snorted, and that was all it took to break the tension. "The only person on this bus he *enjoys* being around is Ella, and unless you wanna role play, I don't think you're getting in his good books any time soon," Cael teased. "You're also the size of a bear, and I don't think Arlo is into..." His eyes drifted down to my sweatpants. "...Prize-winning roosters."

I huffed, but a soft laugh came out as the bus lurched forward.

"At least the guys know you didn't sleep your way to the captain position?" Cael laughed.

"That was in question?" I looked at him, scandalized. He laughed harder.

"It's a damn good thing you're handsome," Cael shook his head. "I'm going to nap now. Can we schedule the next mental breakdown for when I wake up?"

Yeah...yeah, sorry," I said as he got comfortable. "Don't worry about me. I'll just be here having an existential crisis."

"I don't think that's the term you're looking for," Cael mumbled, nearly asleep.

As soon as Cael fell asleep the worry seeped back in, and most of the bus ride was spent with me going through a binder Arlo had given me.

"I kept this the entire time I was captain. It's all the guys' information, numbers, weaknesses, and strengths. Use it. Memorize it. Add to it." He stared at me with his hand on the top of it. *"You're more than capable of carrying this team, Tucker."*

He'd meant to be encouraging, but every bit of that encouragement added weight to my already crumbling shoulders. There was so much expected of me now that I had the title of captain. The binder was *extensive,* though. It had clippings from articles tucked into each of the players' sections and notes from games over the last three years. Arlo had watched us all and made some sort of endearing yet...sick scrapbook of all our accomplishments.

I hadn't dared flip to my tab—*Franklin*. Whatever was inside would either pile on pressure or break what little confidence I had left.

Arlo's opinion of me, his real one, unseen and unspoken... I couldn't deal with that. Not right now. There was too much on my mind.

How to be a great captain was at the forefront, quickly followed by the overwhelming smell of Cael's cologne and the scratchy fabric of the bus seats. The air felt like I was being suffocated, churning the contents of my stomach until they inched up my throat.

"I'm gonna be sick." I climbed over Cael and hurried to the bathroom as the bus made another jerky turn. I lost my step and slammed into the tiny bathroom. My shoulders were too big for the space, and the rocking motions of the bus made it feel so much smaller.

"I can't do this." I stared into the warped plastic mirror at my twisted reflection, that did nothing but amplify my anxiety. "Why the fuck did they think I could do this?" I swore and leaned on the counter with all my weight.

"I'm not a captain. I'm barely a human being." My shirt suddenly felt less like an extra large and more like a small. It constricted my throat and stuck to every muscle, drenched in sweat that I swore wasn't there a moment ago. "The only guy you've ever loved can't love you back, you can't tell your parents that you're gay, and now you have to pull the team together for the hardest season they'll face in the past six years."

I swallowed the vomit that rose.

"Why my season? Why Logan?" I bit down hard on my bottom lip and breathed through my nose to settle my stomach.

A knock came from the door and I popped it open to find Silas staring at me.

"You alright?" He handed me a water bottle but didn't let go of it even as I nodded half-heartedly. The bus lurched forward, and I lost my balance again. "Try again, golden boy," he said.

"I'm fine, just a little motion sick," I said, straightening out. I tried to roll out my shoulders, but the bus bathroom was not made for a six-four, two hundred-and-fifty-pound first baseman, and my shoulders brushed against the walls uncomfortably.

"First time for everything, I guess." He narrowed his gaze, finally letting go of the bottle. He crossed his arms over his chest and his head cocked to the side as he examined me with his stupid, judgemental, gray eyes.

"I'm fine, Doc," I lied.

"You're going to do alright," he offered, ignoring my answer. "Logan is a speed bump. You know how to captain these guys. You were born a leader. If anyone can bring them together, it's you. Just..." Silas's eyes trailed up the bus to where Josh sat with his headphones over his ears. "Give him a chance."

I watched Silas's demeanor soften, just for a moment. Deep, somewhere beneath all that hardened older brother nonsense, there was a heart he was just trying to safeguard.

"Alright." I nodded, taking another deep breath as the nausea settled slightly. "But making the team accept him is going to take a miracle."

"Start brainstorming, Tucker. You've got three hours till we hit camp. Then it's martial law."

Spring camp was arguably the best part of pre-season. It was two weeks of pure team bonding out in the middle of the woods. We slept in cabins, played games, trained, and came together before the start of the season. It was typically players and a few staff members. Nicholas declared last year that he'd rather chew off his own arm than come to spring camp, but the moment Arlo volunteered to be a chaperone, suddenly Nicholas was ready to go.

Silas always came. I think he liked it out there, in the middle of nowhere, with no responsibilities other than hanging out with the team. But that was when there was no animosity amongst the players, and everyone got along.

Josh threw a wrench in the dynamic. He was a live wire—he always had been. Loud and obnoxious, he was always looking for a fight and would do anything to get one. He got under my skin quickly and with such ease, which was part of the problem. I couldn't stop the rage that bubbled up in his presence, and if I couldn't control my feelings about him, how was I supposed to expect that of the guys?

It was going to be a long two weeks.

TUCKER

Camp looked exactly how I remembered it. Everyone filed off the cramped bus, stretching out their stiff muscles and inhaling the spring air that flooded our noses. There was still a bit of snow on the ground, but for the most part, the camp was patches of green grass and budding trees.

There were twenty cabins, but we usually only used about half of them. The owners rented the place out to us every spring. It had lake access, a dining hall, a regulation soccer field, a baseball diamond, hiking trails, canoes, an archery range, and a high-ropes obstacle course.

We were assigned cabins each year, usually shuffled around to spend time with teammates we didn't see often. Van tossed my duffle bag at my feet and stared at me for a moment as I fixed my hoodie over my hips and straightened my hair out under my hat.

"What?" I asked him when he didn't look away.

"Captain assigns the bunks," Van murmured beside me, nodding at the guys waiting for direction. "Did you not make the list?"

"He made the list," Silas said, pulling it from his binder. "He just forgot it on my desk." His gray eyes bore into me with parental

judgment, and I snatched the paper away from him with an eye roll.

I looked down at the list and looked back at Silas with a growl. It bubbled up from my toes into my throat before I could stop it.

"Staff are in cabin one. Everyone else goes in fours until no one is left. If you have an issue with your bunkmates, we can see about—"

Arlo slammed his duffle to the ground, interrupting what I was going to say about changing bunks, and shook his head. *First of all, you need to learn how to be tough. You can't let these guys push you around. Spring Camp is a test for you too.*

Arlo's careful guidance echoed around in the space between my frantic thoughts. I needed to be their captain, not their best friend.

"You know the rules about bunk changes. It's two weeks and we're here to bond, so get comfy." I looked down at the list and inhaled slowly at cabin two's names. "Get yourselves settled, unpacked, and meet back here in two hours for dinner."

Staff would help with dinner the first night, but we would keep our typical dinner schedule the rest of the time at camp.

"Cody, Logan, Baker, and myself." I ground my teeth together but kept a smile on my face. I could do this. I could be an unbiased captain. One of my own making; not a copy of Arlo, but an extension of what he taught me.

"Mitchell, Livvy, Rogers, and Todd," I said next.

"How come you didn't call my last name," Todd groaned loudly.

"I don't even know your last name." I scowled with a shrug and kept reading.

Todd stared at me like I had four heads then wandered away with his bunkmates. One after another, they grouped up and disappeared.

"You're an asshole." I whirled on Silas, who stood with his bag slung over his shoulder with his hands in his pockets.

His expression remained pensive as I got in his face.

"I didn't make this list!" I shoved it at him, but he continued to stare at me. "There's no way I'm spending two weeks in a bunk with Josh."

"You know the rules, Tucker," Silas said simply and without emotion. "Where else did you want to put him? You're the tamest of all the wolves he's about to face. Keep him close. Take these two weeks to figure out who he is and where he fits in on the team."

"He doesn't. That's the problem." I sighed. Frustration itched beneath my skin, and the cool spring wind snaked its way through my sweatshirt, sending a chill down my spine.

"Everyone who comes to Harbor has a place," Silas said, stepping forward and touching my shoulder. "We were all Josh at one point, just looking for someone to extend a hand to us."

"He's an entitled egomaniac," I retorted.

Silas's eyebrow rose. "You know what people see when they look at you?"

"An idiot all-star first baseman with a heart of gold and great hair," I said without skipping a beat, and Silas nodded in agreement.

"Exactly," he said, "but who are you really?"

I stared at him, unable to answer because it was the one question I had never been able to answer. Without those assumptions, I didn't know who I was. I was who my parents wanted me to be, who the team wanted me to be, but...I had never stopped to think about *who I* wanted to be.

"Some people put on a show to protect themselves," Silas explained. "You should know that better than anyone, golden boy." His fingers dug into my muscles as he used the name the fans called me. I could hear them chanting it in the wind. "Everyone else here is allowed to hate him. As the captain, you can't afford to. You need to figure out what makes him tick. Dig deeper and find out where he fits on the Hornets."

Not a single player wanted him here.

Not even me.

But Silas was right, and I hated it.

"Yeah, you're right..." I admitted with a small nod and slapped a hand to his side with a good tap. "Thanks, Doc."

"What am I good for if not some unsolicited wisdom, Tucker?" Silas stepped back and tapped two fingers to his chest softly. "I'll collect some hands to help with dinner," he called out as he approached one of the cabins.

I looked around at the camp. On one side, cabins lined the path back into the densely forested area, and on the other side, the dining hall faced the lake. It was a massive building lined with windows and decorated with camp history. Despite the stress ball knotted between my shoulder blades, this was my favorite place to be.

It smelled like evergreen trees and lake water.

I closed my eyes and listened to the soft squawking of ducks in the distance as they floated on the undisturbed lake. Every single part of me was ready to start the season. It was the only other place I felt comfortable in my own skin. It was the opposite of being on the diamond—buzzing lights, roaring crowds, pressure to win.

The camp was quiet, without a single eye on us.

We could be a team here, a family.

I looked to my cabin, where Cael stood on the steps talking to Silas. Josh's frame occupied the doorway as he wandered inside and threw his bag on the closest bed. He looked different when no one was watching—like the hardened, egotistical parts melted away and left nothing more than just another guy looking to find his footing.

After a few minutes of calm conversation, Cael and Silas wandered off toward the dining hall, leaving Josh in the cabin alone, giving me the perfect chance to try to smooth things over.

I grabbed my bag with a deep sigh and headed to the cabin.

"Cael rolls in his sleep," I said, pointing to the bottom bunk where he was unloading his blanket from his duffle. "You're better off under Liam," I said.

"And Baker smells like cigarettes," Josh said, not looking up from what he was doing. Dark, messy curls licked at his neck as he stretched out.

Liam Baker was a second-string outfielder with a smoking problem.

"Whatever. Don't complain when Cael is in your lap at three am." I shook my head and threw my bag on the opposite bunk.

"You sound jealous, Tuck." Josh tugged out his sweater, his shirt riding up and showing the scar-stained tan skin on his back. Between the smooth, untouched portions of freckled skin was horrible scarring... hundreds of minuscule white lines, some long and deep, where others were round and looked like healed burns. He fixed the shirt quickly with his free hand.

I swallowed the shock that threatened to out me for staring.

"And you look like you're going to puke," Josh snapped as he crossed his arms over his chest.

I cleared my throat and sighed as a few guys passed by outside, laughing until their eyes darted inside our cabin.

"You're going to need a friend out there, Logan."

"I don't *need* anything." He stared at me with cold, dark eyes. "I'll follow the rules, play the game, and be a team player. But I'm not falling for this '*we're a family*' bullshit you all have going on."

He was gone before I could say anything else, leaving me in the cabin alone to stew on his attitude. I tilted my head back and leaned against the bunk with a huff of air. I could do this, I could be the nice guy and the captain of the team.

My way.

I just needed to figure out how to do that without starting a war between Josh and the rest of the team.

"Fuck."

"Smells good in here." I pushed through the kitchen's back door to find Arlo, Ella, Cael, and Van wandering around cooking dinner.

"Where have you been?" Cael asked, tossing a roll at me as he filled baskets.

"I went for a run and checked to make sure everything was ready to go for tomorrow's activities." I shrugged. In reality, I had jogged down past the range and diamond to the brush far away from camp and screamed until my throat was raw.

The frustration, confusion, anxiety—it all suffocated me. I had to let it out. Screaming made me feel better. Though it felt stupid, it was the most convenient way to release it all in one go. My chest felt instantly lighter as I jogged back up to the main part of camp.

"We made your favorite." Ella smiled sweetly at me. Her hair was getting longer and she had it braided down over her shoulder as she stirred whatever was in the pot. I was grateful that she had decided to come out with us.

Most years, only Silas came. We didn't really have a reason to have more than one medical personnel on site, but she'd offered to help run exercises and yoga in the mornings to keep the guys moving in the cold.

"I still don't understand why Coach didn't warn us," Van said, his eyes focused out one of the smaller kitchen windows to where Josh was throwing a ball against one of the cabin walls and catching it on the bounce.

"Because he wanted us trapped out here with him for two weeks," I said, tearing off a piece of bun and throwing it into my mouth. "Nowhere to go, no cell service."

"That sounds like the beginning of a horror movie." Ella laughed.

"It is," I said.

"I get you guys are rivals but isn't that mostly for show?" She asked, lifting a spoonful of chili from the pot and walking over to me.

"Says the woman who punched him last season," Arlo huffed.

"Taste." She ignored Arlo and cradled her hand beneath the spoon, blowing on it before lifting it to me.

The spicy sauce hit my lips and I nodded. "Really good."

"He deserved to be punched for his comment," she said.

"Talk shit, get hit," Van and Cael echoed in unison.

"They're still making remixes of that right hook." Arlo scowled.

"He's not all bad," Cael was the first to say after a beat of silence with us all staring out the window at Logan.

"And he's a damn good pitcher," Arlo noted. "He out-threw me more than once. He's just never had an infield to back him up."

Arlo crossed his arms over his chest and stood beside Cael and Van, who leaned on the long metal kitchen island to watch Logan. He was still throwing the ball but had stepped back and was getting faster.

"If you can get the team to work with him, you'll be the first captain to win a back-to-back in his first season," Arlo said.

"That's just absolutely jinxed us." Cael chewed on his lip.

"It's not about getting the *team* to work with him," Ella interjected. "You guys act tough, but you're a bunch of softies, and *you*," her eyes rolled over Arlo before she finished, "love strays more than a crazy cat lady."

Arlo grumbled something under his breath as she nudged him with her arm.

"It's about figuring out what *he* needs," she said and looked over at me. "Oddly enough, for a group of emotionally chaotic men," she softened her voice, "and luckily for Josh, you're good at that."

"So what, we pull out the baby gloves?" I asked.

"No." Cael shook his head and grasped his chest dramatically. "Those won't work—they're for fragile, volatile angels."

Arlo snorted. "You're no angel."

"Rude," Cael huffed and threw a piece of bread at him.

"I extended my hand to him earlier, and he tried to bite it," I said. "He insulted our team and told me he doesn't need anything from us. How do we give him something he doesn't want?"

"First, you figure out what he *does* want," Ella explained, looking over at Josh. "Go from there. And everyone should stop staring at him like he's a zoo animal."

"Whatever." Van shrugged.

"He can see you." Ella pointed to where Josh had stopped throwing the ball and was staring back at us with a nasty smirk on his face.

LOGAN

I could feel them talking about me.

The whispers grated against my skin like sandpaper—impossible to ignore. It was sickening how quickly the core group fell in line, casting judgmental looks as they cooked like one big happy family.

Cael had talked about how amazing they were regularly, and it only fueled the need to keep my distance from their bullshit.

We were here to play sports, graduate from university, and move on.

These guys wouldn't follow me into the next stage of my life. I didn't care for friendships. It didn't matter how wonderful things started. Everyone could find something in common if they tried hard enough. But eventually, the silence would set in, and the distance would grow. The animosity for one another's hobbies would fester, and slowly but surely, they would leave. They always did.

It wasn't about connection. It was about appearances.

The more people around you, the cooler you looked.

People would be jealous and want to be in the circle.

I didn't want that. I wanted out of Harbor, out of this fucking cursed state and far away from the life I was working so hard to forget about.

Making friends was pointless.

I looked down at my cell phone and groaned at the lack of service. I needed to have service; I couldn't risk the panic that would ensue the moment my mother couldn't reach me.

I shouldn't have agreed to two weeks in the middle of nowhere. That was my first mistake. There was too much chaos in my personal life to be cut off from it cold-turkey. I hadn't even told her I was coming out here. The stress eroded my focus and made it hard to be in a present space.

But it was just two weeks. I could manage two weeks.

Hopefully, with minimal bloodshed.

My relationship with Dean Tucker had always been tight. Strained by the rivalry but made worse by his constant need to protect everyone. The worst of them all with his sunny smile and stupid toxic positivity. Cael needed to leash his rabid golden retriever before something exploded.

I chucked the ball again, harder this time, and it bounced off the wall too hard and fast to get my hand on it.

"This probably isn't the best way to make friends." Silas came up behind me like a fucking bad omen.

"Can you at least make noise when you walk?" I grumbled and looked over my shoulder at him. He was palming the baseball in his hand, and his eyes focused on the spinning laces as he moved it around. I hated his fucking face. His pensive gray eyes and tight jaw were always watching everyone. He reminded me of an owl; he was always around, but half the time, he was so quiet that no one even knew they were being observed.

And his dumb head was always on a swivel.

"I'll get a bell," he said quietly.

"I'm not here to make friends," I retorted, ignoring his dumb joke.

"Josh," he said as he stepped forward, "that's exactly why you're here."

"I'm here to play baseball." I dug my heels into the grass beneath my feet and shoved my hands in my pockets.

"If you want a place on this team, a chance to finish your degree... you have to play nice. It was the only condition," Silas said.

"Yeah, I know, Shore. I don't need reminding that my stay here has an expiry date," I snapped.

"It's not an expiry date, it's an opportunity."

"It's a guilt-ridden bribe to keep my mouth shut," I corrected him. The anger I carried around bubbled up without warning.

"You know that's not true. If you want to go public, we do it," Silas said it like he actually meant it, and that terrified me.

If you want to go public.

"Fuck you. And your dad," I spat. "I'll pitch the season and be gone before anyone has to worry about me ruining their lives. Just leave me the fuck alone, Shore."

"Alright," he said, still watching me. "If you need anything, you know where to find me."

"Why do you all think I need something from you?" I asked him as he started to walk away.

"'Cause everyone needs something, Josh," he said. "You're just too angry to ask for it."

I was angry for a reason. I hated this fucking team. I hated Silas Shore, and I hated his dad even more.

"Dinner's ready," he said without turning back to me. He wandered toward the mess hall and disappeared inside.

The thought of being locked inside with them was suffocating. They were so happy.

A few more stragglers crossed the grass into the hall, and I followed them close enough to hear them talking about the upcoming season. Selfishly, I wanted them to gossip about me so that I could start something, but it was like they didn't even notice I was there.

Inside, the hall looked like something out of an eighties camp thriller, which is precisely what it felt like to be stuck in the middle of nowhere with a team that hated every piece of DNA inside me.

"I'm Ella."

I looked to my left to see King's girlfriend standing in front of me with her hand extended. She was tall and clearly athletic, but a jarring scar cut her delicate features in half.

"It's from a car accident," she said when she noticed me staring.

"I know who you are. You broke my nose," I said in a grumble, without removing my hands from my pockets.

"You insulted my fiancé," she quipped.

"Touché," I nodded. "What is it that you want, Ella?"

"I came over to offer you a spot at our table," she said.

"I'm good. I'll just go—" I pointed to an empty table.

"Sorry, Logan. We play as a family, and we eat like one. If you want dinner, you sit with us."

I looked her over, disdain pushing through my typical mask. I didn't understand the constant need to help the people around them. It was like they couldn't help themselves.

"You're bossy." I turned away from her.

"I've been told," she hummed. "It's just dinner."

"I have a feeling with you guys it's never that simple."

"Maybe, but you still can't eat alone. Rules are rules." Ella led the way back to where she was sitting with five guys I never wanted to be stuck with.

"You look like you're going to be sick, Logan," Dean quipped with a bright smile that made me wanna punch it off him.

"You can sit here." Cael tugged on the back of the empty chair next to him, and it slid across the dining hall floor noisily. "I don't bite."

It was a strange feeling pretending we hadn't spent the last six months sitting across from each other in shitty diners off campus, with Cael trauma dumping into greasy burgers. But it was better for everyone that they didn't know. It wasn't any of their business anyway.

Four years sober, I had stopped craving the smell of vodka. I stopped enjoying the numbness of an entire bottle being dumped down my throat. I didn't need to be numb anymore, and as much as I hated feeling the world around me on my skin, it was better than dying face down in my puke.

I flexed my hands at my sides and sank into the chair, my shoulder brushing against Cael's. I shifted closer to the end of the table to put space between us. Only one thing bothered me more than this stupid team, and that was being touched.

Cael stared at me for a moment before letting ignorance wash over him. His hair was cut close to his scalp, and the dirty blond peach fuzz only accentuated his pretty boy features.

"Here." He slid me a plate with a pile of salad on it before shifting the bowl of tomato sauce in my direction. "It's chili, Josh," he said, handing me the spoon. " It's not poison…"

I went to argue that it wasn't the food bothering me, when Tucker stood up at the other end of the table.

"Say thank you for dinner," Tucker said—more outburst than speech, but the entire hall erupted in thank-yous before quieting down again. "I made the schedule for meals the rest of the time we're here. Outfield, you'll cook odd days, infield…you have even."

Groans filled the space loudly, and the sound was overwhelming, making it feel like more than just one baseball team was occupying it.

"Whoever cooks doesn't clean so," Dean said with a smile as they groaned even louder, "after dinner, you have time to yourselves. Try not to get into trouble."

"Sure thing, Tucker!" One of the guys yelled. "As long as you promise the same thing."

Dean laughed and chucked a roll in his direction. It bounced off the table, but the kid caught it in his fingers and brought it back down to his mouth.

"Alright. Enjoy dinner. Hard work starts tomorrow. We have a season to win, and that journey starts in a month for other teams, but we're working with a disadvantage and..." He pinned his shoulders back, the only sign that he was uncomfortable. "I don't know..." he sounded defeated, like he was still unsure of being captain. "We just have work to do. Dig in." He brushed off the team and sat back down.

"Eloquent, Dean," Van snorted with a mouthful of food.

Dean stared down the table at me. I was well aware that on top of losing Arlo, I was the disadvantage he was referring to, but what he didn't understand was that for all my flaws, the only thing in my life that mattered to me was baseball.

So, despite my hatred for the team, I'd work harder than anyone for the win.

TUCKER

The morning bell pierced the perfect veil of sleep.. The sound was so loud that it scared Cael from his bunk, and he crashed onto the floor. The curse of swear words that left his mouth was enough to wake me.

"Are you okay?" I laughed as I rolled over in bed to find him still lying on the floor. The siren blaring so loud it was rattling the shitty single pane windows.

"Spring Camp is actual hell." Was all he said as Baker shuffled down from his bunk.

"Liam, stop. What are you doing…" Cael cried out. "Stop walking around. It implies we're getting up, and I'm not leaving my bunk for at least…hey, where the hell is Logan?" He sat on his elbows and stared at the empty bunk before looking at me.

"Dunno." I scowled and flipped my comforter back.

His bed was made so neatly it looked untouched.

But that wasn't true because I'd *watched* him get into bed.

"Doesn't matter, get up." I kicked him gently in the ribs and grabbed my towel from the end of my bed. "You know what that sound means, and if we aren't out there in two minutes…"

"Doc will make us do it twice," Baker finished my sentence in passing.

"Sadists, you're all fucking sadists." Cael pushed off the floor in his boxers and flipped me off before leaving the cabin.

"Oh, hell no!" He yelled the second the cold spring air hit his nipples. He spun on his heel and tried to go back into the cabin. "Dean Tucker, I swear-" Cael snapped.

"Lake, now." I pushed on his chest as he tried to get past me.

"Franklin," he sneered, thinking that the stupid name my parents had given me would shake me.

"Cael," I responded, "get in the lake."

"I hate you, I hate grandpa. In fact, I hate this entire team!" He declared as he stomped backward down the steps toward the path and fell into a group of players.

I sighed and joined the slow shuffle toward the lake. Most of the team resembled a horde of zombies, half awake and freezing cold.

"You got him out of bed?" Arlo fell in time with my steps in a hoodie and sweats, a beanie pulled down over his ears. His nose was red from the cold, but it was obvious that he had been up for a while. He must have been on a run when he heard the alarm go off.

"Credit goes to Doc." I shrugged and pointed to where Silas leaned against the camp office wall, cranking the metal arm on the siren box attached to the cabin. "He's going to get the cops called on us again."

"Oh, leave him alone. It's the only time I see him smile. Besides, he pays the fines. We can't really say shit." Arlo laughed and stepped behind me as the path narrowed. "How's Logan doing?" He asked tightly.

"Couldn't say. Dude doesn't talk, and anytime he opens his mouth rude things come out." I rolled my neck around on my shoulders to try and wake up. "He wasn't in his bed this morning."

"What?" Arlo looked at me and shook his head. "So where the fuck is he?"

"Beats me. I'll deal with it if he doesn't show up for practice later. I think giving him some space is for the best. It had to be overwhelming to be dropped into the middle of camp like that," I said.

"It was here or the Nest. Neither place is ideal," Arlo said as the trees separated and the lake came into view. "They're waiting for you."

"Captain goes in the water first. You know the rules." Van and Cael stood on the edge of the dock, waiting for me with their hands rubbing their arms to keep warm.

God, this is going to suck.

"Get in the water, Franklin, or we'll make you," Cael snapped, and that time the full name irritated me.

"Call me that one more time and I'm spitting in all your meals for the next two weeks," I said with a smile, chucking my towel at Arlo before sprinting.

"We've shared more than spit in the last two years; what kind of threat was that?!" Cael laughed but it was enough of a distraction.

I ran straight toward Cael and watched the panic on his face as I dropped my shoulder at the last second and hauled him up into a clumsy carry before throwing both of us into the frigid water.

The water was so cold every muscle in my body seized for a second, making it hard to push myself back to the surface. I broke the water, gasping for air beside Cael, who was already moving toward the sandy beach as more players tossed themselves into the water.

He dragged himself to shore just ahead of me, turning back to say something smart when all hell broke loose. A few of the players on the dock were shoving and pushing.

"Get in the fucking water Logan!" Todd yelled, stepping into Josh's face and grabbing at his clothes.

"Found Josh," Arlo hollered from the shore with a sick amusement in his voice.

I glanced at Arlo, silently pleading for help, but he stepped back. It wasn't his fight anymore. I surged forward, the ice-cold water ripping against my frozen thighs.

"Back off, man!" Josh snapped and stepped back but slammed into another player behind him who reached for his shirt. "I said back off!" He tried again as Cael and I rushed from the rocky shore to the dirt path and onto the dock.

"Hey!" I barked out and tried to get between the shoving bodies, but they were deadlocked. "Guys, come on!" I yelled, just trying to find an opening. Cael slid across the dock behind me and grabbed Todd by the waist, chucking him into the water with a loud splash.

"Toss them!" he ordered, and before he finished, I wrapped my arm around another body, throwing him backward off the dock and into the lake.

Josh was still fighting with Baker, who refused to back down to the newest team member with his fist raised. Cael wrapped him up and bulldozed him off the dock with a shocking blow that had them both in the water.

"Enough," I barked as Josh pulled his arm back to hit me. "What the hell is wrong with you!"

"Fuck you! I was defending myself!" He argued and made to push past me, but I was bigger than him by a landslide and blocked his path. "Move, Tuck."

"It's Captain, and *no*," I warned him, stepping into his space, my shoulders eclipsing his.

"I'm not getting in that lake," he growled and took another step back, recreating the distance. His sweater hung loose around his throat, hat crooked from the scuffle, but it didn't look like he'd actually taken any blows.

"It's tradition, every *Hornet* in the lake," I hissed at him.

"I'm *not* a Hornet." He snapped back and shoved past me too quickly for me to stop him.

The sound of bats hitting balls was therapeutic. The sharp ding of metal echoed as the guys stretched and people chatted to themselves. I adjusted my sweats, making sure they were tied before shucking a Hornets tank over my head and tossing my hat.

I thought I would have to search for Josh, but he paraded into the dining hall for breakfast like nothing had happened at the lake. He confused the hell out of me. One moment, he was shaking with rage, eyes so dark they looked black, and the next, he was plastered with a smug grin, shoving eggs into his mouth.

He tossed a ball with Cael a few feet away, and part of me wanted to march over there and ask him what his problem was, but I knew it wouldn't solve anything. And he wouldn't confess anyway. He was a lockbox. I just couldn't figure out what he was hiding.

Ella's words echoed in the back of my mind: *"figure out what he needs."*

Easier said than done when the guy didn't fucking talk. Even as he warmed up with Cael the two remained silent, Cael taking one for the team by pairing up with Josh. They both focused on the ball hitting their gloves as everyone glanced over with dirty looks that gave away their exact feelings.

Neither side was making this easy; both growing more volatile by the second.

"Alright, huddle up," I called out as I walked to the pitcher's mound. Everyone gathered around in a loose circle. Josh stood back from them with his arms crossed over his chest and a red Lorettes hat pulled down over his dark curls. "And get the new guy a better hat." I scowled, but the sound of Ella giggling echoed from the dugout as she took off in a jog toward the office.

We were supposed to run regular drills that morning to warm everyone up and ease them into the routine, but something was eating at me. With Josh shaking everything up, we needed to think outside the box. Typical drills would keep us active but not unite us as a team.

"I want everyone to form a line," I said with a clap, and they all looked at me like I was insane. "Now!"

Everyone scrambled into line with Josh at the very end, staring at me over Cael's shoulder, his dark eyes always on me.

"Shirt." I snapped my fingers at Van and he nodded. "Skin." I pointed to Jensen. They moved left and right as I went down the single-file line, half the team stripping their shirts until I got to Josh. "Skin."

"No." He shook his head at me, and I could tell it was about to be a fight. His jaw clenched, and his hands flexed at his side as he tilted his chin up at me.

"What is this—authority issues?" I asked him, turning my hat backward on my head and cocking it to the side.

"I just don't have some sick obsession to get naked like the rest of you," he grumbled.

"It's a fucking scrimmage, Logan. It's not a strip club." I laughed. "You're a skin."

"No," he repeated.

"Aye." Cael stepped in, stripping his shirt off in one go. My eyes flickered to his toned chest. I forgot how hard the ridges of his stomach were when he was in shape, making my heart race. "I'll switch with him," he offered, and Josh shrugged.

"Pick your captains," I said to the two teams. I could feel Arlo's eyes on me, and as much as it made me nervous to step outside the box he had drawn for me, I had to do this my way.

Once the boys did as they were told, they stood in awkward huddles, waiting for their next instructions. I stared around at them and smiled. "Good, now even out and pick your positions."

It was clear that they were confused by the way they looked around at each other. Van's eyebrows scrunched together as he turned to Cael.

"Has he lost his mind?" He asked and Cael responded with a flat, "maybe." It was another minute before they started to communicate. They grumbled around for a little while, but after a couple of minutes, they figured it out and returned to me.

"What the hell are you doing, Tucker?" Van asked, standing forward as the shirts' captain.

"First base, third base, left field, and shortstop will all be blindfolded for the game's duration."

Everyone had something to argue about the moment the words left my mouth, but Josh narrowed his eyes at me, silently questioning the order.

"You'll have to rely on each other to catch, hit, and throw the ball," I explained. "Communication is our sharpest tool on the field, and as of right now, some of you don't understand that. So until you do, we play like this."

"This is going to get someone hurt," Jensen grumbled.

"Good thing we've got Doc." I smiled at them. I walked to the benches, digging around in one of the equipment bags until I got my hands on some of the bandanas we kept inside to hand out to fans.

"You sure they aren't going to blow up on each other?" Ella asked as I straightened out.

"I'm counting on it." I winked at her and jogged back to the field, handing each team some blindfolds. "Ella, Arlo, and Nick will be umps. Their word is law. You start arguing you're on laundry for the week."

Cael's eyes caught mine for a second before he covered the bright blue with a sigh. "Atta boy." I clapped a hand to the back of his head and led him to the batter's box. "Shirts, you're in the field first."

"What, no coin toss?" Josh said with a forced grin, making me want to slap the expression off his smug face.

"You burned your one favor, Logan. Mound. Now." I waved him off and stood back. Players were guiding their blindfolded teammates to their positions, and eventually, everyone was ready to go.

"Play ball," Arlo barked out.

"Alright," Josh sighed, rolling the ball in his hand. "Cody," he said, "I'm going to count to three and throw the ball. Underhand, softball," he described.

"Softball?" Cael adjusted his stance. "...alright."

"Just swing," Josh said.

Everyone could hear Cael trying to get the timing right on a softball pitch as Josh counted out loud and released the ball. Everyone fell silent and the sound of the bat cutting through the air with one smooth swoosh echoed through the treetops.

"Strike one." Arlo's voice was harsh compared to the silence.

"Go again," Cael said, pinning his shoulders back, determined to hit his mark. Ella's brows pinched together from behind second base, watching Cael carefully to ensure he didn't hurt himself. "Logan, throw the ball." Cael whistled into the air.

LOGAN

I counted Cael down again, letting the ball leave my fingers in a soft, easy arch. Everyone was on edge, but for the moment it wasn't because of me, and it was a small mercy. His count was better this time, and the bat made sloppy contact with the ball, sending it soaring toward the outfield.

Turning on my heel, I realized no one was talking, "The balls dropping left field!"

No one responded, and the ball was inches from cracking Van in the face.

"Mitchell!" I barked when no one opened their mouths to help. "Put your glove up!"

Thankfully, the tree listened—Van raised his glove just in time... for it to clip off and fall into the center fielder's hands.

"Throw to first!" Van snapped, unable to see what was happening.

"Baker!" I snapped, and he juggled the ball in his fingers before rifling it as hard as he could toward the first basemen. I didn't know the kid, some second-string player who never saw the field unless Tucker was tired, but he wasn't paying attention.

"Hey!" I called out. *I didn't know his name. Fuck.*

Cael was moving too fast—collision was inevitable.

"First, put your fucking glove up!" I yelled, looking around for an ounce of help from the second baseman standing behind me, but he just shrugged.

I fucking hate these guys.

I opened my mouth to order another instruction, but it was too late. The message wasn't relayed fast enough, and Cael took the ball to the shoulder with a heavy slap, knocking him back a step with a string of curse words.

Ella gasped as the two of them went down in a ball of limbs, dirt, and sand kicking up around them as they slid well past first base.

Van was the first to move. He ripped his bandana off his face and threw it down.

Dean moved toward Ella and Silas, who crouched around Cael and the other kid, whispering and talking, but I couldn't tell what they were saying. The entire field was in chaos.

They had pulled out their pitchforks.

"What the fuck was that, Logan?!" He growled as his long legs carried him the length of the outfield in seconds. I stepped back off the pitcher's mound, tossing my glove behind me on instinct, and got ready for the fight.

"You're blaming me for this?" I put my hands up in defense as he closed the gap between us. "No one else was calling plays!"

"You're so arrogant." Van went to shove me, but I slapped his hands away.

"Don't," I snapped. "No one else was helping, and you're blaming me?"

"If either of them are hurt, I'll show you how Ella's right hook feels with an extra hundred pounds of muscle behind it!" Van stepped forward again.

Man, he's the ugly kind of tall. I laughed at the thought, and rage shivered through his muscles, but I leaned back just in time to dodge his long reach and the incoming punch at the end of it.

"They're fine. It was a ball to the shoulder and a tumble," I said, putting that sick grin on my face quickly enough for it to irritate the left fieldman.

A hand wrapped around my shoulder and I whirled, raising my hand to toss a punch. Before I could stop the motion my hand connected with Cael's jaw, sending him stumbling backward with his hands in the air.

"Hey, hey!" He called out, his sharp blue eyes rimmed with water as he fought to blink away the sudden pain. "I'm-"

"Shit," I swore and moved toward him, but he kept his hands up.

"It's okay," Cael grumbled under his breath as he stood back out and stretched out his jaw. "What the fuck, man?"

"You take a punch like a girl," I countered before I could stop the venom that dripped from me.

"Fuck you, Logan, I'm trying to help you!" Cael stepped forward. "Back down."

"Don't tell me what to do!"

"I'm trying to save your ass from being gang beaten in the middle of the forest. Will you chill out?!" Cael practically doubled in size as the frustration bubbled beneath the surface. He straightened out to his six-three form, making me feel more outnumbered.

"I don't need your help, Cody!" I said. "Stop trying to save everyone and focus on the reason why this team is falling apart in the first place. Your fucking drug problem!"

I'd hit a nerve.

I shouldn't have said it, but it slipped out in anger and I instantly regretted the words when the hurt flashed across his face. That was a conversation between the two of us.

It wasn't meant for anyone to hear.

Not even his precious found family.

"You're acting like an asshole," he countered with a fake smile and poked me in the chest with a finger.

"How many times do I have to tell you assholes not to touch me?" I snarled and shoved him back harder that time.

I was swarmed in seconds—piranhas circling blood, ready to tear me limb from limb. They were shoving and yelling, nothing coherent; they all just wanted a piece of me after punching Cael. In hindsight that was stupid, but I hadn't expected the contact, and my first instinct would always be to defend myself when my adrenaline ran rampant.

Van was scrambling to get his hands on me, but a larger set pushed him back as Arlo put himself between me and the mob. Silas was on top of Jensen and Todd before they could slip into the small gap that was left.

"You're a slimy piece of shit," Van spat.

"Enough," Arlo snapped and shoved him back with enough force to really move the oversized lap dog.

Dean filled the space and pointed at me. "Go to the cabins, now!" He ordered.

"You were the one that thought this was a good idea," I snapped at him, throwing my Lorettes hat at his feet. "I don't need this fucking team. I don't need any of this bullshit!" I shoved off another set of hands, chest heaving in fury and stomped back to the cabins.

"Josh!" Cael's voice chimed out as I reached the long line of cabins, but I ignored him and kept my path back to the safety of my bunk. I wanted to slam the door, pack my bags and leave this fucking camp.

I'd walk if I had to.

"Logan, stop and talk to me!" Cael barked. I could hear him with every quickened footstep and slammed the door behind me.

It opened again seconds later, and he stood out of breath in the doorway.

"What the hell was that?" He asked, tossing his hat to his bunk and putting his hands in the air. His jaw was already bruising—red giving way to purple and, soon enough, it would be an ugly purple color staining his skin.

"I'm—" I almost apologized but the anger was still fresh, adrenaline pumped through my veins, and the only thing I wanted to do was tell him to go fuck himself. "Just leave me alone, Cody."

"No." He stepped further into the cabin.

"I'm warning you." I slammed my bag to the floor and squared up to him. One-on-one, the chances of me actually beating him were better.

"Cut the intimidation tactics out. It's just you and me in here." He rolled his eyes at me. "You fucking punched me."

"You deserved it," I countered.

"Man, you are wound up. Where's the Logan from the diner? Calm, cool, and collected?" He asked.

"That's a show, Cael," I lied. "I gave you what you needed to recover. Now, get the hell out of my way. This team doesn't want me. You don't need me. Put some second-string wannabe on the mound. You'll still win."

"It's not about that!" Cael argued. "We're—"

"Let me guess—you're about to preach some family bullshit, but you didn't even tell any of them that we spent six months together? Not a single one of them knows I'm your sponsor! You don't trust me either, Cody, so don't. It's all bullshit."

"We decided together it was best no one knew!" He protested.

"I still expected you to tell King and his little girlfriend, or even Tucker!"

"*You* asked me not to!" Cael growled, actually getting angry for once. "I don't break promises! They didn't need to know, and your little outburst isn't about that!"

"Whatever the hell you psychos are doing here, it's weird. You're all running around with your mommy and daddy issues, diagnosing yourselves." I raised my hands out at my sides. "You're not a family—you're a college baseball team!"

"Why are you fighting this so much?" Cael asked, his calm demeanor pissed me off.

I laughed in his face. "That's what this is, it's a cult."

"Josh." Cael laughed, shaking his head. "It's not a cult. We just have each other's backs, and if you stop fighting it, we can have yours, too."

"I don't *need* friends, Cody," I hissed.

"Everyone needs friends." He smiled at me. It drove me insane how unbothered he was by everything.

"Cael, I just punched you in the face..." I scowled at him.

"Okay, so?" He shrugged. "You've got about thirteen more before you take the championship belt from Arlo for the amount of times he's punched me." Cael laughed.

"You guys are some of the most fucked up people I've ever been around." I sighed.

"But you'll stay?" Cael asked.

Would I? Logically, I needed them—I knew it, and I hated it.. But not in the way they all kept claiming. I needed my spot on the roster to fulfill my scholarship and finish school. Without the Hornets, I didn't have the funds to pay tuition, so technically, I did have to stay.

But the emotions were tearing me to shreds, begging me to explode and take the whole camp with me. The way they seamlessly got along, even in the depths of turmoil, confused me. It went against everything I had been taught about families.

Arlo was a violent dog with a history of biting, Cael was an unhinged alley cat battling drug addiction, and the rest of the team followed them like they were god's word. And then there was Dean, the golden boy. A fitting nickname for a six-three grizzly bear with pure muscle, a rumored heart of gold, and a smile to match.

Team Captain.

Infuriatingly positive and willing to climb mountains to get this to work.

"I'll stay."

"Okay, good," Cael hummed. "Promise me something though?"

"If you're about to let me in on some fucked up Hornets tradition like Coach kisses you all on the forehead before bed, count me out." I snapped, scooping my bag from the floor.

"You wish." Cael chuckled. "No more jabs about my recovery."

"Fair." I nodded. I watched him tap two fingers to his chest. "I'm not doing your stupid Hornet salute." I rolled my eyes. "It further fuels my cult theory."

TUCKER

After yesterday's blow-up, everyone was on edge—some of us even suspicious. Cael was known for being friendly even when he shouldn't be, but there was something about the way he had approached Josh and then chased him down after being punched.

There were secrets cracking down the center of the Hornets, ones that had the potential to screw our season. After a disgusting breakfast of lumpy oatmeal made by Todd and Jensen, everyone started packing their things for the two-night canoe trip.

Arlo, Ella, Silas, and other coaches who made the trip would be staying behind. The canoe trip was for *players only*. The idea of being self-governed in the woods was terrifying—especially when half the team wanted Josh roasted over a fire.

Cael, with all his secrets, managed to talk Josh into sticking around, but I couldn't tell if that was a good thing. We needed a pitcher; our backups were worth nothing, and every time one of them touched the field, even for relief, we ended up making up for it later in the game.

We needed Josh Logan, and it pissed me off.

"You're steaming from the ears, big boy." Cael's voice came from behind me. "Why so tense?"

"This canoe trip is going to end in blood." I cleared my throat.

"I think that's just the theme of spring camp." He laughed. Usually, the sound would ease the tension between my shoulders, but today, it only made everything worse.

"How did you convince him to stay anyway?" I asked, turning to look at him with his hands shoved in the pockets of his hoodie. The bruise on his jaw from where he was punched was festering an ugly, deep purple color.

"We made out for a while, and then I promised him a canoe blow job." Cael smiled.

"Don't be an idiot," I pushed him, "or I'll call Clementine right now."

"She'd be into it." He sighed, but I could tell he was missing her by the way his words trailed off at the end. "Although she's into big, dumb, blonds. Josh isn't really her type." He smacked his hand against my chest.

"Be serious with me. How'd you do it?" I asked him again in a lower tone.

"Josh is my NA sponsor," Cael admitted.

I hadn't seen that coming, and it was written all over my face because Cael started to laugh again.

"I had the same reaction at first," he said quietly. "It worked though. He's not as bad as he makes himself seem. The egomaniac personality? The aggression? It's a defense tactic. Just give him some space to adjust."

"Adjust?" I sighed. We didn't have time for that.

"He's not used to this..." Cael said it like I should understand.

"Used to what, Cael? Stop talking like Yoda."

"That's not..." He started and stopped. "Family. He's not used to people looking out for him. He thinks we're a cult."

"What?" I couldn't help the shocked laughter that bubbled from me.

"Not seriously, but it's a decent way to describe *how* he sees the team. Our relationships," Cael said as Van walked past us and tossed him a sleeping bag. "I don't know much about his life, when we had meetings I usually talked the whole time."

That sounded like Cael.

"So you don't know a single thing about him," I grumbled, sniffling a little as the cold air bit into my skin and ran a chill over my body.

"Even if I knew, it's not my story to tell. You're just going to have to get to know him..." Cael nodded to where Josh crouched on the soft grass loading food into crates as Arlo dropped them at his feet in silence. He looked smaller than usual in a too-big sweater and sweatpants that hugged his athletic thighs.

In quiet moments I thought maybe I could find him attractive. With his dark curls and scruffy jaw that's always so tense, but then he turned those dark brown eyes on me and a chill ran down my spine.

"Cael," I said as he went to walk away, my fingers reaching out and tangling into the fabric to stop him.

"What?" He asked, turning back to look at me.

"Did he help you? You know, with everything?" I asked. Unspoken words—doubt…guilt. *Did he help you in ways I couldn't?*

"Recovery sucks and I'm really lucky to have you all around me, cheering me on even when I don't deserve it," he said. "But I needed balance, and someone to tell me when I was being an asshole. Josh did that for me when no one else could look me in the eye."

I nodded, understanding what he was saying even though it made me feel like shit.

"I'll try," I said with a huff. "If that's what you think I should do, I'll try."

"That's my boy." Cael lifted his hand and clapped it gently against my face. "You should probably bring one of the satellite phones just in case…" He looked around at the team and grimaced. "Because you're right about one thing; this is going to end in bloodshed."

I swallowed tightly, pushing down the anxiety that crawled up my throat as I moved through the different groups double checking their supplies with them.

Silas came down from the camp office with a clipboard in his hands. "Here," he said, handing it to me. "Shit, it's cold out."

"What's this?" I looked down at the papers.

"Emergency numbers, a few first aid things, and canoe safety." Silas pointed at the stuff without looking down from the field. His eyes scanned the players, until they landed on Josh.

"What's the story there?" I asked him. If anyone knew anything about why Josh Logan came to play for us, it was Silas. He always knew everything before we did.

"He just transferred," he said tightly, which was a partial truth but I wanted more than what they were telling the team and press.

"Why did he transfer?" I pushed, tucking the board under my arm.

"He—" Silas stopped and ran a hand through his hair. "There was an incident at Lorette. A couple of guys got into it and Josh took the worst of the punishment. He got expelled."

"No school, no baseball." I looked over my shoulder at Josh.

"Coach found out and we needed a pitcher," Silas said, causing me to turn back and look at him.

"Coach barely tolerates it when we step out of line and he invites a volatile unchecked pitcher to join the team with no conditions?" I asked, curious as to how Silas would navigate the question.

I wasn't an idiot.

The guys loved to pretend I was just because I was slow on pop culture references and confused easily when they talked too fast. I wasn't dumb. I had one of the highest GPAs on the team. The problem was when everyone else was experiencing childhood, I was in the backyard hitting balls. I was at practice, I was running drills. I'd never been giving a moment to breathe between all of it, all that mattered was baseball and family dinners.

Family dinners where I had been subjected to my mom's sickening speeches about people she barely knew and how she couldn't condone their lifestyle because it went against the church. Even though growing up we had been taught to be selfless and caring. To always help those in need. The hard line for my mother was helping people that held different views than her.

"There are conditions," Silas said. "If he screws up spring camp, he's gone."

"Oh, cool, so we're his probation period and this is just another test," I grumbled.

"You're doing good, Dean," Silas said, patting my shoulder.

"There's been two fights, I'm pretty sure we're all going to get food poisoning with Todd on breakfast duty. *And* Josh punched Cael," I scoffed. "I wouldn't consider that a good job."

"You're trying," he said. "That's what matters. You could have taken one look at Logan and sent him home, but you let him get on the bus, you let him interact with the team. The exercise was good yesterday. Keep running it until they start talking."

"You think that's a good idea?" I asked him.

"It got them talking yesterday," he said.

"It got them fighting." I rolled my eyes.

"Fighting, talking—same thing with you guys," Silas said with a laugh. "Just don't give up on them, you're doing it your way and it may not be conventional or even safe but it's working. Look." Silas nodded to the field.

Arlo had crouched beside Josh and was helping him reorganize a crate, which wouldn't necessarily mean anything but they were talking… Arlo was smiling…

"He's playing nice to help me." I rolled my eyes again.

"When have you ever known Arlo to play nice?" He questioned.

"That guy has a smile that they dubbed the *press smile*," I said.

"Dean, look at it, that's not his press smile," Silas argued. "That's a genuine conversation."

"Whatever you say, Doc," I conceded.

"Have a fun canoe trip, Tucker. Try to bring them back in one piece?" Silas laughed as he climbed the stairs back to the office and shut the door behind him.

TUCKER

"Do you want the front or back?" I asked Josh as we stood on the shore. Most of the team had already paddled out—each paired with a senior and carrying maps and supplies in case of separation.

"I've never been in a canoe before, so whatever's easiest…" he said.

"Take the front." I waited until he was in the canoe and positioned at the front before I handed him the paddle and pushed the canoe a little further out. I hopped in with ease, avoided getting my shoes wet, and used the paddle to shove us into the deeper water.

"I'm not going to be in charge of steering this thing am I?" Josh asked and I tried not to laugh at the hint of nervousness in his voice.

"No." I dipped my oar into the water. "Just paddle."

As we moved the canoe out to the middle of the lake, a calm silence fell between us; the water lapping against the wood and the breeze coasting over the surface of the lake. In the distance laughter could be heard as the group travelled.

I opened and closed my mouth a few times, searching for a jumping-off point that wouldn't get me yelled at, but the need to talk was festering. Josh seemed unbothered by the silence which only made me more antsy.

"Cael said-" I started, and Josh shook his head.

"Don't," he said shortly after. "I hate small talk."

"We're going to be in this canoe for three hours, Logan."

The canoe rocked back and forth as Josh's entire body turned to look at me.

"Hey, chill out or we'll both end up in the water, *Mr. I-can't-swim.*" I put my hands up and tried to calm him down.

"I can swim." He scowled and turned back around.

"So why won't you do the polar dips?" I asked him. He had gone M.I.A. that morning again, before anyone could get their hands on him and force him into the water. My thoughts flashed to the scars that littered his skin and I swallowed the cotton ball that became lodged in my throat.

"Because they're stupid," he said, taking little strokes with his oar that weren't really doing much to move us.

"A lot of your comebacks sound like third graders at recess." I rolled my eyes. "If their stupidity is your only reason, I'm going to start forcing you. But if there's another reason..."

"There's not. I just don't want to partake in your cult festivities."

"Right." I laughed. "Cael told me about your theory."

"It's not a theory, it's an observation. If you're just going to mock me, Tuck, I'd rather paddle in silence," he said.

"Yeah, you would," I snapped. "And stop calling me that."

"Why?" He hummed. "Does it bother you?... *Tuck*." Josh's teeth clicked together as the 'k' rolled off his lips.

"You only do it *because* it bothers me."

"If you didn't want to be stuck in a canoe with me, why volunteer? I'm sure Cody would have been a less painful option," he said.

"You don't get to always take the easy way out," I said to him, and watched all the muscles in his back tense. "Did I hit a nerve, Logan?" I teased.

"It's cute you think it's that easy," he responded after a tense moment.

"I've seen you get worked up for less," I said, trying to keep my tone light. I wasn't looking for a fight with him; I *wanted* him to open up to me. to tell me what was going on in that mess of a mind, but I would take whatever the hell this was.

At least he wasn't throwing punches.

"Or is it only fun when you aren't on the receiving end?" I asked him.

"I can take a joke, Tuck. You just haven't said anything funny," Josh said, but I could hear the smile in his voice and I hated that it trickled down my spine in a warm line. I got a budding urge to keep up the banter just to hear that sound again.

"I've won funniest teammate back to back," I said.

"Did Arlo make you all homemade trophies?" He teased, his shoulders shaking with a small laugh.

"No," I grumbled, "Van did."

"Are you serious?" That had his head whipping around to look at me.

The sun caught in his dark brown eyes, and for the first time ever I saw color there that wasn't cold and endless. Amber swam beneath the surface, swirling in waves that drank in the sunlight pouring down on us. His skin was stained with freckles and, in the light, I could see more of those tiny white scars that littered his complexion.

Wind kicked up the curls that rested against his neck and I swallowed tightly, nodding because it was all I could manage as I worked to dampen the sparks lighting fires in the pit of my stomach.

"I'll show it to you if you survive spring camp," I managed to get out after a moment of him staring at me.

"You guys really are a cult." He sighed and carefully turned back around in the canoe.

"Keep this up and you'll win grumpiest Gus," I teased.

"Shut up, Tuck," he growled to get the last word, and I laughed before returning my focus to paddling.

If there was anyone that could break down Josh, it was me. I could do this. I just needed to figure out how. Alone, one-on-one, he wasn't so bad. Maybe he wasn't so overwhelmed or something, but he was different. The jokes were softer, the conversation enjoyable. He wasn't protecting his throat like a dog backed into a corner.

He exuded confidence like a ray of light. Both on and off the field there was a rare time when any of us saw cracks in Josh Logan's armor, but sitting here in the canoe, just the two of us, I was reminded that he was just a kid like the rest of us, trying to navigate his life without fucking it all up too badly.

By the time we got to the island half the team already had their tents up and a few of them were goofing around with a ball as the rest fought with poles and fabric. The sun was high in the sky but it wouldn't be long before it dropped and brought the chill with it.

I hopped out, getting my shoes wet and wandered to the front of the canoe, yanking it with both arms up to the shore so Josh could get out.

"Thanks," he said under his breath, and started to unload what we had brought.

I brought the tent over to the last free spot in the awkwardly arranged circle and pulled everything out, getting mere moments of silence before Cael wandered over, squatting down to my eye level.

"How was the canoe trip?" He asked, in a sing-song voice that made me wanna tie him to a tree.

"Fine." I shrugged and counted the poles at my feet.

"Really?" He smiled at me. "Just fine?"

"Just. Fine." I repeated, and looked over to where Josh was bringing a crate of cans up the shore.

"Oh, god." Cael laughed and fell back on his ass. "You got the gooey look."

"I do not." I shook my head. "Don't start that shit with me. I don't, it's not..." I sighed.

"It is. Josh gave you the goo," Cael said, *way* too loudly.

"What the hell does that even mean, Cael? The *goo?!*" I couldn't keep the laughter from bubbling up. "You're a menace."

"I'm allowed to be, I have a permit," he said, pretending to dig out a piece of paper but flipped me off instead.

"Eat shit." I laughed more and shoved him away playfully.

"Seriously though..."

"Nothing happened. There was no *goo*," I said.

"I wasn't serious about the canoe blowjobs," Cael said, leaning closer and lowering his voice. "Unless it actually happened, then I kind of want details. Clementine will kill me if I don't get the gossip."

I pushed him in the shoulder and knocked him off balance. "You're an asshole." I pointed at him with a scowl on my face.

"A menace, an asshole. Insult me more, it gets my cock hard," Cael purred.

"Cut it out!" I growled. "We just talked..."

"You talked?" Cael's eyebrow raised.

"Yeah, Cael, like normal humans... we talked," I said, as I started to slot the poles into the tent fabric.

"Did you talk about me?" Cael sat up again and brushed his fingers behind his ears as he fluttered his lashes.

"No," I shook my head, "we talked about why he won't do the team dips in the morning."

"Did you get an answer?" He asked.

"No," I responded with a huff.

"Three hours and that's all you talked about?" He questioned.

"Yeah, that was it. Will you go help them start a fire or something?" I brushed him off and he narrowed his eyes at me. "It was nothing. Stop staring at me like you have to plan a wedding."

"In this economy?" He rolled his eyes. "You and Logan can get married at the court house. You kids think I'm made of money." He pushed to his feet and smiled at me.

"Go away, Cael."

I watched his lanky body stumble over the uneven ground toward Josh and groaned. I should have known that he wasn't going to leave this alone. Cael was a cat—sneaky, clumsy, and always causing chaos. It took him seconds to become hyperfixated on causing trouble. He thrived on the attention it brought–and selfishly, I enjoyed it when it didn't involve me.

Josh looked over, brow furrowed as Cael rambled beside him. His eyes flickered back to him and a small, playful smile formed on his face. It was strange to watch them interact with all the assumptions that floated around who exactly we *thought* Josh was.

A piece of hardened shell cracked inside of my chest. I could feel it fall away as I watched him with Cael; his slow, careful patience, the intention behind his eyes as he listened to my best friend run his ear off about nonsense. It was a quiet devotion to a friendship

I couldn't even begin to understand, but one that I was grateful Cael had.

I returned to the tent, fumbling with both poles and emotions as the sun started to drop. Cael helped Van and a few of the boys make lunch, and the rest of the team cleaned up before scattering around camp.

"Sneakers on." I clapped, moving out of my tent with my hoodie pulled around my jaw.

"You're about to ruin our day aren't you?" Jensen sat up on his elbows, bare chested, his tattoos on full display and bathing in the sun despite the frigid breeze.

"Only yours," I grumbled. "We need to move our bodies. Hike time," I said loudly, cutting off whatever was about to come out of Cael's mouth. "Most of you know the trails by heart but if you don't, pair up with someone. I don't want anyone getting lost."

"I mean, there's someone I can think of that can get lost," Todd piped up, and everyone grumbled in unison before pairing up in groups and heading out.

"Good start." Cael pushed off the ground and paired up with Van leaving Jensen with a hopeless look on his face without a partner. "Yee-haw, big boy. To Candy Mountain we go!" He hopped on Van's back and the two of them disappeared down the trail.

Josh sat on his bed roll with his arms hanging over his curled up knees and his dark eyes on the opening to the hiking path.

"Get up and go on the hike." I looked over at him and put my hands on my hips. "Don't give them another reason to hate you."

"I don't know the trails, Tuck," he said in a low, tight tone that suggested he was angry but trying to control himself.

"It's called the buddy system; but if you piss me off I'm leaving you to the wolves." I nodded to the path.

Josh contemplated my offer for a split second too long and I started to walk away. I didn't have to put up with his bullshit. It wasn't in the captain rule book. If anything, I was allowed to show tough love even if the definition was loose. Arlo ruled with tough love, he was born to do it, but I just… couldn't find my line, at least not yet, but with the way Josh challenged every decision, every comment; suddenly I found myself compelled to find it faster.

LOGAN

He left quickly but slowed as I caught up. I approached from behind him on the path and he made space for me to walk beside him. The wind pushed his messy blond curls against his forehead beneath his oversized grey sweatshirt when he turned to look over at me as I matched his pace.

"I would have been fine at camp," I said, clenching my hands in the pockets of my hoodie.

"Oh, I'm sure." Dean laughed. "I wouldn't leave my worst enemy to the bears."

"Is that another term for teammates? Because they're the only dangerous thing in these woods," I snapped, and my eyes were drawn ahead of us to where a group of players were roughhousing as they barreled through the forest.

"They're not all bad, Josh." Dean shook his head. "You just need to open up more."

"This isn't therapy, Tuck, it's a baseball team. Stop trying to drag me into your emotionally messed-up chosen family. You guys are weird. Just let me play baseball." I sighed.

I was so sick of that being their line. Everyone, from Tucker to Cody, all wanted me to acclimate to their offputting, touchy-feely

bullshit. I couldn't do it, not even if it was tempting. It made me sick to my stomach. Families weren't like *this*. They were rough and mean, they were forgetting your kid at school pick-up to score drugs. They were sixteen different boyfriends because your mom couldn't hold one down for more than a few months. It was hiding in your closet, praying that the screaming stopped in time for you to get some sleep so you didn't pass out during your exams.

Family wasn't some cotton candy fairytale they'd dreamed up. Family was the last people you'd choose to share blood with but the first people you'd drop everything for if they called for help.

"Van has two older siblings; a sister who runs an animal shelter and plays for the Harbor Hillcats," Dean said, ignoring my hissy fit. "And a sister who works for the UN overseas. He's the baby of the family and I'm positive that's what will make him a good therapist. He was born listening to everyone talk around him like he wasn't there. He hears everything, so don't say anything stupid or damning around him."

"Good for him. I'm sure the tree will make a great therapist," I grumbled, ignoring the way it made me feel to know that his family was so selfless. I loathed this tactic Dean was playing. He was backing me into a corner by simply being himself and it was infuriating.

"Liam...uh Baker, he grew up in Ontario but got into school in Michigan and then was transferred to us last season. He's a good guy, little weird and pronounces his O's funny, he smokes like three packs a day so if you need one..." He said. "Jensen, he's like an otter. Unsuspectingly kind. He's up for anything, super social and funny.

Unreal hands... he has like photographic memory or some shit, if you give him signals he'll remember every single one."

Jensen, he was the catcher. I remembered his name, only because he woke up with a smile on his face and it pissed me off. No one should be that awake at six am. I kept my head down as Dean went through more guys. "Silas is a saint," he said, and my hands flexed at my sides.

If you only knew.

"Dude would give you the shirt off his back if you asked. We call him Doc, Cael calls him Gramps to get under his skin, but he's not that old. He's an only child. His mom is the sweetest woman in the world. His dad is a fucking tool though," Dean said, and I turned to look at him for the first time since we started walking.

Wrong. It was all so wrong.

"What?" He asked when I stared. "You look offended..."

"Not offended, just surprised. I thought Silas was a daddy's boy," I huffed.

"Alright, that's a strange hill to die on," Dean said, his brows furrowing. "Ok, well you know Arlo."

"Legacy son with the world on his shoulders and perfect season." My jaw tightened at the memory of all the news articles that were waved in my face as the season ended. Coach would have shoved them down my throat if he couldn't get in trouble for it.

"Okay, so you don't know Arlo." Dean laughed. "He's not like that off the field. He's a little rough, kind of like you." He stared at me for a little too long after he said it and it made me wanna push him off the path into the bush, but I clenched my fists again and held back the urge.

Arlo and I were nothing alike.

"Arthur King really is the guy the news paints him as. He's a mean drunk. He pins Nick and Arlo against each other a lot. Just when you think they're in an okay place, Arthur pinches Nick and sets him on a warpath."

"I really don't need the King family drama distracting me from the season, Tuck. They don't even play for the team anymore," I snapped.

"But they're your coaches. Like it or not, you're about to be in the middle of that."

"Like it or not? Maybe the King brothers should learn to be professional and leave their feud off the field. We have games to win. If they want therapy they should walk off a tall cliff with Van Mitchell."

Dean snorted; he actually *laughed* at what I said.

"What?" I snarled, embarrassment creeping up my spine. It wasn't meant to be a joke.

"It would be hard to replace Van. He's the tallest and fastest fieldman in the league and his batting average is nearly .340. And as for Arlo, you'll never have a better pitching coach. I think you're smart enough to know that. So if you want, we can walk them off a cliff but it won't help you or your season."

"You're infuriating," I grumbled and settled back into my indifferent mood.

The trees bristled in the wind, a lot of them only just beginning to bud, with small green leaves sprouting from the dried winter branches. I could see why they came out here for Spring Camp; it was almost serene. We had never done anything like this with Lorette. They weren't sponsored in the way Harbor was. The Shores funneled money into the NCAA programs without batting an eyelid, and it only added to the agitation I felt toward the family.

"Ella," he said, after a beat of silence.

"I know Estella Miele's story." I stopped him with a hand waving in the air. "She killed one of the most promising NFL stars of our generation and walked off scot-free to live her perfect little life."

Dean stopped walking and pulled his hoodie off his head letting the breeze whip through his hair as he stared me down. "Shut the hell up, Josh."

"Or what?" I challenged. "Does the golden boy have any other settling besides happy?"

"You don't get to judge Ella," he warned, his temper simmering and suddenly I was tempted to see how far I could push him.

"There it is. Did I hit a nerve, Tuck? What, do you guys pass around your live-in bat bunny? Is this one of those weird group projects where you all have a schedule for her?" I pushed. "Arlo gets her Mondays, Cael on Wednesdays, you seem like a—"

Before I could finish the joke Dean advanced on me, his hand tangled into my sweater as he shoved me roughly against the nearest tree.

"Get the fuck off me." I pushed on his chest without him budging. He was the biggest player on the team by far and I was strong but he was…made of concrete and rebar.

I could feel his fingertips burning through my sweater. The heat was unbearable, like I had my throat pressed to an element. The panic settled across my chest, suffocating my ability to remain calm. Memories flickered violently, reliving every touch like I was still that little kid unable to protect myself.

Vomit filled my mouth.

"Tucker," I warned.

"You can run your mouth about any guy on this team, Logan," he spat. "But if I ever hear a single bad thing about Ella come out of your mouth again, it'll be me you have to answer to." His tone dropped in pitch, into a territory of anger and loyalty I had never seen from the first baseman.

My chest felt heavy, like he had laid hundreds of rocks on top of it, and no matter how badly I struggled to get free of him, his grip was unwavering. His face was so close to mine that I could see the intricate swirls of sea green that danced in his blue eyes, and smell the sharp sandalwood and amber cologne he had sprayed over himself that morning. I sat there in those colors trying to find reality. A truly desperate attempt to crawl out of the panic attack that was consuming me whole.

"She never did a damn fucking thing to you," he said when I didn't answer.

"She broke my fucking nose."

"You deserved that and you know it." He shoved again and my back scraped roughly against the wood. "You wanna act like that's who she is but I know Cael talked about her. She's his sister in all but DNA and sometimes I even question that. You know what she's done for him, for this team. She's like Cael, like *you*," he spat. "You're so quick to assume we're all bad people but you're the common dementor for our anger, Logan. Keep her name out of your mouth."

"Jesus, Tuck." I shoved again. "Fine, Ella is off limits."

Dean finally let go and stepped back

I stared at him a second longer, composing myself and tugging on the suffocating collar of my hoodie. His grip still burned on my skin like a brand that wouldn't fade.. I could take all the emotional abuse from this team, their taunts and jabs but...

"Don't ever touch me again," I said as he walked past me.

"Keep hiking," he responded, after a long, measured breath. "We have two hours left before we pop out on the other side back at camp. It'll be dark soon."

TUCKER

There was a fire going when we wandered back into camp. Josh trailed behind me, silent after our argument. I know I handled it badly, the anger that had sparked up had been vicious and unpredictable but...

Ella had saved Cael in so many ways the rest of us couldn't have. If she hadn't shown up at Harbor, Cael wouldn't be here today. It was dramatic, a stretch, but deep down we all knew that Cael had been on a path that would have ended with a funeral none of us ever wanted to have.

Ella was our sister and she didn't deserve a lick of the venom that had dripped from Josh. That was a breaking point, but it had also shown something about Josh that I hadn't expected. He had cracked today on the hike, his disdain for families ran deep, almost like he believed his life was worse than anyone else. And maybe it was, but I needed to find out why.

It wasn't Arlo that had triggered him, which is what I would have assumed.

No... It was *Silas*.

I watched as he wandered over to the fire, grabbed food, and secluded himself on his bed roll, away from the rest of the team.

Today had gone terribly, what started as an exercise to help him understand that the guys were people and not just players had completely backfired.

Two steps forward, two steps back.

I grabbed a bowl of stew, staring down at the unevenly cut vegetables and sighed, *they had left Todd in charge again*. I settled down between Van and Cael on a log away from the rest of the team.

"I'm glad it went terribly. That'll teach you to make us hike," Cael was quick to joke but quicker to silence when he saw my jaw tighten. "That bad?"

"He insulted Ella and I shoved him against a tree..." I exhaled a shaky, frustrated breath.

Van giggled, which sounded odd from a man his size, but it was definitely a giggle because Cael leaned forward around me to stare at him in bewilderment.

"What? Sounds like he deserved it. He's not even bruised..." Van extended his bowl in Josh's direction and grumbled.

"The problem is, I'm the captain. I shouldn't have snapped like that but—" I shoved food in my mouth and scowled. "This tastes like lake water."

Both Van and Cael looked at each other before choosing not to tell me the truth about where the water came from.

"Josh can handle it, being roughed up a bit." Cael set his bowl down between his feet and chose the bun in his lap to fill his stomach. "And if he went after Ella he earned it, but that's not you. Try leading him to the carrot without hitting him with the stick?"

"What..." I turned to Cael, feeling like an idiot.

"He means try a softer approach," Van said.

"I am trying, but he has all these preconceived ideas about us as people and it's frustrating to think he believes them. The rumors, the gossip... We aren't the stories the news outlets run." I set my bowl next to my feet.

"If telling him isn't working, figure out how to *show* him we aren't," Van suggested in a surprising turn of events.

"Show him?" I asked.

"Yeah, actions speak louder than words, right? So show him who we are," Van said with a shrug, tipping the rest of the stew into his mouth. I grimaced at the dribbled liquid on his chin. "You gonna finish that?" He asked, pointing to mine. I shook my head.

"How do I *show* him when any time I try to include him in crap, the rest of the team cracks jokes and starts fights?" I said, knowing how defeated and pathetically whiny I sounded.

"You're the captain, man." Van shrugged as he finished his second bowl.

"And you're a garbage disposal," Cael teased. "Neither are helpful additives to this conversation. Let's just get through this canoe trip without any war games?" He suggested.

"I don't know. At this point I'm thinking about chucking the captain title at anyone who'll take it and drowning myself in the lake," I said.

"Oh, dramatic. You could come back as a serial killer and haunt the Hornets for all of eternity. This canoe trip will be legendary." Cael grinned.

"Ha, ha."

"Oh, buck up, big boy. We'll get through this and you'll be leading the way." Cael's hand slapped against my shoulder and gave me a tight squeeze. "We've gotten through a lot worse." He leaned over and tapped his fingers against my chest. "Two steps at a time," he said.

"Preferably forward," I grumbled, but nodded in agreement.

After dinner was cleaned up, the guys settled around the fire for a while before bed but, one by one, they disappeared into their shared tents. Everyone slept with someone; it was still too cold outside at night, and we never had enough tents anyways. Logically, if we had asked, Silas would have forked over the money for more, but there was something about doing things the hard way that made the canoe trip feel more like summer camp.

Pairing up in tents was just another buddy exercise in team bonding. I curled up in my empty tent, shivering beneath my sweater. The temperature had dropped more than I'd expected, and even with two blankets I was freezing. I tried again to tuck down into my hoodie and blankets but something other than the cold was eating away at my peaceful sleep.

Josh.

I pushed from my bed onto my knees, shivering as the frigid air slinked its way under my clothes. *Fuck it was cold.* I just needed some water and a snack; my appetite had been bleak since the news broke about our newest member, but after barely touching dinner my stomach was rumbling and the coolers were across camp.

I pulled on my shoes and unzipped the tent into the pitch-black wild. The stars twinkled brightly in the harsh spring cold and, without clouds in the sky, the moon was uncontested in lighting up camp a hazy blue.

The fire flickered with nothing but dampened sparks that snapped as the wood quietly broke down from the remaining heat. I started to carefully move around the main area, avoiding the rogue baseballs that the guys had dropped and forgot about toward the coolers, but stopped when I saw a body curled up tightly, directly next to the fire.

"Hey." I wandered over to him, knowing that it was Josh from the strands of wavy dark hair that flipped out from under his beanie against his pillow. "Josh." I kicked his restless form gently. "Get up."

It took a little more convincing before he finally opened his eyes and looked up at me.

"You've got to be the worst fake sleeper I've ever seen." I shook my head.

"What do you want, Tuck. It's, like, two am," Josh grumbled.

"Why are you out here? Where's your tent?" I asked, and was met with a scoff.

"Seems your team is a little more unfriendly than you thought," he said, his jaw tight and his words sluggish in the cold.

I looked around at the tents, sighing and giving him a slow nod as I bounced up and down on my toes to keep warm.

"Okay, get up," I grunted.

Josh stared back at me, unmoving, those dark eyes unreadable.

"You can share my tent," I said with chattering teeth. "I can't let you freeze to death out here."

"I'm not even cold," he grumbled, but his frozen red nose and wind burned cheeks suggested otherwise.

"This isn't an argument, it's an order from your captain. Get in the tent, Logan." I dropped my tone so he knew I was serious, but in reality just doing the best I could to keep my teeth from chattering.

I thought he might argue more but he rolled to his knees in a stiff motion before grabbing his blankets and pillow.

"Over there." I pointed.

"Yeah I know, Tuck." I expected to have to fight him on it but he started walking. I jogged over and grabbed a couple of bottles of water and a leftover bun from the coolers, before moving my ass back to the tent to get warm.

Josh had laid out his bed roll, but the tent was so small that our belongings overlapped and tangled together, despite his obvious want for space. He cursed a few choice words before he curled into the blankets and pressed his face into the pillow. I set the bottles down for him and crawled into my own blankets. All the warmth had been sucked from them in my absence and I shivered from the feeling as I wrapped them up to my jaw and curled into a ball. When I opened my eyes he was staring at me with furrowed brows, his lips pressed into a tight line.

He was close enough that I could trace the scattered freckles that stained his permanently sun-soaked skin. I hated that underneath all the hatred I had for him, there was a spark of *want*.

"Can you back up or something?" Josh complained.

"There's no room to move," I snapped back.

"Just like, roll over?" He asked.

"You roll over," I fought back. "This is my tent."

"You made me come in here," Josh argued.

"I'm your captain, I'm not going to let you freeze to death." I closed my eyes, just trying to block out his dumb face.

"So be my captain and give me some space," he mumbled, forcing me to open my eyes again.

"There's no space to give, Logan. Shut up." I pulled the blankets tighter. "Besides, it's a body heat thing, the proximity will keep us warmer..." I tried to explain.

"You wanna snuggle?" He snarled.

"No," I blurted quickly. "We're close enough. Besides, I'm pretty sure you'd gnaw my arm off if I touched you again."

"I will." His tone went frigid.

"It was a joke," I said, and sighed. "You're a jumpy guy," I added.

"I am not," Josh said, following my actions by pulling his blankets tighter around his jaw.

"You are," I argued with my eyes closed.

"How the hell are you so cold? Aren't grizzly bears supposed to be furnaces?" Josh asked in a whisper, avoiding my prodding about his aversion to touch.

"Are you asking because you want to know, or because you want to make fun of me?" I asked.

"Can it be both?" He asked, after a moment of silence.

"I've always run cold and the guys have always made fun of me for it. I—" I stopped.

"Run cold? Like a lizard?" Josh laughed. It was the most genuine thing I'd heard from him all day.

"Yeah, like a lizard," I scoffed. "I was born early and it messed up my body or something. I don't know the science... or whatever."

Josh smiled at me, the sharp points of his teeth showing as his lips parted.

"What?" I snapped.

"Nothing. You just have a really easy time talking about everybody's lives and when you talk about your own you get tongue tied and shut down," he said, curling around himself a little more to pack the heat in.

"Coming from the guy who refuses to get to know any of his teammates, that really isn't an insult." I rolled my eyes.

"It wasn't meant to be one," Josh said.

"Oh?" I said, opening my eyes to look at him. He was staring at me in the darkness and I could feel the tension in the air. "Are you warmer now?" I asked him.

"Nope, still cold, just more annoyed," Josh grumbled, and I sighed.

He was infuriating, exhausting, impossible to pin down.

But he had laughed, and that was something.

LOGAN

We'd been through three days of brutal practice since the torturous canoe trip, and every one of them had ended up in fights. There was no stopping them once they started. One wrong move and they were on me like moths to a flame. It wasn't fair, the way they were treating me.

I was doing my best—trying to be the pitcher I knew I could be.

And every step of the way was blocked by one of them asking for more from me.

Asking me questions about my past, my friends, my family.

I didn't have the time or the patience to entertain their constant need for connection. I'd come to camp under the impression that it was early training for the season, but was shell-shocked to find out it was more team building exercises and campfire sing-alongs. If I had to listen to Cael sing any more *Dua Lipa,* I would find a cliff to throw him off. There had to be one around here.

Routine became my only saving grace. Get out of bed and shower before anyone else, take a run, eat breakfast with the psychotic Brady Bunch, practice, lunch, practice, dinner. Run. I would run until the sky got too dark to see the ground I was stepping on and

the flames from their nightly fires raged in the sky and I would slink into bed unnoticed. And then do it all again the next day.

I stood at the edge of the path and watched the flames dance in the night air.

All I wanted was a moment of peace, but the calm silence was harshly sawed in half by the sound of laughter and happiness. It made me sick to my stomach. I started to walk the shadowed trail against the cabins back to my own when Dean came out of nowhere and stopped me.

"Tonight you sit with us." He pointed to the fire.

"Just let me go to bed, Tuck," I grumbled. "Today was long, and listening to you guys sing makes my ears bleed."

"They aren't singing tonight, listen," he instructed, and I reluctantly turned my head toward the bonfire.

Their voices softly floated through the air; they were talking about baseball.

"For once don't argue with me just... go sit," Dean said again. "*Please.*"

It was the gentle tone in the *please* that got me, because despite the constant beatings that Dean was taking in the form of angry kickback from the team, he was still trying. And he wasn't angry or frustrated, he was just that infuriatingly positive teddy bear he always was.

It was driving me insane.

"Fine." I turned away from him and wandered over to the fire, looking around for a place to sit, but there was none until Van nodded to the space beside him, moving over on the log.

A peace offering.
One I didn't want.

I sank down on the log, resting on my elbows with my hat pulled down over my eyes, and listened. The second baseman, Louis, was telling a story in broken English about a botched play Arlo had made two seasons before. He was from Montreal, from what I could remember about his sheet, a young kid with so much potential. If he wasn't pulled up to the MLB next year it would be a surprise. He had been playing with the Hornets since he turned eighteen.

He recounted the play in so much detail I would have sworn he had been the one to catch the ball and make the out, but he hadn't been drafted to the team yet, he wouldn't have been until six months later.

Van cleared his throat quietly. "Lou spent the entirety of last season with headphones in between practices, hell, between plays, learning English so he could *communicate* with the guys better."

I wanted to snarl at the way he emphasized *communicate* with his judgemental tone. I wasn't an idiot, I understood the importance of communication with the team. On the field it was easy to do call outs, emotion didn't matter out there. What they were doing off the field was a different story; it was emotional connection and it was bullshit. It didn't make them better players, it just wasted time between practices and games.

It had screwed them out of winning when Arlo took over.

He was too emotional, they all were, and it had fucked them over.

"Arlo was an asshole for a week after that game." Dean sank down against the log at Cael's feet and looked up at him with an endearing look on his face.

"That wasn't even the worst day." Cael shook his head with a smile that was highlighted by the warm tones of the fire. "Do you remember when Arlo found out Nicholas was taking over the pitching coach position?"

"Nuclear," Van huffed, and looked at Arlo in his beanie and hoodie. "You made us run sprints the next day until Todd projectile vomited in the dugout."

"And then made us clean the dugout until our hands were raw," Todd added, tipping a beer back into his throat. He crushed the can and threw it into the fire, causing it to spark up in little embers.

"In my defense, it was the anniversary of Mom dying and Nick didn't actually tell anyone he was coming back, so I walked into the stadium to his ugly face," Arlo grumbled, and his brother sighed across the fire from him. Fire danced in Ella's eyes as she watched my every move from her spot behind Arlo, her hands wrapped around his neck and her body curled into his back where he sat in the grass between her legs.

"I'm surprised you didn't hit me that day," Nicholas confessed, taking a swig of beer.

"I should have, but there was a lot of press around and Coach... It wasn't worth it." Arlo shrugged.

A nauseous feeling overwhelmed me at the sight of them. How easily they were able to dance around each other even in turmoil so thick they might as well have been wading through corn syrup.

If it had been me, and I had a brother that so blatantly disregarded me and disrespected me, I wouldn't be anywhere near him. But I didn't have a brother; I barely had a mother to be angry about at the best of times.

It's not that I even wanted those things, it was just that I didn't want them shoved down my throat by the Hornets. It was like being water boarded with family affection that I never fucking asked for.

"None of it mattered. We still beat the shit out of the Lorettes." Arlo grinned at me.

"I was pitching with an injury." I arched my eyebrow at him.

"You came back too soon against the advice of your medical staff and blew it for your team," Jensen added, and I turned my sour look on him.

Dean put his hand up to stop Jensen from saying anything else.

"I could out-pitch Arlo with my eyes closed, Jensen. Which is more than you can say. Any drunk idiot can play back catcher." I looked away from him to Arlo, who was scowling.

Jensen lunged but Dean was faster, shooting from the ground and forcing him back to his seat. "Enough," he barked. This isn't a trial," he added.

"The malice, Logan, *shit*..." Van laughed. "Man, you hate this team more than Ella hates Miles Teller."

Arlo barked a loud, unbridled laugh, and everyone joined in. "Now you've done it," he said, when he finally settled down. I had never seen Arlo King so animated.

"That's a lot of hatred," Ella said, so seriously that her brown eyes unfocused with discontent.

"What?" I asked, confused. "Like the *Top Gun* guy?"

"Don't..." Cael tried to stop what was coming with a quick word, but Ella was already raring to go.

"Tom Cruise? Are you talking about Tom because *he's* the Top Gun guy!" She threw up her hands. It was like a switch had been flipped; her cheeks were flushed and she was ready to go to war. "Miles Teller is *not* the guy. He should never be the guy! He looks like he smells moldy!"

Everyone laughed at her as she rambled on about it and Cael stared at me with a shake of his head.

"You see what you started? This will last hours." He smiled.

"She'll be muttering insults in her sleep," Arlo said with a grin, and it only made her talk louder, arguing with no one but herself.

I smiled back at Cael, and for a split second I wasn't angry at the world, I wasn't angry at the Hornets for being effortlessly welcoming, I just *was*. A calm passed over me as Ella's voice finally died out and Dean cleared his throat.

"My favorite memory from the last few years was the Thanksgiving game two years ago. My brother refused to play because Cael was taunting him and then sat in the bleachers harassing him."

Cael snorted preemptively before the story was over, and Dean nodded down at him with a smile as he went back to where he was sitting.

"Cael caught a rogue liner from Silas's bat." He laughed and did the motions with his hands, turning his body to look at Van.

"Pocketed it, pulled off his glove, and hurled both the glove and the ball at Harvey's face. He didn't know what to stop and ended up getting hit by both in succession."

"He had a bruise the size of an apple and his eye was practically swollen shut," Silas said. I hadn't even noticed him join the fire, but he was standing behind Arlo with his arms crossed staring into the flames.

"And had to skip his office photos the next week because he looked like a criminal." Dean leaned back against the log in a fit of laughter, gripping his chest as Cael followed suit.

"I can up that," Van interrupted the laughter with a loud voice and leaned forward. "Bailing Arlo, Cael, *and* Cosy out of campus lock up for smashing her ex-boyfriend's car with baseball bats."

"They couldn't prove it was us," Arlo said.

"The paint on his car had residue of Harbor blue and yellow from the logos on the bats..." Van reminded them.

"He earned it, and we weren't going to let her do it alone," Cael said loudly.

They had helped Van's sister destroy her ex's car out of sheer loyalty to Van? I swallowed the bile that rose. *Did they always protect each other so fiercely...with such reckless abandon for the rules?*

"Besides, Cosy loves community service." Cael shrugged. "She felt better and we got to destroy some asshole's lifted truck."

"I'm sure the truck is fine, Cody swings like a girl," I added in a gruff teasing tone that made the entire fire go quiet.

"Do I swing like a girl?" Ella's voice cut through the silence like a knife.

I wiggled my nose, it was as if the healed break stung as a reminder of how much weight she'd put behind her punch that day. A faded memory of how much I had deserved it and how little that sentiment mattered to me.

My eyes found her, and for a moment I thought she might be upset, but she was smiling at me with all her teeth and light in her eyes. I didn't know why, but the sheer fact that she wasn't angry at the joke just infuriated me.

"Apparently, Logan *can* take a joke like the rest of us." Van laughed and nudged me with his knee.

I inhaled slowly, pushing down the thoughts of rage as I lifted off the log and left the fire behind. The response was a mixture of cheers and boos as I got further away from the warmth of the burning logs and closer to the dark cabin and my bed.

"Hey," Dean jogged up behind me, "she was joking around, Logan."

"It wasn't Miele. I'm just tired. I did as you asked, I sat around your stupid fire and listened to your fucking fake ass stories, and now I'm going to bed." I waved him off.

"No," Dean snapped and veered around to block my path. "Stop." He put his hands up but kept space between them and my chest. "You're going to tell me why that made you so upset."

"No." I returned his blunt command with a smile on my face. "See, I can use that word too and I don't owe you a story, golden boy. In fact, no one does, and yet you continue to force everyone to sit around your campfires and sing kumbaya."

"I don't even know the words to Kumbaya...whatever, listen." Dean ran his hands through his hair with a small huff. "That's not the real reason you left. You weren't mad..." His tongue darted out to wet his bottom lip, causing it to shine in the moonlight. "You were uncomfortable."

Uncomfortable.

Is that what that feeling was?

Was I uncomfortable that they had a support system? Most of them came from good homes, with good parents and siblings. *Cosy loves community service.* He had said it like she enjoyed being selfless, and it bubbled up inside of me in a vicious way. People like that didn't exist; not true, pure people. Everyone was broken, some with minor cracks but most were barely walking around, chunks of themselves rotting and festering into resentment and depression.

But they didn't care...

They saw each other for their flaws and their strengths and it was fucking infuriating. It was the blind leading the blind but... was it anger that I felt...? Or was Dean right?

Was I uncomfortable that they were a family, chosen and patched together with different threads and fabrics, but a family nonetheless? And it extended down and out. They not only protected and cared for each other; everyone who touched the Hornets was brought under the umbrella.

But being under the umbrella meant being close to people, the space too cramped and tight for anyone to survive. My chest rumbled with panic again and I stepped back from Dean, just trying to catch my breath. The claustrophobia clawed at me like a rabid animal, ripping my conscious thoughts to shreds and leaving nothing but carnage behind.

It hadn't happened in a while; the violent panic attacks, the ones I couldn't control, but I could feel it coming on and there was little I could do to stop it once it started. The nightmares of my life seeped into the cracks and snuffed out whatever lights I had turned on to keep myself company in the darkness.

The worst place to be was inside my own head when it got dark–that's when the memories of what happened played on repeat like bad movies, unable to stop the tape and forced to relive every horrible touch. Every scar on my body itched and stung like they were fresh, and I did everything I could to hide the pain as it surfaced and filled my eyes with water.

"You don't know me, Tuck," I snapped. "Don't pretend like you want to. I'm not like you or your friends. I'm not here to be a part of your little family. I'm here to play baseball and finish my degree."

I stepped around him, not giving him the time to argue as I marched up the steps to our cabin on stiff legs and slammed the door behind me. I sucked in a strangled breath as I collapsed against the door and slid to the floor just trying to breathe.

TUCKER

I wandered into the office the next morning in dirty shorts and a sweat-soaked tank top. The warm air had finally arrived and the sun was beating down on the island. Practice would be hell after breakfast, but maybe I could figure out a way to reward the guys for all their hard work.

"You're going to tell me what's going on," I said, slumping down in the chair across from Silas.

Glasses hung on his nose and he sighed as he slipped them off and leaned back to look at me. His hair was longer than usual; more greys starting to show the longer it got. His mustache had turned into a full beard that I wasn't sure I liked any better, but it made him look tougher. He looked even more serious than before, which I didn't actually think was possible, but under his gaze I was quickly regretting my bossy tone.

"I was trying on my Arlo voice?" I grimaced and he shook his head at me.

"What exactly is it that you want, Tucker?" He asked me, leaning forward on his desk.

"After last night I just..." I grumbled. "I need some more insight on Josh. I need to know why he's here, and I need the real answer, not some bullshit one."

I watched him think on it, his jaw tightening and his shoulders tensing. He was gearing up to lie to me.

"He doesn't want to be here, Doc, and it's causing trouble."

"Just," Silas sighed, "give him a chance to warm up to you."

"It's been a week of camp and he's out-icing ninety percent of the world's glaciers." I sat forward. "He doesn't want to warm up, he wants to run this alone and it's going to kill our season. If I could just figure out how to relate to him, or help him..."

"Dean," Silas started and I cocked my head at him. "Let him play baseball, that's all you need to do."

"No, no, no. That's not all I need to do, Silas." I waved my hands in the air. "I need to captain a team of guys who ruthlessly remind me I'm not Arlo. I have to win this season. I *need* the scouts to see this win."

Letting my parents down isn't an option. The statement went unsaid, but Silas knew better than anyone what it meant.

"I need Joshua Logan to be a fucking pitcher, and I can't get him to do *anything* with the team that he's meant to lead out onto the field every inning. He gets uncomfortable during family meals, he gets angry during team exercises, he doesn't fucking talk during practice!"

"Dean, take a beat." Silas put his hand up to slow me down.

"Letting him just play baseball is easier said than done," I grumbled and slumped back into my chair. "It's like bathing a cat."

Silas chuckled. "Alright, listen. Josh had issues at Lorette—ones that couldn't be solved with tough love or gentle nudges. He was growing more volatile."

"So you and Coach thought *'hey, the Hornets don't have enough trouble, let's bring the spark to the powder keg?'*" I said in shock.

"The problem wasn't *him*, Dean." Silas looked out the window as everyone started to flood into the mess hall for breakfast. "He was expelled for putting a kid in the hospital," he explained, and before I could freak out, which is very much what I wanted to do, he stopped me with a hand. "But Coach and I have a reason to believe that he didn't start the fight. We're trying to figure out what happened but Lorette locked us out of the incident reports."

"So you brought him here knowing what he was capable of and thought, what?" I asked.

"We wanted him under our wing until we could get to the bottom of things, find out what really happened in the locker room that night. It was Ian Peck he put in the hospital."

"Ian? Notorious for his homophobic jokes and relentless taunts, Ian? Those two were thick as thieves on the field. There's no way." The words came out strangled.

Arlo had prevented more than one incident between Cael and Ian in the past. He was infamously big and played first base like a tank. He was a ruddy thing, with beady eyes and a big mouth. Ian was, simply put, a bully, he used the words of my insecurities to get under my skin until I...*snapped*.

"Say they fought, I believe that, but Ian is twice his size," I said in shock. "What was the damage?"

"Three broken ribs, two broken fingers, a shattered orbital bone and a few missing teeth." Silas swallowed tightly. "It was bad."

I sat in shock for a moment. Was he really capable of that kind of carnage? Beating the life out of a guy so badly they had to take him to the emergency room? The thought turned violently in my stomach, and suddenly I wasn't hungry. I had gotten mad before, but never like that. I don't even think I'd ever seen Cael or Arlo that mad, Van maybe, sometimes, but not...like that. Not even in defense of each other.

"Do you think Logan was protecting someone?" I asked.

Silas stared at me for a long moment. "I think Josh was protecting *himself*."

I considered what he was implying, the words unsaid floating between us and it took me too long to put the pieces together.

"You're telling me you think Ian was targeting Josh because he's..." I raised my eyebrows.

"You say that like you aren't..." Silas chuckled tightly. "But yes, Ian isn't exactly known for anything *but* his homophobia. I can't see Josh going that far for anything else, can you?"

"I've seen him have a meltdown about the grass tickling his ankles, so at this point..." I shrugged, there was a chance Ian did nothing. "He really hates being touched, did you know that?"

Silas stared at me and shook his head. "No, what do you mean?"

"I mean, Cael tried to break up a fight and got punched for touching Josh. He's jumpy and unpredictable," I explained, shifting uncomfortably in my sweaty tank top. "Did you—" I stopped myself for a moment, thinking about the implications of the question, and steadied myself on the arms of the chair. "Did you do his physical?" I asked.

"No," Silas shook his head. "He brought signed forms from the Lorettes' Doc that cleared him for play."

"You never looked him over at all?" I asked, just to make sure.

"He insisted he was good to go," Silas said.

"And you just took his word for it?"

"I did."

I stared at Silas wondering what else he was excluding from the conversation. I'd never once, not in the three years of knowing him, known him not to do something himself just to *double check*. He was thorough, direct and careful with every single one of us, but he was *cautious* about Josh and it made me nervous.

"He's covered in scars."

"Everyone has scars, Tucker. It's not exactly cause for alarm," he said.

"Not like childhood scars, or fight scars. I'm talking..." My stomach churned at the memory of Josh's back. "They look inflicted. I don't know."

"Inflicted upon him?" Silas questioned.

"Yeah, like someone hurt him, hundreds of times. They look like scratches or small cuts from a knife and they're all about two inches long. Some overlap." I couldn't help the gag that surfaced from just thinking about the pain he'd felt from whatever happened.

I expected Silas to say something, *anything*, to make me feel better about the situation, but he slumped against his chair with a devastating look on his face. He rubbed his face over his hand

and let his head fall backwards with a huff. I'd never seen him so disgruntled.

"That would explain why he was so insistent," he grumbled.

"That's it?" I scoffed. "No intrigue, no worry?"

"What are we supposed to do about it, Dean? He's made it clear he doesn't want anyone asking questions, he probably forged those clearance papers and now I have phone calls to make so go eat some breakfast and if I find anything out on my end I'll let you know." Silas sat up and went straight back to his paperwork, rifling through them until he found what he needed and grabbed his phone. "Tucker, go eat."

I stared at him for a second longer before pushing out of my seat and leaving the office. Something felt wrong, like the world was off balance. If an incident like Silas was describing occurred...combined with the state of Josh's body. Something bad had happened to turn him so cold and I couldn't figure out for the life of me how to get it out of him. Or if I even wanted to know in the first place.

Maybe ignorance was bliss.

I skipped breakfast and walked my sweaty ass to the baseball field, scooping up a crate of balls and a bat before taking out my frustrations with heavy-hearted swings. Each ball cracked off the bat, loosening the tightness in my shoulders and disconnected me from my problems.

I wasn't exactly grateful for Josh and all his issues, but the distraction from everything else going on in my life had proven to be nice. I'd barely even thought about my parents over the last few days, or the looming cloud that hung over my head over being true to myself and doing it on a public scale.

It was different now though. Would Harbor accept a gay captain? Was that any way to start the season? *"Hey, we're probably going to lose. Oh, and guess what? Your captain's gay! Surprise!"* I huffed and tossed another ball in the air, swinging hard and cracked the ball to the outfield.

"Maybe that's for the best. Rip the bandaid off; have all of Harbor and my entire family disown me in one go..." I said to myself and swung at another ball.

I could hear my mother's disappointment in my head, echoing around like the shrill sounds of a horror movie. *"Franklin, you can't do this to our family. What will your father's colleagues think? What about my future grandchildren?"*

"Hey, Mom, adoption exists..." I grumbled to no one. And even if it didn't, did I even want to have kids? The problems had dog-piled and I'd never had a moment to sort out the important from the frivolous. They all just seemed so heavy when they were weighing down on my chest.

The anxiety of coming out was only worsened by the aftermath of doing something as big as announcing my sexuality to people who wouldn't love me for it. My siblings would call–Anna would flip out and ask me how I could do such a thing to my mother, and Harvey would mail me brochures on conversion camps that his friends passed around the office as they created harmful bills to control the bodies of people they didn't even consider to be human.

It made me sick to my stomach.

"Fuck!" I turned and slammed the bat into the nearest tree, over and over again, until the wood splintered and the handle of the bat rubbed raw against the palms of my hands. Every ounce of frustration vibrated in my forearms and across my chest as the anger and disappointment everyone felt in my presence flooded from me.

I wasn't the golden boy.

I was a fucking failure.

A gay son without anyone to love him, watching a baseball team slip through his fingers. That's who I was and it felt like there was nothing I could do to fix it.

"Fuck, fuck, fuck!" I screamed and threw the destroyed bat into the woods, completely out of breath. I wiped the tears and sweat from my face and then turned around to find Josh, standing by the backstop, watching me with those endless dark eyes.

LOGAN

The sound of wood snapping beneath Dean Tucker's rage-fueled weight echoed in my head as I wandered into the mess hall for lunch.. He had stood there like a child caught red handed but hadn't said a word otherwise.

I backed away from him and didn't see him again until practice. He'd shown up with that dumb, bright smile and positive attitude, like he hadn't disintegrated a wooden bat against a tree an hour earlier. It was both perplexing and infuriating.

He ran practice the same way he had all week—switching players, blindfolding us, forcing communication until we could run a play without stumbles or accidents. I managed to get my hands on a roster. Ella was more than willing to help and I was starting to see why they all went to bat for her so often. It was maddening.

I woke up even earlier and, after a quick run, I found a quiet spot to study their names, but there were so many of them and Dean continued to switch out the teams, forcing me to figure out who was who on a strangled timeline.

The worst part of it all was that seeing Dean so worked up actually made me like him more. The show pony he was in front of everyone else was sickening and fake. I felt drawn to the anger that he was hiding; the frustration he rarely let bubble to the surface. I found myself wanting to know more and that was the last thing I needed. I refused to let the inkling of curiosity derail my focus. Baseball, winning season, graduate. Get the fuck out of Harbor.

That was the short list.

The *only* list.

Figuring out the mystery that was Dean Tucker wasn't on it.

"You like hot dogs?" Cael wandered up behind me in the doorway of the mess hall, keeping his distance but standing shoulder to shoulder with me.

"Sure." I shrugged and started toward one of the tables. I slid into a seat next to him and looked at the bowl in the center of the table. "What the fuck is that?"

"Hot dogs," Van chirped and leaned over the bowl, scooping out a heaping spoonful of noodles and wieners.

"It was Mitchell's turn to make lunch." Arlo stared at the bowl. "He only knows how to make Kraft Dinner and hot dogs, just...eat it."

"It looks like toxic waste," I muttered, taking the spoon from Van but handing it to Cael. I watched them all eat from the bowl like they actually enjoyed it before my eyes wandered, looking around for Dean, but his hulking frame wasn't at any of the tables.

It was weird how often he missed meals but no one called him out for it. Yet if I missed one I'd be hunted down and hogtied. One by one everyone finished their food and left the table, either to help clean or to prepare for the afternoon's exercises. Eventually it was just me, picking away at the gross, swollen sliced pork with a grimace on my face. I forced myself to eat half a bowl of lunch before giving up and finally pushing it away.

"What? Is our food not good enough for you now?" Todd snapped from behind me as he walked by.

"Just not hungry," I said, in a defeated attempt to keep the peace.

"Sure, or..." Todd leaned over the table. "You're a picky asshole just finding reasons to cause trouble."

"Listen, Todd, the only person causing trouble right now is you." I turned my head to look up at him and sighed. "Please just fuck off."

"I've been meaning to ask—why the hell are you here? You clearly don't want to be. The only reason we can come up with is that you're an inside man trying to ruin our season."

"An inside man?" I laughed. "You've been watching too many Mission Impossible movies." I sighed and pushed to get up from the table, but a set of hands shoved me back onto the chair. I snarled and they lifted quickly but the chair was surrounded by a few more of the lesser-known members of the Hornets. Baker, Taylor and Matthenson all hovered around Todd like some sort of half-wit gang, with their arms crossed and scowls on their dumb faces.

It was a win-lose situation. On the one hand, I knew all their names, and on the other, I was probably about to get my ass kicked by them.

"You're going to tell us why the fuck you're here, Logan." Todd looked ready to fight no matter what I said—and that alone was enough to raise my hackles.

"You needed a pitcher." I gave him the most basic answer with a smile, knowing that it would drive him over the edge.

"We had back-up. It had nothing to do with *need*. Why the fuck are you here?" He repeatedly slammed his hand on the table.

"Oooh, some of you Hornets sting after all." I looked him up and down. "You want to know why I'm here, Todd?" I rose slowly from the table.

"Wouldn't have asked the question if I knew the answer, prick." Todd stepped back as I swung my leg around and stepped toward him. The other three tightened the circle but showed no signs of action as Todd went on guard.

"I'm here because I picked out the biggest fucking meat head on our team and I beat the shit out of him so badly he rotted in a hospital bed for three days." I dropped my tone and the words came out tight but smooth off my tongue, like knives to Todd's seemingly tough exterior.

"Yeah fucking right," Todd looked me over. "You're the pussy that got laid out by a girl," he said and I shoved him then, *hard*. He tumbled backwards into a table and scrambled to his feet.

He came at me with his hands raised but missed his swing and lost his balance again, slamming into Baker and needing their help to keep him upright. His anger boiled out of control, rage licking at his usually goofy features, and I could see him losing himself. The weaker their grasp on their static-charged emotions, the sloppier they got.

They needed to learn how to throttle their feelings; to use them in a productive manner.

When he lunged forward again, I didn't hold back. I brought my hand back and drove it into his stomach as he reached for me, knocking the wind out of him and leaving him fighting for his next breath.

The other three weren't having it though; they all jumped on the chance to make up for Todd's shortcomings. Baker had slipped behind me in the jumble, and I could feel his arms slip beneath mine before I could move away. His hands dug into the back of my neck as he held me still. I wriggled to get free, but with my arms pinned upward I didn't have the leverage as Todd composed himself and came at me again.

He pulled back and slammed a fist into my face. The old break in my nose lit up and brought stinging tears to my eyes. I kicked my foot out and shoved him back, but the other two were quick to take his place. I prepared myself for the pain but it never came. Dean wrapped Taylor up in a head lock and grabbed Matthenson by the scruff of his sweater throwing him backward.

"Cut it out!" He warned in a deep voice. "Get the hell out of here before I fucking have you all suspended!" He turned on Todd, who thought about throwing another punch, but Dean squared his shoulders and seemed to double in size, hovering over him in a menacing fashion I never knew Dean had in him. "You and I are going to have a conversation later about your weird need to mark your territory." He pushed on Todd's chest. "Now leave, and take Baker with you."

He was contemplating taking on Dean, I could see it all over his features. Todd squared up, his shoulders nowhere near as large as Dean's, and it was almost laughable. Dean watched him with vicious intent, not backing down for anything.

It was one of the few times he had actually looked like a captain since we'd arrived at camp.

"Yes, Cap." Todd nodded, after a solid minute of silent glaring between them. "Come on," he said, waving off Baker, and the grip on my arms finally loosened.

I shoved him off the rest of the way and stepped back from Dean with cloudy vision and warm blood dripping down my face, the copper tang hitting my lips as it cascaded from my nose.

"What the hell was that about?" He asked me, when the mess hall doors swung shut.

"I didn't start that," I said, trying to clear my head.

"I didn't ask if you started it, I asked what it was about." Dean stepped forward and I stepped back. He sighed and cocked his head to the side with his hands in the air. "I just want to see if it's broken again," he said, pointing at my nose.

"It's not, just agitated," I replied, carefully rubbing the bridge of my nose between two fingers to feel if anything was out of place. "I'll go see, Doc." I said, refusing to use Silas' name. It was definitely broken, but the thought of Dean getting close enough to set it straight made my stomach sick, so I lied.

"Good. Are you okay?" He asked me.

"I'm fine, Tuck," I brushed him off. I was impatient to get out of this conversation. "They were just hazing the new kid. It's out of their system now, so maybe we can finally play some baseball."

Dean watched me for a moment before stepping to the side and letting me walk past him toward the exit. I knew the answer wasn't what he wanted, but it was the only one I had to offer. I turned back to look at him and he was still standing there, muscles tense and chest heaving, as the adrenaline rolled through his body.

"Logan," he warned, before I pushed the door open. "If you don't figure yourself out, I'm going to have to send you home."

"Not sure you have that authority, Tuck. Thanks for the save though. " I pushed out into the sun and heading straight for the cabin. There was about an hour before we had to be grouped up for this afternoon's activities so I was going to clean myself up.

Cael was sitting on his bunk with one of his long legs dangling down from the mattress and his hat pulled down over his face. He tipped the brim up at the sound of the door and eyed me carefully as he sat up.

"What the hell?" He exclaimed, taking in the blood stained collar of my hoodie. "You were alone for, like, ten minutes man!"

"Yeah, well, a nose breaks in under thirty seconds. Will you...help?" I asked him, and approached the bed.

He slipped down and hit the ground softly on both feet, positioning himself in front of me. I braced my hand on the mattress and closed my eyes so I didn't have to stare into his as he reset my nose.

"One, two…" before three he clicked it back into place and pulled back from me to grab a dirty towel that hung on our bunk, handing it to me. "You really need to learn to keep your mouth shut," he said with a smile.

"Wasn't even my fault, Cody. Todd and his band of merry men jumped me in the mess hall." I waved him off and sunk into the rickety chair in the corner of the cabin with my head tilted back to control the nosebleed.

I could see the annoyance on Cael's face as he stared toward the door.

"Tuck dealt with them, it's over. Sit down, you're shaking like a worked up chihuahua," the words came out an exhausted grumble.

I closed my eyes, trying to sit still to let the raging headache I was suffering from pass, as my thoughts were bombarded by old memories. I had made a mistake telling Todd what I did; the chances of him running his mouth were low after he was embarrassed by Tucker, but not zero. Soon, his close friends would know about the fight and the rumors would ripple out until they all had their assumptions about what had happened.

The suffocating truth about that night would stay locked away forever behind walls of concrete and steel. They could assume what they wanted about me; I didn't care and none of them really did either. It was just sick curiosity. They wanted information that could be used in warfare. But I was good at protecting my secrets, and even better at the art of bloodshed than any of them could have imagined. I had been fighting my entire fucking life just to survive, and I wasn't about to let some hyped-up, drunk, college assholes ruin it for me.

My chest tightened and the worry of what my mom was doing flooded back in; whether or not she was okay. It had been nearly a week of no contact and it was eating at me, so badly that sleep was hard to come by, and I spent way too much time wandering around just trying to get a signal on my phone long enough to call the shelters she frequented.

As predicted, spring camp had been a nightmare.

"Are you sure you're okay?" Cael asked as he moved around the cabin. I heard the bed creak and could feel his eyes on me.

"I'm fine." I opened one eye and forced a weak smile to my face. My head was pounding and my nose would hurt pretty badly for the next few days but otherwise I was in good shape. "Ella hits harder," I said, just trying to comfort him.

That was the problem with Cael. No matter how upset I was, or how little the situation had to do with him, I always wanted to make sure he was okay. Comfortable. Safe. That made him laugh though, and he relaxed a little.

"Hey, do you think you could get me a day pass? I need to go into the city." I looked over at Cael.

"I could try." He shrugged and stood up. "Change your shirt before team building." He pointed to the blood drying on the collar, and I nodded at him.

As he left, silence settled in, giving me a few minutes to collect myself before I had to face the wolves again.

TUCKER

The guys all stood around, chatting amongst themselves, when I showed up. I had gone straight to Silas and told him about what had happened so that he could help me keep an eye on Todd and the guys. I knew that ,eventually, they would try to get Josh alone; I just didn't think it would end that way.

I could see Todd's resentment toward me. It was clear from his face that he was pissed off that I'd defended Josh over him, but I didn't care. I wasn't there to just protect them; I needed to be unbiased and captain the team without picking favorites, and that meant sometimes Todd was in the wrong. Which happened more often than not, but never with someone who he'd deemed our enemy.

It had been a week of keeping them apart, only for this to happen the moment I wasn't watching them like a hawk. Arlo stood at the back of the huddle with Ella and his brother, arms crossed, watching and waiting for me to make a move. It was nearly impossible to fill his shoes, and I knew deep down that it wasn't the thing I should be worried about, but the inkling of doubt still pooled in the back of my mind.

Cael stuck his fingers between his lips and blew out a harsh whistle, silencing the separate conversations happening amongst the team.

"We're doing the ropes course today," I explained. "In years past we always did them as a team, but this year I'm separating you into smaller groups. You'll have to work together. The group that finishes the course the fastest, with as few slip ups as possible, doesn't have to practice in the morning."

"Seriously?" Van perked up and I nodded at him. "Hell yeah!" He nudged Baker beside him with an excited smile.

"I'm making the teams though," I said, as Josh wandered gingerly up to the group. "Line up." I pointed, and they scattered into a clumsy line.

I went down it, separating them into five teams by giving them each a number, until I got to the very end and stared at Josh. "Five."

He looked over to where the five were huddled and back at me. "You're an asshole, Tuck," he muttered, backing away and wandering over to where Todd, Baker, Taylor, and Matthenson stood.

"Consider it a teaching moment, tough guy." I smiled at him and looked over the rest of the teams. "Be safe, and listen to the instructors. It's a speed contest, but I don't need any of you hurt. Coach'll kill us all if we come home short of men for the season." I tapped my fingers to my chest and watched them all do it in unison–except Josh. He just stared at me like I had three heads.

"What's with the weird cult tapping anyways?" He asked, as we all made our way down into the wooded area of camp where the ropes course was strung up.

"I don't actually know." I shrugged, and he turned to look at me, confused. "We've always done it as long as I've been a Hornet. I think it was something Coach used to do and it just stuck with Arlo. Now we all do it."

"So it *is* weird cult shit." Josh rolled those sable brown eyes and his lips curled into that infuriating, cocky smile.

"No, it's our handshake, I guess... a way to promise each other, keep each other in check, stuff like that. Sorry it's not an aggressive chant where we smack each other's asses and holler weird shit over and over," I joked.

"Lorette never did anything," he said, and the confession took me aback.

"What?" I said.

"Yeah, nothing. No chants, no sayings, no support..." Josh explained, but he seemed completely unbothered by it all.

"If you think that's bad, wait until you find out that we sacrifice a goat before the season opener for good luck." I smiled over at him, but was met with a nasty glare. "Oh, come on! That was funny!" I laughed.

"You're not funny." Josh shook his head.

"I'm hilarious, you just can't take a joke."

The trees rustled in the wind above our heads; the newly formed bright green leaves catching in the sun and tinting everything with a soft hue.

"Make a funny joke and I'll take it," Josh huffed, looking over at me.

The sun bathed his cold features with warmth and highlighted the undertones of gold in his eyes. The itching feeling returned and I hated that he could bring it the same way Cael used to. That searing heat that licked at my muscles and turned my ears an embarrassing shade of red.

He was infuriatingly handsome in that *'you drive me insane'* kind of way. The bridge of his nose was shorter and his heavy eyebrows were always curled in angrily, even with a smile on his face. My heart was pounding in my chest because, suddenly, I wanted to know how his beard would feel against my skin. I wanted to know if he tasted as warm as he looked and smelled; that woodsy cinnamon cologne he always wore mixed with the lingering smell of pine tar that tickled at my nose.

Every noise around us seemed to mute for a moment, losing its importance as I stared down what felt like the barrel of a loaded gun.

"Tuck?" Josh said, snapping me from the walking wet dream I was having. His hand snapped out and tangled into the fabric of my shirt, tugging me against his shoulder.

"What the hell?" I shoved away from him and he pointed to my left. Not two inches from me was a massive tree. "Oh..."

"We would have matched." He pointed to his nose with a smug look on his face.

"I guess I'm a little out of it," I said, rubbing my hands over my face in a feeble attempt to refocus myself.

"That'll happen when you miss three meals. You're probably starving," Josh said, off the cuff. "How many calories do you take in a day to stay that big, anyways?"

I opened my mouth to tell him I hadn't missed three meals, but then I counted and he was right, which only seemed to bother me more. The number was in the two thousands, but sometimes, when I got side tracked and focused on a task, I just forgot to eat all together. It wasn't good for me, or smart, but my body functioned alright on the rare occasion that it did happen. It wasn't a lack of nutrition causing me to run into trees though—it was the freckle pattern on Josh's face.

The path broke up and opened into a massive area that had been transformed into a high ropes course. Josh tilted his head back and the dark curls spilled down his neck as he surveyed the course. It was a permanent part of the camp, but still in immaculate shape. Silas made sure that they always had the funds for repairs; the camp never wanted for anything all they had to do was pick up the phone.

Rope lines were strung between the tree tops, separated by small platforms along the course. There were ladders, bridges, tight ropes, all suspended nearly fifteen feet off the ground.

"This is intense," Josh grumbled, but his tone was nervous.

"Are you afraid of heights?" I asked him.

"No." His head snapped toward mine and I could see the fear in his eyes. It battled against his usual anger, but I could see it in the way his jaw twitched and his brows softened.

"You are," I whispered with a smirk. It felt good to have the upper hand just this once; even if he was nervous, it was nice to see a different side of him that wasn't created by anger.

"Back off, Tuck." He shook his head and wandered over to the other guys to listen to the instructor explain how to put on a harness. I watched his shoulders square up as he settled in next to the group. He left decent space between him and Todd, which was for the best, but today they would have to work together to finish the course in time. If Josh really was afraid of heights, he was going to need the support of his team to get him through it.

"Not bad." Arlo appeared next to me.

I scoffed and crossed my arms over my chest. "Everything has gone to shit, at this point even getting them to stand next to each is cause for celebration."

"That's not true," Arlo said. "They've made it through a few meals," he offered.

"They have to make it through an entire season without killing each other." I sighed.

"No they don't." He laughed and I turned to look at him, a little confused by his reaction.

"Isn't that the whole point of spring camp? To make them some unbreakable team?" I asked him and he shook his head, looking back to the group of guys laughing and fighting playfully as they got ready.

"It's never been about making them unbreakable, Tucker," he explained. "It's about guiding them in the right direction but giving them the space to make mistakes."

"That binder is messing with my head." I sighed. I had memorized it, front to back, and still had no idea how to captain the way Arlo had. It was eating at me, along with every other problem I was trying to balance on my shoulders.

"The binder is a bible," Arlo said. "Stop trying to mimic and find your heart, Tucker. You need to figure out why Coach made you captain over all the other guys here. Once you do that you'll figure out how to lead them."

"I really hate it when you and Cael start that Yoda crap," I grumbled.

"Never compare me to Yoda again. I'm clearly Obi-wan." Arlo smiled and slapped a hand on my shoulder.

"I hate Star Wars," I complained, throwing my head back.

"You need to lead with this." Arlo pushed two fingers against my chest. "Stop letting this push you around, it's not qualified." He moved and tapped my temple with those same fingers.

"Are you saying I'm dumb?" I asked him, and he laughed again.

"No, Tucker, you just need to get out of your own head and start being you again. Ever since the accident you've been moving around like you're walking on broken glass. No one is mad at you," Arlo said and it unlocked a box that I had closed up tight on purpose. Guilt was a monster I couldn't control and...

"And while you're at it trying to be me; mean and loud doesn't suit you." Arlo backed away with a shrug and found a spot at the base of the course with Ella and Silas.

Lead with this—the problem was, my heart had been untrustworthy lately, more so than my brain ever had been. Wading through the heartbreak that Cael accidentally brought down around us was rough; for a few weeks after the accident I hadn't been sure what to do with myself.

It was hard to even look at him, broken and bruised. The images of him in the hospital were nightmare fuel. His weak shoulder, torn apart and stitched back up again. Seeing the raw skin every time I helped him change his bandages forced horrible feelings to blossom in my chest. I was glued to his side until he went to rehab, and then again when he came home. We had used each other as comfort for so long that it was simple to fall back into it, until it wasn't simple anymore. Guilt ate at me like a rabid dog. It crept up in the most vulnerable of moments to remind me that I had led Cael to his blow up. I'd told him I couldn't love him—that he was too much for me. The fight that led to his downfall had stemmed from my vicious words; simple fear with no reasonable way to project it other than anger and accusation. I knew it wasn't me that put the drugs in his system, I hadn't forced him to drink, but I knew what he was going through and, instead of sucking it up, I let it out and it nearly killed my best friend.

Whether or not the guilt was well-placed or deserved, it was there. Festering.

I just wanted to be loved without conditions or secrets.

I had watched Cael Cody love a shadow for nearly five years. She had always been there and I'd always known I'd lose to her eventually. Whether or not she had returned or Cael ever saw Clementine again, I would have lost him.

It didn't make it hurt any less, but at least I had been bracing for the impact from the moment I'd laid eyes on Cael. He was so loud and so loving. I never meant to drag him into the dark with me—his heart was too big to hide from the world. Cael was happier than I'd ever seen him. Even in her absence his mind was clear, his smile had returned, and he'd be a massive asset this season now that he could play. It was my own problems that needed to be sorted out.

I didn't know how to live in a world where my family hated me for my heart—the real one. Not the one they assumed I had, girl loving, grandchild producing, golden boy. No, the blood that coursed through my veins, and caused my heart to race, had always loved boys. It always would and always in secret until I could figure out how to be honest with myself and my family.

"Earth to Dean." Cael's voice snapped me from my thoughts and his bright smile came into view like a universal reminder that, no matter how I felt, Cael would still be there to love me the way I needed him to. "Your boy is struggling…"

LOGAN

The harness was a death trap—designed to frustrate even the smartest of users. There were way too many buckles, at least sixteen more straps than necessary, and every time I put it on, it felt wrong.

"Fuck." I stepped out of it again and stared at it. I didn't even want to do the ropes course, but I wasn't about to give them another excuse to corner me with their judgmental anger and hair-trigger fists.

"You have it backwards," Dean said as he approached. The sweater he was wearing hugged tightly to his strong shoulders and tapered at his waist. The thin athletic shorts did nothing to hide his huge thighs. I hated to admit that I thought about them more than I should. But it was hard not to, when he was parading them around. I could swear that our only saving grace during a bear attack would be that Dean Tucker could probably choke it out between his legs with little to no effort.

I shook my head clear of the thoughts and cursed again at the tangle of straps in my hands.

"Can I help?" He asked me with his hand extended for the harness.

"I can put on a couple straps, Tuck." I kept the harness close to my body and turned my eyes back to it with a small frustrated sigh.

"I don't want you breaking your legs. Just let me help, it won't kill you." He snapped his finger at me and grumbled.

It might.

I handed him the harness and watched him sink to his knees on the soft forest floor. *Jesus fucking Christ*—those were the only words left in my vocabulary as he tilted his chin up to look at me and the sunlight danced around in those seaglass eyes.

"Right foot," he said, without missing a beat or noticing how flustered I had just become.

Shit.

"This is fucking dumb," I growled, but stuck my leg out for him.

He held out the harness, letting me step into it, and I became oddly aware of his fingers and palms as he lifted it over my hips–careful never to touch me.

"Can you hold this?" He asked, his eyes level with my hips and I gripped the belt as he started to tighten all the straps, one at a time, left to right. He looked at the straps on my inner thighs and paused before looking up at me. "Can I touch you?" He asked, his voice lower than before, and I nodded, turning my head away from his burning gaze.

His fingers smoothed out the strap before he held it flush to my thigh and tightened it up against his hand. I could feel every move he made without looking at him, his knuckles brushing over the other thigh as he repeated the progress. I kept my eyes on everyone else, trying to focus on something or anything else than his touch.

I expected to find people staring, but no one seemed to care that Dean was on his knees helping the 'enemy'. Everyone was too busy tightening their own harnesses or planning strategies for the course. At Lorette, such a public show would have been considered cause for ridicule. The homophobic slurs would have been flying the moment Dean offered his help, but here no one gave a shit.

It was strange being around people who were so well-adjusted.

It didn't excuse the brutal rage that festered between Todd and I, but at least it wasn't being backed into a corner. Here I could breathe long enough to fight back.

Ian's sick smile flashed through my mind, his hands, the running water—

"Okay, enough," I snapped, stepping back from Dean.

He put both hands in the air to show me that he wasn't touching me anymore and rose to hover over me again. It wasn't threatening, but he waited until I'd calmed down before he asked: "Is it tight enough? Check for me." He nodded to my waist and I gave it a tug. There was barely a finger space between the belt and my skin. "Good."

Dean watched for a second longer and I knew he wanted to ask what the outburst was about, but someone called to him.

"Yo, Tucker, can you help me too?" Jensen stood with the harness tangled in a massive knot and a stupid look on his face. Dean looked back at me to check one last time, the pause enough to make me want to tell him to fuck off, but I held my tongue.

I don't need your pity.

I inhaled a breath of clean air, untainted by his scent, and went to stand with the rest of my group. Todd was running his mouth about being the best at the course while the other three were staring up at the ropes like they were going to vomit.

"Who's going first?" The instructor asked, scanning the group.

"Logan." Todd offered me up to the wolves without a second of consideration, but I wasn't going to let him win this stupid game he was playing. If his intention was to rattle me, it wasn't going to work. I was going to run the course, faster than him, and then I'd be done for the day.

"Fine," I said, stepping forward.

Todd glared at me and crossed his arms over his shoulders.

"It'll take a lot more than a punch and some first grade insults to get under my skin, Todd. You and the brat pack can brainstorm while I run the course. Maybe you can come up with something that will actually hurt my feelings?"

"If you fall and fuck up our time, I'll finish what I started." Todd cupped his face and called out to me, but I only responded with laughter.

I'd like to see him try.

I climbed the thick tree trunk one step at a time, using the small wooden boards nailed to its center, until I reached a long, narrow platform that held one of the other instructors.

"I'm going to clip this here." He pointed to the loop on my harness and I nodded, trying not to look down. My hands shook at my side but I was determined to prove them all wrong. I don't think I was actually afraid of heights, but being suspended in the air was a whole other shock to the system.

"You're going to start here and zig zag down to the finish line." He moved his hand through the trees, pointing out the route quickly before asking me if I was ready. I nodded but the contents of my stomach were threatening eviction and I could already feel how much stronger the wind was above the trees.

"Don't fall, Logan!" Todd's irritating voice boomed up through the trees and scared a few birds resting nearby.

I flipped him off and stepped out onto the first bridge, hearing Dean call out that the time had started. I concentrated on the steps ahead of me, focusing on the way the shaking rope bridge felt beneath my feet, and used it to propel myself forward. If I could just count my steps, maybe I could forget the fear that coursed through me.

Being up this high reminded me of the apartment building we lived in. We were in the basement suite, the bars on the window preventing the sun from reaching my skin. So I'd climb the thirteen flights of stairs to the top and pick the lock on the chain that held the roof door closed. I could remember how horrible that part of the city smelled; the rotting homeless flesh that we were just weeks away from becoming, the stench of week-old vodka and smoke from the warehouse factories that our building was crammed between. But still, somehow, up there I felt free, the air tangled into my hair and snuck its way beneath my clothes. It cooled the stinging sensation of new cuts and healing burns. It was salvation to be up that high.

But it was also dangerous.

The ice in winter made the shoddy matting of the roof slippery, and when your boots are so old the treads on them are gone, there was never traction. I had slipped once, right off the side, I fell six feet onto the frozen rusted fire escape and broke my wrist.

I'd hid the bruised arm for weeks until one of my mom's boyfriends saw it and quickly made a game out of the noises he could muster from me as he swung me around the living room. I'd passed out and woke up in the emergency room downtown, my mom nowhere in sight, but the doctors took pity on me and put a cast on me. They whispered around my bed like I couldn't hear them, but the moment child protective services left their mouths, I was gone.

I missed the freedom of the rooftop.

"Good job!" Ella clapped from below as my feet made contact with the first platform. "Keep moving, Josh!"

The way my heart reacted to her positive reinforcement was infuriating.

Everything after that was easy. It took me a second to get into the groove of things, but by the time I came to the last set of ropes I had successfully blocked out the noise. Todd was on my tail. He had caught up when I slipped two stages back, and I could hear his heavy breathing as he pushed himself as fast as he could go.

"You alright back there, Todd? You sound like you're in heat," I called out, stepping onto the rope. It was three ropes, strung out tight in a triangle formation. Two for my hands, and one to balance across to the final platform before the zip line.

"Fuck you, Logan, just mind your business," Todd responded, his words cracking as his balance wavered.

"Don't fall. If you fall, we lose," I said, poking the bear.

"They'll still find a way to make it your fault, Josh. They always will." Todd meant for his words to be a funny jab, but he wasn't wrong. They would find a way to make it my fault if we lost. It wouldn't matter if I ran the course without a slip, what mattered was being able to ostracize me from the team in unimaginable ways until the end of my god forsaken life.

My foot slipped from the rope and my arms tensed around the ones above my head as I hung in the air, dangerously high. My breathing became ragged as my heart rate spiked and I looked down at the ground.

Shit, that's high.

"Get your feet up!" Someone called out to me, but the fear of falling had me gripped tight and my arms felt like lead as I attempted to swing back to the rope. I wasn't going to be able to pull myself up. I was going to fall here and embarrass myself, and then Todd would be right, I would be to blame for the loss.

The rope was taught, dangling from the small carabiner. The only thing stopping me from plummeting to the ground. There was no fire escape to break my fall this time.

"Josh." Dean's voice was quieter than the rest and not below me, but ahead of me. "Hey, tough guy, over here," he said, and my eyes directed upward to where he was crouched on the platform. "I thought you weren't afraid of heights," he mocked.

"I'm not," I said, aware how shaky my voice sounded.

"Then why are you trembling like a wet purse puppy?" Dean teased, and the smile that formed on his face that made my blood boil.

"Shut the fuck up, Tuck," I growled, trying to pull myself up again, but my body was still too heavy and my will to survive this situation was dwindling.

"They'll never let you live this down," Dean said. "But by all means, give up. Show them how much of a coward you are." He cocked his head to the side.

"Whatever fucking mind games—" I grunted. I used all my force to pull myself up and clumsily found the base rope with my sneakers. Dean rose with me, never taking his eyes off me as I found my balance and started moving again "—you think you're playing, they won't work."

"No games," he said with a shrug. "It's not my reputation on the line, Josh. I'm the golden boy–everyone loves me. You're the one who needs to impress, and you weren't going to do it hanging from a rope while Todd teased you like a sixth grade bully."

Dean reached out and grabbed the collar of my sweater, tugging me roughly onto the platform. "Congratulations, tough guy, you didn't die and you finished in fourteen minutes and thirty nine seconds."

"I didn't need your help," I snapped at him, unclipping myself so the last instructor could fasten me to the zipline.

"If you think insulting you is help, Logan, we have work to do."

LOGAN

"Did you ask about the day pass?" I loomed over Cael, muscles aching and head pounding. I hadn't slept in two days and we still had five left at camp.

"What?" Cael's eyes blinked open slowly and I reached out to shake the bunk hard enough for him to sit straight up. "What the hell?" He hissed, scowling at his watch. "It's five am, Logan!"

"Consider it payback," I grumbled. "I *need* to go into the city," I tried again.

Cael opened his mouth to argue but saw the look on my face and nodded. "I'm going to have to run it by Silas, no one leaves camp without his permission. He's the law out here."

"I thought this was martial law—every man for himself?" I snapped.

"That's what he wants us to think, but if we leave without telling him he'll have a conniption so, breakfast first, then let me talk to Silas." Cael laid back against the pillow with a groan.

"Talk to him at breakfast." I must have sounded pathetic because those blue eyes were wide awake with my easy acceptance of his plan.

"What's wrong?" He asked, rolling onto his side and whispering so he didn't wake the other two. Dean looked stupidly peaceful, his arms tucked under his head, his chest rising and falling gently against his messy sheets.

I hated how badly I wanted to touch him.

"Nothing, I just need a meeting, Cody," I growled and retreated. "I'm going for a run. Get up and talk to Silas."

"Fine. There's one on the east side that starts at noon, but you're buying lunch after because this is bullshit." He rolled back over onto his pillow.

I took that as surrender and left the cabin for my run without another word. The sirens for the morning lake dips echoed faintly through the air the further I got from camp, and I only slowed to a walk when my lungs screamed at me to stop.

I slipped down the embankment, something I had become familiar with over the last week, and stripped from my clothes. I left them in a pile by the shore and slowly waded into the frigid water, letting my skin adjust to the temperature and shocking my sore muscles as I dipped beneath the surface.

I sank to the bottom of the lake and held my breath at the bottom for as long as I could. My lungs burned and my head grew empty of all the nightmares that followed me around like shadows. I pushed it a second longer before surfacing.

The moment I broke the water into the mild spring air I knew someone was watching me. There was an eerie feeling to it, and as a child I had never known the silent feeling of being left alone. Someone always wanted something from me; mom always needed more drugs which meant she always needed me to be someone for someone. No matter how wrong it sounded, I was only ever trying to make her love me, so I let them take what they needed so that she could survive another day.

'That's my baby, you're so brave.'

Her voice echoed in my mind and the feeling of her kiss on my head seared hot in the same place it always did.

"Following a guy through the forest is a new low, even for you," I said before turning around.

"Yeah, well, you were the one who chose Cael to be your secret best friend. You'll learn quickly that even when he's trying to be quiet, he's the loudest idiot in the room." Dean's voice was tight and agitated.

"I thought you were asleep," I said. I could have sworn he was.

"I thought you couldn't swim," he countered.

"I never said I couldn't swim, you just keep assuming that." I didn't want to turn around because I could feel his eyes on my back, on my scars, and I couldn't find the courage in me to explain them. They were my best-kept secret and the worst of my memories. Each one still radiated pain long past, caused by men long gone. Scars to remind me how much of a coward I was back then. How little my life really meant to her, compared to her next score.

"You could have told me you were doing the dips out here. I would have gone easier on you," he said, and something about the condescension in his tone had me whirling around in the lake.

"Listen to me, Tucker, because I'm only going to say this once. I don't need your fucking pity. I don't want it. It's flimsy and fake. If you think you're finding common ground with me, you're not. You grew up with a silver spoon in your mouth—pampered and perched on a pedestal made of gold, *just for you*." I pushed through the water to the shore and grabbed my shirt, tugging it over my wet body and pulling on my sweats.

"You're never going to relate to me, you're never going to find any unlocked doors to wander through. I don't want to be friends, and you only keep trying for the sake of a win." I invaded his space. "For the last fucking time, we don't need to be friends for me to play baseball like a God, and that's what I'm going to do. Whether your stupid Manson family cult likes me or not. I'm going to pitch the ball, play the game, and go home every night. End of story."

Dean stayed quiet, his chest rising and falling in the same slow rhythm as when he slept. I despised how easily he stayed calm. I was all but beating the shit out of him and he was just there, like a brick wall, staring down at me with a smile on his face.

He moved his hand and I flinched. "Whoa," he said softly. "Here." He pulled out a set of keys from his pocket. "I got you permission from Silas. Just don't do anything stupid with it."

I stared at the keys and put out my hand for him to drop them into my palm.

I hadn't expected him to be the one to do that for me.

"Thank you," I said tightly, stepping back.

"I'll expect you to make up for the practice you'll be missing."

Cael drove us back into the city and I was filled with instant regret.

"Can you at least try to follow the speed limit?" I asked him, as he pushed twenty over the limit with a smile on his face.

"Don't be such a fun sucker." He rolled his eyes at me and continued his pace. "Just because you were in a foul mood before breakfast doesn't mean you can steal my joy."

"You're a cry baby," I groaned and closed my eyes to at least get a little sleep before we made it to the city. When I opened them again Cael was pulling up to one of the churches I recognized and my phone was vibrating violently in my pocket as the missed calls from my mother flooded in at the first lick of service. It had been a long time since I was in this end of town and my heart seized at the sight of it.

The church loomed over the dirty neighborhood, mocking the poor by implying that if you just believed in something higher than yourself that it would save you. I wish that were true. I wish that faith had been strong enough to heal me, to heal my mother, but it had never been in our cards. It filled me with a resentment I couldn't quite understand, one that maybe I would eventually get past, but for today, I just wanted to watch the world burn.

"You picked this place on purpose," I said as I climbed from the car with him. He looked at me over the roof and propped himself up on his elbows.

"Yeah, and?" He was so honest it was almost a flaw.

"You're an asshole," I added.

"Tell me something I don't know, grumpy groucher." He slapped the hood and the alarm went off loudly in our ears as he panicked to pull the keys back out.

"Oops." He shrugged, shoving the keys back in his pocket as we made our way up the steps to the church doors. It was smaller inside than I remembered as a kid; dustier too. There were less pews and, up at the front where I remember the pedestal being, were a few scattered chairs and a couple of guys hovering around talking to one another.

"Cael!" A shabby looking man with an unruly beard and long brown shaggy hair approached us with an overfilled cup of coffee in his hands. He smelled like mold and had stains down the cuffs of his gray dress shirt. "I'm a bit of a mess today," he said, looking at me like he could read my mind.

"Josh, this is Neil. He runs the meetings here twice a week and I've never seen him put together so…" Cael laughed but hugged the weird man.

He went in on me and I stepped back from him.

"He's jumpy." Neil laughed and clapped Cael on the shoulder. "Grab a seat, we're going to start," he said. He turned to me as Cael walked away and looked me up and down. "You're from around here, aren't you?"

"No," I said tightly. "I'm not."

It was a lie but I had seen that look before and it was always followed by "you're Deedee Logan's son." Which was almost always followed by a fight.

The worst part about Harbor was that everyone knew everyone. When I moved to Lorette for baseball I thought that it was all over, that I never had to hear her name again in that way, but it wasn't the case. We were only an hour apart and Lorette was the bigger city; most people came in for the night life, stayed for the drugs, and died in the dark back alleys completely forgotten.

I had almost died in those back alleys more than once, and many times before I could even get my hands on alcohol. It wasn't until I was fourteen that I started getting into my mom's stash. Whatever would dull the roar of pain and anger that filled my muscles. Vodka was my favorite.

Everyone took their places and the meeting ran through about as normally as those meetings usually do. Everyone explained why they came and we all offered hollow optimism in return. Meetings worked a little differently for my brain. Maybe it was a toxic need to feel shame, but their stories just made me embarrassed enough to never be that person again.

The shame of being a drunk kept me from becoming one again, though it wrecked my mental health, but the anger was better than being face down on the bathroom floor begging for more, just to conceal all the other feelings I didn't want to feel.

"Josh." Neil's weird, grainy voice broke through my sticky thoughts and brought me back to reality. "Anything you wanna share while you're here?"

I stared at him for a second, contemplating telling him no, but people like him, like me, never settled for that kind of answer. "I'm Josh," I muttered, nodding tightly as Cael watched me. He knew some of my story, the things I allowed him to hear, but I was careful to never give too much. A simple, clean alcoholic story was enough to get by in most situations, no one ever questioned when I said I was a party kid, used it to feel alive. That was enough for them and it meant I never had to tell anyone what had really happened. It meant I never had to suffer through the feelings of being a weak, defenseless coward ever again.

"Staying sober has gotten tough lately," I said, with a huff of frustration that sounded a lot like annoyance. "I got in some trouble and had to switch my plans, it uh—" I leaned back in my chair and rolled my shoulders so my back was tight and I could focus on the way the muscles pulled beneath my skin instead of my shame.

"—threw me off a little and it's been a long time since I craved that smell, vodka...but I woke up this morning and I swear I could smell it in the air. So, I'm here." I nodded.

"That matters," Neil said. "You made a choice this morning."

"I could have just as easily made the wrong choice. I almost did," I said, and I could feel Cael tighten beside me, holding his breath at my admission.

"There's no wrong choice, Josh," Neil said, chuckling when my eyebrows scrunched together in confusion.

"There's always a *wrong* choice."

"There can't be, not without the presence of a conscious decision. Which is most cases when we wake up *needing* a fix, it's not a conscious decision. It's exactly that, a need." Neil stared at me and waited for the words to process.

"Maybe for you," I replied. "For me it's a decision to ruin everything. I *want* to make a mess, I *want* to destroy everything. Completely conscious."

Neil nodded gently, sitting quietly in the response without a way to argue back.

That was the problem with these meetings, they did their job to remind me how far I could fall but at what cost. The other members in the room all looked on the brink of relapse except Cael. He stared at me like I was a shiny beacon of hope, and that alone would be the reason I fell from grace.

I pushed from the chair and left the circle without another word. Cael didn't follow, no one did, as I wandered out into the open air. I jogged down the steps looking up and down the familiar street before I started walking to my right. There was a diner two blocks over but I circled the crumbling concrete sidewalks for nearly an hour before stepping inside and letting the smell of week old grease and onions hit my nose.

Swallowing past the cotton lodged in my throat, I found a booth at the back along the only wall without windows and slid in against the cracked leather.

"Can I get you anything?" A waitress asked from over the counter at me, her dark hair was grayed and pulled up tightly off her old face.

"Just water," I said, turning away from her to stare at my hands. I pressed them flat against the rickety diner table top and counted the scars one at a time until my breathing slowed down. I slipped my phone from my jeans and set it on the table; it was still vibrating on and off. Mom had called three times since we had been in the city.

"Fuck."

A plate of fries slid across the table and with it Cael's dumb fucking face.

"Go away, Cody." I waved him off and rested my head against the booth, hoping that closing my eyes would get him to disappear.

"Eat," he urged, "and then tell me what the hell is going on with you."

"Not hungry," I said. "Just leave me alone for an hour and then we can go back to the torture camp."

"You're always hungry," he insisted. "So eat—then talk."

"How the hell did you even find me anyways?" I asked, opening one eye to look at him. His hat was turned backwards over his buzz cut and he had a serious look on his face that was rare from him.

"You're *always* hungry," he repeated gently. "We never met anywhere but a diner when it was time to talk, and this was the closest one. I've been sitting here for nearly an hour waiting for you, for a second there I thought maybe I was wrong, but then I remembered something," he paused.

"What?" I asked.

"I'm never fucking wrong." Cael chuckled, a smile forming on his face as he pushed the plate toward me again. "Eat—"

"Talk, yeah, yeah, I heard you." I shoved a fry in my mouth, hoping maybe just the eating would be enough to get him to leave me alone, but I could tell by the look on his face I wasn't getting off the hook that easily.

"You aren't the only one with a shitty parent," I said to him. "In fact, your dad isn't even shitty, he's just really bad at communicating…"

"What's your point?" Cael asked in a soft tone before stealing a fry.

"I grew up down the street, in the run down apartment building behind the church. I could see the iron peaks from the small window in the bathroom." I stared at the front door, my mind trying to convince my heart to bolt before I told him too much.

"You grew up in Lorette? I thought you were a transfer…" Cael sounded confused and rightfully so. That was what had been told to everyone, but I'd forged the address on my admissions to Lorette.

"My high school teacher, Mr. Campbell, he always said that if I wanted to be someone else I just had to try, so I reinvented myself. I worked hard and got that scholarship. Mr. C let me use his address so that my mail didn't get stolen by my mom," I explained.

"She's clearly your catalyst," Cael hummed, nudging my vibrating phone and I sighed, flipping it over.

"She's always had problems; I don't remember a time in my life when she didn't."

"Never thought I'd hear the day that Joshua Logan blamed anything in his life on another person," Cael said.

"Yeah, well, sometimes there is someone to blame." I shrugged just wanting the conversation to be over with.

"Why'd you get kicked off Lorette?" He asked next; I knew the question was coming but I wasn't in the mood to budge.

"I didn't, I transferred. Drop it."

"Josh, you preach letting shit go but you're so wound up over something that you don't seem to wanna feel, and I don't understand why you aren't being honest?" Cael pushed. His blue eyes seemed to sting as he surveyed my tight posture and squared off shoulders.

"This is different from a long-lost girlfriend and a dead mom, Cael. What I have to feel will kill me." I stared him down for a second longer before shoving the plate back toward him. "Take me back to camp."

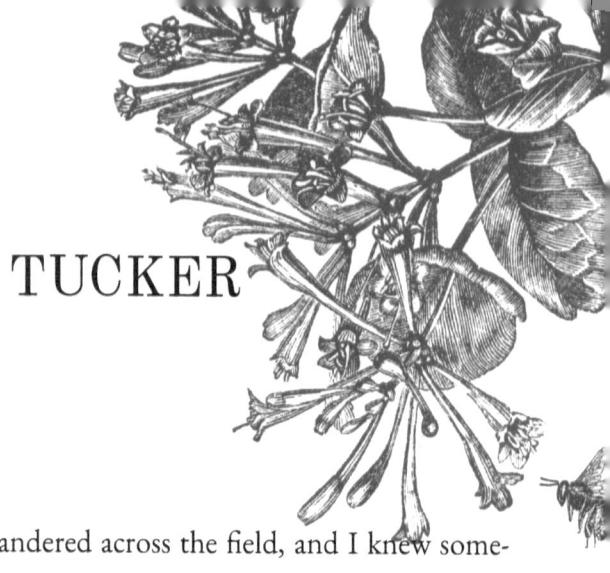

TUCKER

Cael and Josh wandered across the field, and I knew something had happened by the look on Cael's face. His expression was tight, the smile brittle—secrets clearly gnawing at him. I clapped Van on the shoulder and met them in the middle, only for Josh to walk around me like I didn't exist.

"Great," I huffed as Cael lobbed the keys through the air at me.

He looked over my shoulder at the team and then back to me. "I tried."

"If you can't get him to talk, I don't know what I'm supposed to do," I said.

"I think..." He paused, lowering his voice. "Even though he knows we're not, I'm pretty sure he's stuck on this idea that we're perfect. That none of us has anything to be sad or stressed about. Like, he's having a trauma dick-measuring contest, but none of the rest of us were aware we entered."

"Was that really the best way to describe that?" I laughed, and Cael shrugged.

"Whatever..." He laughed with me. "Maybe if he sees how imperfect we can be, he'll open up a bit."

"Anytime I try to explain to him, he walls up and flips out," I admitted.

"Stop trying one-on-one," he suggested.

"What do you mean?" I turned and started to walk with him over to the diamond.

"It's time you share your story, big boy, and not just with Josh. With all of them." Cael winked and backed away to start warming up before I could argue with him that it was a dumb idea.

Even more dumb than trying to figure out what Josh needed. Every time he was met with even a flicker of kindness, he pushed back, claiming he didn't need this or that. It was infuriating, and there was little I could do to stop the outbursts.

My mind was flooded with the image of him in the lake that morning. His back was a mess of scars that ran so much deeper than I had expected. With my new perspective of his skin, I could see the trauma seeping from him, but instead of being scared of it, all I wanted to do was ask him how it had happened.

At this point, I could barely get him to tell me his middle name. He wasn't going to trauma dump over a can of Dr. Pepper at Hilly's with me. I kicked at the dirt with my sneaker and made my way over to where they were standing, waiting for me to tell them what we were going to be doing that day. There were only a few days left at camp, and we really hadn't gotten anywhere as a team. If we expected to go back and even compete in the exhibition game scheduled for the end of next week, we needed to start working as a team–and we needed to do it now.

"Alright, I'm going to give you a position, and you're stuck there for the day. No arguments," I followed up quickly as they all started to rumble and huff at the announcement. "Van, move to catcher. Todd to pitcher, Jensen to third, Cael go *first*."

I gave the last of them positions, and they moved, but not in total silence. Cael gave me a death glare as he shifted from his rooted position at shortstop, but I needed to teach Josh and Todd a lesson in cooperation, and the best place to do that was with Logan as Todd's backup.

"Josh, shortstop."

I watched him open his mouth to argue and then close it again when I put my arms out to welcome the fight. He shoved his hand in his glove and wandered across the field, no doubt feeling more out of place than ever.

"Arlo, hit some balls for them?" I asked, moving to second base.

"I thought you'd never ask." He smiled and tugged off his sweater, throwing it toward Ella before swiping a bat from the dugout and warming up his arm. It was always nice to see Arlo in his element; practices gave us that sense of familiarity that we all craved now that he was a coach. I could feel the tension lifting as he stepped into the batter's box.

Todd pitched the first ball the minute Ella shouted "game on", with the pitch soaring too high past Arlo and into the cage.

"Have you ever pitched a ball, Todd? Or are your skills limited to rifling them back to the pitcher?" Arlo grumbled as Todd reset on the mound and inhaled loudly.

"This is bullshit, Tucker. What's the point of us being all messed up?" He complained, but he threw the ball and again it soared wide.

"Ask for instruction, Todd," I said to his back instead of giving him a straight answer.

"Instruction?" He asked, only pausing to grunt as Van put the ball hard into the back of his mitt. "You're fucking ten feet from me Mitchell. Soften up, man!"

"Throw a straight pitch, Todd!" Van yelled back. His arm wasn't made for short distance throws, and he had a cannon on a bad day. I didn't envy the sting that was no doubt spreading out like wildfire across Todd's palm.

"Ask for help, Todd," I said again, when the two stopped bickering.

He turned those shit-brown eyes on me and scowled, before turning to his newly appointed shortstop. "Help me," he barked.

Josh chuckled and looked up from the dirt with a smug smile that was only going to cause another fight, but then he opened his mouth and "move back a step and aim for Arlo's shoulder," came out of it.

Todd looked unimpressed that Josh hadn't pushed back more, but turned around, stepped back on full step, and did as he was told. By some miracle, the ball whirled passed Arlo, into Van's waiting glove.

Todd glanced back at Josh, who just put his arms out and laughed.

"Not as easy as it looks," he muttered, dropping back into ready position, completely ignoring Todd's fuming glare.

The game continued with Todd finding a clumsy groove that looked similar to a toddler learning how to walk for the first time. But he figured it out with a few more pointers from Josh that sounded more like mocking than helping.

Cael didn't catch a single ball all game, and it was hilarious to watch him get worked up every time Arlo scored a run. Jensen, on the other hand, was happy at third, spouting off nonsense about enjoying the backward view of the diamond. But then again, nothing ever bothered that guy.

"How many times are we going to run this fucking play?" Cael yelled finally, snatching his mitt off in frustration.

"You're the only person that hasn't caught a ball," I called out to him. "So you tell me?"

"Is that what it'll take for you to let us free?" He asked me with a loud groan. "First base is stupid and so is your face, Tucker."

"Kitten's grumpy," Arlo mocked from the batter's box.

"Shut up, Princess." Cael whirled on Arlo with his finger pointed and shook it. "You're having fun because you have torture kink. This is brutal–we all know I can't play first and it's cruel!"

"Switch then; play outfield." Van shrugged. "Logan can take first, his reflexes are better, and Todd can move to shortstop because Arlo never hits left field unless he has to."

Arlo scoffed.

"Where will you go?" Cael flipped his hat backward with the brim, seemingly frustrated but definitely listening to the plan.

In fact... *everyone* was.

"Pitcher. Move Baker to catcher where he's not in the way..." Josh cut in. "Put Dean at third–he'll cover Todd in case Arlo switches hits, and fill the gaps in outfield with Jensen and Louis, Riley can play second."

And Josh had learned everyone's names...

"It'll work," Van said, surveying the field and nodding toward Josh in agreement. "Everyone switch!"

I caught Arlo's expression as he crossed his arms over his chest and watched them all willingly switch their positions in the field.

Cael flipped me off as he wandered to right field, but I could tell he was instantly more comfortable in the position. Arlo waited until they were ready before taking a perfectly timed pitch from Van that flew over the infield heads straight toward Cael.

Todd hollered out before anyone else could. "First!"

Cael didn't hesitate as the ball hit his glove. His fingers scooped it effortlessly from his palm and hurled it toward Josh, who was ready on base. Arlo pushed the pace, but he wasn't fast enough. The sound of the ball kissing leather as Ella yelled Arlo out echoed almost simultaneously through the air.

It didn't take them long to get back into the swing of things; Cael even started catching more balls. Logan's voice carried cleanly across the bases, cutting through the noise with ease, which only meant good things for a loud stadium.

"They're going to be ok, Tucker." Arlo nudged me as he came to a slow stop at third. "If you can get Cael and Logan on the same page for the season..."

"We can win." I finished his sentence with a small proud nod. He completed his circle just in time for Silas to sound the siren that told us dinner was ready. "Alright, go shower and meet for dinner."

The guys piled off the field, chatting with each other, and I watched as Van turned to Josh. I was ready to get between them, but Van's brows scrunched together before he asked him a question about his back foot placement on the mound.

Josh explained it to him slowly, and twice over, Van mimicking the movement in choppy steps as they walked. Even afterwards, with everyone packed into the dining hall, dinner went alright. Josh sat with us again and actually ate a full plate of pasta. Whatever it was, it smelled delicious, but I was still too stressed to have an appetite, and the four small bites that hit my stomach weighed a thousand pounds.

I leaned back in my chair and watched everyone finish.

In a few days, we'd be back in Harbor—and I'd be a caged animal again. Forced to put on fake smiles that meant nothing to people who didn't really know me. I was already over it, and the suffocating pinch of my parents' expectations for me loomed.

I could hear my mother's voice, peaking and pulling at the back of my mind. She would want to know who I was taking to the Gala that season. Being captain had brought down so many more problems on my head than I'd expected from her. All of a sudden, the pressure of having a partner or, in her words, a *girlfriend*, was exponential. It had to be one the family would be proud of and that the press could gawk over as the season progressed.

Not a word out of her mouth had been about my needs.

It would kill her to know that Cael and I had gone together last year, in quiet solidarity. We told her that it was because 'we wanted to keep our options open' when, in reality, I just wanted to fuck Cael in the locker room showers.

He'd had other plans for the occasion.

But that's how it had always been. Me expecting Cael to be there for me, and Cael not understanding what that meant. It was odd to think how far we'd come since that night. There were no more overdoses, but there was also no more '*us*'.

I sighed, heavy with the weight of it all.

"What's up with you?" Silas leaned over the table, and it was only then that I realized I had been sitting, staring at the ceiling. Everyone had left, and the dining hall was quiet except for the players in the kitchen doing dishes.

"Nothing, just tired. The bunks aren't exactly made for anyone of exceptional height." I looked up at him. "You fit because you're 5'10"."

"First of all, I'm 6'2", and it's not my fault they don't sell bunks made for overgrown children or *Hulklings*." Silas sank into the chair across from me.

"You've had nothing but toast and three bites of pasta in—" he paused to think about it, "oh, I don't know, six days?"

"I've eaten, Doc, thanks though. You don't get a body like this from toast." I gave him a half-hearted flex, and he scowled at me in response.

"We're not doing this again, Tucker." He slid his elbows against the table and stared me down with his judgmental glare.

"It's not that," I stopped him quickly. Fresh out of high school, coming off an impressive senior baseball season, I was distracted. So distracted that I'd lost nearly sixty pounds in my first semester at Harbor. Silas had caught it quickly, but it had taken me another forty pounds and an embarrassing collapse during a game for me to admit to it. I had dropped to one hundred and sixty pounds.

"It is that." Silas pressed his lips into a thin line and shook his head at me. "A lot is riding on your shoulders now, but if you need help, say it and I'm there."

"I'm fine, Silas." I pushed up from the table and inhaled slowly. "Food at camp just sucks."

"It's the same food as home, Tucker. Do not walk away from me," Silas grumbled, his tone becoming increasingly annoyed with my dismissal.

I turned and looked at him from the end of the table.

"I thought we'd figured this out," he said, standing to match my gaze. "You've got to prioritize yourself, Dean. Focusing too narrowly on a win is dangerous. You can't win from a facility, and I warned you, if you couldn't manage your eating dis—"

"It's not a disorder, don't say that." I waved my hands in front of my body and stepped closer to him, lowering my voice so the guys in the kitchen couldn't hear. "I'm not sick, it's not that. I'm fine, I'm eating, it's fine."

Silas chuckled. "You've said that word three times in two sentences. You're not sick, but you're also *not* fine, and you're not eating. It's not just me that's noticed."

I swallowed tightly and folded my arms over my chest, ready to argue.

"Cael is a busybody. He doesn't have problems of his own anymore, so he's trying to dig them out—"

"It was Josh." Silas cut me off in a quiet tone.

"What?" I scowled.

"He came to me after they got back from the city for a conversation, and he mentioned that you'd been skipping breakfast," Silas explained. "I didn't push for more, but the slope is slippery, and if you're not eating breakfast..."

"I am—a piece of toast, *remember*?" I rolled my eyes and sighed.

"Dean, come on." Silas pushed, stepping toward me and running a hand through his dark hair. "The last thing I want to do is force you to get help, I'm not qualified to coach you through this, or I would. But I will not pick you up off the field again. It was scary enough the first time."

He was right. The first time I'd collapsed because of the neglect was in the middle of a game with a stadium full of people. The lights had been so hot and the noise from the stands had made me dizzy. It was like my muscles all went slack at the same time, and everything went black before I hit the ground.

He placed a hand on my shoulder, holding my gaze for a moment. "I know that everything is messy right now. I know that your family is suffocating and the stress of taking captain has got a chokehold on you..." He paused, feeling me tense under his fingertips. "I'm not saying you can't handle it, I know you can. I'm saying you don't have to do it alone."

"Two steps at a time," I grumbled under my breath and looked down between us. "I'll stop skipping breakfast."

"If I don't see you in this hall, I'll send Arlo after you," he threatened.

"Not funny." I shuddered.

"Wasn't a joke." He smiled, but it didn't reach his eyes.

LOGAN

"You coming over?" Van asked, before I could slip away after dinner. The fire had already started, the last one before we packed up and left the camp. There was no way I could refuse, not after how well the practice had gone, but I wasn't really in the mood to be surrounded by their toxic love for one another.

Not with my mom's missed calls still lighting up my phone. I hadn't gotten the chance to call her before I lost service again, and I wasn't going to do it around Cael. She was calling for money; she always was.

"Uh yeah..." I sighed and changed my direction to follow him over toward the glowing ember haze and the sounds of laughter.

I watched as he settled down against the log between Cael's legs and floundered. His long arms rested across Cody's knees, and he leaned his body into him to listen to whatever story Nicholas was telling.

I looked around at them all and noticed Dean was missing. So was Silas, and my thoughts flickered to the brief conversation we'd had earlier.

"*Where did you and Cael go?" Silas asked.*

"*Into town for a meeting. He needed one," I lied.*

"Funny, he said it was you who needed one." Silas narrowed his eyes at me.

"Why ask if you knew what we were doing?" I slumped against the door frame and looked over my shoulder to make sure we were alone. More than one Hornet player had a bad habit of sneaking up behind people and eavesdropping.

"I wanted to see if you were going to lie to me again," he answered, resting his hands on his hips. He shifted uncomfortably in the navy polo and jeans, his lips pressed into a tight line.

"I'm not the liar in the room, Shore," I reminded him.

Silas sighed. "I'm not a liar, I was an unaware party and the moment—"

"Yeah, did you call me in here for excuses or?..." I offered him a tight, annoyed smile and stood up straight in the doorway.

"No, I wanted to see how you were doing," he said.

I let out an unimpressed chuckle and shook my head. "Stop it."

"What?" He asked, and I couldn't tell if he was genuinely confused or just being an asshole and baiting the answer out of me.

"Acting like my brother."

"I am your brother."

I swallowed tightly and shook my head in disbelief at his calm tone. I hated that he just so easily accepted it. He should be angry, wound up and mean about all of it. But instead he was just there, asking me what I needed, and it was infuriating.

"No, we share the same bastard blood, but we're not brothers, Silas. You're just some rich asshole with a guilty conscience and too *much time on your hands. How about you focus on your real family? Tucker's missed 14 of the last 21 meals."*

I watched him open his mouth to argue with me and then close it again, his hands tightening around his hips. The look on his face went from frustration to concern with a single blink.

This had happened before.

"14?" Silas asked. "You counted?"

"He's the size of a bear. It's pretty easy to notice when he's not around," I deflected. "You have too many eggs in your basket to be worried about your daddy's bastard son. Leave me alone and do your job so I can do mine."

"Josh!" Silas called out as I left the office and went down to practice.

I pushed the argument to the back of my mind and focused on practice, putting one foot in front of the other and keeping my head down. My priorities were baseball and school, not on making Silas feel better about himself in a situation I never asked to be in the middle of.

I remembered catching her on the phone with my biological father... Mom was crying, asking him for more money. She had mumbled about it my entire life but I never believed her. I was thirteen when I found out that I had the blood of a Shore running through my veins with evidence that wasn't spilling from some drunks mouth. Thirteen, and every time I walked to school, I had to see his stupid face in the newspaper or on bus benches.

Charles. Mr. Shore.

Dickbag, deadbeat, dad.

It took another three years until I found out the story of how they knew each other. And knowing the story was more painful than the truth of who I really was. The bastard baby who was thrown away because I had the potential to topple an empire. She had been healthy, thriving almost, working as a nurse at St. Christian's downtown. But Charles was handsome and persuasive; it wasn't long before he was banging my mom in storage closets like a bad episode of some medical sitcom.

I wasn't part of the plan, though, and the moment she had gotten pregnant, Charles found any reason to get rid of her. He paid her to get rid of me and then continued to threaten her after she didn't. Eventually, he started sending her money to keep her quiet.

That paper trail was how Silas found me.

I wanted nothing to do with them. I had worked hard to get where I was, and I did it without their help. I never saw a cent of that money, it had been funneled into drugs just to keep my mother's heart pumping.

Every day of my life was spent listening to her blame me for our situation.

You ruined everything.
You look just like him.
You're a piece of shit just like your Dad.
You'll never be anything, just a rat scurrying around begging for scraps from a family that wanted you dead.

She tried more than once to see it through. When money was tight she'd let her shitty boyfriends into my room. They'd do what they wanted, take what they needed, and time after time it left me as a husk. An angry kid with a deadly codependency with vodka and enough PTSD to put down an army vet. I tugged at the collar of my sweater as my thoughts stirred.

I should have known from the moment Silas showed up at Lorette that day he'd be annoying about the entire thing. He'd claimed no one knew—that he'd found out by accident when the family accounts were transferred to him. But I didn't believe him. His father—our father—had been keeping me a secret my entire life, and he'd just slipped up?

It felt slimy.

I didn't want what Silas was offering: the truth, freedom, and money.

That was until Ian attacked me in the showers that night and, suddenly, I was in more trouble than ever expected. Trouble that I couldn't talk or pitch my way out of. Silas had almost sounded excited when I called.

Only three people knew the truth: Silas, Coach Cody, and me. It had to stay that way. I was almost free, and I never wanted the Shore name; I just wanted to be clean of my past.

"What about you?" Arlo kicked his foot out and it connected with mine, bringing me back to the bonfire raging before me.

"What?" I shook out of my dissociation.

"Favorite holiday?" Ella asked for Arlo.

"Uh, I don't know, I don't really have one." I shrugged.

"What do you mean you don't have one?" Cael asked, as his fingers raked through Van's chocolate brown mullet in circles. It weirded me out how comfortable they were with one another, and I was almost eighty percent sure that it had sent Mitchell to sleep.

"What's yours?" I asked him.

"My birthday, duh." He answered like it was obvious.

"The one day of the year where everyone is forced to pay attention to him for hours on end," Dean said, coming up behind us and sitting down on the log beside me. "Last time we lucked out because Clem showed up and we didn't see him for twelve hours after."

"We fucked on every surface at the stadium and then got French fries." Cael grinned lecherously, and I scowled back.

"That's a disgusting overshare," I said.

"I could go into detail, Logan. If you think that was an overshare, you have no idea," Cael hummed and Dean practically growled.

"Not tonight," he said, before Arlo could get the words out.

"Mine's this," Dean said from beside me. "I know it's not a holiday, but these weeks out here with you guys. It's my favorite time of the year."

"Awe, Deano," Van purred with his eyes still closed, but it confirmed that he was still awake enough to pay attention to the conversation.

"It's just better out here, away from everything and everyone. The last few years have been rough on us; we all know it even when we're ignoring the truth. This season won't be much different. The second the world finds out that you have a gay captain, our lives are going to get harder."

No one flinched from the sudden change in conversation except for me.

I had known of the whispers about Dean and Cael, it had been obvious for a long time that there was something there. And Cael Cody, for all his trouble, had never once hidden who he was as a person. He had flirted with me throughout our entire friendship... But to hear Dean Tucker, six foot something, two hundred and fifty pounds of sunshine, first baseman and captain of one of the best team in the NCAA, say it out loud and with no shame or remorse... something stirred inside of me.

"But we have what it takes to win this season, to prove to everyone in Harbor that you can break us down, switch us around, throw us in the dirt, but we're always going to get back up again. It's who we are," he added, looking around at everyone. "I know it's a lot to ask for you guys to have my back this season with more than just baseball," he started and was cut off.

"You don't have to ask," Van said, his eyes cracking open and every player that sat around the fire in one form or another confirmed with a nod or a tap to the chest.

"We already knew you were Bi, Tucker," Louis said.

"Not Bi... Louis. Gay. Full gay," Dean said like he was choking on the words.

"We're a family, Tucker, and as long as you stop fucking rival players in the back of my truck, I don't care where you stick your dick." Van filled the awkward silence that followed.

Everyone laughed, and Cael shrugged, almost like he knew Dean was worried about the outcome of the conversation long before it had started.

"Gay Captain has a nice ring to it. You think when we win the series back to back, they'll make it the headline?" Todd asked, and Dean laughed.

So simple was the decision to protect Dean from the world that I envied how quickly they all jumped to shield him from the realities of homophobia in male-led sports.

He was right about one thing; it would make everything a lot harder the second word got out about his sexuality. I knew it intimately, only, yet again, I was alienated by the way the Hornets handled it. No horrible jokes or slurs were rolling off their tongues. Only acceptance and love.

I had worked hard to hide my own sexuality from the world, from the Lorettes, but every secret has an expiry date, and the moment Ian saw the texts on my phone from my recent interests, I knew that trouble would follow.

It had taken him less than a week to corner me.

Less than five minutes for him to have me shoved up against a wall with my back exposed to him and no way out.

No more than thirty seconds for him to strip away every ounce of my remaining dignity, leaving me back in my bedroom, begging every boyfriend my mother had brought home to stop. It was like I had been locked in my own mind with my nightmares. Ian had no idea what he'd done, not really. Maybe I had snapped that day, gone too far, but he'd deserved every ounce of anger that flooded from me.

The only thing I wanted to remember from that night was how strong I felt.

It consumed me.

The scars on my knuckles from that night stung.

"You alright?" Dean's voice broke through the veil.

"Yeah," I answered. Turning to look at him, and finding that I hated the green in his eyes and how soft the hues became every time he looked at me. At first I thought it was pity or sympathy but now I understood the look and it terrified me. "Just tired."

I pushed off the log and made my way to the cabin.

This time, Dean didn't follow me, and I wasn't sure if I was grateful—or disappointed.

TUCKER

The bus was loaded, and Silas was running final checks before we hit the road back to Harbor. I stood to the side, staring at the camp, wishing that I could just stay here for a day or two more. I needed to sit in the silence and try to figure out exactly what I wanted from everything. Maybe find the courage to tell my family before they find out from a news source or school gossip.

Silas wandered over, handed me an apple, and crossed his arms.

"Thanks for skipping breakfast this morning." He scowled.

"I was packing," I said with a shrug, ignoring him and the way my thoughts felt sluggish, rolling around in the back of my mind.

"That's probably the most bullshit answer you've given me to date." He shook his head. "Eat."

I took a bite of the apple, counting each chew before swallowing and stared at him. "Happy now?"

"Do I look happy?" He asked, and the answer was obviously no. "I want you back with Riona when we get home, no more of this bullshit."

"Seriously, Doc?" I groaned. I didn't have time for mandated therapy right now.

"Deadly," he snapped. "You don't wanna listen to my advice? You deal with her. She won't let you get away with this shit and you know it."

"She's terrifying," I whined, knowing exactly how pathetic I sounded.

"You should have thought about that before you decided to open Pandora's box," he reminded me. "I'll call her on the way home and make you an appointment."

"I can do it myself," I said as he patted my shoulder and made his way to the bus.

"I know you can, but you won't. So I'm skipping the middleman—just like you skipped breakfast." He stared at me one last time before disappearing up the stairs.

I sighed, still stalled out and unable to move my feet.

Leaving meant dealing with every complicated puzzle piece back home. All I wanted to do was play baseball and forget about all of it. I was half tempted to pull them off the bus just for one last practice. Inhaling the smell of camp, pine trees and lake water, I let it fill my lungs and wash down the stress. The trees rustled in the wind as the clouds moved in; there was a storm coming in more ways than one, and I wasn't ready to weather either of them.

"Tuck," Josh's voice came from behind me, and I turned to look at him. "Get on the bus."

I nodded and followed him up the steps to the only open seats on the bus. I looked around hesitantly before sinking into the seat next to him. Cael winked at me and gave me two thumbs up as I took the seat. I had a feeling the ride back wouldn't be a thumbs-up situation, more like awkward silence with a few choice words that would surely piss one of us off.

That seemed to be the circle we had drawn out, uncomfortable silence followed by me saying something stupid that set Josh off, only for him to prove my point. I turned to speak—though I didn't even know what I was going to say, but he was staring out the window, completely oblivious to my struggle.

How did I ask him about his past without starting a fight?

And how the fuck was Cael so good at doing it? When I tried to get to know people, they just talked to me like I was a toddler or yelled at me like I was prying into things I wasn't allowed to know.

"What's your favorite color?" I blurted out and immediately regretted it.

"What?" Josh turned to look at me.

I cleared my throat and shifted in my seat to give him as much space as I could manage. "Your favorite color..."

"I don't have one." Josh stared at me as if I were insane.

"You don't have a favorite color?" I asked him, confused by his answer. He could have said anything, blue, red... but instead he said he didn't have one.

"Nope," he grumbled. It looked like he was going to turn back around, but he stayed staring at me. I could smell the cologne he used that morning, and it tangled with the faint smell of generic camp shampoo and the pine tar he used on his bats; it lingered on his skin and tickled my nose. I inhaled slowly, filling my chest with air and living in that scent because it was a small piece of my haven left behind for another year.

"Mine's yellow," I said to him when I finally collected my thoughts.

"You would love the most obnoxious color in the rainbow, Tuck." Josh shook his head at me. "What's appealing about yellow?"

"Golden retrievers, buttercups, bananas..." I shrugged.

"You did not just list off yellow *things*." Josh smiled at me and the lines around his eyes crinkled in the softest way. I'd never noticed how gentle his face looked when it wasn't scrunched angrily.

"The sun, cheese, lemon cookies..."

"Please stop." He sighed, but the smile remained.

"It's easy to pick a favorite color, you just have to think about things that you love," I explained to him. "Honey," I added. "It's yellow..."

"Yeah, I know that honey is yellow, Tuck," he said, but went quiet. I didn't think it was even possible for someone to not have a favorite color, but the question weighed heavily on his shoulders in an unexpected way.

I should have known it was coming, it was just a part of the circle. We had slipped unknowingly into awkward silence all because Josh didn't have a favorite color.

"Favorite food?" I asked.

"All food is food," he fired back.

"Mine's chili, or actually... when Ella gets french fries from Hilly's and we eat them with the leftover chili, that's the best," I clarified.

"Surprised you actually have a favorite, considering you didn't eat dinner yesterday or breakfast today before we got on the bus," he said, completely ignoring the light tone in my voice. I was trying, and he just wanted to fight, as per usual.

I chose to ignore his jab and moved on. "What music do you listen to?"

"I don't," he said.

"You don't listen to music? Like at all?" I was growing increasingly worried for Josh's well-being. At this point in the conversation, it seemed like all he could manage was baseball and angry contemplation.

"I like silence, Tuck." It was a pointed response, aimed at me to get me to shut up, but if there was one thing I was bad at, it was social cues, so I kept talking, if only to get under his skin.

"Void of color, eats to survive, and hates music..." I hummed. "Do you read?"

"No."

"What about movies?"

Josh shook his head.

"Seriously?" I grumbled. "Do you watch other sports?"

"Nope."

"Ok," I said, refusing to give up. "Favorite thing to do outside of playing baseball?" I asked him. There had to be something he enjoyed other than the sport.

He scowled at me, his lips pressing into that typical Josh expression. Anger and annoyance. "Baseball is the only thing I *do*."

"That can't be true. There has to be something you do other than baseball," I said, refusing to take his answer at face value.

"I study," he muttered, clipped and flat.

"You study?" I scoffed and flipped my hat into my lap before brushing the knots from my hair with my fingers.

"Yup."

"Shit, Logan, I'm trying to get to know you... You can't just study and pitch," I complained, the frustration coming out in my voice.

"I can, because that's what I do, Tuck, and if you need something more exciting than that, go harass someone else because that's my life," he muttered under his breath, but his voice had fallen into an irritated territory.

"There's got to be more!" I urged, and Josh finally broke. He shifted in his seat and stared at me.

"There's nothing more," he said, his voice low but steady. "That's it. I'm sorry that my life isn't sunshine and favorite foods. We didn't have a TV growing up, and the only music I ever heard was from the apartment above us when they turned it up to drown out the sounds coming from ours," he snarled. His cheeks were red and his eyes were darker than I had ever seen them. His confession turned my mouth dry.

"I didn't have a golden retriever, or a mom who made me dinner every night. I didn't have a dad who played catch with me, or siblings to carry the blame when something got broken by accident. It was just me and my mom in some shitty apartment that permanently smelled like smoke and sex. Quit trying to fucking relate to me Dean. You're from the side of the tracks where boys get yellow as a favorite color. You don't get it—you never will."

"I'm sorry," I said, and the fact that I meant it rattled him. It was written all over his face as his shoulders relaxed and he settled back into his seat. He pressed himself up against the window and turned away from me.

It wasn't his whole story, but it was something to go on, and by the sounds of it, nothing in his life had been even close to normal. The bus jolted, and I swallowed tightly to keep the nausea from rising as I leaned back against the seat for a split second before sitting up again.

"You know what? No," I argued. "No."

He didn't move, but I saw his brow arch.

"You think my life is perfect just because I grew up with money?" I bit out. "It wasn't. I grew up in a house where I couldn't be anything but what *they* wanted me to be. A gilded cage is still a fucking cage, Josh. Say what you want, but my life was far from perfect."

Silence.

"Yeah, Dad played catch with me, but the second he finds out he's never getting a daughter-in-law out of his golden children, he'll never look me in the eyes again. My Mom? She openly talks about how horrible of a sin gay people are at the fucking dinner table on Sundays. And sure, I'm eating my favorite food, but I'm doing it while she rants about how people like me don't deserve to breathe the same air as her at the grocery store. So, maybe it looks perfect—but it's fucking not. I'm not taking that shit from you."

"Why not?" Josh laughed, it was hollow and quiet, and he didn't bother to look at me when he asked. "You take it from everyone else."

LOGAN

I dozed off on the bus, my thoughts plagued by the look on Dean's face when he fought back about his family. It was startling to see him so heated—rare for Dean—but clearly, there was a lot to unpack about his mother.

What he told me didn't compare to or dismiss my own past, but it showed me a different side of him that I hadn't realized existed before that moment. That was the Dean who disintegrated a bat against a tree, the one I had been looking for since the first time I saw him.

It rattled me.

The buzz of my phone finding service woke me, forty minutes from Harbor, and I was scared to look at how many more messages had flooded in since the other day. Once she realized they were being delivered again, she probably flipped out. Dealing with the fallout from camp was oddly worth it? The last few practices had been promising for a season that might actually be good. We had a chance to win if we could just keep our focus on the game and not on the issues underlying each and every player. Our personal problems needed to be left in the parking lot, which, for this group, was easier said than done. They wore their grievances like patches on their jerseys, on display for the world to see. It was more annoying than Dean trying to pry my favorite color out of me.

My answer wasn't meant to get under his skin; I'd truly never had one.

I'd never stopped to think about it long enough to pick one.

Even after he had yelled at me, I sat there staring out the window, trying to decide, but nothing came to mind. Green was too... green. And blue was too bright, but also too dark and sad. Red seemed obnoxious, and maybe I only owned so much red because we got handouts at Lorette. Yellow was his, so I couldn't have that or it would seem like I liked yellow because he liked yellow.

After a while, I realized that I was arguing with myself about the rainbow and got mad at the distraction. For a whole hour, I had forgotten every problem that itched under my skin whilst I just tried to pick a color.

Unsuccessfully.

Dean fell asleep an hour into the bus ride; his head leaned back against the seat, exposing his strong neck. His lips were slightly parted, his chest slowly rising and falling as he found peace in his dreams.

I was envious that his life didn't seep into his sleep; it wasn't easy to close your eyes and see your demons waiting for you.

An hour later, the bus turned, and his body shifted, the full weight sliding across the seat and resting against my shoulder. I hissed from the contact at first, but didn't push him away. I just breathed through the burning that the connection brought on, and slowly counted the curls of his hair to distract myself. Each one was perfect—like honey-dipped straw.

I lifted my hand and ghosted around a solitary curl that rested against his forehead, wanting to touch it–needing to know how soft it was, but unable to bring myself to do it. His breathing hitched, and I dropped my hand as he stirred from his sleep to the realization that he had fallen over.

"Sorry," he mumbled in a sleepy tone.

"You weigh more asleep," I muttered, shifting away from him, creating space and wishing I hadn't all at the same time.

"Where are we?" He asked, brushing his hair back and flipping his hat over on his head to conceal his messy curls.

"Twenty minutes out," I estimated. "You snore."

"I do not." Dean rolled his eyes and looked around the bus. Everyone was awake, give or take, from what I could see, and their anxiousness to get home and into their beds was tangible.

My anxiety was high for a whole other reason.

The last two weeks at camp had been hard, but they were nothing compared to being stuck inside Dansby House with them. We hadn't even pulled up to the stadium, and I could already feel the walls closing in on me.

As if he could read my mind, Silas's head popped over the chair in front of us. His hair was messy from sleep, and he was definitely half awake, but he gripped the chair as he spoke. "I have you in the guest room downstairs on the main floor until we can figure out a room to put you in that won't cause a fight."

"You can put him in my room," Dean offered, before I could say anything, and I groaned. "Ella is with Arlo, which means *my* room is the guest room, and I'm sick of sleeping with Van. He smells like an overheated hippo," Dean complained.

"Uh—" Silas stopped to think about it.

"He can either bunk with me, or bunk with Mitchell..." Dean shrugged. "But I'm captain now. It's literally the rule that I get my room back, and if it's not, I'm making one right now."

"Alright, alright." Silas laughed. "You can have the captain's room." He put his hands up in defeat and almost lost his balance as the bus turned into the Harbor stadium parking lot. "Your choice, Logan. Do you want the hippo or the chainsaw?"

"I do not snore!" Dean scowled.

I didn't want either of them. I would almost have rather slept on the couch than have to share a room, but from the looks on their faces, it wasn't an option.

"Tuck." I shrugged. "I don't want to know what an overheated hippo smells like."

"Disgusting. It smells disgusting..." Dean grumbled and started to pack his backpack up, before slinging it over his shoulder and climbing off the bus.

I stayed in my seat until everyone else was off, and then slid my phone out of my pocket to finally answer a call from my mom.

It barely rang once.

"Joshua?" Her voice was manic through the phone, and I had to take a deep breath before confirming to her that it was me. "Where have you been? It's been... it's been..."

"Two weeks, Mom. I had a baseball thing," I explained quietly.

"A baseball thing?" She scoffed. "That was more important than me? A *baseball* thing? You sound like *him*."

I resisted the urge to snap at her. "What do you need, Mom?"

"I need my son to love me the way a son should love his mother." She said it like it should have been under her breath, but she made sure it was loud enough for me to hear.

"Anything else?" I asked gently, just trying to avoid her getting wound up.

"Jimmy left and—", she stuttered over her words, "he took that new stereo I bought and I was going to pawn it for cash..."

"How much do you need, Mom?" I asked her. The story didn't matter. I didn't even know who Jimmy was, and he couldn't have been any better than the previous fifty guys.

She didn't answer, and I could hear her in the background, rifling through cupboards, looking for something. My eyes were focused on the small crowd of players in the parking lot, just outside the blue-tinted bus window. They were so blissfully unaware of the challenges everyone else suffered.

"Mom," I said again to get her attention. "How much money do you need?"

"This is your fault, you know." She came back to the receiver. "If you were normal like the rest of us, you wouldn't have gotten kicked off that team. But no...my crooked son had to fuck other little boys and now we've been cut off from..." She stopped, unable to say his name, but I could hear the pain in her voice. "And I can't pay rent or buy groceries without that, Joshua. But you just *had* to play baseball! Follow in *his* footsteps!" She snarled. "Is it worth it?"

"Mom." I sighed. "How much money do you need?"

"Throwing balls with your new family while your mother is starving!" She hissed.

"I'll be there in an hour," I said to her, knowing that visiting was the only thing that would stop the spiral of vicious insults happening over the phone. "Don't leave the apartment. Don't go looking for..."

"Jimmy?" She said, as if I should know his name. "That bastard is never getting back in my bed; piece of shit..." She trailed off in a slew of insults before she set the phone down on the counter without hanging up or saying goodbye.

I sat, listening to her destroy her apartment, the familiar sounds of her crashing from a high echoed through the receiver. Going down there was exactly what she wanted; yelling at me through the phone never gave her the same rush as doing it to my face.

Hanging up, knowing full well she'd call back the second she realized, I climbed off the bus and started toward my car. It was the oldest piece of shit on the lot, but it ran and that's all that I needed. A way of getting to and from Lorette to keep my mother from ending up face down in an alley.

"Where are you going?" Dean's voice was too warm and worried at my back.

"I have to go into the city," I said.

"You were just there."

"Some of us have lives outside of Harbor," I bit out, reaching through the open window in the backseat to pop the lock on the car. I chucked my duffle bag in and turned to look at him. "I'll be back. You can tuck me in later—how's that sound?"

"Patronizing." He rolled his pretty blue eyes at me, and I had to shove back the snarl that formed on my lips at the traitorous feeling of thinking it was cute. "Your girlfriend might not like it, though." He smiled.

"If that's you fishing, I don't have a girlfriend," I said as my phone vibrated again. I looked down to see the texts rolling through and shoved it away in my back pocket.

"Tell your girlfriend that." Dean looked at the phone with a smug expression.

"You're going to have to work a lot harder than that to get under my skin, Tuck," I said. My tone was controlled, but all I wanted to do was get on the highway and scream at the top of my lungs.

The irritation building from the constant vibrating in my pocket, combined with Dean's incessant need to figure me out, was making me lose my mind.

"Doesn't look all that hard." Dean smirked.

I wanted to hit him.

What would that solve? Nothing. It would simply be kicking the Hornet's nest, and they were already operating on a hair trigger with me as the target.

"You gonna make it into Lorette in that thing?" He asked next, when I didn't respond fast enough.

"I made it here in this thing." I scowled at him and popped the driver's side door. "Not everyone has a daddy to buy them a brand new truck," I snapped, looking at the deep red vehicle behind him.

"It's been sitting on the lot in the cold, but…whatever you say, Logan." He stepped back from the car. "And it's a *Jeep*, not a truck."

"Oh, so twice as expensive. Did he wrap it up with a bow for you?" I rolled my eyes and slammed the car door in Dean's face. I shoved the keys in the ignition and prayed that the car didn't embarrass me. For the first time since I pulled it from the junkyard on Twenty-second Street, it started without trouble.

It had taken me two weeks to get it running—and a new block heater to *keep* it running—but it did its job when I needed it to, and I didn't have to bus anymore. I pulled noisily from the parking lot, leaving the team behind, and for the first time in two weeks, I was finally alone.

I gripped the wheel tightly, inhaling as deeply as I could, and screamed.

I didn't stop until I couldn't breathe, and then I did it all over again.

It felt fucking amazing.

Every ounce of malice poured out and dissipated into the air. I hadn't realized how much pent-up aggression I was holding onto until that point, but with it all out of my body, I loosened my grip on the wheel and let my shoulders relax back against the cracked leather seat.

The engine gurgled, causing the car to sputter and skip.

"Fuck," I swore, as smoke began to billow from beneath the hood.

TUCKER

The smoke was the first tell that his car was on my side.

I pulled up behind him on the road and hopped out onto the pavement, checking for cars before heading to his driver's side.

I watched his chest rise and fall in one very angry breath before he rolled the window down. "Don't say it," he grumbled.

"I won't." I shrugged; I felt bad for him. His comment about my vehicle hadn't been wrong. My parents had bought it for me on my eighteenth birthday. It was a present for graduating and I was making payments on it, but that wasn't the point.

It was a show of wealth, and I had rubbed it in his face.

"Get in the *Jeep*," I teased.

"I'll call a cab, Tuck. I don't need your charity." He waved me off, but I didn't move.

"It's not charity. You can take my dinner schedule for the week to pay for gas," I offered, knowing that showing him it wasn't a handout would help. That was the thing about Josh—he needed to feel like he was doing it on his own or he wouldn't do it at all. I had figured that much out over the last two weeks.

"Fine," he groaned, climbing from the car.

"Don't leave your bag," I said, pointing to it. I checked for cars again and started back toward my own. Pulling out my cell phone, I texted the group chat.

> **Someone come grab Logan's heap of garbage.**

Cael

> What happened?

> It broke down on the nineteen, I'm taking him into Lorette. Just tow it back up to the house, or, Arlo, can you look at it? If you have time?

Arlo

> Get Van and the truck, we'll get it back to the Nest. I can't promise to get it running. It sounded like it was full of water, leaving the lot.

> Just try, please?

Arlo

> You owe me

Cael

> Do you ever collect on those, or do you just say them to scare us?

I shoved the phone back in my pocket, looking up in time to see Josh throwing his bag into the back and climbing into the passenger seat. His dark eyes widened as they took in the console.

"God, this must have cost a fortune," he whistled.

"Buckle up." I pointed to his seatbelt and he scowled at me, but I waited until he did it up. "Thank you, and it costs me seven hundred dollars a month to pay for it," I added, just to see the dumbfounded look on his face.

"You have a job?" He said in a shocked tone.

"Yeah, I do contract construction jobs with Van when I have the time." I pulled off the shoulder and onto the highway. Josh was silent for a while, the only sound was his phone going off in his pocket. "You can get that," I said to him.

"No," he clipped quickly and went back to being silent.

"Touchy," I hummed, turning onto the highway toward Lorette. It was another hour of uncomfortable silence before Josh started giving me directions. When I'd imagined all the places he might be going, the rough side of Lorette hadn't been on my list.

Rent-controlled and overpopulated, this side of the city was littered with homeless people and run by some street gang that no one really messed around with. I was ashamed to say that I'd always been too scared to come over here.

"Stay here," he barked as we pulled up to a ratty-looking apartment building.

"No." I shook my head. "You aren't going out there alone..."

"Tuck, listen." He sighed. "I'll be fine. Stay put and lock the doors."

I had offended him.

"I'm coming." I cut the engine and climbed out of the car, pushing the fob and listening to it beep as I jogged up the sidewalk behind him.

"You should have stayed in the fucking car," Josh snarled.

"It's a Jeep," I reminded him, trying to lighten the mood.

"It's going to have one less window, leaving it parked there unattended," Josh muttered darkly, swinging the shattered door open into the main lobby. My eye caught sight of the out-of-service sign on the elevator as Josh ignored my hesitation, already climbing the dirty stairs. The whole place reeked of piss and smoke, and the stairs felt endless.

"How many floors?" I queried.

"Fifteen," he answered as we hit the fourth floor.

"Where are we going?" I asked, rounding the corner of five.

"Seven," he answered, not sounding even a little out of breath.

"How many times have you done these stairs?" I asked as we reached six, my breath had started to get shallow and quick.

"All my life," he replied, stopping at the first door off the seventh-floor landing and spinning on me so he was in my face. "If you tell a soul about what you see in here, I'll fucking kill you, Tucker."

I would have laughed, but something about the way Josh said it meant he was serious, so I nodded and waited as he popped the lock on the apartment door. The intense smell of vodka, smoke and rotten fruit washed into my nose, and it took everything in me not to gag.

"Mom," Josh called out, stepping over a leaning pile of newspapers with his long legs. I stepped inside the apartment and shut the door behind us as my eyes scanned my surroundings.

The walls, which I could only assume were white at some point, had been stained yellow from smoke and were littered with holes. The windows were covered with film and newspapers to block the light from pouring in onto the dirty couch and the glass coffee table that was piled high with garbage.

The kitchen off to my right was barely that; dishes and rotten food piled in toppling towers of plastic and mold. The rotten stench of beer cans festering with fruit flies filled the air and seeped into my clothes and against my skin.

"Fuck," I swore under my breath, seeing the discarded needles, and crossed my arms over my chest as I looked around for Josh.

He was in a room to my left, talking to someone that I couldn't see, but could hear.

"You came." Her voice was strained, and she sounded weak as Josh helped her off the floor and onto the dirty mattress piled with clothes and blankets. "That's my boy."

Josh's body went rigid as her hand touched his cheek. Gently, he pulled her wrist away and reached for his wallet to dig through it.

"This is all I have," he said. "I'll stop by Mark's office and get him to change the lock on the door." He moved with the kind of fluidity that only came from having done this a hundred times before. As if caring for her this way was second nature.

I looked around as Josh lowered his voice, clearly not wanting me to hear what was next. I stepped back and scanned the hall, taking in the peeling paint in the corners and the piles of dust that lined the baseboards. The door at the end of the hall had three chain locks—all of them had been snapped off and reinstalled, again and again.

The pit in my stomach grew as I stepped toward it.

I put my hand out to open it; the cool metal pressing against my palm, begging to be turned.

"Don't." Josh's voice was harsh and laced with impatience. "Let's go."

I didn't turn the handle, but my heart ached from the strained way he demanded it, and I knew that the door led to his room. The frame was etched with scratch marks made by small hands.

"Tuck," he said again, his tone more strangled the longer I stood staring. "*Please.*"

I let go of the door knob and turned to look at him. He suddenly seemed so much smaller than usual, but I nodded and followed him out of the apartment. I kept my eyes trained on the center of his back, right between his tense shoulder blades, as we walked down each flight of stairs.

"Give me a second," he said, knocking on a door off the main lobby.

An older gentleman with an unruly beard and mean dark eyes answered, but his expression grew more gentle at the sight of Josh.

"Mr. Logan!" His voice softened as he opened the door wider. "I didn't expect to see you— is your—?"

"She's alright, Mark. How are you?" Josh's tone was so different with this stranger. It was considerate and patient, just like he'd been with his mother, but his shoulders had relaxed and he even had a smile on his face that I'd never seen before.

"Surviving," the old man coughed out into a rag. "What can I do for you, Josh?"

"Mom had another unwanted visitor while she wasn't home. Do you think you could change out her lock again?" He asked. "Do you still have that box?"

"You saved me a lot of money with that idea," Mark said. "I'll change it out for one of the old ones. What about Darren's?"

"Yeah, I haven't seen that guy since eighth grade. That'll work." Josh nodded. "Thanks, Mark."

"Anything for you, kid," he said, without hesitation. "When does the season start?"

"Two weeks," Josh replied. "We're gonna have to upgrade that radio to a TV soon. Can't have you listening to MLB games. Gotta be able to see me pitching, right?"

"Dream big, boy." Mark slapped his shoulder, and Josh flinched, but he swallowed the discomfort. "You got your schedule for the season?"

"Uh n—"

"Right here," I said, pulling out my phone. "You got a piece of paper?" I asked, and the old man looked at me. "Dean Tucker, first baseman for the Harbor Hornets." I held out my other hand for him to shake.

"Well, damn, you're a big fucker," Mark huffed, amused by the sight of me. "I know those announcers are dramatic, but they weren't lying about you, golden boy."

"Paper?" I reminded him, and he nodded, swinging the door open and wandering into the kitchen. He brought back a pen and paper, and I jotted down what was on our schedule for the first month. "I'll get Josh here, an official one. We have magnets, you like magnets?" I asked, still scribbling.

Mark nodded.

"Maybe a Logan jersey?" I suggested, and Josh sighed. "You look like you fit a large, you'll look good in navy too–get you out of that Lorettes red. What do you say?"

Mark laughed. "I like this one, he's pushy."

"And proud." I smiled at him. "I'll make you a bag and have Josh bring it over next week, before the exhibition game."

Josh was about to open his mouth when a group of rowdy teenagers busted through the front doors, screaming and arguing with one another about a video they were watching.

"You boys should get going. I'll get her lock changed after dinner." Mark turned to Josh and shooed us away.

I made room for Josh to walk by me in the small hallway and held my hand out for Mark again, who finally took it in a tight handshake. He held on as Josh pushed out the front door.

"Tell me the truth. Is he okay?" Mark asked, in a low, serious tone.

"He will be," I said with a nod. "Promise."

A sick, unfamiliar feeling turned in my gut as Mark let go of my hand.

Josh's hatred for the Hornets and everything we stood for went so much deeper than just a rivalry. His hatred was bone deep; not for the team but for the family he never had.

"Shit." I exhaled and pushed open the door.

Josh climbed into the Jeep as soon as I pressed the fob and slammed the door behind him. *Good to know we're back to our old attitudes.* The silence was raw when I closed the door and started the engine.

I hadn't forgotten about the state of his childhood; still so present in his adulthood. My brain wandered into darker territory, thinking about how often he'd had to step back in there and relive it just because his mom called. His phone had stopped vibrating and I felt like a dick for assuming that we were going to see a girlfriend.

Sadly, everything made a little more sense.

I didn't know what to say. Every question that formed felt too rude, too raw, or too soon. I wanted to know how long he'd been taking care of his mom like that, how many times he had been locked in his room as a child, if he'd always lived in that filth. But the words wouldn't come, so more silence filled the space, and it felt wrong.

So instead of asking a question, I apologized.

"I'm sorry. I didn't know that's where you were going tonight. The caretaker seems like a nice guy. Has he always—"

"Shut up, Tuck," Josh snapped. He didn't look in from the window as the trees whipped past us back toward Harbor.

"I'm just trying—"

"I don't give a shit what you're doing," he growled, cutting me off again. "It's none of your fucking business, and don't ever overstep in my life ever again. You don't get to offer shit to people just because you want to clear your little rich boy's conscience."

"That's not what I was doing." I gripped the wheel tighter. "I was just... trying to talk."

"By offering him a ton of shit that he can't use? He doesn't need your fucking magnets, or your jerseys." Josh whirled on me with eyes full of hatred. "You don't know the first thing about my life, or his, and just because you barreled into it today uninvited, doesn't mean you get to try to fix problems with your saintly attitude."

I sighed.

It was useless. In the eyes of Josh Logan, I couldn't do a damn thing right.

TUCKER

It had been a fucking week.

Josh had been sleeping across from me every night—and he hadn't said a word.

Arlo had managed to get him out into the garage to work on his car. They'd switched a few parts out and thrifted a few more. The car would run, for now, but not for long. Josh had taken our deal seriously, slipping into cooking dinner with surprising ease. We actually ate better than usual; it was a surprise that someone who'd grown up eating canned pasta and boxed soup knew how to cook better than half the guys in the house.

But that was just my privilege showing again. We didn't know how to cook because we never did it for ourselves until Lorraine had taught us how...

Logan knew how to cook out of survival.

It only made me feel more guilty for the shit I'd said to him.

And the fact that, no matter what he set on the dinner table every night, it all made my stomach churn with disgust. There wasn't room to eat when stress was consuming me whole. Josh took offence every single time; it was written all over his face.

The preseason game was today–the first of a very long, rough season if Josh decided that what I'd done last weekend was completely unforgivable. I snuck out of bed in the dark and changed into a clean sweater, pulling it over my shoulders as I left the room, quietly shutting the door behind me.

I wandered into the kitchen and leaned against the doorframe—Ella and Arlo were already there. Arlo's arms were wrapped around her with his head on her shoulder, whispering something as she tried to make a pot of coffee.

"Don't you want someone to celebrate with when we win—or go home to when we lose?"

I could hear Cael in the back of my head, clawing around in my thoughts and reminding me at every turn that I deserved better, but I didn't know how to take it or earn it without blowing up my life.

"Tucker," Arlo's voice grumbled, and my eyes focused back on the kitchen. "It's early. You look like you're sleepwalking."

"I'm awake," I said, stepping forward and sliding onto a stool. "Just wound up about today, I guess," I offered, because it was that, but it was also a mixture of things I could and couldn't control.

"It's just Philly," he said. "Worst team in the league. You could beat them with your eyes closed." Ella nodded her agreement as she started the coffee machine.

"We can't beat them without you," I argued.

"That's nonsense, and you don't have to stroke his ego anymore; he's not your captain." Ella kissed Arlo's cheek when he scowled. "You proved how good you are over the last three weeks. Even

Coach said you came back a different team. Cael's shoulder is loose, the guys are excited to play..."

"Logan is ready to pitch," Arlo added. "We made sure of it."

It wasn't the team or the game I was worried about. The look on Ella's face told me she knew that but Arlo, that grouchy oblivious asshole, remained blissfully unaware. The only blessing of the evening would be that my parents would be absent. They were on a trip visiting Anna, and it meant that I could find my groove without them looming over my shoulder.

It gave me a chance to breathe the stadium air without choking on my mother's judgment.

Arlo tapped the counter with a finger, his eyes roaming quickly over the two of us before straightening out. "I'm going to go for my run."

He leaned over and kissed Ella, his big hands squeezing her cheeks tightly before he took off through the back door. Ella turned back to me and narrowed her eyes.

"Now that the brick wall's gone—what's really going on?"

I shook my head and laughed gently. "You're more observant than Riona, and it's annoying. I hope you know that."

"I do. She and I have had conversations about it." Ella smiled at me. "Now spill," she insisted.

"It's Logan," I said quietly. "He's messing with my head."

"He seems to be getting along with the guys; he's been cooking dinner with Todd and Jensen all week without issues," she pointed out.

"Jensen could make anyone get along," I mumbled, "it's that insufferable charm."

"But you're withholding information." Ella said, and ignored my whining.

"The Josh everyone knows—it's all a show," I said. "He acts like some egotistical showboat; loud, cocky...came from upper class but..."

Ella scoffed.

"What?" I said.

I was confused more than ever.

"He doesn't hide it, Dean," she said. "His cleats are from three seasons ago—they're the Nike series that was put out when the Braves won. His glove is even older. He cuts his own hair, and he eats every bit of food you put in front of him, even if he doesn't like it. He also flinches when you walk by him too fast, hates to be touched so much that he's willing to fight Cael about it, and..." She paused, lowering her voice but never breaking eye contact. "I'm pretty sure the smell of smoke gives him panic attacks," she said.

"How do you..." I slumped against the counter.

"Oh, wow, okay." She sighed, and I could see her working out a way to explain things to me. "Uh... Have any of you ever asked Van where he grew up?" She asked, and I just shook my head. What did Van have to do with any of this? "He and his sisters grew up in the trailer park behind Zoey's house. I know a homegrown haircut when I see one."

"Really?"

The conversation had never been brought up by us or him; we all just knew he had a good family. But it also tracked that all three siblings were pursuing careers that gave back. The Mitchells were selfless and kind; it was a coveted trait, and they never failed to prove how big their hearts were. Trailer park or not, it was nothing like what I'd seen from Josh's mom that day. They were still two very different versions of low income.

"I see the gears turning," she said, walking around the island to stand closer to me. "You didn't do anything wrong by not noticing, but you'll do him a disservice if you keep being ignorant of who he is. He didn't grow up with puppies on Christmas and family vacations to Disney."

"Right." I nodded. "I think maybe we should get him in to see Riona, it might help him with the anger," I suggested. "And I'll stop trying to impress him with generosity…"

"Now you're thinking with that beautiful brain of yours." She smiled up at me. Ella was the only one who never resorted to treating me like an idiot. She was the sister I never had, and I didn't say it enough, but I was grateful for her patience.

"We don't deserve you, El."

"Mmm," she hummed, and scrunched her face up at me before moving back around the counter and pouring coffee. "Impress him?" She asked, passing me a mug. "How did we go from acclimating him to impressing him?"

"I barely noticed that he was struggling," I said. "Don't ask such complicated questions."

Ella laughed. "Alright, alright. Something has to have happened to soften you up a little–or him. What changed?"

I thought about her question. What had changed between us that made it feel like I wanted to do things *for him* but not to spite him? I had never hated Josh, not really. There weren't many people I *did* hate. I couldn't even figure out how to hate my own mother for all the mean things she's said around me and *to* me.

But I had reasons I should hate Josh. He was terrible for the team morale; we've always been at each other's throats, he refused to get along with anyone, and he liked to keep secrets.

He wasn't keeping secrets. He was protecting himself.
Just like me.

"Common ground," I whispered, and Ella waited for me to figure it out. "We both had a secret that we didn't... *don't*... want to share because of how it'll affect our lives. How we'll look to the people in our lives."

"That's good," she said. "Dean, just be yourself and show Josh that it's okay to have secrets as long as he has people he feels comfortable sharing them with."

"Do you wanna do something with me today?" I asked her, suddenly having an idea. "I have to stop by the stadium and then go into Lorette."

"Sure." She set her coffee down and eyed me carefully. "Let me get dressed?"

"I'll swing by the stadium and come back up in thirty. Does that work?" I asked her, and she nodded as I backed away from the island.

I grabbed a hat and took the road down to the stadium. It was early, but Susanna would be around to help me with what I needed. I swung by the small coffee shop on campus and grabbed some sweets before hitting up the stadium. The parking lot was dead except for her car and Coach's truck, so I parked close and used my card to get into the building.

"Dean Tucker," she waddled up to the desk with a smile on her face as I handed her the box along with a warm coffee. "Now, there has to be a reason behind this." She smiled at the pastries.

"I need your help with something," I said to her, her smile growing wider as she let me behind the desk to sit with her. We talked for almost twenty minutes and she wrote everything down; on a mission to get it all done before the game today.

"I also need the key to the shop." I smiled and she eyed me dubiously, but dug it out regardless. "I promise to leave some money in the register." I waved them at her and ran through the building.

I despised being in the stadium this early; the quiet ate away at me, and the brick felt cold and suffocating when there weren't a thousand voices causing it to vibrate. I grabbed what I needed from the shop and, by the time I returned to Susanna, she had printed out what I needed and was working on the next step of our plan.

"You're a goddess," I whispered to her, taking the envelope with a smile.

Ella was waiting on the steps in her hoodie and jeans when I returned, and it didn't take me long to fill her in on the plan as we drove into Lorette. It was still early, but we stopped at the grocery store and loaded up a cart with food that I put on my credit card without remorse. I would deal with those consequences later.

I could feel her get nervous as we drove into the rougher area of town, but the streets were pretty quiet as I pulled up to the apartment building. "You can stay here, if you want," I told her, but she shook her head, leaning over the seat to grab a few of the bags from the back.

Balancing a few more with the bag from the Hornets gift shop, I pressed the buzzer with my elbow and hoped that someone was home. The old man's grumpy voice came over the staticky intercom.

"I told you kids to stop pressing that button," he grumbled.

"Uh, Mark," I said, "it's... Dean Tucker. I was here the other day with Josh," I said, turning to Ella with a nervous expression, unsure if he'd remember me, but the door buzzed loudly and clicked open for us.

I led Ella down the hallway to where Mark was waiting with his door open.

"Where's Josh?" He asked, looking at me and then Ella.

"He had morning practice, but I wanted to bring over something from him," I answered, holding up the bags.

"It's from Josh?" He eyed me and I nodded. I couldn't tell if he could see through my lie or not but, either way, I would try.

"He picked it all out himself. It was very cute." Ella smiled and peeked her head out from behind my shoulder. "I'm Ella, the team's physical therapist."

She tried to extend a hand but fumbled with the bags, making Mark chuckle. "You let this angel carry all those bags herself? Shame on you," Mark scolded me playfully and took a few of the bags from Ella, who shrugged and grinned at me.

"Hear that? I'm an angel." She winked in passing as Mark allowed us into his small apartment. The space was much cleaner and organized. It was warm and full of little things that Mark had obviously collected over the years. Weird art, a mix of mismatched furniture, but it felt like a home.

"There's a lot more than just a jersey here, Mr. Tucker." Mark set the bags on the cracked vinyl counter and turned to me.

"There is." I nodded at him. "I also have…" I dug out the envelope from my back pocket and handed it to him. "Tickets for today's game, above the dugout, if you want—"

"For me?" He cut me off and took the envelope with shaky hands. All of his knuckles were swollen and scarred from what was, without doubt, a hard life. He carefully removed the tickets from the paper and smiled down at them. "You know Josh used to hit balls off the roof when his Mom wasn't around? Broke a few windows that had to be explained away, but he's always had a knack for the game."

"He's a damn good pitcher," I agreed.

"I've listened to every Lorette game on that radio, but I've never seen him play," he said, looking down at the tickets.

"Today's your chance." Ella smiled. "But you can't be seen wearing red; Hornets' law," she teased, pointing to the gift shop bag.

Mark set down the tickets, eyeing the two of us, and pulled out a jersey stitched with Logan across the back in the perfect size. He then retrieved a beanie, a pair of socks, a few magnets, a signed baseball, and a navy blue sweater.

"You weren't kidding about getting me out of the red!" Mark barked, his grin stretching wide. He tugged the jersey on, and it fit like a glove as he buttoned it up and straightened himself out.

"The navy is handsome," Ella cooed and crossed her arms.

"This was very kind of you," he said to me with a fading smile, but the sentiment was still there. "Most folks say they'll do something and then forget—or just don't make the time."

"It was all Josh," I said. "I'm just the messenger, and you didn't hear it from me, but any game you want to be at, you've got a seat at the Hornet stadium, you just call me."

Mark studied my expression, and I know he saw through the lie, but he didn't say anything else on the matter. Ella stood by, proudly staring at me with a smile on her face and, even though Josh's voice was in the back of my mind, telling me that I was wrong, or overstepping, I knew that I had extended what I could and done it in a way that helped everyone.

"Alright, back to Harbor. Coach is going to be pissed that I'm running errands instead of being at practice." I clapped Mark on the shoulder and shooed Ella from the apartment.

LOGAN

I stared at the donation box and cursed Dean Tucker under my breath. The large crates were positioned by each gate into the stadium, with signs asking for food donations. After spotting the first one, I walked the whole damn stadium loop until I was back at the start. I should have known that he would take what I said about being a spoiled rich kid to heart and try to rewrite the situation with kindness.

God, I hated how soft and unaware he was.

I hated that it made me want to be protective.

I chewed the inside of my lip, desperate to feel anything other than the possessive warmth that simmered just beneath my skin.

"You should be in the locker room," Dean's voice sounded from behind me. "People are going to start flooding in here and the team may have come around..."

"But the crowd hasn't." I inhaled slowly, swallowing the rest of my complaints as I looked over my shoulder at him.

"You're still a Lorette to them; at least until after today."

He looked good–*too good*. His blond curls had been cut a little shorter and his cheeks were flushed with color. He was in a dark purple dress shirt that barely fit the rolling curves of his strong arms and a pair of matching dress pants that hugged tightly to his generous thighs.

It was a stark contrast to the white dress shirt and jeans I wore at every game. I felt stupid and underdressed.

"You look good," he said, as if he could read my mind. "Your knot is horrible, though." He pointed to my black tie and stepped forward. "Can I?" He checked before touching me.

I watched the muscles in his forearms tighten as he raised his hands and tried to push down the feelings of panic as he approached. I nodded and turned my face away to focus on the running length of the hallway to my left.

His hands worked at the tie, undoing it and straightening it out before retying it and pushing it up against my throat.

"Too tight?" He asked, his warm breath fanning over my jaw.

I turned slowly to look down at the tie, his hands still on the fabric and so close to my skin, and I swallowed. I tilted my chin up and our eyes met in a strangled, silent moment as he waited for a verbal answer I was too distracted to give.

Flecks of dark green danced around in the lighter shades of his eyes beneath his stupidly long eyelashes, and the panic in my chest dissipated.

"It's fine," I gritted out, and he took the cue to step back. "Thank you."

"You're welcome," he said, shifting on his feet.

"You shouldn't have done that." I pointed to the donation bin.

"I didn't." He shrugged. "It was Susanna. S he wanted to give back to the community; help the people struggling in Harbor."

The secretary?

"This about Mark? Because I said he wasn't your charity case—that he didn't need your magnets? "How about you just own up to the guilt when you say something privileged. You can't fix everything, Dean. You're acting like an idiot." I growled. Of course, he had taken that argument and flipped it on its head to give back in a way that mattered. *I hated him.*

"It was Susanna," he repeated. I could see that he was lying; his stupid smile gave him away at all times, but I let it go. *Why did I let it go?*

"Come on," he said quickly as the sounds of people laughing and talking echoed through the open doors of the stadium.

I followed him down the tunnel to the inner staff entrance, holding my breath the entire time, until we were safely behind the big blue doors. The tunnels were quiet as we took the stairs down to the locker rooms. I had walked these halls as the enemy before, but never as a Hornet, and it was instantly a different atmosphere.

The grey bricks looked warmer; the Hornets logos were brighter, and the concrete floors didn't echo in the same way they had when we were stomping down them in angry silence.

"You okay?" Dean stopped outside the Hornets' locker room. The massive hornet painted perfectly on the side-by-side navy doors mocked me.

"Yeah, Tuck," I snapped, unable to hold back. "Stop babying me." I shoved past him into the locker room and immediately wished I hadn't. Every player in the room stopped what they were doing and went quiet. "Right, who's ready to get their asses kicked?" I joked.

"Go get changed before they decide to eat you in a pre-game ritual," Cael said as he wandered up from his locker with his jersey undone and his ballpants hanging loose over his hips.

He stayed and said something to Dean as I walked over to my new locker. Reality hit me seeing the Hornets' jersey hanging there with *new* navy cleats and clean pressed ball pants. Reading Logan across the jersey in bright yellow lettering was weird. I reached out and brushed my fingers against it as I set my bag at my feet. The chaos of the locker room returned, the excitement of my entrance wearing off and leaving me in a buzzing hive of unintelligible noise.

I didn't know if it was on purpose or not, but Dean's locker was right beside mine, and the sound of his bag hitting the wood made me flinch.

"Sorry," he apologized, stripping his shirt without a second thought.

"Was this you?" I pointed to the cleats and he shook his head.

"El said your old cleats were bad luck. She found a pair of extras in the equipment locker; they should fit." Dean continued to get ready, taking off his pants before glancing quickly at me.

I looked around at the crowded room and cursed myself for not wearing a T-shirt beneath my dress shirt.

"There's a bathroom," Dean said quietly, "off the showers, to your left."

I looked up at him, his eyes burning my skin with concern and care.

"Cool. Thanks for the tip," I muttered. I didn't need him looking out for me. I didn't need him to be worrying about changing in front of all the guys. The scars I carried weren't his problem.

"Whatever, Logan." He turned back to his locker and shuffled into his uniform. Once he was dressed, he wandered away and left me where I stood, still staring at my own, paralyzed with fear. He flipped his hat over his head and climbed up on the bench in the middle of the locker room.

"Hornets!" He whistled, and the majority settled down immediately. "We've worked hard to get ourselves to this point, and it shows. You're more of a team than you were two weeks ago, and we can only get better as the season progresses."

With everyone's eyes on Dean, it gave me a split second to strip from my dress shirt. I unbuttoned it as he talked, and his eyes flickered to me with a small smirk of accomplishment that infuriated me.

He had won again.

"Today won't be easy, even for a pre-season game. We're going out there to win against the odds and despite the expectations. Remember what Arlo always says, 'don't play for anyone but yourself and the man next to you'. I'm not buying you a keg though, I'm broke..." He curled into a ball to protect himself as clothing flew at him in an uproar of boos and yelling. "Ow! Who threw a fucking shoe?!" He burst into laughter and chucked it back from where it came.

"Two steps at a time, Hornets."

The entire room tapped their two fingers to their hearts.

Cult.

I finished buttoning up my jersey and quickly slid into my pants as the room went back to its typical chaos. I could feel Silas's eyes on me from the main door where he stood talking to Coach, but his attention was on me.

It drove me nuts how much of myself I could see in him at that moment. The same hardened jaw, both dusted with a dark scruff. If his hair were longer, it would be wavy and messy, just like mine, but he kept it short and pushed back off his face.

I had spent all my life staring at the scowl in the mirror; I knew it intimately and it pissed me off that Silas did too. When he excused himself to come over to me, I grabbed my shoes and turned my back to him, using the locker to tie them up tight.

My toes wiggled freely in the cleats; it was either Ella or Dean that had noticed I was wearing a size too small at camp and I felt ashamed.

"Are you ready for today?" Silas asked me over my shoulder.

"I don't know how many times I have to tell you to fuck off." I turned my head to look at him and glared.

"Josh," Silas started, but I cut him off.

"Just leave me the hell alone, Silas."

"You need to know something—"

The room erupted in the sound of cheers and cleats as the guys started to flood from the locker room and into the hallway. I shrugged and backed away from Silas, not giving a damn what he had to say in that moment. I joined the team, keeping my distance and waiting in the tunnel for the announcement.

The Harbor stadium had always been twice as loud as Lorette. We only had a thousand or so more seats to fill, but the fans in Harbor were insane. More insane then they had the right to be over a college baseball team. The entire stadium was vibrating as the announcer fought over the volume of the screaming crowd.

One by one, the starting lineup was announced, with me being the last of the starters to be welcomed onto the field. As predicted, and honestly warranted, the crowd swelled and the sound of hatred rolled down from the stands onto the diamond.

"Go home, Logan", they chanted—a pulsing, hateful chorus of voices as I made my way to the middle of the lineup, sandwiched between Dean and Cael.

"They could have at least come up with something clever," I growled, and Cael started to laugh to my right.

"You have two first names as a name, give them a week," Cael said in their defense, and to ease the tension between my shoulders.

The sound of screamed insults was only silenced by the announcer introducing the game's opening host.

"Please welcome your most generous sponsor and Hornets alum, Charles Shore."

My heart felt like it was clawing out of my chest at the sight of him. Why had no one warned me that he was going to be here today? As far as I knew, he had been all but cut out of the family's dealings with the baseball team.

You need to know something...

Silas had tried.

"Good afternoon, Harbor!" His cracked voice boomed through the microphone, and the stadium cheered for him. The sound of their adoration only made me more sick to my stomach. They had no idea who he really was; it was hidden beneath walls of smiles and donations that satiated the masses. The ones who never did their research past a simple newsletter or article in the paper.

Charles Shore was a slimy asshole with darker secrets than anyone on this field outside Silas and myself knew. His bullshit speech was drowned out by the hatred that was coursing through my veins. This was the closest we had ever been.

Even after I found out who I was, I had never confronted him.

I had, on many occasions, stood outside the hospital he worked at and stared up at the shiny glass windows just wanting to fucking kill him but never finding the courage to go inside. I smashed the shit out of his car one time; spent three days hiding from the cops when they came looking for a kid with my description.

I gave up trying to make him see me after that. It wasn't worth the heat from the cops, and he had replaced the car with something newer before I could even blink. People like him—money didn't matter, and neither did their mistakes.

He was the reason my mother started using drugs.

He was the reason she started selling my body for money.

For all the scars and nightmares.

The reason I couldn't breathe when someone stood too close.

And he didn't give a shit.

I stared at the back of his head in disgust, just praying it would end soon so we could play baseball.

"Our new captain, Dean Tucker, and our new starting pitcher, Joshua Logan."

He had no idea.

I almost vomited hearing my name roll off his lips so casually.

My eyes immediately locked onto Silas, standing on the stairs in the dugout, worry straining over his features as Dean started forward to stand with Charles Shore, but I remained frozen.

"You have to do it"—that's what he was saying without words, waiting for me to cause a scene, but I was so rooted in the ground I couldn't move to try.

"Josh," Cael mumbled under his breath. "He wants you to throw the first pitch... move, man."

I cleared my throat and stepped forward to where Dean stood next to him, my jaw clenched so tightly I could feel the muscles that ached down through my shoulders and spine. I came shoulder to shoulder with the man who'd thrown me out like trash and stared straight ahead.

Silas' hands were wrapped tightly around the bannister, watching and waiting to intervene, but frozen just the same.

I flinched when a hand came down on my shoulder and dug into my skin. "Logan will lead us to another win, so let's start treating him like family!"

I gagged, bile rising, and I choked on it in my throat.

"You alright, son?" Charles turned to me and squeezed my shoulder tighter.

Son.

He hadn't meant it in the way I took it, but it churned viciously in my stomach nonetheless. I glared at him and nodded slowly and carefully. Each small movement felt like my skin was peeling and pulling.

"Let's throw that pitch," I gritted out, forcing a smile that didn't reach my eyes.

TUCKER

"Nothing fancy," I said to Josh as I walked to the catcher's spot with my glove.

His dark eyes were glassy, fixed somewhere far away. His whole body had looked like it might curl into a ball when Mr. Shore laid his hand on him. I braced for a snapped comment or an angry remark, but Josh stayed quieter than I'd ever seen him.

He threw the ball without a word, he barely even set up, but he put his hand in the air as the crowd's chorus of boo's turned to cheers for him. We needed them on our side, and I appreciated the effort he was putting in despite clearly being very uncomfortable.

I did the coin toss after the national anthem played, before making my way to the rowdy dugout with the rest of the team. I looked over at Josh, but he avoided my gaze and continued to bother with the laces on his glove.

"What the hell was that?" I asked Cael, sliding down onto the bench beside him.

"No idea, but whatever it was, it's got him in knots, and that's not good for us. This game was already going to be a hard win... without Josh in focus..." Cael's tongue ran along his bottom lip,

and he pushed up from the bench. "We're going to have to play a lot of defense today." He nodded.

Unfortunately, he was right.

I needed to give Josh a reason to loosen up. I needed smug, asshole Josh for this game, not whatever tangled ball of yarn he had turned into since stepping on the field.

"Hey." I passed by Josh, then stopped. "Come here."

"What?" He scoffed at me, his brows coming together in confusion.

"Stand up, tough guy," I said; a feeble attempt to push his buttons.

"You're getting on my nerves today, Tuck." He pushed from the bench, making his way over to me, and his eyes trailed my arm to where I was pointing into the stands.

Mark stood with Zoey, who was decked out in Hornets' gear with a bright smile on her pretty face. The introduction had gone perfectly and Mark was more than willing to '*keep Zoey entertained*' for the game. They both waved down at us and Mark gave Josh an enthusiastic thumbs up.

"You brought him down here?" Josh said, not taking his eyes off Mark.

"He said he's never seen you play," I replied, still looking at Josh.

His brown eyes watered but were quickly blinked clear as he turned to look at me.

"Thank you," he said tightly, and despite the lack of enthusiasm, I knew that Josh meant the gratitude this time.

"Yeah, so don't embarrass yourself," I teased with a smile. "It would be a shame if you lost today in front of him."

"You're an asshole," Josh growled, but that smug smile formed on his face.

"Say it like you mean it, Logan," I murmured, leaning in until only he could hear me above the noise.

"You're an asshole, Dean." His voice dipped lower than I'd ever heard it, but the sound of my actual name on his lips was like a balm to my fried nerves. The heat coming off him was intoxicating, and it took everything in me not to get even closer.

"Ouch." I clutched my chest playfully and finally looked away from him. "Now go pitch a perfect first inning. Give them something to love you for, because once they see how big of a dickhead you are in post game interviews they're going to need a reminder."

"Ha," Josh barked and flipped me off. Stepping out onto the field, the resounding chorus of disgruntled fans returned, but he didn't seem phased this time. He was ready to prove himself.

"Good work, big boy. I think you might have cracked Josh's concrete heart," Cael said as he followed me out onto the field. The groaning turned to cheers and the guys all shook out their tense spring nerves, replacing them with excitement and focus.

Josh closed his eyes on the pitcher's mound and rolled his neck out before palming the baseball and staring down the pipe at Jensen, behind the batter. I lowered my stance and Louis, on second, followed suit. Cael inched to his right, his shoulder lining up with Josh's, and his eyes widened ready for the pitch.

Ritchie Levson was their lead off, and for a damn good reason.

He hit hard and had the disgusting capability of dropping balls into tiny gaps left in the outfield.

Josh inhaled one more time before angling his body backward in a fluid motion as he shifted his feet and threw the first true pitch of the season.

The sound of the bat meeting the ball was loud and followed by chaos.

No one was talking to each other.

Josh turned to track the ball, and I shifted off base to prepare for Mitchell's cannon from his scattered position.

"First!" I called out, but he couldn't hear me and the sound of the crowd drowned out any echo that might have followed. The ball hit the turf in center field, just beyond Todd, and had Van sliding through the grass to collect it in his long arms.

Ritchie bulleted past me onto second and Louis wasn't ready.

"Second!" I barked, but instead of putting his glove up, Louis turned to look at me. "What are you doing?" I pointed as the ball ripped past him, bouncing hard into the sand and rebounding upward toward Josh's glove.

He turned on his heel, but it was too late for Taylor on third.

Ritchie was gone, cheering and hollering from home as he scored the first run off the first bat. I shook out the frustration, slapping my hand into my glove a few times.

"It's alright just..." I huffed and got louder for them, "talk to each other!" I ordered. Louis gave me a pained look that was more of a silent apology than anything else.

The instruction fell on deaf ears. We let in another three runs before Josh found his groove and managed to shut down batters in the box with some strikes.

The guys were frustrated, and rightfully so; Philly was mocking us with loud laughter and big smiles. They were under our skin and it showed.

"Alright, hold up." I shoved Cael back down into the dugout, even though he was called to bat. "We didn't come out here to let some last place team push us around. Start communicating. I don't care if you're screaming about the grass tickling your fucking ankles, just give something more than silence!"

"Yes, Cap." Cael tapped his chest, his voice booming through the dugout, and scooted past me to take lead off while the rest of them swallowed the order.

With Cael's boisterous cooperation, the team seemed to find their footing. Nerves had taken the first half of the inning, but it was clear they weren't going down without a fight.

We scored to even the game and took the field again; out of breath and riding on adrenaline. The communication that had formed so stiffly at spring camp reappeared, and as the game went on we worked out the kinks. Cael and Josh became a single thought, contributing to nearly half the outs between the two of them.

It was in the second half of the game when things started to go downhill. Down a single run and in desperate need of a winning push, Philly started to get chippy.

Noah Hudson was up to bat, a second string shortstop with a violent attitude and a habit of running squeeze plays. With a player on third, it was clear what was about to happen. Josh flicked his dark eyes to me, and I knew he was on the same page as he leaned back and let go of the ball in a straight, fast line toward Hudson's bat.

The bunt dropped toward Josh's feet, but he scooped it up fast and threw it even quicker to force the ball in my direction. I caught it before Hudson could blink and tagged him out as I hurled the ball toward Jensen.

"Out!" The ump called twice, back to back, and the diamond erupted.

"Nice catch, faggot," Hudson growled from beside me, and my entire body seized up at the sound. I had become desensitized to the word, but in sports it was everywhere. Especially when guys got angry. It was what we were raised on; our dads used it, theirs before them. It was as common as asshole and prick, but it felt worse.

Most ignored it, brushed it off, but for me, it sank deep into my bones and reminded me that they thought I was disgusting, that they saw me as nothing more than something to tease each other about. My sexuality, my life–I was a slur to them, not a human. It was the first word they went for, and there was nothing I could do against it, because if I argued it, then I *was* one.

"What the fuck did you say to him?" Josh stepped off the mound as Hudson started back to his dugout, and I remained silent. My shoulders were pinned back as I tried to ignore how the slur rolled down my spine.

"Piss off, Logan!" Hudson waved him off and kept walking, but Josh wasn't satisfied with the answer and picked up his pace.

His hand wrapped around the back of Hudson's jersey and tugged him backwards. "What did you say?" He snarled, as Hudson shoved him off.

"I said, nice catch *fa*—-"

Hudson wasn't given the chance to finish his sentence. The word died on his lips as the sound of flesh on flesh echoed out, followed by a quick, nasty crunch.

"You're not so tough with a mouthful of blood. Say it again, pussy!" Josh demanded as Hudson attempted a retaliation swing. The ump tried to get between them but the dugouts flooded onto the field and soon both teams were locked in a massive, uncontrollable fist fight, fueled by the chanting of a bloodthirsty crowd.

Coach was the first to interject himself, grabbing Van by the waist as Arlo caught Cael by the collar of his jersey and dragged him back.

"Go!" he barked at Cael, who had a thick stream of blood running down from his nose, filling his smile and making it red.

"Dean!" Cael yelled over Arlo's shoulder, spitting the collection of blood in his mouth to the dirt. "Dean!" He yelled again when I didn't move. "Get him!" He demanded and Arlo turned around to find me frozen.

"Go." He shoved Cael's chest, causing him to stumble back on his feet, but he listened and grabbed Baker by the jersey, pushing him toward the dugout.

"Hey, Tucker." Arlo's hand slapped against my neck and gripped me tightly to break me out of my dissociation. "Snap out of it, dumbass, before you get smacked around!"

I wanted to, but my eyes stayed on Josh—still looming over Hudson, still swinging, and I knew I couldn't leave. I pushed past Arlo and shoved through the violent mess of players to get to Josh. I grabbed him roughly by the arms, hauling him off Hudson as he fought against me until he realized who it was and he kicked away, brushing himself off.

"Get off me!" He snapped, shoving me back.

"It's me!" I stepped forward, our chests brushing together as Josh's pulsed rapidly.

He had a nasty cut across his freckled cheek, and his pupils were blown with rage as Hudson climbed from the ground with a busted lip and a bloody nose.

"Keep your faggot away from me!" Hudson snarled, and at first I thought Josh might go in for another round, but it was Arlo who whirled on the player that time. I half expected him to hit him, but instead he grabbed him by the collar and lifted him up until his toes were dragging on the ground, and hurled him backwards into a group of his own players.

"Get out of our stadium," he snapped, stepping forward when the Philly coaches came to the defense of their players.

"We have an inning to play, King," their head coach said.

"Play it on your bus ride home, this game is over."

"You don't have the authority to end games. You're an assistant coach!" They hollered at him.

"He doesn't, but I do." Coach Cody pushed forward, controlled rage engrained on his face as his jaw ticked. "Take your team home, Albie. Teach them some fucking manners before you come back or I'll report you to the committee." His voice dropped low.

"For what?" The Philly coach was red in the face, his hands balled at his side.

"You know what." Coach smiled at him but there was no humor in the action.

"If you end it here, Ryan, it's a forfeit. Philly gets the win," the ump warned.

"Let them." He shrugged, turning his back on Philly. "It's the only win they'll get this season."

Arlo laughed and followed Coach back to the mess of players still pushing and shoving. "Harbor. Locker room. Now." He didn't yell, but we moved anyway—a loose line of battered and bruised faces in the dugout.

"You alright?" Cael asked as I stepped down into the dugout, and I nodded my head in passing. "Hey, hey!" He grabbed me and stopped me from going any further. "Are you sure?"

"I'm alright, Cael," I answered him properly that time and curled my fingers into his jersey for balance as my adrenaline rush crashed through my bloodstream. "Not a great start to the season," I grumbled, but a smile formed on Cael's stupid face. "What are you smiling about? We lost," I scowled at him.

"Look around, Deano." The guys stood shoulder to shoulder in blood-stained jerseys, with bruises blossoming and big grins. "We're a team, that's better than a pre-season win."

TUCKER

"Sit down!" Coach demanded, and we all sank stiffly against the lockers. Arlo, Silas and a few of the other coaches flanked him with serious looks on their faces. "What the hell is wrong with you guys?"

"He called Dean a..." Cael piped up the fastest, but his words died on his lips as Coach shook his head. He didn't need to finish.

"I know what he called him, we all heard it." Coach turned his fiery stare on his son. "Since when do we throw punches to solve problems on the diamond?" He asked.

The locker room was quieter than it ever had been.

"Alright, fair. Dumb question." Coach ran his hands through his graying, dirty blond hair, pushing his hat off his head as he went. He took a long, deep breath before he spoke again. "I know that I'm not always the most aware, or present," he said, looking over at Cael again. "But when you sink to their level, they win. You always protect one of your own, but when it comes to slurs, homophobic or racist..." he said with a pause.

We all remembered the year a kid from Boston went after Arlo. It had ended the same way as today. Bloody lips and a softcore

scolding that sounded more like a *"good job boys"* rather than a *"you're idiots"* speech.

"So what, we let them?" Van asked, his brown hair sticky against a nasty cut that sliced through his eyebrow.

"No," Coach said. "These guys don't see the problem with using words like that because they're coached by men who don't see the problem with it."

"Well now they've been taught a lesson!" Todd hollered. "They can't get away with it. If we can learn—"

"Let me deal with it through the right channels. Hudson will go back to Philly proud of himself for getting his team a win," Coach interrupted whatever Todd was going to say next.

"That wasn't a win!" Cael argued.

"It is on paper, because you're all hot-headed…" He trailed off, looking around at us. "Where the fuck is Logan?"

We all stopped to look at who was sitting beside us, but Josh was nowhere to be found. Silas' jaw tensed, and without a word, he was out of the locker room, the heavy blue doors swinging behind him as he went.

"Clean yourselves up, shower, tomorrow you run a double practice for this bullshit," Coach said. "Tucker, you gotta talk to the press."

"Don't make me," I almost begged, rolling my shoulders back, but I pushed from my seated position regardless because of the look he gave me.

"You're the captain—you don't get a choice. Come on." He waved me over and tossed his hand around my shoulder. "You'll be okay. You don't have to answer any questions about the fight. Deflect them into game tactics and season projections."

"Easier said than done," I grumbled, but put a smile on my face as we reached the press room.

"You're already more likeable than Arlo," he teased, opening the door for me. The cameras' clicking and the low buzz of reporters talking amongst themselves were enough to have me turning and leaving, but Coach was blocking the doorway. "Sit."

There was a small chair behind the desk for me and I pulled it out, the legs grinding loudly against the concrete floor. The sound was obnoxious enough to awkwardly silence everyone in the room.

"Dean Tucker," I said. A few of them chuckled. "Right. Guess you knew that..."

"Mr. Tucker, what was the fight about today?" The first question came from a slender male reporter with horrible posture and large teeth.

I was in the wolf's den now.

"Unclear." I shrugged and tried to sound dismissive.

I picked at the tablecloth spread beneath my fingertips to keep myself calm.

"Noah Hudson said something to you that set off Joshua Logan. Care to elaborate?" He pushed and I knew he would, the question had the room in chaos.

"No, I came down here to talk to you about baseball, not politics," I said just loudly enough to seem brave, but my legs were shaking under the table.

"Baseball *is* politics," the reporter sneered. "Did the fight have anything to do with your activities outside the game?"

"If you're referring to my private life, no," I said, the lie was tight on my lips.

"So your pitcher, who has a violent past, jumped a Philly player for no reason?"

"Do you have any questions about the game?" I said.

"Listen, kid—"

"It's *Captain*," I corrected. The word *kid* slipped past my defenses, and I could hear my brother in the back of my mind, teasing me for being too slow, or too stupid to keep up with him. "We went out and played hard. What happened wasn't a result of anything the Hornets did or didn't do; at the end of the day, we can't control what other players bring to the game."

"So he did say something?" Another reporter got louder.

"You'll have to watch the Philly conference to find out." I shrugged. "Do you have any questions about the season?" I asked.

The room went quiet.

Until one reporter near the back stood, I recognized him immediately. He was the reporter who wrote the piece on Ella after Cael's accident. A reporter who would do anything he could to manipulate a narrative for a rumor mill piece. Whatever came out of his mouth next would be said with the intent to rattle me. I pushed my feet into the soles of my cleats and tried to breathe.

"The team seems to be struggling after your rough season last year? Does it have anything to do with the shoddy dynamics now that Arlo King is gone?" He asked.

Shoddy dynamics. Great.

"The team is solid and ready to work towards a successful season," I answered smoothly. "Today was a hiccup, but that's what exhibition games are for."

"It's apparent that there's animosity among the team after Cael Cody's accident. Has this created more strain between the players?" He asked.

He was trying to find loose threads to pull.

He wanted me to unravel.

"We're finding our groove, and if you give us a few days, we'll prove just how well we work together," I said, ignoring his probing about the accident.

"So you and Cael Cody are on good terms?" He asked.

What the hell was that supposed to mean?

I could feel the panic building, I could see the path he wanted to take with his story, and it all ended with public humiliation and my name at the forefront of it.

"We're fine."

"Did the fight have anything to do with your romantic relationship with Cael Cody?" He asked, and my throat tightened. My muscles seized as my heart started to race.

"I—" I opened my mouth to speak, but nothing came out as more reporters stood, and the room erupted into more questions I didn't know how to answer.

"Mr. Tucker." He stared at me like I was enemy number one; his impatience was clear. "It was rumored that last season, the reason

Cael broke down was because of you. Because of your complicated history with one another. Is that true?"

My throat felt tight, and I shook my head.

"It's not true?" He probed.

"The reason behind the accident—"

"Isn't true, or..." He continued to cut me off, and the more he did it, the more frustrated I became. It was sitting on my chest like a thousand pounds, and there was nothing I could do to control the narrative unfolding in front of me, short of flipping out on the entire room of reporters. "Mr. Tucker, are you capable of answering a single question?" His tone was harsh.

"The accident had nothing to do with Cael and me," I said, and it ripped from me in a clumsy bark that made Silas flinch in the corner of my eye.

"So the rumors are true, you were in a relationship with Mr. Cody, you *are* homosexual."

Bile rose, and my hands flexed on the tabletop, just needed something to grasp onto before I completely lost control of myself. Head was spinning violently from the accusation... but it wasn't one, it *was* the truth. I was gay. But...

"What—" I meant to say yes, to say no. To give them anything that might just get them to leave me alone long enough for my heart to stop thudding painfully in my chest. "I—"

"Cat got your tongue, Mr. Tucker?" the reporter smiled. That broke down whatever confidence I had left.

I opened my mouth to talk again, unsure what would come out, but it wasn't going to be good. "Fuc—" My breath was stolen from my lungs, the anxiety stealing everything I had and making me numb.

Coach was at my side and pushed me from my chair.

"Go," he whispered and I didn't hesitate to listen. "Interviews over gentleman," he snapped. The echoes from the press boomed down the hallway as I jogged down toward the locker room. But the noise from inside was just as loud and it made me freeze.

I couldn't breathe.

They'd all see that news.

My reaction would be posted everywhere come morning.

Fuck.

I pressed my hand to the door, I knew that behind it they'd all be waiting for updates and that they'd have my back no matter what happens but it was…overwhelming and suffocating. I veered left toward the visitors' locker room—empty, dirty from Philly's quick departure. The silence hit me like a warm blanket.

Tears were streaming from my face but I couldn't do a damn thing to stop them.

I stripped my jersey off, barely bothering with the buttons and threw it away. I just needed to be free from the restricting, itchy fabric. I walked toward the showers, just needing to shock my system with the frigid, harsh water pressure.

"Shit," I stopped, my whole body coming to a halt seeing him there. He was drenched, still wearing his ball pants, but they were soaked through as he ran a sponge over his torso. He didn't notice me in the doorway, too busy scrubbing his skin raw under the scalding water.

Every other problem in my life was muted by the sound of his sobs.

I stepped forward slowly, watching the water pour from his dark curls against his chest, dripping down and diluting the stream of blood from his nose.

"Josh," I said. He didn't hear me over the water, so I moved closer. My fingers brushed over the sponge, ghosting his skin, and his head snapped up as he pressed himself against the cold shower wall.

"Don't touch me," he snapped, his eyes fluttering closed and his breathing harsh and shallow. Like I didn't even interrupt him, his hands returned to their scrubbing motion.

"What are you doing?" I asked him, trying to be gentle, curbing the need to yell at him or break him from the trance.

Again he ignored me, and continued to scrub frantically like he was trying to remove permanent marks, but there was nothing on his skin except for a few bruises, the cut that split through his bottom lip and the one that bit into his cheek. I knew getting in his face wouldn't work, he barely wanted me there when he was coherent. And whatever he was going through, he wasn't himself.

I stepped into the hot water, wincing at the temperature as it burned my unprepared skin, and I reached out for the sponge for a second time. He held onto it tightly, his fingernails raw from the grip.

"Trade me," I said, pulling on the sponge.

"Go away, Tucker." He squeezed tighter, and I could see beneath the sponge that he had scrubbed the skin so raw it was bleeding under his assault.

"No," I shook my head, trying again. "You helped me today," I swallowed, "which means I owe you, remember? We don't do charity," I reminded him. "If you don't let me help, then you're no better than me."

"Shut up," he growled and stepped closer. The water ran slick down his features and when he turned his face up toward me I could see the shame raging behind those brown eyes, pupils still flared and angry.

I stared back at him, raising my hands at a torturous pace so as not to startle him before I pressed them against his jaw on either side. His whole body tensed under the contact, but I felt him lean into the touch and breathe. It was ragged and heavy, releasing whatever pain he was clutching to, and he closed his eyes. His lashes were soaked with water and made him look so sad as he broke down a little further.

"Let me help," I gritted out, just trying to convince him that I wasn't there to hurt him. My thumb brushed over the cut on his cheek, and he didn't say a word, but his brows pulled together in pain. "I'm sorry," I whispered, suddenly very aware of how close he was to me. I could feel the heat that radiated from his body, and I could smell the sweat and blood that tangled with the hot steam that rose around us.

His eyes opened at the sound of my apology, and he grabbed my wrists, his nails digging into my skin. Josh's bottom lip trembled as he brought in another strangled gasp of air and moved us in a rough motion. He slammed my back against the tiles, staring at me with bloodshot eyes that screamed for help.

"Take it back," he growled.

"No," I said, shaking my head. I wouldn't. I was sorry. He was here, like this, because of something I did... I just know it. I could feel it under my skin, picking at my muscles. There was guilt there, I just didn't know why.

"Don't look at me like that," he snapped and dug his nails deeper.

"Like what?" I whispered over the running water, his lips were so close to mine that I could feel the shaky exhale that came, it was cold compared to the heat of the water and fanned down my skin, kissing my overheated body.

"You aren't allowed to feel sorry for me," he said, his eyes flickering across my face.

"I don't," I lied.

"You do, I can smell the pity on your skin and it's driving me nuts," he groaned. "Just don't."

"Alright," I said, just trying to understand what was going on behind his eyes. "What do you want then? Because whatever you're doing isn't going to work, I won't let you—"

Josh didn't let me finish, he surged forward and captured my open mouth against his. The force slammed my head into the tiles, but the sting was drowned out by the hungry way his tongue pushed into my mouth. I allowed my hands to drift back through his soaked waves of hair and gripped him tightly. The kiss was needy, it was hot and full of hatred, but he was kissing me, and much to my surprise, *I was enjoying it.*

Teeth clashed as he fought for dominance, but I didn't care; he could have whatever he wanted. I was completely at his mercy, in a trance under his harsh touch and painful grip. I wanted every mark he planned to leave in his wake. It was all I could think about as his fingernails scraped against the soft skin of my wrist, leaving little raw lines that proved I wasn't dreaming.

I closed my eyes and sank into the kiss as he leaned against me, but as quickly as he had initiated it, he was gone. I felt his touch dissipate, and when I opened my eyes, he was already gone. Leaving the shower room without another word.

LOGAN

I sat in the closet for three hours before the door to our room at Dansby finally opened. I knew he'd come looking for me eventually, I just wished he hadn't. Now I'd have to explain myself.

"Josh?" His voice was sturdy as always, kind and searching for me in the darkness despite our last rough interaction.

My lip throbbed and my cheek probably needed ice but I had gotten dressed and came straight here to find the solace in the silence. The rest of the team had gone to a party somewhere on campus and I was grateful when the loudest thing to welcome me into Dansby House was the creaking of the old floorboards.

I heard Dean stop, turn back and flick on the lamp beside his bed.

His tall frame cast a shadow across the floor to where I sat huddled in the closet and I did my best to straighten up and not seem so small but in his presence there was no denying how little I felt.

"What?" I said, harsher than I meant to be, but he didn't flinch at my tone.

He kicked off his sneakers and peeled off the hoodie he was wearing as he walked toward me and sat on the floor across from me.

"Shouldn't you be at a party?" I looked at him, curling up against the wall to keep myself from reaching out to him.

"You weren't there," he said, like it was just a simple fact and it resonated against the steel cage I kept my heart in.

"I should've known you wouldn't take the hint. I don't want to be around you," I lied.

Dean just laughed at me.

"Liar," he said gently. "We need to talk." Dean chewed on the inside of his mouth.

"Do we?" I scowled at him but tried to keep my voice lighter.

"You kissed me, Josh. And... I..."

"Spit it out, Tuck," I snapped.

"I liked it," he confessed as he rubbed the crescent-shaped bruises that stained his inner wrist with the pad of his thumb. I had hurt him.

"I was fucking with you," I said, trying to push him away but he just smiled at me.

"No, you weren't," he chuckled. "You don't have to be that guy in here, it's just us." He looked around our room, his side so full of life, and mine was bare. No posters, no life. Just my bed and my bag.

"You don't know me." I rolled my eyes and sighed. "Stop pretending like you do, I'm not going to be Cael, I'm not going to fuck you in secret to make you feel better about yourself."

"Hey now," he smiled, and it was like the room got warmer. So easily he was able to change how I felt, balm the anger, soothe the pain. It was infuriating and exhausting for me. "I'm not the one sitting in the closet," he joked.

He was smiling at me... I scoffed. Where was his anger? His frustration?

"And I don't know you because you won't tell me," he said instead of getting mad about the Cael comment. "And for the record? You don't get to use Cael's secrets as ammo in this firefight."

"Is that what this is? A firefight?" I snarled at him. "Or is this an integration?"

"Have you ever had a normal conversation, tough guy? Or is everything with you an argument?" Dean asked.

When you were born into a life that never wanted you, the answer to that question was always yes. The only thing I knew how to be and how to be well was angry. Argumentative. It kept me alive for all these years, and now Dean Tucker wanted something else? Something softer?

Fuck that.

"Do you even know what you're arguing about?" he asked.

"God, go back to your party, Tuck, I don't want you here." I turned my head away to stare at the closet wall.

"There you go lying again," Dean said. "I brought..." he looked around, his eyes catching his bag, he slid it over to us and pulled out some ice and Tylenol. "For..." he pointed to his own cheek and I reached out for the ice.

It stung as I pressed it to the open cut.

"Why did you do that for me?" He asked me after a tortuous beat of silence.

"I didn't," I denied it.

"Josh!" He snapped, his voice rising higher than I've ever heard from him, and I smiled in shock. "Now you're smiling?" His entire body deflated.

"It's funny when you get loud," I said genuinely.

His cheeks turned red and he rolled back against the hardwood floor with a soft thud, closing his eyes and ignoring my jab.

"It's a shitty word, and he directed it at you but it wasn't just about *you*," I explained.

He sat back up on his elbows and looked at me.

"I got expelled from Lorette for attacking a fellow player," I confessed to him. "Which, by the look on your face, you already knew. Silas is a *rat*."

Dean tried to hide the smile that formed on his face at the insult.

"Ian," he confirmed.

"Ian." I nodded. I chewed on the inside of my mouth, unsure if I should even tell him the reason why, but the way he was looking at me told me that he was ready to hear it, whether or not I was ready to tell it.

"He found out some shit about my life, things I kept well hidden. He had been harassing me, minor stuff, things I could handle, brush off or ignore. I used to shower alone after all the guys left to hide the…"

Scars.

Dean sat up more and moved closer to me as he listened.

"He got the jump on me in the locker room showers one night," I stopped because the bile was rising in my throat over the next sentence. I could feel the scar above my eye… "He slammed my head into the wall and I blacked out… When I woke up, he was—" I paused, trying to find a less harsh word, but there was nothing. "He was raping me with a smile on his face."

Dean watched my every movement; each flinch, each twitch. Every single tense muscle he took note and he waited. I could see the questions on his face and the need to ask them, the want to understand but he stayed quiet.

"He wanted power over me and he got it," I said with malice in my voice. "But he couldn't hold on to it because he was stupid for thinking that I would just give in to it. I got up and I beat him until he couldn't open his eyes because it felt good to do it. I could have stopped, but I didn't."

He remained silent, listening to every word I spoke.

"He wasn't conscious when they dragged me out of the locker room, and I prayed to whoever would listen that he'd stay that way. Lifeless and unable to harm anyone." I felt the cool water of the melting ice against my palm and realized I'd dug my nails deep into the plastic, and it was leaking down my wrist.

"I fought because I have had to for my entire life, and the moment I thought that I had found a safe place, somewhere I could let my guard down. Ian reminded me that a place like that doesn't exist. Nowhere is safe, every conversation is a fight, no one has my best interest in mind, harming someone else is easy when it makes you feel better about yourself, and I will never let anyone do that to me again."

"Understood," Dean said quietly.

I quietly scoffed, of course, he'd just agree. Like it was that simple.

"Why does no one know what he did to you? They all think you snapped."

"Because that's what I told them at the committee meeting," I said.

"That's why you're here," Dean said, he was finally starting to connect the dots. "Silas was at that meeting, they were going to strip you of your position."

"They were, but he convinced them that he could find me a place with the Hornets so I could finish my last year of school," I said. "At the time I didn't give a shit, I just wanted out of Lorette."

"And now?" Dean asked.

"Now what?" I shrugged.

"Do you give a shit now?" His lips curled into a soft smile as I nodded.

I envied how easily he just listened.

"I'm sorry that happened," he said just after, in the most delicate voice I had ever heard.

"It wasn't the first time, but it *was* the last." I swallowed, and I could tell he knew what I meant. He had seen the locks on my bedroom door. Locks I'd ripped off again and again, hauling on the doorknob and begging to be let out..

The sound of them clicking open as my mom got ready to let in another random man was branded into my conscious thoughts. Everywhere I went, so did that noise.

"How many?" Dean asked, clearly uncomfortable but still trying.

I curled my fingers into the hem of my shirt and tugged it gingerly over my head to expose my chest to him, sliding out from the shadows of the closet into the moonlight that shone through the window.

"She did it for money," I said, looking down at the scars. "People will pay a lot for discretion and who better to keep secrets than a junkie desperate for money."

I kept my head down as he slid closer, his leg brushing against mine but he was careful to create space. He was cautious not to touch me. I looked up at him and I could feel the tremble in my jaw as the water welled in my eyes.

"There's that pity again, Tuck," I murmured, barely getting the words out.

"Not pity, tough guy." Dean shook his head.

"What is it then?" I asked.

"Admiration," Dean whispered, his own voice tight with emotion.

It was hard to wrap my head around the idea that maybe instead of Dean being ashamed of me he was praising me for my strength. I wanted to fall back on my anger and snap at him, tell him he's wrong or stupid but before I could even open my mouth to insult him and retreat back to my safe space he spoke again.

"You know that you're safe here, right? You might not be happy, but…you're safe."

I'd just spent the last fifteen minutes stumbling through my trauma, pouring it out like it meant nothing. And Dean had successfully collected all the blood I spilled into his palms, looked me dead in the eye, and told me the one thing I've never heard in my entire broken and battered life.

You're safe.

TUCKER

Dinner Sunday.

Awesome.

Just great. My heart raced as I stared at the text in my lap. I was curled up half awake and half dressed in my bed with Josh sleeping in the bed across from me. His hair stuck to his forehead, matted against the crusted cut on his cheek.

It looked painful—but he looked peaceful.

He had exposed so much about himself sitting on the floor in the closet the night before that I didn't even see that mean, cocky pitcher anymore. My opinion of him hadn't necessarily changed—but it had shifted, there was an understanding now that wasn't there before. A reason why he was the way he was.

I just wish I had his courage.

Maybe if I had some of that unbridled rage I wouldn't be such a coward about facing my family. Mom's silence was deafening, it had practically woken me up at three am just thinking about it.

Stewing preemptively in her disappointment. I flipped my phone over and rolled back in my bed to stare at the ceiling.

I knew that eventually everything had to come out, that the press would figure it out. Cael and I hadn't necessarily been careful about things. We were quiet when we needed to be, but we had never cared at parties or on the road. It was just a matter of time before the world outside the Nest put the puzzle pieces together.

Dean Tucker, *gay.*

I could see the words written in dark ink across the newspaper's front page.

There would be more tact to it.

Some may even spin it to make it a humanitarian piece.

But most would use my sexual orientation as rage bait; it would give cause to blame whatever faults that arise during the season on me. It was unfair, and bullshit but true. It was human nature to be afraid of something they didn't understand. I just wish more people were willing to learn before they cast judgment.

"Why are you awake?" Josh's voice was husky and full of sleep.

I don't answer him, keeping my eyes closed. We had enough sharing secrets for the last twenty-four hours, and whatever advice he might have, I'd heard it before.

Be honest.

Be brave.

Be you.

It was all nonsense from people who didn't understand the consequences of being those things with people who only cared about how it made them look.

"I know you're awake, you aren't snoring," he said.

"I don't snore," I muttered, opening my eyes to look over at him, still tucked tightly against his pillow with his jaw nestled into the loose collar of his old hoodie. Even in his sleep, he protected his skin, and it made me unreasonably sad.

It was too hot in the Nest to be sleeping like that. I was sweating in my pajama pants and I could see the beads of sweat that stuck to his neck as he pushed up on his elbow to look over at me. The moonlight was fading as the sun started to rise and it was casting the prettiest shade of purple into the room that made Josh glow.

"Alright, up," he grumbled and flipped his blankets back.

"What?"

"Get. Up."

I stared at him for a few minutes longer as he shuffled across the room and pressed his feet into his sneakers left by the door.

"If you're going to keep us awake, we might as well go for a run," he explained. "The fresh air and forced exercise will guilt you into telling me why you're not sleeping, or eating." His eyes rolled over my chest as I rose from bed, he looked around, and when he found what he was looking for, a sweater was hurled at my head.

"Put some clothes on," he sighed.

I laughed under my breath and pulled on the sweater, grabbing a clean pair of sweats. He crossed his arms and leaned against the door frame with his eyes closed. No doubt still fighting away the sleep as I tied my shoes in double knots.

Stretching out as I stood I took in Josh one last time in the cover of darkness, admiring the way his sleepy curls stuck to the sweaty nape of his neck and how grumpy he looked with his hands shoved into his sweater pocket.

He led the way from the Nest without a word, the cold spring air hit my face instantly startling me from my sluggish state. For a while the only sound between us was the pounding of our shoes on the pavement and the occasional songbird. It was too early for much else. As we rounded the base of the hill the sun had started to peek over the roof of the stadium and melt the thin layer of frost that covered the steel structure.

Josh pushed the pace, barely even fazed by the frigid air in his lungs as he swiped his card on the players entry and opened the door for me. We slowed down into the tunnels and when we came to the entrance of the field he stopped, staring out at the grass and inhaled.

"The only place I feel normal is on a baseball diamond," he confessed quietly.

There was a lot that came out of Josh's mouth that I didn't understand, even less that I could relate to. But the feeling of complete contentment that settled over me during a game was different. It was the only place I could control my actions and the outcomes of what was next.

There was no anxiety, no stress. It was just me and the ball.

And thousands of screaming fans.

The diamond was a safe place. A place where I could feel like a god despite everything going on outside in the world. But today it felt like a coffin.

The clock on the scoreboard blinked five am, people would be watching the news.

Watching the highlights.

Soon my face would be plastered across every TV in Harbor.

The panic that rose was violent and red across my vision. It felt like the sirens were blaring, and I couldn't focus on what was in front of me with all the noise.

"Come feel normal, Tuck." His voice was softer than I'd ever heard it, but still demanding and it made my skin itch to deny him. "Just for a little longer."

Josh had stepped out from under the tunnel onto the grass and was looking over his shoulder at me, frozen in place with my chest heavy. It was like he knew what had choked me up, and gone was the mean demeanor he usually carried, replaced with that guy huddled in the closet staring up at me with fear and disgust for himself in his eyes.

We were so different—and somehow, so alike.

"My family didn't know," I said, my throat felt so dry. "My mom had ideas, there were a few incidents last year, but for the most part she thought it was just my rebellious stage…"

"You, rebellious?" He scoffed.

When I didn't find amusement in his joke, he watched me with curious intent and turned around to face me completely, his back to the field and our hearts perfectly parallel.

"They didn't know what?" He asked.

"Don't be an asshole," I sighed.

Josh stared at me.

"Say it, Dean. They didn't know what?" he pressed. "That you were sucking Cael's dick in the locker room?"

"Fuck off, Josh." My voice cracked.

"That you have a laundry list of ass under your belt," he sneered.

"Enough," I growled.

"What do you think is going to happen when your mommy finds out that her little golden boy is a—"

"Shut up!" I cut him off.

"No, you think that the press will stop at one politely worded question?" Josh growled. "They're going to pick you apart like vultures, you'll be nothing but bones when they're done with you!"

"I can—"

"Avoid it? You're captain, Dean, there's no avoiding this anymore!" Josh reminded me and put his arms out at his side, a smug smile on his face. "Hudson was the tip of the iceberg, the homophobia that you saw yesterday is nothing compared to what runs deep in this league, and that's when they all thought you were *normal*." He said it like an insult. "You don't get to pretend you're straight anymore, you have to lead the way!"

"Why me?" I snapped. "Let someone else do it!"

"Coach Cody chose you for a reason," Josh said. "It wasn't just because you're a pretty face."

"I'm a good ball player." I shrugged, my emotions were frayed and sparking like live wires.

"You're gay, Tuck!" Josh yelled.

"Shut the fuck up before someone hears you!" I snapped.

"Own it!" He demanded. "Why is it theirs to control?" He asked.

"It's not," I argued, and he stepped forward, the shadows casting over his face as he re-entered the tunnel.

"Then why do they shame you for it? Why do you let them?" He asked.

"I don't." I shook my head, but I could feel his question slithering around under my skin.

"You do, you let them tell you how to feel. You aren't in control, Tuck."

"Don't fucking call me that," I said, the frustrating mounting. "You're mouthy for a guy in the same position."

"I'm bi-sexual, no one even believes my sexuality is real. I'm just an attention whore, a slut, a fuck bag," Josh's voice was sick with anger. "And I'm not the captain, they don't care about where I stick my dick."

"I don't want to have this conversation." I stepped back and tried to inhale but it was like all the air had been sucked from the stadium. "Not with you."

He ignored me with a smile on his face.

"If you control it, control the narrative, then you control the emotions. You want to pretend that you have a handle on everything, and for a while there, I questioned whether or not you were even human, but I see the cracks now."

"Stop it," I said to him, my jaw clenched to keep from crying and my hands balling into a fist. "You can't force me to tell them!"

"Maybe," he admitted, "but it's too late for confessions." Josh continued his slow, methodical steps. "They run the news at five am. Highlights start right after the weather. You left your phone at Dansby House, but it's probably ringing. How many missed calls from your dad before you fall apart?"

I hated how easily he dissected it all.

I needed him to stop, I couldn't catch my breath, and the dread seeped into my bones.

"Own it before they *take* it from you," Josh demanded. He moved forward some more, completely unaware of our closeness in his effort to make me see what he saw. "Come on, Tuck, who are you? After they pull you apart for the good of their own twisted morals, who the hell is Dean Tucker?"

"Son," I whispered.

"No," he stopped me. "Who are *you,* not who do you want to be for *them?*"

"Captain," I corrected myself with a short nod, and Josh watched me carefully, his dark eyes flickering between mine. "Friend," I added.

"What else?" He pushed.

The word was there. I knew what he wanted, but I wasn't sure that I could take control of that just yet. Even in the face of his certainty, I just...

"Come on, Tuck, don't be a coward." His voice was so low and demanding.

"Gay," I whispered it—my breath ragged, heart racing. "I'm gay."

"That's right," Josh's eyes flickered to my lips. "Don't move," he said quietly, and all I wanted to do was obey.

I stayed perfectly still as he lifted his chin and captured my bottom lip between his. The kiss was more gentle than before, slow and soft without the harsh intrusion of his tongue. His fingers relaxed, and for a second, they brushed against my chest as his teeth dragged over my bottom lip, and he pulled away.

"What was that for?" I asked him.

"It was necessary," he said simply before going back out onto the field and leaving me wanting more from him.

TUCKER

E verything had changed.

I wasn't sure if it was for better or worse, but Josh had shed a piece of his armor—and let me see the horrors he kept tucked so close to his chest. It pained me to know that he was keeping all those secrets to himself, and for so long.

I had shed the weight of shame, at least in the face of Josh.

I hadn't picked up my phone for anyone in my family since the news broke, and with Sunday quickly approaching, the knot in my chest grew tighter with every passing hour. But I did my best to focus on our team and the way Josh's lips felt against mine.

Noah Hudson got a ten game suspension, Josh got two. Reyes filled in for the next two pre-season games—we won, but they were hard-fought and the field felt unbalanced without Josh.

Which is odd because two months ago I would have died on my '*I hate Joshua Logan*' hill. But now he was sitting in the dining room with his nose in a book, the cut on his cheek finally less irritated and completely unaware that I was staring at him from across the kitchen.

"Shouldn't you be making dinner?" Cael whispered to me and I nearly jumped out of my skin.

"I thought you were at Clem's?" I looked over at him and he shrugged.

"Everyone has to come up for air sometime. I was getting homesick," he said, leaning his head back with a smile. The peach fuzz on his scalp was growing in, and I just knew it was because Clementine had flipped out about the impromptu haircut.

"Homesick?" I shook my head and pushed on his shoulder. "Or nosy?"

"I'm hurt," he feigned offense and turned to the fridge. "What are you making anyway?"

I ignored him and watched the way Josh balanced his pen on his fingers as he cross referenced something in his notes. He needed a laptop, it had been a long time since I saw anyone do notes with a pen and paper but I was scared to ask him.

Scared to offer mine.

"Something happened..." Cael slid up onto the counter, his thigh brushing against my shoulder, and he leaned down, blocking my view of Josh with a stupid smile.

"You're being annoying again," I grumbled.

"Annoying is my middle name, big boy."

"I thought it was '*I'm bored*,'" I shot back.

Cael laughed but looked over his shoulder at an oblivious Josh.

"He's doing better," Cael said quietly. "Thanks to you."

"I didn't do anything, he just likes to be left alone and if that's what works then whatever," I dismissed Cael's gratitude and praise.

"Yeah, 'cause he risked a suspension over you because he likes to be left alone..." Cael scoffed. "Big, dumb, and pretty," he sang under his breath, and I looked up at him. "You did that."

I shrugged.

"Josh craves violence; he would have gotten in a fight that game over anything," I said.

My skin shivered thinking about how rough he loved.

I shifted at the island, stretching out my arms across it and rolling out my back to hide my sexual frustration from my best friend.

Cael tsked and tugged on one of the curls near my ear.

"The last person I saw go full doberman was Arlo, on Nicholas the day he hurt Ella." Cael's voice was quiet and serious. "He didn't attack Hudson for fun, Deano..."

"Did he tell you why he left Lorette?" I asked Cael, who just shook his head at me.

I couldn't tell if I liked being the bearer of that secret or hated it.

"Can you two stop staring at me?" Josh set down his pen and turned his head to look at us in the kitchen. "You're five feet away, I can hear every word you're saying."

Cael snorted, but I turned six shades of red, dropping my forehead to the counter.

"How's the hand?" Cael asked as Josh wandered into the kitchen and crossed his arms slowly at the other end of the island.

"Fine," Josh huffed.

Blue eyes flickered between Josh and me, gauging our body language before he slipped from the counter and backed away.

"I thought you were hungry?" I said, my voice begging him to stay and fill the awkward silence that would no doubt fall over the kitchen the moment he left.

"Yeah..." he looked over at Josh and back at me with a suspicious look on his face. "I'm going to go crawl back to Clem, Josh has murder eyes and that's your problem now!"

Before I could argue, Cael was gone, slipping from the back door of the Nest out into the warming spring air. *Fuck.*

"Honestly, I'm surprised he doesn't get punched *more*," Josh said with a tight smile.

"Yeah, I think about that every day," I shook my head and tried to recover from how embarrassed I felt. "About the conversation..."

"You're the captain, he's your best friend, you're allowed to talk about the team with him..." Josh shrugged like it didn't bother him.

"The team, right." I nodded. My fingers twitched at my side, filled with the urge to close the gap. I needed something to do with my hands. I wasn't sure where we stood after the entire conversation and the fight, we hadn't... kissed again but we also hadn't really spoken.

Josh was either asleep or gone by the time I crawled out of bed most mornings and he was so focused on school that all his spare time outside the stadium was spent studying. But now he was standing in front of me, those dark brown eyes waiting for me to make a move but I couldn't because I wasn't sure what move to make.

"You know, I don't think I ever asked you what you were studying?" I asked him, just trying to break the tension.

"It's stupid," he dismissed it and I stared at him until he broke. "I want to be a social worker," he confessed. That was a surprise, I figured he would pick something that made him money... Money meant the ability to leave, to feel respected. Social work was exhausting, it was hard work and *it hit close to home.*

"That's cool, Josh," I said, surprised.

He eyed me trying to figure out if I was being serious or not before he nodded gently. "It's how I make a difference, maybe if I can learn how to prevent what happened to me, I can stop it from happening to other kids."

It was brave, selfless.

"You surprise me every day," I said. He swallowed tightly, the silence stretching over us again. I don't know why small talk felt so hard between us now. It was like the kiss had broken down a boundary, and now we didn't know what to do with ourselves.

"What are you making for dinner?" He asked, cutting through the silence.

I looked around the kitchen, realizing I'd have to run into town—we were completely out of real food. The cupboards were empty except for some fruit and junk food. I chewed on my tongue and tried to ignore the way I wanted to have a different conversation with him, one that wasn't about baseball or dinner.

I just needed a minute where someone wasn't expecting something from me.

"Sundaes," I declared and plastered a smile on my face. "Put a sweater on, it's still chilly outside." I pointed to his light t-shirt and grabbed my keys from the hook by the back door.

Josh stared at me for a second before grabbing his hoodie and following me out to the garage. I could feel his judgmental smile between my shoulder blades when I wandered around to the passenger side and opened his door for him. My fingers gripped the frame as he climbed in quietly, hauling the hoodie over his shoulders and messing up his chocolate curls. I wanted to put my fingers in them, to remind myself of how soft they can be even when Josh is so hardened and angry. The feelings were so contradictory and yet...

"What?" He snapped, but there was a hint of softness to the angry question.

I wanted to say nothing, to brush off the way I felt every time I looked at him lately, but I couldn't ignore the feelings that coursed through me.

"Promise not to punch me?" I asked him with a smile that clearly made him nervous because he cocked his head to the side and narrowed his eyes on me.

"Nope," he said. I should have expected that response.

"It's worth it anyways." I shrugged slightly. "You look cute when your hair is messy, those days when you forget a hat."

Josh's cheeks flushed with color, and he grumbled something under his breath before grabbing the door handle and shutting the door on my face.

"At least it wasn't a punch," I chuckled as I walked to the driver's side.

"Push this," I said, handing him the cart and walking ahead of him into the grocery store. Josh leaned over the bar of the shopping cart and lazily walked along behind me. Every so often, I'd turn around to see if he was still following me in his hoodie and jeans, mindlessly looking around at the shelves.

It was odd to see Josh in such a mundane light.

"What are we here for again?" He asked as we circled into the freezer section.

"Ice cream, sprinkles, toppings, syrup...lots of syrup." I opened the door and grabbed a pail of vanilla and a pail of chocolate before tossing them both into the cart.

"You really are an overgrown child, aren't you, Tuck?" He asked.

"Are you gonna look me in the eyes and tell me that you don't like ice cream?" I asked him and grabbed a pail of strawberry, just in case.

"I don't like ice cream." He shrugged.

"Liar, you're a tiny bundle of angry lies." I put my hands in the air.

"Get it off your chest." Josh laughed, and his smile was bright across his face.

"Are you laughing at me right now?" I said, leading the cart toward the candy aisle.

"You're not preparing for war, Tuck. You're shopping for candy to feed a championship college baseball team ice cream sundaes for dinner..." he followed closely, and the sound of him teasing was warm and familiar. I missed it. The mockery. He had been so tense and quiet for the last few days, hearing the ridicule back in his voice and seeing the smugness back on his face made me feel better about everything.

"Don't diminish the sundaes, tough guy. Just because you don't know how to have fun doesn't mean you can make everyone else miserable!" I called out and collected a few bags of candy into my arms. "Catch." I tossed them in the direction of the cart, and Josh zig-zagged to catch them all.

"I'm not making anyone miserable," he groaned as he walked closer.

"Me, I'm miserable."

Josh rolled his eyes. "Yah, you look real miserable, Tuck."

"You know I hate when you call me that, right?" I reminded him, and he just shrugged. "You're not going to stop, are you?"

"It makes your ears turn red," Josh said, and for a moment I thought he was teasing me, but then I turned to look at him again with a bag of marshmallows in my hands. There was a genuine smile on his face, and the urge to kiss him returned, even after trying so hard to push it down.

"Can't be worse than Franklin," I sighed.

"You have a point," Josh laughed and took the marshmallows from me. "The banana ones," he said, pointing at a hot pink bag that contained those synthetic chewy banana marshmallows. "What's with *Franklin* anyways?"

I chucked him the banana candy and sighed. "It's my grandpa's name. I think they meant me to be more Prince William and less Prince Harry."

Josh's face scrunched up. "What?"

"So everyone else is allowed to make obscure pop culture references but I'm not?" I groaned.

"Well, they make ones about Star Wars... you're talking about the royal family..." Josh laughed loudly. "Sorry, sorry." He put his hands in the air, mocking surrender when I glared at him. "Never took you as a Queen Elizabeth junkie," Josh teased.

I turned away from him so he couldn't see the enjoyment that flashed across my face at the randomness of the conversation. It felt unforced and normal. Nothing like anything we'd done before.

"So why do you know so much about them?" he teased.

"Knowing the difference between Diana's sons hardly makes me an expert." I avoided his intense stare, searching the shelves for more candy.

"Oh my god, it's not the Royal family, you're a fucking Downton Abbey dork!"

"Lower your voice." I chucked a bag of chocolate chips at him, and he caught it with a grunt.

"Admit it, Tuck!" He got louder. "You get riled up by those spoiled British brats!"

"They're the Royal family, Joshua!" I scoffed. *God, I loved that show.*

"Ha!" Josh burst out laughing, the sound echoing through the aisle as I stepped closer and braced my hands on either side of the cart to stare him down. "I've never watched. It's too much drama for me."

"Seriously?" I huffed, realizing that I gave myself away.

"Say it," he lowered his voice, and his lips pressed into a serious line. "*Please*, Tuck."

"I'm a Downton Abbey dork." I caved the second the word left his lips and hated how easily he pried it from me.

"I'm surprised you weren't disowned sooner." His smile returned, along with the light in his eyes. He paused and then opened his mouth again. "Have you talked to them?"

"Uh…" I let go of a nervous breath, "no."

"Why not?" He asked me as I dropped the syrups into the cart and led him to the fruit aisle.

"Saying it out loud didn't make me more ready to be shunned." I rolled my eyes and grabbed some bananas.

"It's their loss, Tuck." There was conviction in his voice that I wasn't expecting but it made the breath catch in my throat.

"I have dinner with them tomorrow," I said and grabbed a package of strawberries. "Fruit," I shook it at him.

"Sundaes can be healthy," he mocked me. "I forgot you guys have Sunday dinner rules," he said in an almost sad voice.

"Ella will be home, Arlo usually doesn't get far from her and I think he'd rather commit a serious crime then bring her over to his dads, so if you don't have plans they'll take pity on you," I explained.

Josh nodded but I could tell that the idea of family dinners on Sundays would eat at him. I couldn't imagine he would be rushing back into Lorette to have dinner with his mother any time soon. It made me feel a little bad to leave him sitting at the Nest but I also wasn't in the position to bring him to mine.

That would be like bringing spectators to my death.

"I think we have enough." I looked over the cart, ignoring the guilt that ate at me. "Let's get back before the ice cream melts."

TUCKER

That evening, after the mess from the ice cream was cleaned up and everyone had slunk off to their corners of the Nest, I climbed the stairs to our room. I curled into bed but sleep never found me, it was like the clock was mocking me, flashing hour after hour with echoing ticks to remind me that Sunday was here and I had no options left.

I was out of time.

The floorboards creaked.

"Against the wall," Josh said quietly, and I listened without argument, curling up against the far side so he could lie down. He left a gap between us, throwing his pillow down and rolling onto his side into the mess of blankets.

I didn't say a word as I hugged my pillow and pressed my cheek into it, watching him as he got comfortable in silence. He turned his head away from me, and for some reason, I didn't mind that he had. There was a tender comfort in how easily he had just found a place there, and even though he was still cagey about touch, he had sought out the closeness.

"Go to sleep, Tuck," he grumbled after a few minutes, like he could feel me staring.

I hated how quickly my body obeyed him, every little request I caved to without conscious thought. I closed my eyes and his cinnamon cologne filled my nose, lulling me to sleep for the first time in three days. When I woke he was still there, fast asleep with his sweaty curls pressed to his freckled skin and all I wanted to do was touch him.

But I knew it had to be on his terms. He had to ask. He had to want it.

If I touched him without permission, I was no better than Ian in his mind, no better than his mom. So I'd wait for him to ask, or to kiss me first because that's what he needed. I lay there for another hour until his breathing changed and his eyes fluttered open in the warm sunlight of Sunday morning.

"Are you staring at me?" He grumbled and closed his eyes again.

"No," I lied.

"What time is it?" He asked, and I couldn't help but smile at his grumpy, sleepy voice. The combination of him being in my bed and the husky tone he was using with me made my chest warm.

"Eleven," I said, glancing quickly at the clock.

He tensed and looked up at the clock from his position in the bed.

Even I was surprised, I hadn't slept in for years and never without worry the way I had last night. Sleeping in was reserved for hangovers and even then...the dependency was thick in the air and Josh slid from bed, throwing his pillow back to his bed.

"Don't make it a habit," he muttered, a small snarl at the edge of his voice before rifling through his duffle bag.

I wasn't about to argue that he was the one who crawled into my bed, because pushing my luck meant it probably wouldn't happen again, and I couldn't have that.

"Practice in an hour," I said, sitting up in bed.

"Yeah, I know the schedule, Tuck," he said, pulling out a clean shirt. He stared at it in his hands, no doubt contemplating whether or not he felt comfortable enough to change in front of me. "I'm going to shower," he lied and left the room without another word.

"Right." I clicked my teeth together and pushed off the bed.

I spent ten minutes stretching out my muscles on the floor before I pulled on clean shorts and a t-shirt. I had a quick meeting with Riona before practice and was already running late when I pushed into the stadium and took the stairs up to her office.

"Mr. Tucker," she said, handing me a cup of coffee as she settled behind her desk with a folder and a knowing look on her face. "You look more rested than the last time we spoke," she said.

I had stumbled into her office the day after we got home from spring camp, running on two hours of sleep and a protein shake sloshing around in my stomach.

"Yeah, I'm sleeping better, I guess." I sank down into the chair and lifted the coffee to my lips to find out that it was tea and scowled.

"Caffeine isn't good on an empty stomach," she raised her eyebrow at me and set down her mug.

"I ate today," I lied, and she saw right through it. "I woke up late, I'll eat after practice."

"Mmm," she looked down at her desk, reaching for something in a drawer and then back up at me as she tossed a container of fruit through the air. "Eat." She commanded, and I was going to argue that I couldn't eat her lunch, but she glared at me. "You're a smart man, Mr. Tucker, but you're valuing your worth over your well-being."

"I'm not great with riddles," I muttered, setting the tea down on the desk in front of me.

"You would rather run yourself into the ground to be worthy of captain and son than take care of yourself with things like eating and slowing down."

That hit home, and I swallowed tightly as she stared me down.

"Do you understand now?" She asked.

"Sort of." I fought with the urge to scream.

"You're a very busy man this season, there's a lot more riding on your shoulders than ever before, Mr. Tucker, but you cannot survive what's to come if you continue to neglect yourself," she warned. "I know that it's hard, and that you aren't doing it on purpose. That your appetite is minimal, but it's the stress, your body needs fuel, and your brain is tricking you."

"I'm eating," I lied.

"If you were eating, I wouldn't have been fielding phone calls from Shore. This meeting has to be quick because if I keep you from practice, Ryan will be in my office throwing a hissy fit, and I can't deal with him or his manchild attitude today, so I have a challenge for you," she said.

"Great. More responsibilities," I muttered.

"Think of it as one you already had—but *neglected*," she said. "I want you to start eating lunch," she said.

"That's not a challenge..."

She cocked her head sideways and waited for me to surrender.

"Don't interrupt me," she commanded.

"Fine, lunch." I shrugged and stood from the chair.

"I want you to start eating lunch with me," she said as I backed away, causing me to stop.

I knew what she was doing and I hated it.

"I'm so busy lately that I don't ever get to talk to any of you outside of this room, so I'd like you to keep me company." She tapped her fingers against her mug and smiled at me. "I take my lunch at eleven," she said with a smile.

"This is manipulative," I grumbled.

"Unfortunately, Mr. Tucker, I know you better than most of the players because of your activities with my nephew, and there's one thing I know about you... That's your love language," she said. "You take care of me, I'll take care of you. Simple as that."

I stared at her and her stern green eyes never faltered as I tried to come up with reasons why she was wrong. I picked at my fingernails nervously, just wanting this to be over.

"Has anyone ever told a Cody no in their lives?" I asked with a defeated sigh.

"Eleven." She reminded me instead of giving me an answer.

"Eleven..." I shook my head and left the room.

I walked the hallways down back to the locker room and changed into my cleats before jogging out to meet the guys on the field. Coach gave me a dirty look but I wasn't focused on him as I joined the team jogging around the diamond. I was too busy being overwhelmed that Silas was pushing me around and that Riona agreed. I was fine, I was eating...

Okay, maybe I had skipped breakfast this morning, but I had slept in.

"Tucker?" Coach called to me and I turned to look at him, pushing the eating issue aside to deal with another day. He nodded his head for me to come over, and I broke from the group, sauntering over to where he leaned against the padded banister of the dugout.

"Yeah, Coach?" I crossed my arms.

"How are you feeling?" He asked me.

Those same Cody green eyes, always judging, rolled over me. He was gauging my reaction, trying to figure out if I was going to lie to him or tell him the truth. But the truth would only have more people worried about me for reasons that didn't matter. The season mattered, the win. Why didn't they understand that? If I were Arlo, they wouldn't care; they would just trust me to handle it, but I'm being babied and manhandled by people who think they know better.

"I'm fine," I said.

"You're fine?" He chuckled, his head bobbing as he looked down between us. "Alright, kid, what is it gonna take to get you to talk to me?"

"I mean it, Coach. I'm alright," I tried to insist.

"I wish I believed that," he said, pushing up from his leaning position. "Dealing with problems off the field is the only way to keep your head straight, and if you can't do that, you block it out while you're here."

"Right," I said, just needing the ping pong effect to stop. I was being slammed around by both him and Riona emotionally and I was ready to explode. "I just need to get through dinner tonight and I'll get straight Coach, promise."

He studied me for a second longer, no doubt trying to figure out if I was still lying, but that was the truth. My life outside of baseball was practically over. My skin was itchy thinking about stepping into that house for dinner later because I knew what was coming.

"Alright, back on the field." Coach waved me off, but I could tell that he wasn't convinced.

I had played the argument over and over again in my head. When I couldn't sleep I thought about it, when I did sleep, I had nightmares about it. I couldn't figure out why I cared so much about what they thought, but no matter how hard I tried to shove back those feelings of disappointment that my family would rather ignore who I am, then have me in their lives, they seemed to embed themselves into the fibre of who I was.

They weighed me down, and every step back onto the diamond felt like quicksand.

Coach ran us harder than usual, but with the season opener right around the corner, he didn't have much of a choice. We needed to get our shit together. The burn in my lungs and the sting of my muscles felt good and combated all the dark thoughts swirling around in my mind. Focusing on the ball, the smell of the grass, the feel of the leather. It helped center me.

Each thrown ball, each perfected play was a breath taken without the aftertaste of failure and disgust. *I could do this.*

"There's a party at Hilly's tomorrow for Todd," Jensen said as we started off the field.

"I don't know if I'm in the mood for that man." I shook him off and kept walking toward the lockers.

"Since when?" Jensen questioned, his hair pushed back off his face in damp, sweaty bundles.

"Is this because of camp?" Todd huffed. "We were just hazing him, he's fine. It's not like he hasn't taken a few shots before!"

I whirled on him in the tunnel, my hand coming up to his chest as I shoved him against the wall.

"Hey, man!" He clawed at my arm, but I was twice his size.

"I don't care about what you were doing, we don't haze our own. You were being assholes," I snapped.

"We were just joking around, no need to flip out!" A crowd of players formed in the tunnel, watching us as Todd tried to get out of my hold.

"You broke his nose," I snapped. "You weren't joking around and I'm sick of you all fucking around behind my back." I dropped my hold and turned to the crowd that formed.

"I know what the hell you're all thinking," I said in a huff, opening my mouth to say something more but couldn't find the words to express my frustration. I pushed through them all into the locker room and grabbed my duffle bag from the bench.

I would shower at the Nest because I couldn't stand being around any of them. It felt like the entire world was nipping at my heels. Like all of a sudden, their opinion of me had changed simply because of one news article.

I threw my shit into the jeep and slammed the door.

"Fuck!" I screamed and rested my hands on the side of the vehicle. My chest was falling in rapid time, and it felt like my heart might claw its way out of me. It didn't even want to be around me at that moment. I tried to work myself up, to bring the rage to a head, but the problem was I wasn't Arlo, deep down I'd never be him. And that's what the guys wanted, tough guidance with a strong hand and wise advice.

Meanwhile, I couldn't even get mad properly, I didn't even want to be mad. I just wanted everything to stop feeling so overwhelming all the time. I felt like I was drowning on dry land.

"Just get angry, you pussy," I whispered to myself. I had every right to be. The world was crashing in around me, and within the next few hours, I'd basically be an emotional orphan. But still, even with the looming threat of my parents disowning me, the anger was absent and only guilt lingered.

"What the hell am I even feeling guilty for?" I rolled my eyes and tapped my fingers over the Jeep just trying to find a calm rhythm that would help me think, or at least slow down my thoughts enough to drive back to the Nest and panic in private.

"Alright Tucker, get your shit together. We can do this, face your parents, deal with the emotional torment and inevitable fall out, come home, do it all again in the morning when the press rides your ass for your sexual preferences..." I sighed. "Go to class, be ridiculed, go to games, avoid having tomatoes thrown at me..."

"Do they even throw tomatoes anymore?" Josh's voice broke through the very private outside thoughts I was having as he rounded the Jeep. "I'd think they'd get more violent."

"Announce yourself when you sneak up on people!" I scoffed.

"I did," he said dryly. "You were in the middle of your monologue." He shifted with his bag, and it was clear he hadn't showered either. I could smell the sweet sweat and sticky remnants of pine tar from practice that rolled off him as he got closer.

"I'll deal with Jensen's attitude tomorrow." I waved Josh off.

"Cool," he said with a tight smile, clearly he didn't give a shit what had happened in the hallway minutes before. "I need to shower before dinner."

Before I could argue what that meant he was moving around to the passenger side and slamming the door behind him.

TUCKER

Josh was waiting in the garage, damp dark hair curling against his forehead, wearing the same dress shirt he wore to games. I had been so worked up in the shower that my muscles were still cramping across my back, but seeing him standing there was like someone had found the pressure point and rubbed out all the knots.

He looked good, he always did, even in a cheap shirt and pants he had probably owned most of his life. It never mattered because he looked at me with all the confidence in the world, determined to prove himself past the assumptions.

I could learn lessons from Josh.

But not today, there was too much going on inside my mind to take notes on how he handled adversity. Today there was only crippling anxiety and incoming heartbreak.

"You look nice," I said, and he rolled his eyes.

I tossed on a plum sweater that Mom had given me a few Christmases ago that was too tight around my shoulders and a pair of slacks. It was impressive that Josh even thought about dressing up.

Or even offered to come.

Which I had assumed was what he was doing by standing there.

"You don't have to do this," I said, my voice barely a whisper. *Please don't back out now.*

"Get in the car, Tuck."

I watched him wander around to his side and climb in, the motion was becoming normal and I liked it. I liked Josh Logan in my Jeep, at my side, in my life.

Shit.

"It's a Jeep," I reminded him as he shut the door in my face, but the jab was enough to get my feet moving.

The entire front seat smelled like cinnamon, and it was distracting as I threw my arm over the seats and pulled out of the garage in one quick motion. Josh stayed silent the entire drive to my parents'. They lived on the other side of Harbor, and while it wasn't a long drive, the silence made it feel like it was.

I pulled up the driveway and swallowed tightly, staring up at the three-story brick townhouse. Unlike most of the guys on the team, I was Harbor born and raised. I had never known anywhere else, these walls had protected me and nurtured me growing up but now they were a cage.

"You *should* feel guilty," Josh said as the sounds of the engine died.

"What?" I turned to look at him, but he was staring up at the house.

"You want to be angry, but..." he paused, body rigid. It made me want to reach out and comfort him but that would only make it worse. "Anger doesn't get anyone anywhere," he said.

"You aren't making sense," I sighed, I would never understand why none of them couldn't just tell me straight what they meant. I hated riddles.

"Your guilt, that'll get something done. You can use it to fix problems, but anger doesn't solve anything. Guilt can. Even misplaced guilt."

Josh finally turned in his seat.

"*They* may hate you for this." He pointed at the house without looking at it. "But there are easily a hundred other kids that need someone like you."

I stared at him and tried desperately to understand where he was coming from.

"Feel guilty because you grew up with every opportunity to be something and you're sitting here scared and ready to throw it away because of the opinions of your out of touch parents," he said and ran a hand through his hair to fix all the little waves that fell out of place.

"I..." I opened my mouth and closed it again.

He was right, this shouldn't be that hard. I had everything I ever wanted, and if they couldn't see that, what did it matter?

"They're family, Josh. They're my blood. It matters," I argued half heartedly.

"You have a family, Tuck. It isn't about blood. Whoever is behind that door is an insult to the Brady Bunch," his voice was tight and quiet. "Even if you all participate in cult activities, at least they have your back."

I offered him a tiny laugh.

"If you think they'll pull their punches tonight just because you came with me, they won't," I warned him. My parents were the kind of rich that didn't believe in consequences for the stuff they said. Josh wouldn't be able to buffer their conversation, it was going to be rough.

"You saw my Mom's drug den," he whispered, and I know there was a joke in there somewhere, but he barely got it out without a snarl. "I think I can handle your nuclear family dinner."

"Alright," I said. I wanted to tell him that his mom was sick, she wasn't in control of herself, but somehow I knew the sentiment was futile. My parents were of sound mind and body, they were just cruel and unwavering in their hatred. I was still worried that he didn't quite understand, but I tried to get my breathing in control before I nodded, ready to go inside and face the wolves. He waited for my cue and only climbed from the Jeep when I was sure I wanted to go inside.

Looking back at him as his feet connected with the pavement I had a wave of gratitude wash over me. Months ago if someone had asked me about Josh, I'd have a handful of nasty things to say about him. I would have taken pleasure in shredding him apart, piece by piece. But now…

Josh looked up from fixing his belt, and our eyes met.

Those sable brown eyes were usually hard, angry.

But today, they held a softer concern that spoke volumes about the guy that Josh actually was beneath all the anger. Sure his jaw was tense and his hands were usually balled into fists, but he was kind, and intelligent. I just hoped he knew that he wasn't just his anger and trauma.

Lately, I felt like it was up to me to show him… but it would have to wait until after we got through dinner. I couldn't manage the two things at once, and as the front door swung open, my fight-or-flight response was triggered, and nothing else was as urgent.

"Franklin." My father stood in the doorway in a navy sweater, his glasses low on his nose and his lips pressed into a tight line. "We've been waiting."

"Practice ran late, sir," I said quickly. I apologized with my head down. I stepped to the door, and it was only then that he noticed Josh behind me.

"Walt Tucker," he held out his hand to Josh, and I bit down on my tongue as Josh stepped forward and extended his hand.

I looked down at his palm and tensed. The lengths he was going to, just to be here, didn't go unnoticed.

"Joshua Logan." He shook my father's hand without a fuss, but I could tell that his palm was itching from the unwelcome skin-to-skin contact.

"The new pitcher," my father noted.

"I apologize for the intrusion. I don't have any family in Harbor, and Dean is doing his captain duties by dragging me along for Sunday dinner," Josh said. His diplomatic tone made me uncomfortable, but it was impressive enough that my father smiled and let us into the house.

"We're happy to have you!" My father said, his voice more chipper than before. "We have more than enough food and are proud of Franklin's new status," he added, the words more clipped that time.

Josh didn't look over at me but I could feel how uncomfortable he was as we were led back past the large staircase to the living room. The townhouse was old, hundreds of years old and was laid out in tight hallways with too many rooms for afternoon tea and gentlemen hours. My fathers study was across the hall from the living room, and the kitchen was at the back of the house, connected to the massive dining room.

"Can I get you a drink?" My father asked Josh, and before I could tell him no, Josh politely declined. "Sober for the season, I get it. Baseball is hard on the body."

He wandered around me as I sat down on the couch, and his fingers dug into my shoulder in passing before he sat in his chair at the head of the living room. I could hear Mom moving around in the kitchen, surprised she hadn't come to check on us yet, but too scared to go see if she needed help. I closed my hands in my lap and tried to slow the tempo of my racing heart.

Josh sat on the couch next to me, leaving a gap between us like always, but his foot pressed against mine on the floor, and I inhaled slowly, grounding myself to him.

"How are you settling into Harbor?" My father asked and I couldn't tell if the mundane small talk was welcome or not, I almost wanted him to flip out and get it over with.

Whatever the hell he was doing felt like he was playing with his food.

"It was an adjustment, they do things a little differently than Lorette, but good. The team is ready for the season, and I'm excited to pitch," Josh answered. He was so unbothered and smooth with every answer. I was jealous of his ability to just *be himself*.

"They do, don't they?" My father said, his head slowly turning to look at me.

There it was.

The other shoe.

"Can we just have dinner?" I asked him as he lifted the glass of whiskey to his lips.

"We will, and you'll sit there and listen to every word your mother has to say and then you'll thank her for dinner just like you always do," he said, no doubt having more to add but there was a knock at the door.

It opened before he could get up, and Harvey piled in with his kids and wife. The noise volume in the house exploded as everyone barreled through the hallways to the kitchen, where my mom's voice echoed with laughter.

"Franklin." Harvey stopped in the hallway and shoved his hands in his pockets as his wife rounded the corner with a flip of her hair and a disgusted look on her plastic face.

"Harvey," I responded. "Lianna," I nodded to her, but she just looked me over and disappeared in her heels toward the kitchen. Most likely to gossip with my mother about me before we all sat at the dinner table, so she could berate me in front of everyone.

"Is Anna coming?" My brother ignored me and Josh to look at my father.

"No, she's stuck at work, it'll just be us."

"Stuck at work or couldn't stomach it?" Harvey sneered, and Josh tensed on the couch.

"I don't think we've met, I'm Josh." He stood off the couch and approached my brother, who stared him down before slowly taking the offered hand in a firm shake. "Harbor's new starting pitcher," he said, and smiled at my brother.

I could feel my father watching me instead of them, and I turned to look at him, only to be slapped with all the judgment in his cold, old stare. *Awesome.* Even though I knew it wouldn't protect me from my mother, my brother and father seemed to be swayed into silence by Josh's confident presence.

They talked around me for a little while longer before dinner was called, and we all made our way into the dining room. Josh introduced himself to Lianna and all the kids before turning to my mother.

For a split second, I watched the anger bubble to the surface behind those brown eyes, but he plastered on a sweet smile and shook her hand before taking his spot at the table beside me. I wasn't extended the same kindness from her; she ignored me most of dinner, chewing her food and asking Harvey weird questions.

Josh ate his food without hesitation, the roasted chicken and potatoes smelled delicious but my stomach was tight with anxiety and all I did was pick at it as everyone talked around me like I didn't exist. It was when she set her fork down and stared at me from the other end of the table that I knew I was about to hear it.

"Are you going to explain yourself or sit there and eat our food like nothing is wrong?" She asked.

Our food.

I was already being talked about like I wasn't a part of the family.

"What do you want me to explain?" I asked politely as I pushed around the barely eaten food on my plate. "You haven't asked me a question."

"Watch your attitude," my father interjected, and I chewed on the inside of my mouth.

"Yes, Sir." I nodded, turning to my mother. "I'm sorry," I said to her tightly and I felt Josh's mood shift beside me. "I'm feeling a little cornered about this entire thing."

"Cornered? When you received the mantle of captain, Franklin. We expected you to make us proud, but imagine how I felt when I opened the newspaper to see your name in bold letters heading an article about your homosexuality," my mother said.

"I'm sorry, Ma'am," I repeated, because I didn't know what else to say to her.

"You're sorry?" She sighed but didn't relent. "The words you're using, you're making yourself a victim, Franklin. Are you the victim here? Do you know how hard it was to walk into the club the next day when everyone was asking me questions about my gay son? How dare you do that to me, to this family. *We're* the victims. We gave you everything, supported every dream you had."

"I know, Ma'am, I'm sorry." I swallowed the copper tang of blood, my teeth tearing into the inside of my cheek just to keep from puking or screaming.

"Did you not receive enough love? Enough attention?" She questioned, her tone becoming harsh and tight. "Did I not love you enough? Is this punishment for something?"

"No, Ma'am."

I wanted to scream *yes*, that she had never shown me an ounce of love. Not in the way that I needed, only in the way she deemed fit for her perfect little son. But I wasn't who she raised, not in her eyes. I was now nothing but a disgusting sin, a stranger sitting at her dinner table, sharing her last name but not her sick, homophobic ideals.

Harvey was thriving in the tense atmosphere with a smile on his stupid face. His wife, Lianna also seemed to be enjoying the way my mother tore into me. The kids all ate unbothered, frankly it wasn't even a family dinner if Mom wasn't ranting about something. I had just never been the subject at hand.

"You'll hold a press conference," Harvey said in his office voice, and Mom looked pleased with him. "Tell them that it's rumors, that you're not...*gay*." The word rolled off his tongue like it stung him to say it, and I tensed. "I've spoken with Mom and found three suitable rehab centers, all specializing in your illness."

Conversion therapy.

My heart sank.

"You're sick, Franklin, and I'm sorry it took me so long to notice but we can help you get back on a proper path. An acceptable one," Mom said, reaching out to touch my hand.

It was still clenched tightly around my fork, I could feel the silver digging into my palm, and it was the only thing keeping me from lashing out. They wanted to send me away to a conversion facility because they thought I was mentally ill. *You're sick.*

"They're the best centers in the state, they have an eighty-eight percent success rate," Lianna chimed in like she knew what she was talking about.

My mind was spinning; in fact, the entire room was. I felt like I was going to be sick, and the feeling of my mother's touch against my hand was hot and sticky. I choked back a gag and did my best to inhale quietly as they talked about me like I wasn't even there.

"One is only a few hours away," Harvey explained.

A few hours?

"You see, Baby, we'll fix this together." My mother's voice scraped down my spine like razor blades.

LOGAN

He was struggling.

Suffocating.

I reached out under the table, swallowing my own panic and wrapped my fingers around his thigh, squeezing just enough to get him to breathe.

When I had climbed into the passenger seat I couldn't have imagined dinner going like this. Dean had a tendency to dramatize but his family was whole other level of fucked up. They passed information about conversion clinics back and forth while stuffing their mouths with food.

The kids laughed and Dean's father just kept drinking his whiskey in judgmental silence like nothing was happening. It was baffling that none of them realized how dehumanizing their conversation was and worse that they weren't even including Dean in it.

The first time he said Sir, instead of Dad was a shock. But to hear him call his Mother ma'am as she berated his life and choices. I rarely felt the need to be angry for others, my own life was full to

the brim with hate but today, in that moment of absolute disrespect; I made space for Dean.

I squeezed his thigh again and he inhaled a shaky breath as his mother continued to question him about things.

"I don't know if I can..." Dean stumbled over the words. "Maybe a press release?"

He was caving to their requests.

The man I was so sure was made of stone was crumbling like a sandcastle in the tide.

He was going to write a statement and say what? Lie to everyone, tell them he wasn't gay? Live his life still suffocating from the pressure of his family and buried beneath all the lies they want him to tell.

I watched as he stumbled through the degrading conversation and pulled my phone from my pocket.

911

Where are you?

I dropped the pin with our location and shoved the phone back in my pocket, turning my attention back on Dean who looked like he was going to be sick. They weren't anywhere near finished with him.

His brother had pulled out his phone and was going through his contacts of women to set Dean up with all while Dean sat there and took the abuse. Part of me was tempted to flip out, to get him out of there but the logical part of me could see that it wouldn't make anything better.

And Dean and I weren't close enough for me to play white knight.

It was awkward and frustrating.

Time seemed to crawl by as they listed off women, each name making Dean flinch in protest, but he continued to offer them a soft smile that made me sick.

"What about Kerri-Ann?" Lianna asked, and Harvey scowled. "She's pretty, brown hair," she described her to him but it wasn't getting them anywhere until she said, "smart but not smart enough to realize your brother is gay."

"Oh! Kerri! Yeah..." Harvey nodded but I still wasn't sure if he actually knew what his wife was talking about. "You just need to buckle down, show them they were wrong until we can get this fixed," he said to Dean.

"Franklin," his mother chimed in again, her voice sickly sweet like nails scraping along chalkboards. I knew the tone well, my mother used it often when she wanted something or was about to say the most fucked up thing she could think of in the moment.

Dean tensed in my grip, bracing for impact.

"We love you and we love who you are, but as a family we've worked too hard for our stations in life for something like this to come out. You're so sick and we can see you struggling, the cry for help was heard so just let us take care of you now?" She said and it felt like someone had poured ice water down my back.

I could only imagine how jarring that was for him.

"Yes, Ma'am."

The words were strangled, like he was choking on the air in his lungs, but he got them out, his eyes watering and his muscles so tight I could see the way they flexed in his neck.

She opened her mouth to say more but was interrupted by a knock on the door.

"Franklin, answer the door," his father said, and I watched Dean rise from the table.

"Yes, Sir," he said through a clenched jaw before leaving me at the table with the vultures.

"My apologies for the brash conversation, Josh," his mother cooed. "We don't see Franklin much these days, and some heavy topics were discussed, but I can trust you'll keep all this to yourself?"

I smiled at her but didn't answer.

It was tight, and laced with disgust so loud that her expression changed from uneducated confidence to panicked fear the longer she stared at me.

"I should check on Dean," I said, using the name he liked rather than Franklin on purpose to let her know exactly where my loyalty lay. I rose from the table slowly. "Dinner was delicious," I said, looking down the table at everyone else before meeting her gaze again. "The chicken was overdone."

I pushed my chair in and made my way through the house without another word, stopping only because Dean stood just outside the open front door. His entire body was curled against Silas, I had never seen a man that size break down so hard. Silas's hand was against Dean's neck, holding him still while he sobbed. The guy we had once assumed never broke, the unshakeable golden retriever, had been split in two and was hemorrhaging on the front step of his family's townhouse.

I hadn't thought Silas would actually show—my faith in him was still strangled by the past but without questions he had dropped whatever he was doing and had been here in record time. For the first time since meeting him, I was grateful. Gray eyes watched me as I walked from the house and closed the door behind me, giving the two privacy from everyone inside. The sound of the door clicking had Dean standing up straight and turning away from me to wipe his face with his hands.

Silas patted his back and waited until he was ready.

"I should go back in there," Dean's voice cracked, and Silas grabbed him by the arm.

"Absolutely not," he growled.

"They'll just take it as an act of hostility." He cleared his throat but Silas's grip held firm.

"From where I'm standing you and Josh did the least hostile thing you could have done," he said. "From here on out you leave the communication with them to me."

Dean scowled. "I can't ask you to do that," he said.

"You aren't asking, I'm telling you. It's an order." Silas adjusted his grip to pull Dean down off the step gently. "Whatever happened in there was bad enough for that asshole to text me. You do not go back in that house or I'll drag you out of here."

I snorted that time and both of them looked at me with dirty expressions. "What?" I shrugged. "The guy weighs, like, two-fifty—no way you're dragging him anywhere."

"It was..." Silas sighed but the joke had returned a light to Dean's blue eyes that I hadn't seen for nearly two hours.

"It's okay," Dean said with a tight nod. "I hear you, Doc, but it's not that simple," he said.

"*It is*, walk yourself to your car, get in and go back to the Nest. Now." Silas stared at him, and I could see Dean thinking about the options but Silas wasn't going to back down and I was glad for his pushy attitude for the first time ever.

"It's a Jeep," Dean groaned and rolled his eyes but I could see him relaxing a little bit with the way the conversation was going. "Thank you for coming," he said.

"Always." Silas tapped two fingers against his chest, then clapped Dean's shoulder to move him in the right direction. "Go," he said as the front door opened again. "Mr. Tucker, how's your Sunday?" I heard Silas turn on his business voice as Dean and I started toward his Jeep.

There was an inkling of guilt leaving Silas to deal with the fallout, but the main priority was getting Dean away from it.

"Keys," I said to him as we approached the curb.

"No." He shook his head and tried to walk around me but I stepped in front of him and held out my palm with one hand, yanking open the passenger door with the other.

"You aren't driving like this," I said. I didn't care that he had painted some fake smile on, I'd seen that look a hundred times—standing in my bathroom mirror, practicing it so no one would ask questions. Becoming Joshua Logan, pitcher with the cocky attitude and handsome smile all to protect Josh, the beaten down, angry little kid.

Dean watched me for another moment before digging the keys out and dropping them in my palm. He slipped into the seat in silence, and I closed the door on him. Silas heard the sound, briefly looking over his shoulder at me and nodded at me as Dean's father continued to speak in quiet, quick sentences.

I climbed in and closed the door behind me, starting the engine before he could argue, getting us out of there. It wasn't until we were moments from the house that Dean finally opened his mouth.

"Thank you," he said, the sound was too quiet and too broken. It slithered beneath my armor and inched its way toward my guarded heart.

"I'll help you with the press statement," I said, ignoring the way his little, cracked gratitude made me feel and turning into the driveway of Dansby House.

"Okay," he said and as soon as the engine died he was out of his seat and disappearing into the house. I tried to follow but it was clear he didn't want that so I grabbed my books from the dining room table and sat down to write.

TUCKER

*Y*ou're sick.
    You're sick.
You're sick.
You're sick.
You're sick.

A piece of paper landed on my chest. I opened my eyes to see Josh standing over me. I didn't want to deal with the statement right now, I didn't even want to think about it. I just wanted to rot in my bed and hopefully pass away peacefully into the darkness where all of the nasty things my mother said about me couldn't be heard.

I grumbled at my own dark humor and shifted in the bed, still in my dress clothes and shoes. I felt stuffy and stiff. Seeing Silas when I opened that door had been unexpected—I couldn't stop the reaction as I stepped through the frame. He just nodded at me like he understood what was happening and didn't need the explanation. He was just there. The tears started from a place of desperation and fear. It was embarrassing that I had broken down

like that. I'd have to explain myself to him later, and the stress of it piled precariously on my back.

I kicked off the shoes and curled my knee up with my arm extended over it to read what Josh had brought me. It started like any normal statement, apologizing for my outburst during last week's press table and went on to explain why I left so abruptly, but quickly changed tones.

I, however, will not apologize for my personal life. It comes as no surprise to my teammates or my friends that I am a gay man. I have been open with them from the very beginning, only protecting myself from the harsh judgment of the media. I am a gay man in sports. I know that this will create a multitude of headlines, some refreshing and kind, but most hateful and worrisome. But none of these words, these articles or gossip change who I am, or how good I am at baseball.

"I can't read this," I shook my head. "This is the opposite of what they want, and it makes me sound insane."

I set the paper down on the bed, not bothering to read the rest because it was making me nauseous. That statement would fan the fires, not put them out.

"What do *you* want?" Josh squatted on the floor, dropping his eyeline below mine and tilting his chin up to look at me.

"I want to curl up and die," I muttered, mostly dramatic. Josh just scowled.

"Tuck," he groaned, but it was soft and encouraging.

"I just want to be left alone like everyone else," I answered honestly that time.

"The only way you do that is by getting ahead of everyone, if you sit back and let your parents control the narrative…" he said, pausing with a sigh. "Then they will always have it."

"Why are you pushing this so hard?" I fought back. "It's not like you're running around with a Bi flag, screaming from the rooftops that you swing both ways! Why do I have to defend myself?"

"Because no one cares about my life," he said to me. "They care about yours because you're the captain of a national championship team and being gay in sports is a conversation no one is ready to have!"

"Why do I have to have it?" I surged forward, and he flinched. "I'm sorry." I put both my hands in the air, instantly feeling bad for scaring him and pushed back against the wall to put more space between us.

"You don't," Josh said, pinning his shoulders back and rising from the floor. "But there are kids out there living like you, under the weight of their families and maybe if just one man stands up there, proud of who he is…" he said. "Then maybe there will be hope for them in the future."

"I don't want to be a role model, Josh. I just want to get through college and this season," I said, completely defeated and now feeling more guilty than ever over a thousand unheard voices.

"Too bad," Josh responded. "If you don't then guys like Noah Hudson will always get away with their shit. It takes one person. If it were anyone else, I wouldn't trust them with something so important. But it's you, you're the golden boy, the kid with all the heart. Lead with it."

"Josh," I groaned. My chest was so tight, I could barely breathe.

Cael would have told me it was fine, he would have hid in my room with me for a week and just let me be but Josh was not Cael and he would not be denied.

"You're a captain, Tuck. You don't get the option to just get through stuff, you have to lead the rest of us out of it." He stepped backward. "Read it or don't, but don't go into that press conference with the mentality of making a bunch of homophobes comfortable."

His eyes were dark, but I could see the silent plea behind them. He had been one of those kids, searching for a light in the darkness. He had never found it, never had anyone. The guilt was enough to consume me whole.

"They don't deserve peace."

He left the room without arguing further, and I was alone again.

Only this time I couldn't get the disappointed look on his face out of my mind.

All I did lately was let people down.

I kept the press statement folded up in my binder as I climbed the stairs to my class the next day, sliding into the seat next to Van. It was the only class we had together. It was a basic course, one I could take in my sleep but today it felt like everything was in one ear, out the other.

It had taken me nearly an hour to get out of bed and I spent another forty-five in the shower. I didn't want to be on campus. I could hear them whispering about me but no one had the balls to actually ask me.

Van shared his notes with me that I missed from the class before so I spent most of the time typing them up into my own.

"You alright?" He asked, noticing the muted mood.

"Yeah, just stressed out." I shrugged, handing the papers back to him.

"You've been vibrating negative energy since Sunday, dude. I've never seen you so balled up." Van pushed. "Spill."

I dug the statement out of my jeans and handed it to him behind our laptops as the professor rattled on about the negative effects of something that I couldn't find the time to care about. Van was quiet for five minutes before he scoffed and handed it back to me.

"You didn't write this," he looked at me, and I scowled. "I've proofread every essay you've handed in for the last three years, *you* didn't write this."

Sinking lower in my chair, I pulled my hat down over my eyes and sighed. "Josh wrote it."

"Yeah, that explains the 'sexual preferences' line. Dude made it sound like you were in court, not the press room. It's too harsh, hold on…" Van said, and before I could stop him, he was scribbling out lines and rewriting them. It didn't matter what he did to it, I wasn't reading it. "Have we gotten him checked for robot parts?" He joked but I was too busy being wound up to laugh.

I couldn't even figure out why the fuck I was carrying it around, other than the fact that I was trying to find my courage. Even if I didn't announce myself to a room full of blood-hungry reporters, I would have to stand up for myself eventually.

"There." Van handed it back to me, and as soon as I started, I knew that whatever magic he had worked actually made it a viable option. "Less Josh, more Dean."

"Thanks," I said with a small nod before I folded it up and stuffed it into my pocket again. It would rot there until I found my voice. Who knows when that would be.

When class was done I went down through the cafeteria to some of the study halls and found a spot to sit quietly. Going back to the Nest meant facing Josh or Cael and going down to the stadium meant facing Coach and Silas.

Nowhere felt safe.

"Franklin," my Father's voice inched across the divide and felt like a thousand small cuts.

Great.

I pushed from my chair, turning to face him and tried to hide the disappointment in my voice as I acknowledged him.

"Good to know you haven't abandoned everything," he jabbed with his grip tightening around his briefcase. "Your mother expects you at dinner on Sunday."

I scoffed before I could stop myself.

His brow rose, and he stared me down when I didn't elaborate on the outburst.

"What happened yesterday may have been uncomfortable for you son but you needed to hear it, there comes a day when you need to answer for yourself." He shifted uncomfortably looking around to see if any of the other students studying were listening.

"Answer for myself?" I said, trying my best to sound anything but combative.

"Your explicit and sinful actions have consequences, Franklin. It was time that you learned that, and having your friends step in for you when you were being a spineless coward didn't help your case," he said tightly. "You'll come to dinner Sunday, there's more to discuss."

Without another word, he walked around me and out of study hall.

My chest burned. My thoughts turned to slush. I stood staring out the glass doors to the hallway where he disappeared and let myself go numb again.

They didn't give a shit about me, they never had. It had always been about what I could do for them, and never about familial love. I was a trophy to them, stuffed away in a display case to be fawned over during important holidays. Nothing more.

I didn't want to stand on the pedestal they had built for me anymore.

They don't deserve peace.

LOGAN

The early bi-week helped us regroup, but the tension in the locker room since the last game was palpable. Dean hadn't said a word to the press, Coach had been running interference. The problem was the longer he waited to do it, the more *suspicious* it all looked. The reporters all had their own narratives now, and there wasn't a damn thing Dean could do about it.

Cael sat beside me in silence, tying his shoes—a quiet confirmation of my point. Everyone was walking on glass—and it wasn't because Dean was gay; no one gave a shit about that, it was the fact that none of them could do interviews without the reporters pressing them about their captain and no one wanted to be the one that said the wrong thing.

Coach cleared his throat as he stepped into the center of the locker room, every eye turning toward him as they finished getting ready for the game.

"Today is going to suck," he said, and Cael snorted from beside me with the shake of his head.

"He's horrible at the whole speech thing," Cael whispered under his breath, causing my lip to curl up in amusement.

"It's the last week of pre-season and your last opportunity to show everyone out there exactly who you mean to be this season. I want you to be composed, focused and driven. We win this game as clean as possible, boys; no fights, no suspensions. I don't want to spend the three hours after the game on the phone negotiating terms," he warned.

"Yes, Coach," the locker room responded in unison.

"They're going to fuck with Tucker," Coach said. Dean, noticeably absent from locker room prep, would've hated being talked about like that. "And when they do, you do not react. If anyone has an issue with your captain, come to me and I'll deal with it outside the game. Breaking your hands on their faces isn't going to stop them from being assholes. Do you understand me?"

Again, understanding was barked out from each Hornets player.

"Win the game to prove everyone wrong, don't give them any more reasons to alienate him," he said as the doors swung open and Dean stumbled in. His tie was already loosened, and his fingers were working at the buttons on his dark dress shirt.

"Where the hell have you been?" Coach asked him.

"Meeting with Ms. Cody," Dean grumbled and threw his duffle into a locker.

"I'll talk to her about scheduling them this close to game time."

"It wasn't her, I scheduled it. I'm ready though, I'm sorry." The words came out tight and strung together in a mumbled mess as he kicked off his shoes.

Coach wrapped up his speech, leaving behind a blend of confidence and just enough fear. The team didn't move though, they waited for Dean to dress in his jersey in silence. Hoping maybe he'd find the courage to say something.

He could feel their eyes on him and he sighed, turning on his heel to look over them as he did up the last of the buttons.

"What?" he asked, but it clicked almost immediately after, and he sighed, knowing what they wanted. "Right..." he pulled his hat down over his eyes and put his hands on his hips. When he looked up from the ground, there was a fake, full sparkle to his eyes, and he had forced a smile on his face. "I know this season is off to a rocky start, but we'll find our groove and prove to everyone how good Hornets' ball is. Go out there and play tight, communicate and kick ass."

That seemed to satisfy them—they hollered, thumped their chests with those dumb handshake taps, and flooded out of the locker room. I waited, tying the last knot on my cleat and grabbed my hat.

"Nice fake smile, Tuck," I muttered as I passed him.

"What, this? All real," he chuckled, but it was tight and wrong. I knew when it was real.

"If you're going to be depressed, you need to hide it better," I warned him as he walked around me to get to the tunnel.

"I'm not depressed," he deflected.

"Sure," I said. "You go to class, you go to practice, you go to bed. Not depressed, gotcha." I scoffed at him. It was a mirror of the schedule I used at spring camp, just less dinner with the Manson family.

"Is my healthy routine bothering you?" Dean rolled his eyes.

"If you were anyone else, that might be healthy." We rounded the corner to the players' entrance, where the entire team was getting ready to take the field. "But you?" I scowled. "There's nothing healthy about what you're doing."

"Yeah, because you know me so well, tough guy. Focus on the game, Logan—stop worrying about me." Dean pushed past me and smiled as he patted a few of the guys on the back, starting a loud, rhythmic chant that had them jumping and swaying.

I ground my teeth together. He hadn't called me Logan in a while, and I don't know why it bothered me as much as it did, but I could do what I was told.

Right now, the priority was the game.

The lights on the field were unforgiving as we stepped out and waved to the fans as we made our way down to the dugout. Coach called out the batting order, and it was the same as usual. Dean lost the coin toss, and we started the game. The first few innings weren't bad; we were down three runs, but it would be easy to catch up in the back half. Some hard hits and a few tight outfield moments had us back in the lead at the bottom of the seventh.

Dean never missed a swing, it was like every ounce of worry and frustration he had been feeling was channeled into the game. His feet planted hard in the clay as he rounded third and cemented the win for the Hornets, *for us.*

Coach ushered everyone down the tunnel, ignoring the protests of the press as he closed the heavy navy doors to the locker room behind us.

"They're fucking insufferable," Van sighed and tugged his jersey over his head, tossing it into the locker and undoing the belt on his pants. "You'd think they'd give up on it."

"You know they're relentless, the second they smell fresh meat, they're out for blood," Cael said, stripping the majority of his clothes in one swoop of his long arms.

"I'm exhausted." Dean slumped against his locker beside me and closed his eyes.

"Fuck Delta tonight," Van said, sweat dripping from his chocolate brown mullet as he collapsed to the ground in nothing but his boxers.

I untied my shoes and shoved them into my locker between my feet before unbuttoning my jersey. I had been smart about wearing a t-shirt under my jersey, and so far, the only person who had given me stink eyes about it was Cael. I could tell he wanted to ask again, but he didn't want to be pushy. Which was an odd revelation for Cael to have, since he had lived his entire life to push buttons.

"I'm calling in an orange duck," Dean grumbled.

"A what?" I asked, looking around at them as they all agreed.

"Chinese food and TV," Cael explained. "We call it an orange duck because one year Arlo-"

"I don't need to hear the story that's behind your latest toddler code word," I scowled at him and tugged my sweater over my head. "But I'm in," I grumbled.

"Logan's in," Cael smiled and slapped Van in the shoulder like it was a big deal.

"I'm just hungry," I added, and Cael gave me a *'sure, that's what it is'* look in the form of a wide smile and his eyebrow raising.

"Shower and then meet back at the Nest." Van clapped his hands into Cael's who hauled him off the ground and followed him into the showers, arguing over who would call to order the takeout.

Dean didn't move from his sleepy position on the locker bench, his eyes still closed. I sat with him, quickly changing out of my ball pants while the others were distracted.

"You alright?" I asked him.

"Fine," he said. And that's all I got out of him.

We drove back up to Dansby house because my car was still ripped apart in the garage. Arlo had invited me in to help fix it more than once, but I knew less about cars than I did about loving someone. And being locked in a garage with Arlo King still felt like a death sentence, so I avoided him to keep the peace.

Dean looked wrecked behind the wheel. His hair hung limp under his Hornets cap, and the usual bright blue in his eyes had dulled. His hands gripped the wheel with white knuckles, and it was obvious that pretending to be okay was eating away at him.

I didn't say anything as we all flooded into the house, running upstairs for a shower as the rest of them all found comfort in the living room on the main floor. I could hear them laughing and talking through the floor while I ran the shower hot and stepped under the water. For a moment the silence was perfect, there wasn't a sound except the running water and my slowing breaths but it was interrupted by a small knock on the door.

Before I could say anything, the door was pushed open.

"Hey—"

"It's just me," Dean's voice interrupted me.

"What do you want?" I asked, muscles locked with tension.

"I—" He stumbled over his words, and I could feel him standing there awkwardly, waiting for the invitation, but I couldn't seem to get them out. "This was stupid, I'm being s—"

"Get in," I snapped, before he could call himself stupid. Hearing the need in his voice was enough to break away another piece of the concrete that surrounded my heart. His clothes fell away in shuffled motions and the curtain pulled back just enough for his giant frame to slip into the shower.

His eyes caught mine, and uncomfortable heat filled my chest.

"Face the wall," I ordered him. I reached up and angled the shower head so that it ran over my shoulder against his skin.

He nodded and turned around in the shower, offering the toned muscles of his back to me, and I eased out of my discomfort a little further. I wasn't sure what he was trying to do by coming in here or why I even let him get in, but beneath all the anxiety that seemed to be itching its way to the surface was a want for him to stay.

I think that he had also sought out the quiet and that, maybe, I was that for him the way the shower was for me. Just like the night I had joined him in his bed; if he was able to focus on the one problem in front of him, all of his problems didn't feel so scary.

"Tuck," I said over the sound of the running water. "Are you okay?" I asked him, trying to curb the annoyance in my voice as I braced for him to lie to me again.

"I don't have the time to be anything else, Josh."

His answer didn't make me feel better, but there wasn't much else I could do. If he wanted to be sad and cover it with fake niceties, then I couldn't push for more, not without breaking out the paper-thin trust we had built with one another.

I washed the dirt and sweat off my body, handing him the soap so he could do the same. The motions are slow and methodical, neither of us coming in contact but sharing the silence for what it was. It was mesmerizing how gentle he was for his size; his arms and back tensed periodically, but for the most part, he took the form of a rolling wave. His tan skin pulled tight as he rolled the soap over his body, his shoulder blades flexing with his back muscles as he angled side to side for the water to reach every spot.

I kept my eyes trained on his back as I washed my hair. I thought about giving him the bottle and slipping from the shower so he could finish, but the want to touch him that nipped at the back of my mind was loud today.

"Put your head back," I ordered him and there was a brief pause, but he stepped back once and tilted his head back toward me.

The gap between us was minimal, and I could feel the heat rising off him as I filled my palm with shampoo and inched closer. Never touching skin to skin, but leaving inches between our naked bodies.

I paused, counting myself backward from ten with the simple reminders that I was in control and that I wanted to feel him, to do this for him. I chewed the inside of my lip as I reached one and ghosted my hand over the first set of curls that fell limp at his neck, saturated with water. His shoulders softened the moment I found my courage and sank my fingers into his hair.

Applying pressure, I massaged my fingers through the hair and watched carefully as he struggled to keep his balance as he relaxed further. His eyes were closed, but his hand was pressed flat against the shower wall to keep him upright as I worked the shampoo in his scalp slowly and carefully. I realized at that moment, Dean had never been taken care of. Our loneliness had stemmed from different trauma, manifested differently as we grew older, but festered with the most toxic need for independence.

I angled to the side to let the water rinse through his hair, helping the more stubborn curls with the pads of my fingers until all the soap was gone.

"Done," I said and felt him straighten out and pull away from my touch.

I held my breath as the strange feeling of disappointment filled me. I hadn't wanted him to pull away—and I'd never felt so hollow not touching him.. I swallowed the unusual emotion and slipped from the shower before he could do something stupid during our moment of vulnerability.

TUCKER

Josh had left the shower so quickly I didn't even get the chance to thank him—to tell him how fast his touch had silenced all the noise. I was fucked, royally and down bad fucked up over Joshua Logan.

And I couldn't do a damn thing about it. I stayed in the shower until the water ran cold and bit into my skin. Panicking over how quickly I had eased back into a situation that looked so much like my previous one. Hidden rendezvous, sneaking around, never telling anyone who or what we were.

"Fuck," I grumbled and got out. I got dressed quickly, the smell of Chinese food and the sound of laughter beckoning me to the living room where all the guys were piled on the furniture and spread across the floor.

"Here." Cael handed me a box of fried noodles and vegetables. I took it and settled on the floor at his feet, setting it beside me and looking up at what they were watching.

"You guys are watching Transformers without Arlo?" I asked, and in unison, three of the guys, including Cael, mocked his voice.

"*Why would they take the fight to the city when they were already in the desert? This movie is stupid!*"

If there was one thing we could all count on, it was Arlo's love-hate relationship with these movies. I'm surprised he wasn't grumbling in the corner about the cleanup expenses in Las Vegas.

"He took Peachy out for dinner." Cael leaned back on the couch and sank against the cushion between him and Van. "Figured we could watch the movie in peace," he said after a long yawn.

We were halfway through the movie when I noticed Josh... standing in the doorway in a long sleeve and sweats watching the tv quietly. I know better than to tell him to come sit but the fact that he's even trying to partake in the evening is something more than he did yesterday.

I could still feel his fingers in my hair, and it was the only thing keeping me from going insane. Coach had taken care of the press, but I still felt guilty for not doing my job. I was supposed to be able to put my personal issues aside, be able to lead the team without problems, but lately it just felt like all I did was mess it up more.

I knew that the guys didn't care, they just wanted to play ball and they would continue to show up to do that no matter what happened next. But I felt bad because they were all being quarantined because of me. The vicious rumors and questions weren't just slung in my direction, each and everyone of them had been subject to the wickedness of the press this week. And it was my fault.

Cael passed out with a string of tiny snores, and Van was drooling in his hair before the movie even ended... so I pushed off the floor, handed the box of food to Jensen and made my way to my room. I just needed some sleep and time to figure out what I was going to do. I couldn't keep letting everyone push me around, but I didn't want to disappoint anyone either.

One statement would prove my family right, and I'd never see a day of peace in my life knowing that I'd been disowned. I had spent every single day of my childhood in that house and had never missed a Sunday dinner until now. It was eating at me.

The other statement would allow me to keep my family but I wasn't sure I even wanted to keep them half the time if it meant losing my dignity. Which is exactly what lying would do, I'd be able to return home for dinner, see my mom and dad. But looking them in the eye would make me sick and how was I supposed to lead the team if I couldn't even stand up for myself and my morals.

I closed the door behind me, tugging off the clean shirt and throwing it to the side before I crawled into bed and pressed my face into the pillow. I wanted to scream, to just let it all out, and in that moment, completely alone, I did. The pillow ate most of the sound, and it felt good to let it all out in one explosive go.

"That was dramatic," Josh said, closing the door behind him. "You forgot to eat," he said, handing me a bowl of fried rice and shrimp. Food I had no intention of eating.

"Not hungry." I took it but set it on the side table next to my bed.

"You played seven innings as a one-man team and haven't touched anything that will actually replenish that spent energy. What's the point of those meetings with Ms. Cody if you aren't going to listen to her?" Josh picked the bowl back up and handed it to me again.

Relentless asshole.

"Why are you being so nice to me?" I asked, sitting up on the bed, curling my knees up and took the bowl from him as I scooted back against the wall.

"If you think this is nice, we have some work to do," he said, and I heard myself in his voice. That day at camp. I was being such an idiot.

"I can't eat that, even the thought of it is making my stomach turn," I admitted. Josh nodded, grabbing the bowl without a word and disappeared. *Fuck.*

I hadn't meant to upset him, I just...

I curled my legs up and let my head fall against the wall behind me. I was fucking everything up, and now Logan was even fed up with my shit. I heard a small creak in the floorboards, and his voice made me open my eyes.

"What about now?" He asked, and when I looked down at what he had in his hand, a small smile formed on my lips.

"Ice cream?" I said, taking the bowl from him. It was exactly how I had made it the other night, right down to the syrup.

"Eat." That was all I got in return as he lowered to the floor beside the bed. I held the bowl in my hand, staring at the sprinkles like they'd somehow have the answers to all life's questions, but I was only met with silence.

"The first time I had ice cream was last week," Josh said, and I looked over at him.

"What?" The confusion was raw because Josh chuckled and looked back at me.

"Yeah." He shrugged. "I was scared you were going to ask for my favorite flavor that day."

There was something so innocent in the confession, the way his eyes drifted to the floor and his shoulders relaxed forward.

"Because I don't have one, I guess vanilla if I had to pick, but only because it's a flavor, not because I actually know if it's my favorite." He played with the fabric of my comforter. "But I definitely don't like chocolate syrup," he said, and I huffed a little laugh out, one that after two weeks finally felt genuine.

"That's because you hate fun," I said with a small smile.

"We just couldn't afford stuff like that, ice cream is a luxury," he said and I understood where he was coming from but it didn't make me less sad for him.

"Want to share?" I asked, mostly because I couldn't fathom eating this much alone. "I'll eat off all the syrup," I added.

Josh looked back at me, pushing off the floor and climbing into the bed. Keeping his distance, he curled one of his legs up and held out his hand for the bowl. "Bite for bite, you aren't getting out of eating it," he warned.

"Deal," I said, watching him press the spoon between his lips. "Can I ask you something?" I took the bowl back and he waited to answer me until I took a bite of the ice cream.

Satisfied with my spoonful, he nodded.

"Why did you..." I stopped. I hated how easily I lost my nerve around him. "Why were you so nice to me today?" I asked, my voice quieter than usual.

"For the same reason you came to find me," he answered. "I needed it."

Needed it.

It felt like such a heavy statement from Josh.

But he wasn't wrong, I had needed it. Needed *him.*

I came home and all the noise had just been too much, but it was like my subconscious knew where he'd be and the next thing I knew I was standing in the steamed up bathroom asking to get into the shower like some lost puppy.

Josh took another bite of ice cream, never breaking eye contact with me.

"What are we doing?" I asked him, and took the bowl back.

"Eating ice cream," he said, like it was the only correct answer.

"No, I mean…like us." I took another nervous bite.

"You have enough going on in your life to figure out without trying to dissect whatever the hell this is, Tuck. Why don't you just eat your ice cream and shut up," Josh suggested.

"So you sleeping in my bed, us showering together…" I listed the suspicious activity off for him. "It's nothing?"

"It's necessary." He shook his head, then shoved the bowl back into my hands. "Finish," he said.

Necessary. He had said that before, and it confused me then, just as much as it did now. It was as if those miniscule mundane tasks were the only thing holding us together. And maybe they were, but it felt like it was snowballing into something that neither of us were ready for, and I was scared that if it got too big, it would scare him. Just like it had scared Cael.

I set the empty bowl down between us and shifted back on the bed against the wall laying down and covering myself with the blankets. Josh put the bowl on the table, kicked off his shoes and grabbed his pillow. Settling on the bed next to me, leaving a little less space between us than the times before.

Unnecessary, I thought. Everything he was doing felt unnecessary. He just needed an excuse for his kindness. A small, genuine smile formed on my face, staring at the back of his head. His dark wavy curls were within reach, and his cinnamon cologne filled my nose. I could let him think it was necessary, if that's what he needed. As long as it meant he kept sleeping in my bed.

LOGAN

I'd shifted in my sleep and ended up pressed against Dean, his head tucked between my shoulder blades, completely unaware. I inhaled a shaky breath and held the monstrous feelings at bay, slipping out of his hold without waking him up.

I made it to the bathroom without breaking down, but the second the door clicked shut, I was hunched over the toilet, emptying my stomach in violent heaves. I tried to count myself down, but couldn't get past seven before more nausea hit.

I collapsed against the wall ten minutes later, just wading through a waking nightmare. I wanted to be close to Dean so badly that even in sleep, I reached for him—but someone's touch still sent rage spiraling through me. It was hard to imagine ever being okay to the point that I could be normal with him.

What are we?

I wanted to say nothing because I couldn't even bring myself to lie next to him without having the nasty thoughts creep in. But I was trying, and until I could trust my own mind, trying was all I could offer him. I also wanted to say something, because the lines that had once been drawn were fading, and with every day close to Dean Tucker, I found myself closing the gap between us. I wanted to be *something*, but how did I do that without breaking both of us more than we already were? I couldn't promise him that we, *together*, would fix anything. I had slept with people before, drunk and unbothered, but never...

I'd never crossed the line into intimacy while sober.

I wasn't even sure I could bring myself to do it. But there had never been an urge to do it until Dean. I wanted to feel him, to be surrounded by him. Engulfed in him. And that fact alone made me sick to my stomach.

The door to the bathroom opened, and I reached out to push it closed again, but Dean slipped in, his eyes squinting from the light. "Your phone was ringing."

Mom's name flashed across the screen, and I groaned, setting the phone on the floor. *Perfect.*

I buckled down, ignoring the nauseous feeling in the pit of my stomach and pushed off the floor to answer it. Dean stepped back, leaning against the counter to give me space. His blond curls were stuck to his forehead and he barely looked awake as I hit answer.

"Hey," I said.

"*Where are you?*" Mom asked. "*You're not in your room!*"

"Yeah, Mom, I don't live there anymore, remember?" I said with a low groan. "Why were you looking for me?"

"*You weren't in your room, Joshua. I told you to stay in your room.*" She repeated herself, and I could hear her banging around on the other end.

"Mom, you called me, do you remember why?" I asked her. Dean watched my every move as I sank to the side of the tub and ran my hand through my hair.

In her drugged-up state, she flip-flopped between past and present. In her mind, I was still ten years old some days, unable to make the connection to her timeline when she was so worked up. When she didn't answer, I asked her again why she called, but that time she just hung up on me.

I tossed the phone on the bathroom floor and shut my eyes. I couldn't bring myself to look at Dean, not at that moment. The judgment in his sea-glass eyes would eat through my defenses like acid.

"Is she okay?" He asked after a beat of silence. He stared at me like he wanted to ask if I was okay, but he knew that the answer was moot.

"She's never okay," I chuckled, a hollow, breathy sound that came out of the depths of my defeat. "Do you think I could borrow your keys? I can't leave her like that."

"Let me get dressed," Dean said, with a shake of his head as he started out of the bathroom.

"Just give me your keys, Tuck." I followed after him, the vomit taste still lingering in my mouth as we made our way back to the room.

He was digging in his closet when I got inside and shut the door behind me. "Tucker!" I hollered, but he didn't listen. He only turned around as he tugged the hoodie down over his head.

"Get dressed," he said, like it wasn't an argument to begin with as he pushed his feet into a pair of sneakers.

"Just stop for a second," I demanded, and he stopped fidgeting with his shoe laces to look up at me. "I don't need to be babysat," I said to him.

"You can fill the gas tank." Dean offered me a soft smile and pissed me off. He was bargaining with me, trying to make it feel like this wasn't a favor but an exchange.

"I don't want to fill the tank, I want you to stop whatever the hell this is and just let me go deal with her quietly." I slammed the door behind me.

"I can be quiet." Dean stood off the bed, his size doubling mine. "You aren't doing this alone, so please stop arguing with me and let's go. We have practice this afternoon. We need to be back for it."

I sighed, there was no way I was going to win the argument. He was set on helping me with my mom and as much as I hated the idea of bringing anyone back into that apartment. He continued to stare at me, waiting patiently for me to make up my mind. I shook my head, grabbed my hoodie and admitted defeat.

"Good." He nodded and tossed a hat over his hair.

I knocked on the door, but she didn't answer right away, so I started to pull out my keys. Dean leaned on the wall beside the frame, staring down at the dingy glass panes at the other end of the narrow space. His jaw was tight, and it was clear that he hated being here.

I wanted to say I hated bringing him here—but that would imply we were something, and I was still clinging to the façade that we weren't.

Just as I went to shove the key in the lock, the door opened. My mom's hair was messy and pulled into a thin bun at the back of her head. She looked like she hadn't slept in weeks, dressed in a flimsy satin tank and ratty pajama pants that cut off above her skinny ankles.

"Where have you been?" She said, walking away from the door in a huff. She stumbled and knocked over a pile of magazines and cans that toppled to the floor.

I looked back at Dean as I wandered into the living room, but his eyes were on the door at the end of the hallway. I could barely bring myself to look at it without hearing the screams that echoed from inside. I swallowed down the anger and tried to focus on my mom, who was wound up and screaming.

"Calm down." I put my hands out to stop her and when she touched me I suppressed the hiss that bubbled from me. "Sit down," I instructed her and it took her a moment but eventually she listened and settled to the couch. "What is going on?"

Mom looked up from her lap with tears in her eyes, and it wasn't something new. She typically liked to weaponize her sadness to get her way. I was ashamed to say it worked more often than not. I took a deep breath upon seeing her face, and tried to focus on her instead of Dean. He was standing off to the side, minding his business, but his presence gave me a new confidence that I hadn't felt before. Almost like because I wasn't alone with her, she couldn't do anything nearly as bad as she used to. That didn't mean she wouldn't try—but now I had someone to fall back on if she did.

"I can't pay rent, and I got fired," she said in a repetition of mumbled words, over and over until I pieced it together enough to understand what she was saying.

"How did you get fired?" I asked her, the last I heard, she was working down on Fifteenth as a waitress. And I asked her, but I knew the answer before she even opened her mouth to explain. And, as expected, it was a string of excuses that didn't make sense, and the reality was she got high, probably missed her shift and got fired the next time she actually did show up.

Mom avoided answering and instead turned her sights on me again. "You can pay the rent until I can get it covered, can't you?" She asked.

"I don't know, Mom," I answered honestly. "Everything is a little tight right now, and paying rent wasn't really exactly in the plans for this month." I kept my voice low, just trying to avoid Dean hearing every single tidbit about my life as he found a space to stand that didn't disturb anything.

"What do you mean you can't?" She hissed. "You don't want to take care of your mom anymore? Do you hate me now?" Her voice started to get louder, and there was very little I could do to stop her as she wound herself up again. "I knew you going to that school would screw everything up. They're poisoning you. Soon you won't even visit anymore."

"Mom, it has nothing to do with that. I'm an adult. I went to school to get a better job so I could take care of you," I snapped. The reality was I was just telling her what she wanted to hear, not the actual truth. I wanted out of here, as far away from her as possible.

"You did this to hurt me." She shot up from her position, knocking me backwards and started to pace. "Is it because of them?" She whipped around and looked at me, her head was limp on her shoulders, and her body was trembling.

"Mom," I tried to get her to calm down before she said something I had to explain, but I was too slow. The thought process was already completed, and I had no control over the situation.

"It's your father, he's in your head, he got under your skin!" She stepped forward and reached out to scratch me, but I was faster and stepped back from her.

"That's enough, it has nothing to do with that. I don't have the money to give you," I attempted the explanation again but she wasn't hearing anything I said anymore.

"It has everything to do with them! The Shores ruin everything they touch, you were ruined the day you were born!" She hissed and tried to lunge at me again. "Why don't you just ask them for money? They're swimming in it!"

Fuck.

"Mom," I barked, louder than usual, and her whole body seized up at the demand. "Enough, there's no money to give."

"You aren't my son," she whispered. "You're what they want you to be. You've fallen so far, such a disappointment. I should have known you'd grow up to be just like *him*." She started rambling again, retreating into the back rooms and slamming the door behind her.

I kept my back to Dean, knowing the minute I turned around, he would question everything that had just been brought up. My skin was crawling from her touch as I ran my hands over my face and tried to sort through my thoughts. She had outed me in front of Dean, and now there was no way around telling him the actual secrets. All this time, he'd thought it was just a bad home life—he never pieced together that Silas and I were half brothers, that Shore blood ran in my veins.

"Josh," his voice was quiet but closer than I expected as I turned around to finally face him. I didn't know why it was so hard to meet his eyes. I had never been ashamed up to that point, only angry and resentful. But with Dean, I was scared, embarrassed, maybe? Of who I was, guilt racked me for keeping it from him.

I expected him to start yelling or bombarding me with questions but his hand reached out and before he could touch me, he stopped himself. "She got you," he murmured, and I looked down at the angry red scratches on my forearm. I hadn't even felt her nails in my skin, too worried over what was being said.

"It's fine." I stepped back from him and swallowed tightly. She had done worse before. "About what she said..."

Dean shook his head.

"Not here." He stepped aside to give me room to walk toward the door, guarding my back, even if that wasn't his intention. I looked over my shoulder, feeling guilty for leaving her like that, but there wasn't much more I could do for her right now. She was too worked up. She would just have to stay angry with me.

TUCKER

"Practice isn't for another two hours," Josh said as we pulled into the stadium.

My mind was still spinning from what his mother said. Josh was somehow mixed up with Silas and the Shores and I couldn't for the life of me figure out how or why. I shut off the engine and hopped out without answering him before wandering over to the players entrance and going inside. I needed to talk to him but I didn't know where to start. All I knew was that if I wanted him to be honest with me I needed to distract him from what was really going on.

I stopped by the medical offices to grab a first aid kit. Josh followed behind, still grumbling and muttering questions about what we were doing.

"Do you ever stop being cranky?" I laughed and pushed open the main doors that led out to the concourse. I waved to one of the security guards and started out on the field with the kit and on a mission. "Sit," I said to him and pointed to the dugout bench.

"I don't need first aid for a scratch, Tuck." He scowled and stayed standing.

"Humor me?" I asked, and it took him a minute, but eventually he caved.

I pulled some of the antibiotic wipes out that Silas always uses on our scrapes and handed them to him, but he'd already got his arm out to me. I looked down at it, and when my brows furrowed, he huffed.

"Fine, I'll do it myself." He tried to snatch the wipe, and I held firm to it.

"No it's just... I wasn't expecting you to let me," I said. He stared me down, the angry expression on his face never faltering as I worked up the courage to take his arm in my palm. When my fingers brushed against his skin I felt him bristle but he sat as still as possible as I cleaned the scratches.

"Are you okay?" I asked him when he closed his eyes and inhaled deeply, but he nodded and I tried to finish up as quickly as possible. "Done," I told him as I pulled away and headed toward the bats. I turned my back to him to give him a moment to regain his composure and grabbed the handle of my favorite bat.

"Here," I said, extending it to him.

"What the hell are you doing, Tuck?" He asked, but took the bat.

"Distracting you. Arlo does it with us sometimes," I explained and climbed from the dugout. "Makes it easier to talk about shit if you're concentrating on pitching balls."

"What do you think I need to be distracted from exactly?" He asked me but followed me out to the batter's box.

"The questions I'm about to ask you," I said, with unbridled honesty.

"I don't want to do this." Josh shook his head and turned on his heel, but I caught the bat he was holding and pulled him back.

"Doesn't matter, you either answer my questions or I'll go ask Silas," I said and Josh rolled his eyes. It was glaringly obvious that Josh did not want Silas's side of the story told. "Give me the bat," I said and handed him a crate of baseballs.

He huffed, trading me and wandering out to the pitcher's mound with a scowl on his face and an attitude in his step. "This is stupid," he said, but rolled the ball in his hand.

"What did your mom mean?" I asked him and he looked up at me with a frown. "She said a lot about the Shores, what did she mean?"

"Maybe you should mind your business," he said, his arm pulled back, and he let go of the ball in a smooth motion that looked like a rolling wave. I wasn't ready for it, but I made contact regardless, and the ball cracked against the wooden bat, soaring through the infield and landing deep in the left grass.

"You are my business, tough guy," I said softly, smiling at him as I readied for the next pitch.

Josh scowled at me, his dark brown eyes narrowing at my jab, and he threw a second ball. That one flew right out of the box and almost hit me in the shoulder before it bounced off the back cage and into the dirt.

"What did your mom mean?" I asked again, my mind twisted in knots of possibilities, each one worse than the last. "Do you owe the Shores money?" I asked him.

"No," he laughed, like it was a ridiculous stream of thoughts.

"Then what?" I got frustrated and snapped at him. I fought against the urge to push him, the deep down need to know that it wasn't bad but that wasn't me, and that wasn't us.

"Silas is my brother," Josh said and suddenly everything that I had been thinking of wasn't so bad. "Half brother," he corrected himself.

"What?" I asked, stunned by the confession, dropping my bat from my shoulder.

"When a man gaslights a woman..." Josh started in a grumpy tone.

"So your dad is Charles Shore?" I asked, cutting him off from his angry explanation of the birds and the bees.

"My biological father is Charles. I never had a dad," he corrected and threw the ball hard that time. It whizzed by my head and I ducked to the side before it hit my face, a stinging sensation telling me it didn't miss clipping me in the ear.

"Hey!" I said, pointing my bat at him.

"This was your idea," he snapped, hurling another ball. Each one was harder than the last, and he wasn't giving me much time to prepare for them.

"You seriously have anger issues," I muttered, shifting the bat in my grip.

"Get better insults, Tuck." His serious expression faltered for a second with the twitch of his lip as it curled into a tiny smirk. He threw a few more balls and I hit each one without effort, cursing myself each time they dropped into the outfield. I'd have to collect each one when we were finished.

"When did you find out?" I asked him between the next pitch.

"A couple of months ago." He shrugged. "I guess Charles was frozen out of his accounts, cut off from the family. So Silas took them over. He found out his dad was giving my mom money, and the bastard didn't hide his trail very well. I'm just another one of his indiscretions, he was paying her to keep her quiet."

Charles had been cut off? That was news to me. Silas was pretty good at keeping things close to his chest, but that seemed big. I wondered if Arlo knew about Josh...

"Does Arlo know?" I blurted and missed the next ball in my confusion. I caught the tail end of it and it skipped through the out field near Josh, who scooped it up into his glove effortlessly.

"I don't know." Josh shrugged. "If he does, he hasn't said anything to me."

I chewed on the inside of my lip and nodded. "So no one knows but you and Silas?"

"And you," he added.

"And me..." I huffed. "Your mom doesn't exactly seem like the kind of person to keep secrets."

"She told me, she's been telling me my entire life. I never believed her. She's a drug addict, Tuck, she said a lot of shit to a lot of people. Would you have taken her at her word if she told you that your father was one of the richest men in Harbor?" Josh rolled the ball in his palm but kept his eyes trained on me. Waiting for an answer.

I couldn't understand how he was so nonchalant about all of this, his mood never shifting even after telling me his secret. Joshua Logan wasn't even Logan. He was Joshua Shore.

"Yeah, right..." I processed the information. "And Silas knew before your hearing?"

"He did," Josh said. "I didn't want his help, though. This wasn't some weird blood-pact thing. I didn't want to come to the Hornets. I still don't want to be here," he added.

Ouch.

I guess I couldn't expect him to change his tune, after all, it was he who kept swearing we were nothing but a necessity to each other. *A way to survive.* What I didn't understand was the definition of necessity because it clearly meant something different to him.

As if I was like sleep or food, he needed it in his daily life to get through the day but to me necessity meant something so much more. It was water, it was air... I looked at him, the way the sun kissed his sculpted cheeks and scarred skin under the light of the open roof. His eyes casted upwards and the sun reflected around in the hazy gold color that hid beneath the darkness.

When did needing Josh to survive become second nature?

His shoulders were so tense, and his strong arms flexed as he focused on the ball in his hand and the stadium around us. The breeze kicked around his chocolate curls against his neck, and he shifted in his hoodie as he prepared to throw another ball, distracting himself like I meant for him to do, but suddenly it was me who was in knots.

"So you're a Shore…" I whispered as it all fell into place. "And he knew it and he left you…he left you in that place?"

Josh growled, the memory of his childhood bubbled up so quickly he couldn't prevent the animalistic reaction.

I dropped my bat again, my arms going slack and swallowed tightly. "I get your anger now," I said after a beat, watching his expression harden. "But I don't know how to help you with it…"

"I didn't ask for your help, Tuck." He pulled his mitt off and chucked it into the crate.

"You should go see Ms. Cody," I said to him, ignoring the way the heat and stress rolled off of him in waves as he turned around on the mound to avoid my gaze.

"No." He shook his head. "I don't need another Cody telling me how to feel about something they don't understand," he grumbled.

"This is different." I pushed. "It's not…" I stepped forward, closing the gap between us. "It's not her telling you how it feels, it's her helping you manage it."

"I'm managing just fine," I snapped.

"No you're not, you're still angry and you're allowed to be, shit Josh. But… It's not healthy," I said.

"Don't preach to me about what's healthy." He whipped around and looked me up and down. "I was doing just fine until you started to dig under my skin. Why can't you just leave me alone?" The words came out of his mouth, but I could tell that he didn't mean them; it was just him pushing back like he was so used to doing.

"I can't, Josh," I said softly, dropping my gaze to the turf for a split second before reconnecting my gaze with his. I dug deep for the courage to say what I felt.

"You've been left alone enough," I said. "It's about time someone pushed their way in—because that anger you're carrying is going to eat you alive. You don't want to hear it, but that anger is a threat to everything you've built, despite your mother and in spite of him."

"Big talk from a boy who can't even face the press, Tuck," he snipped.

"You can't turn this on me, it's not about me. I'll deal with my shit, if you deal with yours," I said to him.

Josh's tongue slid out over his bottom lip in frustration as he looked away from me. Hook, line and sinker. He couldn't resist having the power in the situation.

"Fine," he said. "I'll go see her, but if she starts bossing me around, Tuck, I'm out."

I laughed, a smile forming on my face. "She's a Cody," I said, my tone lightening. "Bossy is her only setting."

LOGAN

Dean sat beside me, knees pulled to his chest and arms wrapped around them, silent for nearly an hour.

"As far as I know he promised my mom that he was going to leave Mrs. Shore and then it all got screwed up. The second she got pregnant, he was done; he wanted her to get rid of me, and maybe she should have. It would have saved us all the trouble."

Dean flinched at the dark humor.

"When she threatened to go to Mrs. Shore, he started paying her off with monthly checks but..." I sighed.

"She loved him," Dean said softly, finishing the thought for me.

"Stupidly so, she was naïve. The way she talks about him to this day is like he'll come home to us, as if we were some happy family." I picked at my sweater. "She blames my... grandfather," I stumbled over the word. "And Mrs. Shore, like they're holding him captive," I chuckled. "When she realized he wasn't coming back, she started drinking, and then it shifted into drugs to numb it all. She felt pretty again, adored. But she was a revolving door for junkies and abusers."

I bit the inside of my cheek, the taste of copper spreading across my tongue. "When the money was tight..." I took a long, shaky breath just to steady myself. I had never told anyone any of this, and I wasn't even sure why I was sitting here telling him. But he was so quiet and patient with me that I *wanted* to tell him more even if I knew it was a bad idea.

All I could think was, *he's going to think you're fucked up beyond repair*, as he waited for the next part of the story.

"The world is full of fucked up people, ones that find pleasure in things they shouldn't, like little kids and hurting people..." I said with a tiny sniffle. "I don't know how she did it, but she found all the worst of them, and she'd lock me in that room with them for the price of a bump of coke. She's never been any better than Charles, she just was delusional enough to think she was."

Dean's jaw was tight as I explained to him what happened in that room, the details of nearly nine years of my life laid out on the turf in front of him as I quietly begged him not to leave me there. A silent plea to see past how messed up I was and see the person I could be, the person I had left on the other side of that locked door.

"I drank myself stupid for a lot of it, which sounds crazy." A defeated chuckle left me. "A fourteen-year-old blitzed off vodka. But I understood why she did drugs then. It was the only thing that blurred the screaming and pain. The visits only stopped when I could get a job. I worked hard and gave all my money to her while I changed my grades, and did my best to get sober. It was hard, it's still hard every day to know where I came from. And before you say shit about leaving her behind, I can't..." I said, looking at him. "They all left her, it's why she is that way and I..." I choked up and closed my eyes, my fingers brushed over the irritated scratches on my forearm.

"I know she's done bad shit, but she's sick—and I'd be just as bad as him if I walked away from her," I said, eyes still shut.. I wasn't able to look at him, to see the pity or anger in his eyes. I couldn't handle his judgment.

"Josh," Dean's voice was quiet, and he silently shifted over closer to me. He held out his hand flat to me. "It's *necessary*."

He looked at my hand clenched around my forearm, and only then did I notice my nails digging into my skin. Little crescent shaped indents that melted into the lines my mother had left behind. I scowled and uncurled my hand allowing him to slip his palm under mine and tangle our fingers together.

I swallowed the urge to run. Bracing for that little voice inside my head that threatened to rage at another's touch, but it never came. I could feel the blisters on his fingers from the bat and all the healed scarring against my skin, but the nausea that typically followed wasn't there. My heart slowed down as I stared down at our hands, and I was finally able to take a full breath.

When I took the chance to look over at him I noticed that there was no malice or judgement, just Dean Tucker being himself. Kind, soft and incredibly patient.

All the while being infuriatingly handsome. Each dumb golden blond curl I counted was a step toward calming down. Each shade of blue that danced in his eyes, all framed by long, thick lashes, reminded me to breathe through the pain that threatened to swallow me whole in the moment.

"I used to hate that smell," he said quietly, his eyes flickering to our hands.

"What?" I asked.

"The pine tar you use for the grip on your bat, I fucking hated that smell and now..." He smiled. "I don't know, I kinda like it."

I hated how effortlessly he existed in these tense moments.

Like his only job was to make sure I felt... seen.

He was changing the subject for me so that I didn't have to feel tied down by the trauma. I pulled my hand away gently and cleared my throat, pushing off the ground.

"We should change for practice before the team gets here," I said, brushing my face with the back of my hands just in case the tears streaming down my face were real. Dean watched me for a second, hesitant to rise, but followed a moment later.

He thankfully left the issue alone after that. Other players flooded the stadium for practice, and before long, I was running out the negativity in angry sprints that caused the sweat to pool between my shoulder blades.

I watched as Dean talked to Arlo on first base and wondered if he was as twisted up as I was inside about everything. The second the guys started to arrive, it was like a whole new version of him came out. There was a bright smile on his face that hid any trace that an hour ago we were fighting about who was more screwed up.

It pissed me off to no end that he could flip the switch like that.

Even worse, everyone had shown up today, the field was overwhelmed with noise and unnecessary bodies. Silas leaned against the banister beside Ella, the two of them going over notes. They were keeping a close eye on Cael, who was still tensing up everytime he had to swing a bat but he was getting better at hiding it. All the injuries on the team were minor, strains and pulls, nothing to be overly worried about going into the season.

Our next game was against Lorette and I already knew that it was going to be a disaster. Tension was high without the added pressure of it being the first time I was facing my old team. In a usual circumstance, it would be fun to see old teammates, to catch up and enjoy the sport as rivals. But I hadn't left on good terms, I didn't even leave of my own free will. I was banished after being attacked in the locker room and protecting myself.

I was a pariah.

A loose canon.

An animal to them.

The thought of tomorrow was making me sick to my stomach, and there was nothing I could do about it but wait it out. Dean's laughter echoed across the field as he wandered from Arlo, who gave him the middle finger, and joined Nicholas and Coach.

I stopped to catch my breath, doubling over in the grass as the rest of the team continued the sprints around me and everything felt like a blur. It was unfair that they could all just carry on the way they did.

You're not my son.

The secret of who I was didn't bother me—I could deny being a Shore until my last breath. But having my mother remind me constantly... That was different. She had a way of getting under my skin quicker than anyone else. With such ease, she disrupted what progress I made; every step away from that apartment was a day cleansed of its torture and trauma. But she found me wherever I went and now... Dean was tangled up in it.

There was no doubt that he would keep my secret; he was good at shoving down the bad stuff, ignoring it like it never existed in the first place. The way he joked around with Cael in the outfield as they tossed a ball around proved that much. But I had a feeling he'd weaponize his knowledge to hold me to my promise.

I needed to make a meeting with Riona before he called my bluff.

Practice went well and before going back to the nest I found myself knocking on her office door. She looked up from her desk with a smile, those bright eyes and friendly smile a Cody staple. She looked like Coach—if he were a woman who dressed much better.

"Joshua Logan," she set her pen down and leaned back in her chair with a smug look on her face. "Thank you."

"For what?" I said, my tone already annoyed. Every member of the Cody family had this annoying personality trait that made them feel untouchable. They spoke in goofy Texan riddles and never got to the point of things without *making a point*.

"Ryan owes me fifty bucks," she said. "He said you wouldn't darken my doorstep until long after the Lorettes' game, but I was sure you'd make it in here before."

"You made a bet with Coach on when I'd come see you..." I narrowed my eyes on her, but I found myself wandering further into the office. It was nice inside, clean and comfortable. It felt like being in someone's home, a dark plush couch, a few matching chairs. It smelled like citrus and flowers.

"And Silas," she added. "He also owes me money."

"What was his wager?" I asked, suddenly a little more curious.

"Oh, he was sure you'd never come up here," she said with that same smug smile. "But here you are."

"Here I am," I nodded and pulled my hand from my sweater pocket to offer it to her, despite not wanting to touch her. It was polite, and shaking hands usually kept people from asking questions. Rude is the word they often used when I refused to do so.

She finally stood, and she was taller than I had expected, her blonde hair short to her scalp, and big jade earrings dangled from her ears. She looked down at my hand and back up to me without shaking it.

"What has he told you?" I snapped, my tone sharper than intended.

"Who?" She asked, it was her turn to narrow her eyes on me.

"Silas," I said, retracting my hand. She hadn't shaken it for a reason, and I wanted to know what Silas had said to her, and I wanted to know now.

"The last time I spoke to Silas about you was to make that bet," she chuckled softly. "Your hand was shaking, and I've noticed from press conferences, player lineups... You rarely offer your hand to anyone. You don't even high-five after a home run."

She was good, I'd give her that.

"You went back and watched old press tapes?" I asked, incredulous.

"I like to know the players," she said. "You can learn a lot from a person from how they act under public scrutiny."

"That must be hundreds of players," I scoffed. "There's no way."

"Two hundred and sixteen athletes come in and out of this office, to be exact. I'm the therapist for all the teams at Harbor, it was very important to Seymour Shore that players were of healthy body and mind," she explained.

"Feels phony," I said, just being honest with her.

"You can say what you want about Seymour, but phony, he's not." She defended him.

"I get it, you're under the Shores payroll so you pump their egos, get a little extra on the side…" I said. "Makes sense, it's why Coach Cody has a job. What did you have to do for yours?"

Riona laughed at me as she wandered around her desk and leaned against it beside me. She kept a fair distance, but she constantly kept her eyes trained on mine.

"Six years of school while raising a daughter on my own, living out of a car, and fighting through about nineteen other very highly qualified candidates." She answered the question without skipping a beat. "I don't pump egos, Mr. Logan." She smiled, keeping her voice professional. "I deflate them because typically overconfident, brash egos attached to men who are usually described as bullies can only mean one thing."

"What's that?" I asked her, knowing I probably wouldn't like whatever shrink answer she decided to throw at me next.

"Trauma," she simply said, crossing her arms over her chest.

"I'm not traumatized," I argued and rolled my eyes.

"But you are an overconfident, brash bully with an inflated ego?" She asked, a smirk curling at the corner of her mouth that mimicked the same one Cael had.

"That's your assumption," I said.

"Alright, so why did you come up here then, Logan, if not for open communication and a good bickering session? I'm sure if you ask him nicely, Arlo or... Mitchell, maybe, would verbally spar with you. Mitchell pretends to be a softy, but he's..." she widened her eyes and scoffed as she rounded her desk again, going back to her chair.

"I was going to set up a meeting, but this clearly isn't going to work," I muttered, stepping back.

"On the contrary, Josh, I've never seen you so uncomfortable," she said, picking up her pen and flipping the page in her book. "Tuesday, after practice."

I shook my head, my tongue pressed to my teeth. She was going to be my worst nightmare, but I liked how easily she ignored my gruff nature, and it was almost fun to argue with her, if that was what we were doing...

"Tuesday," I repeated with a nod, then turned and left her office.

TUCKER

Friday night games were, without question, my least favorite thing on the planet. The boys were restless after a long week, wanting to spend the night getting wasted at Delta and forgetting all the crap we learned in school. No one wanted to be dressing for a game beneath a concrete pad that held thousands of cheering fans.

But tonight was even worse, it would be the first time we were facing Lorette since Josh had transferred to Harbor. Transfers weren't usually a big deal—they happened all the time—but Josh hadn't exactly left Lorette on good terms.

After our conversation about what happened with Ian, I reached out to a few of the guys over at Lorette. I was nosy and wanted to know if Josh had told me the entire truth. I realized quickly that he had been ostracized there long before Ian had snapped. It was like I'd slapped them—the mood shifted instantly the second I brought him up.

Nothing about Josh's sexual orientation was mentioned, but I could feel them holding back almost as if they weren't sure how truthful they could be with me. Ian was a sore topic; turns out

whatever Josh had done had serious consequences. He'd spend the majority of the season in the dugout.

Tonight would be a bloodbath.

"Earth to big boy." Cael sat on the bench next to me. I had all but sleepwalked through getting dressed. I knew Josh was beside me because the only thing I could smell was that spicy, woody cologne he was always wearing. I just wanted to be at the Nest, hiding from the world, tangled in the sheet that smelled like him. It had taken a week for me to understand why Cael washed his bedding with lavender all those years.

It was addicting.

It was comforting.

The way Josh had crawled into all the dark spaces beneath the surface was unbelievable.

"You gonna be alright?" Cael asked, flipping his hat over his head.

"Yeah, I was just spaced out. I'm good." I brushed him off and finished tying my shoes before standing. I looked around at them all, quietly getting ready, everyone already bracing for the impact of tonight's game. "No one is more stressed about tonight than me..." I said loudly, getting their attention. "But this is just another game, just another team... We beat them before, we'll beat them again. We do this as a team," I said, looking around at them before stopping on Josh. "We have each other's back and no one gets left on the field."

The boys clapped, hollered, and tapped their chests in agreement, each one rising and filing out of the locker room. The tunnel's energy before the starting announcements was charged, I could feel the electricity in the air, it tingled at my fingers and made my tongue fuzzy.

Josh was the last out of the locker room as per usual, and I thought about saying something to him, but when I looked back at him, he was steel. There wasn't anything on his face but anger and determination. It wouldn't have mattered what I said; he knew what he wanted out of the game tonight, and he'd get it.

I sighed, rubbing my hands on my pants to get rid of the nervous sweat and led the team out onto the field with a bright smile and a few waves. Lorette was already lined up near the dugout, murmuring to each other like the stadium had been vacuum-sealed of air.

I looked back at Josh, who seemed indifferent, but I knew better, his fingers curled at his side and his shoulders tightened beneath his jersey. Ian was standing with the Lorette's head coach, his ugly glare tucked beneath a red cap. There was a thick cast around his right arm and he looked like every breath was painful.

Good. I thought when I saw him. The sound of Josh's voice when he told his story echoed in the back of my mind, and it took everything in me to turn to the dugout at that moment.

"Looks like Ian found his legs," Cael whispered from beside me as Van came to stand at my back. It wasn't a secret that he was a homophobic asshole. He made it clear every chance he got. Arlo used to work harder to strike him out just so no one had to stand on base with him during the games.

Every interaction I'd ever had with Ian was horrible.

"Unfortunately," Van said, crossing his arms over his chest. "This is going to suck," he added, before following Coach's voice to the dugout.

"Tucker, Cael—" he called to us, and Cael tugged on the back of my jersey to get my feet moving. My stomach was in knots, he wasn't supposed to be here today. My previous statement of today's game being a bloodbath was an understatement. Josh's focus was still on Ian even as Coach ran through some last-minute updates. His jaw was so tight I could feel it in my own, and all I wanted to do was check on him, but I couldn't. Not here, not now.

Fuck.

I turned to Coach, completely unaware that he had stopped talking and was ordering me out on the field.

"Get focused. There's nothing you could have done to stop it." He gripped my shoulder and caught my worried gaze. I had forgotten that Coach knew about the fight. I wasn't sure how much he knew, but he knew enough to be concerned about the game. I could see it in his eyes. I nodded, and he tapped his fingers to my chest before shoving me up and out of the dugout.

We needed to win this toss, we needed the advantage.

"Hey, Tuck." Yuri stepped up to the plate with the ump, and I shook his hand.

"Fortuna," I said back. "Good to see Ian on his feet," I said politely and Yuri looked over his shoulder with a scoff. *Everyone* knew the kind of person Ian was.

"He might even get to play this season." Yuri's weasel-like features curled into satisfaction.

"Alright, men, no funny business today, keep the game clean and keep it fair. If you have issues, I'm the first to hear about them. No bench brawls today, I got a date later and I don't need a black eye," the ump joked.

"Chicks dig that stuff," Yuri joked with the Ump. I could have cared less, with one eye on Ian in the dugout I shook hands before walking back to my own.

"Get in the field," I barked as I came down the stairs and grabbed my glove. First base was directly beside the Lorette's dugout. I swallowed tightly and shoved my hand into my mitt as we all marched out onto the field. I whirled on Josh as he came out of the dugout, the words caught in my throat as his dark eyes panned over me.

"What Tuck?" He snapped.

I'm here, I know he wouldn't understand the sentiment of what I did next but I hoped that even through his hatred for the tradition he'd see what I was trying to say. I pressed my two fingers to my heart, no tapping, and all the silence of the moment swallowed by the stadium noise. *I have your back.*

Josh's gaze flicked to my fingers, narrowed briefly, then snapped back to meet mine. "Quit being fucking weird," he snapped and pushed past me but his shoulder brushed against mine and he tapped his mitt against my hand gently.

Okay.

I settled my nerves and made my way to first, watching Josh pace on the pitcher's mound for a moment. He looked like a caged animal, the anxiety and anger rolling off him in thick, tense waves.

When he finally settled, Yuri was readying in the batter's box. Swinging his bat back and forth before settling it on his shoulders.

Jensen nodded twice to Josh before pushing his cage over his face and sinking low. It had taken a second but it seemed like the two had finally started to find a groove. Josh double checked his surroundings making sure that Cael was ready over his shoulder and that Louis was paying attention to the gap.

From this distance, it was hard to tell what he was thinking, but I watched the methodical, slow rise and fall of his chest as he counted his breaths and rolled the ball over in his palm.

"Game on," the ump called, and it was like a switch had been flipped.

Josh's jaw ticked, his back foot grinding into the mound like he was anchoring himself in place. He inhaled deeply as his arm pulled back over his head and his body arched in a graceful curve that turned into a wave of power as he threw the ball with everything he had, and it slapped into Jensen's mitt behind Yuri.

Watching Josh pitch was art, like those moments in movies when the sound fades away from the shot and all you hear is the soft orchestra of music building in the background. His fingers curled around the ball, his thighs tightened as he moved his feet with practiced precision, and his eyes never left Yuri's.

Another strike.

Maybe we can do this...maybe we can win.

Yuri rolled his neck out and re-adjusted in the box as the batting coach screamed something at him from the side. I scanned the field as Josh readied and saw what the batting coach saw, a pocket in left. I swore as the ball was released and sank low on the base as the ball cracked loudly against the bat and soared over the infield head to that unprotected patch of grass. Van was quick on his feet, the anticipation building as he flung himself to the ground to try to catch the ball, but it bounced passed his sliding body to Todd as Yuri rounded first and moved toward Louis at second.

"Lou!" Cael shouted, but it was too late; the second baseman wasn't going to be fast enough. The ball hit his mitt mere seconds after Yuri found home beside him on the base with a cocky smile on his face.

"Nice team, Tucker." A twisted, malicious jab floated from the dugout, and I tried to ignore it, but he tried again. "You guys might actually make it to the playoffs if you can pull your dicks out of each others asses and get it together."

The Lorette crowd cheered loudly as the next batter, Steve Keery, placed a ball in left field and pushed Yuri home. Ian was still leaning against the banister, I could feel his gaze on my cheek as I tried to focus on something else.

All I want to do is put my fist through your face.

"How's Logan?" Ian's voice echoed around my head, and I pulled my hat down over my eyebrows. "Is he fitting in on your happy little gay team?" Every word Ian spat was crafted to get a rise out of me.

"Did you give him the Tucker special welcome when he arrived?" Ian hissed.

If you don't stop, you'll never play baseball again, and I'll be in jail.

I flexed my hand inside my mitt and ignored him as another batter stepped up, hitting the ball to Cael. He yelled my name but I barely heard it over the sound of my own frustration. The ball soared into my mitt clumsily and the batter settled on first safely, that run was enough to load the bases.

Josh readied for the next pitch, and just like the one before, the batter easily hit the ball, which soared over the heads of the outfield and over the back end of the Hornets stadium into the stands. *Shit.* A home run grand slam. *Perfect.*

Everything went downhill from there, we couldn't keep ourselves together long enough to score a run in the first three innings. It wasn't until the fourth that Van finally connected with a ball and put it out to bring me and Todd home for three runs.

We were down seven to three and everyone had seemed to lose their fight. Arlo was getting short with Josh as Nicholas tried to run Reyes through a warm up to take his place on the pitcher's mound.

"You're not taking me out!" Josh snapped, and Arlo growled in response.

"You've handed over seven runs, Logan, this isn't about me questioning your abilities, it's about Lorette getting in your head!" Arlo threw his clipboard on the bench beside him and crossed his arms over his chest. "You aren't ready for this, not for them!"

"You don't get to fucking decide what I'm ready for," Josh bit out.

"I do!" Arlo stepped forward to get in his face. "It's my job. I'm your coach. Which means if I say you aren't ready, you don't go on the field. You need a break!"

"It's bullshit!" Josh got louder and pinned his shoulders back as he moved closer.

"It's law," Arlo said, clearly very finished with the conversation.

"Give me one more inning!" Josh wasn't going to beg, but it was close enough as his voice got lower, practically pleading with Arlo.

"It's an inning we need, Logan, we have to put Reyes in," Arlo said, his voice calmer than before. "I'm sorry."

TUCKER

Leaving Josh on the bench was torture.

He looked like he might tear himself apart, his hands digging roughly into his leather mitt. He kept his dark eyes trained on the field, but there wasn't a thought behind them besides anger, at himself and at Arlo.

I had never once in my life dreaded standing on first base, it was where I felt the most at home. Untouchable, and free. That was where my heart was, where it had always been. I walked the foul line straight and true, never once looking back—until now.

"Move your ass, Tucker." Coach clapped his hands and broke me from my trance.

I grumbled, turning around to see Ian hovering in the dugout like he had been all game. He wouldn't stop, each jab was another reason for me to kick his ass. I just wanted this god forsaken game to be over and done with.

Reyes did no better than Josh, the Lorettes had inched their way under all our skin and there was no getting rid of them. We needed off the field, hidden behind the wall of the Nest. Maybe it was cowardice or defeat, but I didn't care. Every muscle in my body

felt like it was one insult away from snapping like a rubber band beneath my skin and I couldn't promise myself or the team that I could control it once it happened.

I've never once in my life been an angry person... Sad, depressed, frustrated, happy and hopeful for sure. But never truly angry, I didn't have the space for it. But Ian was dragging that raw, unbridled and unchecked emotion from the depths of my system, and it wouldn't take much for me to learn what a rage-filled adrenaline rush felt like.

Josh didn't want that though, I knew he didn't and it was the only thing keeping me in check. The idea of starting a war with Lorette over a few homophobic jabs from Ian—only to humiliate Josh—was the only thing keeping me focused on the game. Even if we were losing.

And we did, we lost badly. Cael and Van tried their best to do damage control, both bringing a few more runs, but by the last inning, we were still down five, and there was no hope. Coach was pissed and Arlo was slamming things around in the dugout as we walked onto the field to shake hands with Lorette. Josh thought about not going, but Coach made him, and he stepped slowly into the sand with cautious steps. I followed him in time, keeping close but giving him some space as we lined up and waited.

I knew the moment he stepped into line with us, the tension would rise and, as predicted, it built from the ground and consumed him like a dark wave. He didn't shake a single hand, only nodded as he went through, but it was almost as if the Lorette players knew better than to touch him.

As we approached Yuri and the tail end of the list I could see their eyes on Josh. I braced for impact as we approached them, pulling my other hand out of my pocket and inhaling a dirty breath of air that smelled like clay and sweat. I searched for that cinnamon scent, but he'd moved too far ahead—and I missed whatever Yuri said that made the team laugh.

I watched it happen in slow motion as Ian slipped out from behind the pitcher, hidden from sight and laid his hand on Josh's shoulder. *I was going to kill someone.*

I stepped forward, unable to focus on the words coming out of Ian's mouth and shoved him backwards with both my hands, making sure that he wasn't in reach of Josh.

"Should've known you'd let that snake into your bed." Ian's smile curled with pride as the teams surrounded us. What remained of the dissipating crowd rumbled with excitement over the sudden aggression.

"Keep your fucking hands off him," I warned, and Ian just laughed in my face.

"Or what?" Ian righted himself, his arm tucked to his side as his team protected his back.

The darkest kind of anger bubbled up from me with Josh's broken voice echoing in my mind and the smell of his cologne over my shoulder. He was still right there behind my back, quiet and so still I almost missed him, but he hadn't slipped away in the crowd.

"You'll have to find a sport you can play from a wheelchair." I licked my bottom lip and stepped forward, but his team met me.

"Ooh, Tucker found his balls! For a while there I was thinking that Cody had them in a box somewhere," Ian sneered, and looked around at the faceless idiots that laughed at his joke.

I laughed, the sound escaping me uncontrollably and catching Ian off caught. I wasn't sure what response he had been expecting, but it wasn't laughter. His face twisted into confusion for a brief second before falling back into a confident falsehood with an equally fake smile.

"What's so funny?" He asked me, and I could hear the coaches starting to get restless. They couldn't see into the center of the huddle what was happening, and it was setting them on edge. Two bench brawls for the Hornets in two weeks wasn't exactly a good look as the new captain but I didn't really give a shit. They had tried to attack one of our own and I'd be damned if Ian got away without repercussions a second time.

"You." I smiled and shook my head softly as I stepped forward. There was always a sick thrill in going toe to toe with Ian. He was quite possibly one of the only players we saw regularly that matched me in size, and if we were to ever fight, it would be a real challenge. One I wanted to give a shot at that very moment.

"Me?" His stupid eyes rolled. "You really need to work on your insults, Dean; that was very first grade of you."

"Yeah, probably." I shrugged. "But then again why would I want to practice being an asshole?" I said, and Cael huffed a tiny laugh from my side. The funny thing about the Hornets was that their support was endless, I could have been lobbying to jump off a bridge and they'd be there, kicking off their shoes and getting ready for the plunge.

And no matter how much they hated Josh, how hard the last weeks had been trying to find a way to work together with him and acclimate to his presence in our lives. He was a Hornet, like it or not. So the moment Ian became a threat, the team surrounded Josh and me, waiting for the word but not acting on their own.

You never got just one Hornet when you kicked the Nest. You got swarmed.

"Maybe being an asshole would make you a better captain," Ian said, and I wanted nothing more than to knock that stupid smirk off his face. "Less time butt fucking eachother and more time practicing baseball," Ian jabbed.

"Last I heard you like a good butt fucking, Ian," Cael was quick to insult him, and I heard the sound of satisfied amusement leave Josh from behind me.

"Fuck you, Cody." Ian stepped forward, and I stepped in front of Cael, blocking his path with the shake of my head. Ian looked me up and down, no doubt trying to decide whether or not it was worth it, but he shook his head and stepped back. "This was getting boring anyway."

"Yeah." I nodded. "*Boring*."

The rest of the Lorettes backed away from Ian, all of them moving with caution, but with the tension easing and the threat of a fight fading, they didn't care much anymore. I turned around, and the Hornets hadn't moved. Cael, Van, and Arlo had formed a tight line around Josh directly behind me. I hadn't even heard

Arlo's arrival, but having him there had been a silent confidence boost.

It wasn't until I tapped my fingers to my chest that the team started to funnel away from us back to the dugout. Josh's eyes never moved from mine, a quiet thank you for taking control of the situation. I nodded toward the dugout, and he took the cue.

"Hey, Tucker," Ian called out, and I turned to look at him over my shoulder as the rest of the team wandered out of earshot. A sick, twisted smile formed on the first baseman's face. "His favorite date spot is the shower room."

The rage boiled in my chest and spilled over as my vision blurred at the corners. Every muscle in my body tightened painfully, and I almost asked him to repeat himself, because there was no way he was stupid enough to bring that up.

I'd never felt anger the way I did as I spun on my heel towards him. Blinded by the fury, I felt Josh's finger tips brush against mine in an attempt to hold me back, but it was too late. I heard him scramble after me in the clay, but I was faster, and before I could be stopped, my arms were wrapped around Ian's middle, and we were slamming into the hard ground.

Ian tried to protect his face, but my fist found it before he could get his arms up. I didn't pull it either, I put the full force of two-hundred-and-fifty pounds behind it. I wanted him to feel the bones in his face break; I needed him to.

Losing control was too easy. All the frustration, shame and anger that I had been storing away for weeks was overflowing. It felt good—too good. Effortless, almost addictive, to pummel Ian, he was the face of homophobia in the league, and he was just as bad as my mother and family. It all melted together, and suddenly I could hear all of them hounding me for answers, begging me to be *normal*. To fit in. But I did fit in, just not to their narrative!

"Fight me back!" I screamed at him and cocked my arm back for another punch but he just cowered below me and before I could throw the punch fingers wrapped around my elbow.

"Enough." Arlo was there, the only person that could truly silence the anger with just a look and I felt it rush from me, down through my toes into the unsettled dirt like a shot of electricity. His dark eyes screamed understanding but his tight grip and tense jaw communicated authority.

An unfamiliar growl of annoyance left my throat as I climbed off Ian, still whimpering as the blood poured from his nose. I stared down at my bruised knuckles and inhaled once before turning to the Lorette's dugout.

"Keep your dog on a leash!" I snapped, pointing at Ian. and stomped back to our dugout, passed Josh who was standing where I left him. His face was completely unreadable as Cael approached him. I ignored Cael, shaking him off as he reached out to check on me.

I marched down the steps, aware that everyone was watching me. Coach was waiting with his arms crossed. "I guess you missed the '*no breaking your hands on faces*' memo," he huffed.

I ignored the need to obey him or feel ashamed of what I had done and looked over at Josh, who was talking to Cael quietly. His eyes locked on mine over Cael's shoulder.

"Why isn't there a restraining order in place?" I asked Coach as Silas wandered over to take in the conversation.

"Not here, Tucker." Coach shook his head.

"Tell me," I snapped, wincing at Coach's expression at the demand. I was letting Ian get to me, it was making me irrational and mean. "Sorry, I just—"

"I know, let me deal with Lorette. You'll probably get suspended for this, Tucker, but you did the right thing," Coach said, putting his hand on my shoulder. He made sure I was looking at him, listening completely. "Take that anger and go talk to the press," he said.

"Ryan," Silas said, a soft warning that it might not be the best idea.

"No, this is the only time when he's going to have the courage to do this," Coach argued without looking away from me. "Ride that adrenaline rush, answer their questions, but don't let them push you around. You understand me, son?"

I nodded, swallowing the bile that stung my throat.

"I'll go with him," Silas said, and he tapped his fingers over his heart as my eyes flickered to him.

I wanted to say something to Josh, but when I stepped toward him, he shook his head and broke eye contact with me. *Fuck.* I followed Silas down the tunnel, and only when we were alone did he turn to me.

"Are you okay?" He asked, holding out his hand for mine. I gave it to him and nodded. "Good, are you also out of your mind?" He scowled as he inspected the irritated knuckles. "Since when do you pick fights?"

"He baited me and I fell for it, I'm sorry," I mumbled, and Silas narrowed his grey eyes on me.

"Josh told you," he said quietly, and I nodded.

"He told you?" I asked, confused that he had shared something like that with Silas.

"I know enough, and it wasn't his choice," Silas said. "I told him that he either told me what started the fight or he didn't get a chance with Harbor."

"Oh," I said, and let my hand fall back at my side.

"Are you sure you want to do this? They aren't going to be nice," Silas said, double-checking my mood.

"I can do it," I said, my confidence was waning, but I couldn't feel anything. My blood was pumping too quickly to pause for fear.

"Alright, kid." Silas didn't seem convinced, but he nodded. "If you need a rescue, slip pineapple into the conversation. It'll be our emergency code word."

"Pineapple?" I huffed a laugh—ridiculous, but kind of perfect.

He clapped me on the shoulders and spun me back toward the lion's den. I was going to be torn to shreds on local television, and I was expected to do it with a smile on my face.

I took one last deep breath and pushed through the doors.

LOGAN

The most attractive thing Dean Tucker had ever done wasn't beating the shit out of Ian in front of everyone. It was how he was sitting at the table in the press room with his shoulders pinned back and his bloody knuckles flexed on the table for the cameras to see.

He looked like an enraged god—sweaty blond curls clinging to his neck, his scruffy jaw set tight with anguish. I wanted to make it all stop, quiet the noise, break the cameras. He hated every second of being on display, but he was doing it with a brave face.

His bright blue eyes were blown out and dark as he rode the wave of his adrenaline rush. Coach putting him out there was smart, but also torture to watch from the hall when we could barely hear anything they were asking.

Van hovered beside me, outside the door's small window, not ten minutes after we all left the field. The sound of Dean's fist connecting with Ian's face still echoed in my mind as everyone, quietly and patiently, waited for the word that Dean had entered the press room.

"Josh," Cael's voice hissed from my left, he waved me over and I followed him down around a smaller hallway to a door that opened into what looked like another hallway but the door on the other end was open and from it we could see *and* hear Dean.

I snuck in quietly behind Cael as we tucked against the wall hidden by a few standing journalists. Cael's hands found someone, and from the giggle that followed, I knew Clementine Matthews was on the other side. She wiggled her fingers at me in a little wave and went back to focusing on Dean.

From this angle I could see his foot shaking beneath the table, his entire body was vibrating as the media started to ply him with questions.

"Lawson Gall." A stout man with a ruddy beard stood up near us. "Welcome back to the table, Mr. Tucker. Was today's loss attributed to the distractions in your personal life?"

"What?" Dean said, his face scrunching in confusion.

"You've been under a fair amount of scrutiny. Was that pressure a direct result of today's game?" He asked.

"I'm very capable of separating my personal life and the game, Mr. Gall. We went out, we played hard, but we lost our focus. Lorette has a strong team this year, we just need to figure out how to be stronger." Dean sidestepped the loaded question with grace and a touch of anger lacing his otherwise professional tone.

"So none of it has to do with your tumultuous relationship with Cael Cody?" He asked.

"Mr. Gall, can you spell that for me?" Dean asked him, and the man looked confused, but Cael barked out a loud, amused laugh that made a few reporters turn before he ducked down out of sight again. The reporter, unaware that he had been made the butt of some inside joke, sat back down.

"Frank Keller," the next man introduced himself as he stood. "You've been hiding from us, Mr. Tucker." He smiled. "Why? Did the fight on the field today have anything to do with your avoidance?"

Dean's shoulders tensed. "If you can call that a fight, I guess." He flicked his eyebrow as his tongue pressed against the inside of his bottom lip.

"There are rumors that the committee have already suspended you, is that true?" He asked next.

"No." Dean shook his head. "We have to have a hearing meeting before that happens, but you know that Mr.—"

"Keller," he offered. "Back to the reason behind the scuffle, was it because of the comments made last conference?"

"You mean when I was outed to everyone in my life without my consent?" Dean questioned him, his voice flat and riddled with discontent.

My chest filled with pride, another new emotion that until recently I had never experienced or least never in the way I had before.

"Uh—Yeah," the reporter tripped over his words, clearly not expecting something so blunt from the team's resident golden boy.

"No, the beating didn't have anything to do with me being gay, Mr. Keller." Dean looked around the room. "Do any of you have questions for me that don't involve my sexual preferences?"

The room went silent.

His direct approach to their nonsense had sucked all the air from the room.

"Mr. Tucker." Clementine stepped into the light in her dark skirt and tight white blouse, and it was like a blanket had been wrapped around Dean. His expression softened, and a genuine smile curled on his lips. "Clementine Matthews, Independent." She smiled back. "We haven't heard much from you since the season started. How has the team adjusted to Joshua Logan's presence? That must have been quite the shake-up."

He relaxed a little, his chest rising and falling with a long, steady breath. "Josh came to Harbor during a transition period, and losing Arlo was rough, but we gained a great pitcher, and with his help, we stand a shot for back to back titles."

Dean couldn't see me from where Cael and I were hidden, but I wish he could have.

"So you're saying Josh is a better pitcher than Arlo?" Clementine's eyebrow raised.

"Line them up," Dean laughed, and the entire room was in the dark when Clementine mirrored his expression. He cleared his throat, and it was clear Clementine's calm conversation was having the right effect on him. "No, Arlo was one of a kind, no one could fill his shoes, but Josh has the ability to walk in them, even in a size too big."

Cael huffed and looked at me. "Big boy's good with his words when he's not saying something stupid," he said with a cheeky smile.

"He's tiptoeing around shit, but holding his own. I expected tears by now," I muttered, just trying to hide the pride in my voice.

His eyes narrowed on me, and his head turned to the side. "Mm, the goo…"

"What the hell is wrong with you?" I stared at him with disgust.

"I've seen that look before. Arlo used to look at Ella like that. It's almost like you're constipated trying to hide your attraction," Cael teased, and I wanted to shove him, but we weren't supposed to be in here, and I wasn't ready to get kicked out just yet.

Dean fielded about nineteen more questions once the reporters started asking about the game and not about him. He didn't entertain anything about his personal life, shutting them down with a hard no or a walk-around joke. It was like he had climbed out of the hole he'd been hiding in to prove to the world that they couldn't push him around.

By the time he was done, it was easy to see how exhausted he'd gotten. The adrenaline had worn off, and his hands were starting to shake. Silas followed his tail out of the room as the reporters went into a frenzy upon his departure. He noticed Cael and me on the way out and called us over, funneling us out in front of him and taking the rear. Silas whispered something to Cael that I didn't catch because my eyes were focused on the space between Dean's shoulder blades. It's where he carried all of his tension, balled up and tight. I wanted to put my hands on it, to ease it from beneath his skin, but it wasn't the time or the place.

I wasn't even sure I could make myself do it.

But the need was violent.

Any other day, the locker room would be empty—everyone would have showered and disappeared by now. But every member of the team, including most of the coaches and Ella, was still waiting patiently for him to return. They sat quietly as Dean entered the room in his baseball gear, sweaty and uncomfortable.

Cael and I wandered around him to our lockers as he stood in the middle of the giant hornets logo and stared at the carpet with his bottom lip between his teeth.

Coach almost stepped in when the silence dragged, but Dean lifted his head and opened his mouth before it could happen. "Sorry, I just... the silence was kinda nice..." he chuckled half-heartedly. "I'm sorry about today's game, I failed you guys as a captain, and I promise from here on out that I'll be there, heart and head. I should have told the reporters off the day they backed me in a corner, but instead I let them cage us all up like animals because I was too scared to be who I am."

He pulled on the collar of his jersey with a shaky, bruised hand and popped the top buttons free so he could breathe a little easier. "No more hiding, we play as ourselves and we play hard. And maybe no more fighting, but no promises," he said with a small smile as he looked over his shoulder at Coach. "Sorry, Coach."

"None of that tonight, Dean. You defended your home," he said, his expression never wavering from the utmost of pride. "Enough apologies will be made tomorrow, double practice and Tucker, you and I have a meeting with the board tomorrow at noon. Showers, food, sleep, get to it, boys."

Coach clapped his hands, and everyone moved into action, but Dean stayed frozen in the center of the blur like the people moving around him were nothing but noise. I untied my cleats one lace at a time while I kept my eyes on him, and slowly the locker room emptied. He never moved, and I knew what it was, it was paralysis from the events that had transpired over the last four hours.

He hadn't come to the stadium today expecting to fight or sit under a media spotlight for an hour. The adrenaline of the fight had gotten him through it, but now that it was wearing off, he was stuck, replaying it all back in his mind, wishing he had done things differently.

Cael stood by the door and looked over at me, he wanted to know if I could handle it and to be honest, I wasn't sure if I could. Not in the way anyone else would have, I didn't know Dean as well as them and I was scared to screw it up. For the first time in my life, I was wading into unfamiliar waters, scared that at any time I'd wade too far, lose my footing and slip beneath the surface.

But also curious, *brazen maybe*? It wasn't the water that scared me, it was the unknown of what was below, the dangers I couldn't see in the depths. The only sure thought I had was that I wanted nothing more than to drown in Dean Tucker.

I nodded to Cael, and he took it as a sign that he was safe to leave his best friend in my hands. I wasn't exactly confident in that trust, but I had it regardless. He left and flipped the lock to give us privacy before the door clicked shut and left us alone. When the locker room was finally empty, I pushed off the bench in my sweaty gear and made my way across the carpet in exactly thirteen agonizing steps.

"Tuck," I said. "You gotta shower, you smell like dirt and blood." I looked down at his jersey, and a messy dark red stain splattered across the Hornets logo. My hands shook, but not nearly as much as his. I inhaled, filling my lungs with a rush of air before I stepped forward and lifted my hands to the buttons of his jersey.

Dean was completely checked out as I undid each button and rolled the fabric away from his skin. I did my best not to touch him, I couldn't battle my own demons while battling Dean's, even if it meant holding on to the one thing that he might need from me.

"Asshole," I muttered, not sure if tough love was the right approach but I had to try something. I'd never seen him so far gone. "Snap out of it, it's over. The world knows, you're free. Whatever comes next, we deal with it."

Dean looked down at me then, his eyes finally meeting mine, and there was so much uncertainty behind him. I nodded at him, understanding the rush of emotions that was coursing through his veins. Words weren't needed between us to convey how overwhelmed he had gotten in mere moments of slowing down and really realizing what he'd done.

"I can do it." Dean lifted his hands as I started on his belt but stopped before he touched me. At least he was talking to me.

"I didn't ask if you could do it," I said and popped the belt off, pulling it out of the loops and throwing it with his jersey.

"You don't want to do this," Dean tried to brush me off again, his voice thick with burden.

"You need me too," I argued and ignored the way he tried to move away from me as I counted to ten in my head and inhaled again. "It's necessary."

He stopped fighting it then, slipping back into his awkward uncertainty and remained quiet as I knelt to the floor and started to untie his shoes. Once he was half undressed I stepped back so he could shuck out of his pants. I walked over to the showers, disappearing out of his sight and ran one of the showers hot for him.

When I returned, he was rubbing the back of his unhurt hand across his cheeks, and he was staring away from the showers, completely naked but not unaware of my presence. His knuckles were still red and raw, and his eyes were glassy with exhaustion.

"Go clean up. I'll wait and drive us to Dansby house," I said to him, and pointed to the showers.

TUCKER

The Nest was quiet when we arrived, everyone had either gone to dinner or retreated to their rooms to study or do school work. I was hoping that someone would be around to buffer the awkwardness between Josh and me. It took twice as long for me to shower than usual, but when I'd returned to the locker room Josh was still there waiting patiently for me to get my shit together.

I'd done it, I took the questions like bullets to my chest. I'd answered what I could, shut down what I couldn't or shouldn't. I knew that no one would be satisfied, and I could hear my cell phone buzzing in my locker like an incessant reminder that my parents' wrath loomed like a thunder cloud.

"*Whatever comes next.*"

That's what he said.

But what came next was war, of the mind and body.

He disappeared to shower and for a moment I almost followed him like some lost puppy unable to navigate my own emotions. I would have just sat there on the counter until he was finished but it felt like too much. *Unnecessary.* So I wandered into the kitchen and

stared at the fridge like something I actually wanted to eat might crawl out and nourish me with zero effort.

"I ordered pizza," Josh's voice broke me from the trance, and I couldn't be sure how long I'd been standing there, but it didn't feel like that long.

"Oh." I flipped off the hat I was wearing and threw it on the counter. "Thanks."

"Do you want to watch a movie or something?" Josh asked, he looked uncomfortable even though he was wearing the faded red Lorette hoodie and same sweats he wore after every game. He was being so normal, but I could see through it, and it unexpectedly frustrated me.

"What are you doing?" I asked him as he wandered around to grab his water from the fridge.

"Asking you if you want to watch a movie and eat pizza?" His brows scrunched together in confusion as the fridge door clicked shut between us.

"Stop being nice to me," I snapped, shaking my head. "Be angry or mad at me—something!"

"What exactly do you want me to be angry about, Tuck?" Josh asked and set the bottle down on the countertop. "Defending me? Defending yourself?"

He made it sound so simple.

"I lost control, I let my temper take the wheel, and I could have hurt someone!" I argued loudly, not caring who was listening.

"You hurt Ian." Josh's laugh was gentle and surprising.

"That's not who I am, I don't punch people," I tried to explain to him.

"I'm thanking you for punching him." Josh flashed that cocky smile and I wanted to shove him, to make him understand that what happened was bad. It wasn't anything to smile over. "You told me I was safe here," he reminded me.

"You are."

"You were just keeping your promise." He never took his eyes off mine, the weight of his words settling heavy against my aching chest. "If it counts for anything, you looked in control to me. Well, in the moment, after not so much," he added.

I had embarrassed myself in the locker room, and I'd be thinking about it for weeks. How stupid I must have looked. It was a fight and a shitty press conference. No one had died, my life wasn't falling apart, but everything had hit me like a ton of bricks. It weighed so heavily on my chest that it was hard to breathe if I moved. So instead I shut down, I stayed so still that I could feel my muscles contracting with each breath. A sure way to tell that I had started breathing again after so long holding my breath.

I probably looked like an idiot to Josh, and that's why he was teasing me now. Because in a trauma contest, I lost every round. Compared to the shit that he'd gone through in his life, a few shitty family members I could escape and press I could ignore. My life had been golden.

I stopped, shaking my head at my own thoughts. I looked up at Josh.

My life *is* golden.

Josh would hate the idea of someone describing him in such a way, he'd argue that he was cold and harsh like a bathroom floor in the morning after a bad sleep or the raw, upsetting feeling of disappointment. But he wasn't, he was that first ray of sunshine sneaking through the dark curtains after the longest winter. Warm and annoyingly welcome even if he wakes you up at the crack of dawn.

Pay attention, Ella whispered in the back of my mind, and I looked closer at what Josh was saying to me.

Defending me?

I chuckled under my breath. It wasn't about the punch or the violence. It never was. Josh was thanking me for protecting him, for standing up for him. Years spent defending himself, from every person that stepped dangerously into his life, his own mother, his team, people he no doubt thought were his friends. No one had ever stepped *up* for him.

"What movie?" I finally asked him.

He smiled at me. "You pick, the last movie I watched was..." he shrugged and a few of those dark damp waves fell out of place against his temple. "I don't even remember?"

"My favorite is The Outsiders," I said, and Josh's face scrunched up in a funny but adorable way.

"Isn't that movie a hundred years old?" He asked, nodding toward the living room. I followed him like I always did, settling down on the couch with some distance between us.

"Cael's mom loved it. When she got really sick, we all used to read her pages of the book so it's kinda a staple of the Nest," I said.

"I never really slowed down enough to pick a favorite movie of my own."

"Too busy being Harbor's golden boy?" Josh jabbed.

"Luckily, I think tonight stripped me of that stupid title." I shook my head and used my phone to flip on the movie.

"You're beating yourself up, the crowd isn't going to turn on you. If anything I think they respect you more, Tuck," Josh said. "I'm not the only one that's been waiting for you to explode. You bottle shit up because it's what you think they want from you, that fake sunshine bullshit." Josh rolled those deep brown eyes at me.

"You say the most inspiring things," I scoffed, and the doorbell rang.

"That's pizza, be right back." Josh pushed off the couch.

"My wallet's on the—"

"Shut up, Tuck." He flipped me off and disappeared around the corner of the hallway. The smell of pizza was quick to fill the living room and Josh set it on the coffee table in front of us, grabbing his own piece. "I didn't waste my money on this date for you to starve to death," he grumbled.

"Date?" I laughed nervously and pinned my shoulders back to keep myself from falling apart completely.

Josh ignored my question and stared at me until I grabbed a piece and pressed the warm crust and cheese to my lips. Once he seemed satisfied with how much I'd eaten he went back to his own, melting into the couch and watching the movie.

I spent more time watching him. '*Date*'. He had said it, not me, but what the fuck did he mean, date? My heart was pounding faster in my chest now than it had been on the field, and it felt like my body was a hundred degrees.

"*Date?*" I said out loud that time.

Josh laughed and looked at me. "Will you relax?"

"You can't just drop bombs and go back to eating pizza," I said with shock, badly hidden in my voice.

"I was doing just fine, it's you not eating." He pointed to my half-gone slice of pizza as he grabbed a second one.

"I'm eating," I said, taking another bite. "Eating and melting down here, dude."

"Don't call me dude, I'm not your dude," he corrected me.

"'*Dude*' is your limit?" I teased, the tension between my shoulders starting to relax.

"It is my limit." He turned back to the movie.

"Why?" I pushed, because if I was going to have the term date thrust upon me, I wanted to know why he hated being called dude.

"Cause I'm not your friend, Dean," he said it so easily that it took a moment to register that he called me Dean.

"Isn't the mortal enemies thing getting old? We've made out," I said with a small smile.

"That wasn't making out, one kiss *isn't* making out," Josh said, the slight tinge of red in his cheeks only made me smile more. It was the first time he had been visibly flustered.

"Alright," I said, popping the rest of the crust in my mouth. It filled my stomach and I was starting to feel a little better about everything. How easily Josh had walked me back from the edge was baffling. It was like I didn't even know it was happening until I was situated safely away from the cliff.

He finished his piece and turned on the couch to look at me, closer now I could see the soft trace of freckles that lived beneath the tan tone of his skin and the weather worn scars from life that painted his features.

"I..." He started and stopped.

"Are you nervous?" I laughed and he tossed me a dirty look that made me raise both hands in surrender.

"A little, just *shut up*." He rose to his knees and moved closer to me on the couch and I held my breath. It burned in my lungs as my heart started to race uncomfortably fast.

"What are you—"

"Please shut up?" He cut me off with a pathetic whisper, and I nodded, willing to do whatever he wanted if it meant he was going to take the leap and touch me.

I wanted to know every single violent thought that was floating around in his head at that moment, when he leaned down with his hands resting against his thighs and his lips slightly parted. *Was he scared? Did he want to kiss me, or was he doing it for me?*

"Stay still," he said quietly and shifted on the couch, his hand pressed flat against my chest. He pushed me into the pillows, but it wasn't rough or forceful, it was just direction. I hooked my arms up over the back of the couch, careful not to interrupt him as he lifted off his knees.

"Josh," I whispered, suddenly so unsure that I wasn't forcing him into something he didn't want.

"Dean," he inhaled my name like it was a breath of air he desperately needed, and inched closer. His leg hooked over mine, and he hovered over my lap, staring down at me with a tight, nervous jaw.

"Are you okay?" I asked him. I needed to know. I dug my fingers into the fabric of the couch to hold myself still as he lowered onto my lap. I ground my teeth together as his weight settled comfortably around me, and I wanted to hold him, to kiss him, to tell him how proud I was of him for doing any of this, but I couldn't open my mouth.

I relinquished all the control to him.

His eyes darted to mine from my lips, and I could see how terrified he was, but there was something else there, certainty? Confidence? *Need*.

"Don't move, okay?" The question came out a whisper and I wanted to nod but he told me not to move so I was going to listen and sit still for him while he worked out what he wanted just hoping that the want led to *us*.

I closed my eyes in hopes that it would help him calm down, but he paused.

"Look at me," he said

I opened them, and he was staring at me so nervously that he was practically vibrating. I stifled the anxious laughter that threatened to bubble up from me, knowing that it would scare him away and instead breathed through my nose. The cinnamon kissed every sense as Josh rebuilt his courage and leaned in. His fingers dug into his sweats, pulling the fabric under his intense touch in a feeble attempt to hide his emotions.

Our bottom lips collided in a delicate kiss that wasn't angry or rushed; it was just him and I. Quiet seeped in around us, and it took everything in me not to reach for his sides and pull him deeper into my lap. I wanted his body flush to mine, I wanted my arms around his back. His lips were so feathery and distracting from the tension he was clearly fighting as butterflies ran rampant in my stomach and my heart beat skipped around in my chest like a ping pong ball.

He retreated, and I felt myself follow him, my hips involuntarily lifting from the couch as my body gravitated toward him, daring to steal more from his trembling lip.

Josh paused, briefly letting me take the kiss that I needed, but one that scared him to no end. He licked his bottom lip and settled back on my thighs, his fingers still tangled into the fabric and his shoulders so tense I could snap him in half with the poke of a finger.

"What was that for?" I asked, reeling from the contact, wanting so much more. The couch creaked beneath my grip, and Josh's eyes flicked to my white knuckles with a quiet hum.

I had never been that high in my life.

Everything was quiet except for Josh's heavy breathing and the sting left on my lips from his absence. It was the longest moment of my life, wondering when and if he'd come back for more. He sat so quietly that I wasn't sure he'd even heard me ask. I wanted to put my hands on him, to feel his skin, but without permission,

I was stuck waiting for him to figure out what he wanted, what he needed.

When Josh decided to come back, I think my chest exploded with frantic impatience. It was such a small kiss but I had never been touched like that, with such careful exploration. It was new, but with Josh it felt familiar.

My palms were sweaty against the itchy fabric of the couch, but my mind was lost in the way our lips crushed together, sealing in the air and making me dizzy from the lack of oxygen. I wanted to devour him, to explore every inch of his freckled, scarred skin until I knew it by heart. So it would show up in my dreams on those days he couldn't bear to crawl into my bed.

Suddenly, the meaning of need felt new—loud, and ringing in my ears.

I needed Josh.

A low whine of disappointment slipped out of me—pathetic, but Josh's kiss-bitten lips curled into a tiny smirk.

"Thank you," he said in a tone so soft I couldn't believe that it had left Josh.

"You're welcome?" My voice lifted in a confused question.

"For making it easy," he finished, clearing the air.

"That was easy?" I laughed softly.

He shook his head.

"No, you fucking idiot, that was agony," he said and I knew he didn't mean because of me but because of all the trauma he had just waded through *for* me. "For making the last few days easy, you could have flipped out the moment you found everything out, my mom, the Shores."

I waited patiently for him to get through it.

"Just thank you," he said, swallowing hard. His hand lifted, and I wasn't sure what he was going to do, but his fingers brushed over my bruised knuckles on the couch, a ghost of a touch that barely felt real.

"If all your gratitude feels like that..." I lowered my voice, leaning into his gravity. "Then you're welcome, but—"

Josh's lips curled into a gentle smirk. "Spit it out, Tuck."

"I don't want you to feel like you *have* to show it, ever," I said to him. I wasn't here for the sex or the makeouts. Hell, I didn't even need him to hold my hand or even pretend he liked me around the guys. "That part doesn't have to be necessary," I said to him, trying to get him to understand.

"Our definitions of necessary will never align," he said.

"Isn't that a bad thing?" I sighed and he shook his head, causing his hair to fall loose from the pushed-back style he had combed it into after his shower. I was so nervous to do it wrong that I hadn't noticed Josh leaving out all the instructions on how to love him right.

"No, Tuck," he said. "But we do what we can, when we can. And right now, I'm fucking exhausted and want to go to bed."

"The movie isn't even over," I complained, lifting my hand finally and pointing at the screen. Josh laughed at me.

"Fine, you stay here and finish. I'm going to bed," he said, and I knew it meant that if I didn't come now, he'd spend the night on his side of the room because getting comfortable together was a process.

He climbed out of my lap, leaving nothing but cold, aching loneliness behind, tugging off his sweater at the bottom of the stairs and disappearing out of sight.

"Fine," I grumbled to myself and rolled off the couch, jogging after him. I wasn't ready to be left behind just yet.

He was already tossing his pillow on my bed when I closed the door behind me, and he pointed.

"Against the wall," he said, for what felt like the hundredth time in the last two weeks, and I listened without a shred of hesitation every single time.

I stripped off my clothes down to my boxers and slipped against the wall, pulling my blankets up around my waist and shoving my arm under my pillow to crumple it up under my head. Josh waited until I settled, then climbed in beside me. Only that time when he crawled into the bed, he lay facing me. For weeks, I've slept staring at his back, and having access to the look in his eyes and the sharp lines of his cheeks and jaw was rattling.

It was like a gift.

The silence stretched on for a moment before he asked. "How's your hand?"

I looked down at it and took in the ugly irritation. The red was settling into a dark purple color that would be sprawled across the top of my hand come morning. I had hit Ian harder than I had ever hit anyone in my entire life and was paying the price.

"Fine." I tried to flex my fingers and groaned as the muscles screamed for me to stop. "Okay, not great."

"You have to stretch it out, you're seizing up." Josh held out his hand, and before I could stop him, he was pressing his hand into mine. His fingers were long and soft, with small reminders of his occupation in the form of rough healed blisters. It was a little smaller in size as he pushed against my palm and the whimper that left me was embarrassing as he flexed the fingers to full extension.

"Breathe, Tuck," he warned as he let them fall limp and did it again without warning or the same delicate touch. A thick, painful growl left my throat at the movement, but they went easier that time. You're a baby," he laughed through his own discomfort and pulled his hand away, but I wasn't ready to let go of his touch just yet, tangling my fingers down around his with a stiff curl.

"Please?" I asked as he hesitated. "Give me this, I behaved earlier," I said, I wasn't above begging him for the contact.

He mumbled something under his breath but didn't move as our hands came together and rested in the bed between us, his arm pulled closer to my side of the bed.

"I went to see Ms. Cody," he confessed. "Just so you know."

He listened.

"Thank you," I said to him.

"She's worse than both Cael and Coach," he said, a tightness to his tone no doubt a result of the contact.

"She likes those fancy daisies, the bright colored ones and that sushi place down the block from Hillys," I suggested. "Maybe you can bring her lunch this week."

"You want me to bribe my therapist?" Josh questioned.

"Oh no," I laughed quietly. "I want you to apologize to her because there's no doubt in my mind that you pissed her off with the first sentence you spoke," I teased.

"Fuck you, Tuck," he said but a soft laugh tumbled from him as he shut his eyes. After a beat of silence, his eye crack opened and his brows furrowed as he asked. "Wait, why do you know that about her?"

TUCKER

"Hey Doc." I slid into the chair across from Silas.

"Hand," he said, rifling through his drawer and pulling out his glasses. He looked so much older with them on, but he never wore them outside his office. I set my bruised hand on the table and looked around his office. The walls were bare as always except for his degree and a photo of him and Mrs. Shore.

"Did you ice it yesterday?" He asked me and I nodded, I did for a bit, but I got a little distracted by the whole Josh-in-my-lap moment. "Are you lying to me?" He looked up from my hand and narrowed his grey on me.

"Not for long," I admitted. "Are *you* lying to *me*?" I asked after a beat of silence.

Silas looked up from my hand again, this time his expression was puzzled but defensive. "About what, Tucker?" he challenged with his eyebrow raised. It was apparent that he didn't have the patience to deal with my shit today but I was going to lay it out anyways.

"Why didn't you tell anyone you and Josh were brothers?" I asked, not cutting corners.

"He told you," Silas said as he set my hand down, he rose from his chair and wandered across his office to the cupboards. He pulled out a box and brought disinfectant, and a wrap back to the desk.

"Everything," I said as Silas popped the cap on the bottle, pressing the opening to a cloth with a tight jaw.

"You did it," Silas smiled when he looked up at me, but that only led to further confusion. "You figured out what he needed."

"I wouldn't go that far," I chuckled, but it felt good to have the effort recognized.

"He threatened to burn down my house when I suggested we tell my mother that we know, I told her anyway, you should have seen that fight," Silas said, swallowing tightly. "If he told you out of his own free will... It's a step in the right direction.

"It wasn't necessarily out of his own free will," I sighed.

"What does that mean?" He asked.

"It means we went to Lorette, his mom called him, and he needed a ride, so I took him. She's..." I trailed off, the pit in my stomach growing with every passing moment, thinking about that lock on his room.

"A monster," Silas finished for me. "She's sick. I know that much. I remember the day I showed up there to help him, she thought I was there for her. She gave me a list of prices before the door had even fully opened."

"Have you been inside?" I asked him.

"Josh stopped me before I could get inside," Silas sighed, the grey hair was more prominent in his exhausted state, like he had aged ten years from the mention of her.

"There's a lock...locks..." I said, counting them in my head. "On the outside of his old bedroom door. And scratch marks," I said, my voice getting quiet. "She locked him in there."

"Are you sure?" He asked me and I nodded.

"She really messed him up." I looked up from the table and met Silas' grey stare.

"He's good at hiding it with his anger, but he's..."

"Yeah, I only know the pieces I was able to string together through my father's transactions," Silas said.

"She still loves him, you know, your father. It seems like that's why she resents Josh so much, because she thinks he ruined it for her." My voice cracked at the thought of anyone treating Josh in such a disgusting way.

"She was sick, Dean. Really sick. She still is. I can't change the mistakes my father made. I can't rewrite the past to save him from what he is today, but I'll work harder to give him the life he was meant to have," Silas said, and I believed him. "Bringing him here was a fight. He would have rather gone anywhere else."

"But after Ian," I said with a sigh.

"He told you *everything* about Ian?" Silas leaned forward.

"He told me the truth about Ian," I corrected him. "He attacked him, he..." I paused, unsure if it was even something I should be sharing, but I needed Silas's help. "Ian raped Josh that day in the showers, it's why he fought back so hard. That's why he nearly killed him."

"Fuck." Silas slumped back in his chair and ran his hands through his hair. "I knew it was bad, that Ian had done something...he told me and the council it was just a fight, that Ian pushed him too far and the two went at it."

"Did anyone look at Josh after the fight? Did he go to the hospital?" I asked Silas who seemed caught off guard from the question. He rose from his desk to his filing cabinet and tugged it open in silence, digging through it until he pulled out a light blue folder. He flipped through it, each passing moment the lack of noise ate at my resolve.

"He did," Silas finally said. "The Lorette team reported a few bruises, cuts, but nothing serious. But in his file, a week before the fight, there's something that was added to his file. It's in a different pen..." Silas grumbled under his breath. "It says he suffered a concussion in practice when he was struck by a ball."

He pushed me, I hit the shower wall and when I woke up...

"It wasn't a ball," I said. "He told me Ian shoved him and he hit his head on the tiles." He's got a scar," I said, lifting my other hand to my eyebrow. "It's fresh, still pink. It can only be a few months old at most."

"Lorette is covering for Ian." Silas slammed the drawer closed and threw Josh's folder on his desk sending the papers scattering across. His school picture stared up at me from the desk, he was still sporting a dark bruise under his right eye from the fight and his eyes were so dark that the iris were lost in a sea of black.

"That's why you attacked him," Silas said, leaning over the table to look me in the eye. "What did Ian say to you?"

"It doesn't matter." I shook my head.

"Everything matters now, every single detail. We aren't going to get rid of him unless I know exactly what happened, to you, to Josh." Silas's arms flexed tightly; he was trying not to get worked up, but I could see it all over his face.

"Josh was alright lying that day. What makes you think he'll help now?" I asked him.

"You," Silas said plainly and looked up at me. "What did Ian say to you?"

I contemplated lying, but all I wanted to do was get Josh free of this. "He said that Logan's favorite date spot was the shower room," I said. "I wasn't thinking, I just... I swung."

"You didn't hit him hard enough," Silas said instantly as he sank into his chair again, his shoulders relaxing a touch.

"What do we do now?" I asked Silas, trying not to smile at his quiet pride for my out-of-character moment of violence.

"If I take this to the committee again. The proof is clear if I can get photos of the scar, combined with the tampered medical records. The problem is I need Josh to testify," Silas explained. "It's going to be a pain in the ass anyways because coming back months later with new information and a changed story. They probably won't believe him—not this long after, not with the story changed."

"I don't want to put him through that," I said. *I can't, I won't.* That searing hot wave of protectiveness washed up over my chest, and there was nothing I could do to stop it. I just had to let it pull me below the surface.

"If we don't, Ian just gets to go on, he'll be back on the field by season end... You can't fight him every time he makes a sleazy remark," Silas said.

"I can try," I argued, but he wasn't impressed by that. "This, combined with your family secret, it's too much. We just got him working with the team... it'll disrupt everything."

"I wanted to go to my Grandfather, to deal with it directly before the news gets wind of it," he said. "It's going to blow up in our faces if they find it."

"Vultures," I agreed with him.

"Exactly, but Josh is confident he can keep it quiet until the season is over," Silas said, I hissed as he pressed the cloth to the open cuts embedded between my knuckles. "Don't hit people if you can't handle antiseptic, Tucker," he grumbled.

"Doc, you and I both know that he can't keep it quiet, not now..." I ground my teeth together in frustration. "They're going to dig now, for anything they can find. I shut them down too hard...if anything comes out. It'll be my fault," I said with a grimace as he cleaned another cut.

"You're stupid, Golden Boy, but you aren't that stupid," Silas groaned and pulled off his glasses.

"They don't have a story anymore, Silas," I said, deliberately using his real name. He huffed out a frustrated sigh, but it meant that I was serious; this wasn't a joke to me. "I was their story, *gay captain destroys winning team.*" I winced as he wrapped my hand tightly in the bandage.

"You still have time to chase all those dreams—if you don't lose focus on what's really important," he warned. "Entertaining the idea that if the story breaks on Josh and my family, it's your fault because they didn't have a better story is stupid, it's a notion. It's your anxiety talking, you're stacking a bunch of 'what ifs' and preparing for a war that might not come."

"And if it does?" I questioned. "What then?"

"Can I ask you a question?" Silas said, and I nodded. "Are you sure about this?" He asked me after a long moment.

"About what?" I asked, the confusion palpable.

"It wasn't your fault that day," he said. "I know that you think Cael getting in that car, reaching that point, was something you did in your relationship. But he was a ticking time bomb."

"Yeah, and I lit the fuse," I scoffed.

"Maybe you did, maybe it was already lit... Josh is a different kind of doomsday clock Dean, just make sure that you're ready for it when the time comes because Cael had everyone to fall back on. Josh has no one." He looked at me, really wanting what he had just said to sink in.

"Josh has me," I said without missing a beat.

A small smile crept over his lips, nodding once. "Alright, then we handle it."

"Together," I said.

Silas tapped his fingers to his chest gently.

"Two steps at a time."

TUCKER

A three game suspension, a week of exhausting classes later, and lunch everyday that week with Riona had worn me out. She watched my every move and I hated every second of it but I'd been taking the time to get in one meal and she enjoyed watching old baseball tapes with me so it wasn't awful. She never asked me invasive questions, she let me lead the conversation and I usually felt better after.

But the week had been a lot, and now Jensen was dragging me up the steps of Delta. "Man, I don't wanna be here." I shook my head.

"Yeah, well, you've spent way, *way*, too much time in your bed lately, it's time to have some fun." He argued, slapping his hand against my shoulder.

It wasn't the bed keeping me in my room, it was Josh. I wanted to say but kept my mouth shut. After the talk with Silas, I had been keeping him close. I didn't care that I looked like a lost dog following him around. I didn't want him out of my sight, not even for a second.

It had become increasingly apparent that my feelings for Josh were snowballing into something bigger. Every time I saw him,

it bettered my mood. I had caught myself complaining that his sweaters were too small, I just wanted to tuck down inside and lose myself in the smell. The next morning, he left his bottle of cologne out in the open, clearly on purpose, and I sprayed my favorite sweater with it before tugging it on and leaving for class.

My feelings for Josh weren't like the ones I'd had for Cael—those burned hot when we were together, but cooled easily when we were apart. Being apart from Josh felt like torture.

"Surprise!" Delta erupted into cheers and hollering as the lights flickered on and my eyes adjusted to the darkness. *What the hell?*

Everyone was standing in front of me in an assortment of jerseys, sweaters and t-shirts, their hats backwards on their heads and big smiles on their faces. Every single person in the room was dressed like...me.

"We wanted to congratulate you!" Zoey squealed. I should have known that she was behind the party. Anytime there was a theme to be had, Zoey made sure it happened.

"And the theme is?..." I looked around at everyone with an awkward smile on my face.

"You!" Ella laughed, she was tucked into Arlo's side, wearing a home jersey to match his away one.

"Wow," I looked around again, I couldn't believe they had gone out of their way to do something so grand for me. My cheeks hurt from smiling as Zoey dragged me through the house toward the kitchen. Everyone convened around the island as Van lifted Zoey to the counter behind him.

Cael appeared on my left with Clementine—wearing my Halloween costume... I looked him up and down, scowling. "Is that my toga?"

"It's a blanket and you left it in my room," he shrugged. Clementine was wearing a sweater and sweats with her hair tucked behind her ears and a hat over her hair. She scrunched up her nose when I winked at her.

"Congratulations," she whispered as Cael went to get her a drink. "You did good the other day, with the press. The whispers and gossip have subsided, at least in my neck of the woods."

"Thank you for asking questions that didn't involve my... well, you know," I said at a loss for words.

"You didn't need my help, Dean. You just need a little more faith in yourself, and pride... definitely more pride." She took the glass from Cael as he returned, kissing her on the cheek in passing before he grabbed me by the face and kissed me without consent or warning.

"Cael, come on!" I shoved him off, laughing.

"Congrats, big boy." He backed off, scooping Clem up in his arms and whispering something in her ear before setting her back on her feet. "Dancing, we should all be dancing!"

"How is it possible that you're more obnoxious, sober?" Arlo groaned but conceded when Ella pouted.

"Two against one!" Cael pointed to Ella's sad bottom lip with a wicked grin.

Van helped Zoey from the counter, kissing her gently before the five of them disappeared into the crowd, leaving Van and me to field nonsense from the team. But something felt off, missing.

"Did Logan come?" I asked Van.

He pulled off his hat and smoothed out his hair with his hands as he shook his head. "I tried to get him to, but he said he had too much studying to do."

"Studying?" I scowled. "He did that all morning…"

"How's he doing?" Van asked me, his voice so quiet in comparison to the sounds of the party as Cael took over the sound system and started blasting TLC.

"It's Josh, he's fine, I think… I don't think he would tell me even if I asked." I took the cup that Van held out for me and sniffed it before scowling at the warm whiskey scent. I set it on the counter, and he eyed me uncomfortably.

"So why are you so on edge?" Van asked and took a swig of his beer.

"Me? I'm not, I'm fine—" I said and was cut off by laughter.

"You're not fine, the second you realized he wasn't here you clammed up and now you're being weird," Van said, pointing at my drink. "You never say no to whiskey," he noted.

"Don't therapist me, we're at a party," I said to him and rolled my eyes.

"Be honest, then, what's got you so wound up?" He asked, leaning across the shitty island on his elbows. He stared at me for a long while, I knew he wanted answers about everything: baseball, Riona, my parents…

"I haven't heard from them." I shrugged.

Van's face scrunched up momentarily as he tried to figure out who I meant, but it wasn't long before he nodded softly. "Your parents."

"Yeah, I expected some blow up but it's just silence and it feels like I'm walking on glass, especially at school when I could run into Dad anywhere," I said. "I googled other schools' baseball programs, Van," I added and he grimaced.

"Bad, bad." Van swallowed down the rest of his beer and circled the island. "If you haven't seen your dad in a week, good chance he's avoiding you too. You take three classes in his building," he said.

"Is that supposed to be advice?" I said, with a defeated huff.

"No, it's just the reality of the situation, your parents never understood your value, Tucker. They saw you as a trophy, maybe it's a good thing to be free of them, of that." Van smiled at me, his brown eyes soft and understanding.

"It doesn't feel like a good thing, I feel guilty," I confessed.

"For what?" Van asked, and I knew I had walked into a trap.

I stared at him, all the answers on the tip of my tongue and knowing that he had a rebuttal for every single one of them. I was acutely aware of how stupid I sounded, but I just couldn't get my brain to follow my heart. Logically, everything I had done was warfare in their eyes, refusing their help, turning my back on my blood because I was *sick*. Emotionally, I felt free, like I could finally just be who I wanted without the fear of upsetting my family. But the guilt sat between those things, eating away at my logic and happiness until all that was left was shame and guilt.

"I see the gears turning, Tucker, but you aren't going to come up with something that outweighs your heart. There's pure stupidity in letting them make you feel guilty for who you are. You're not hurting anyone by loving men. And Dean—you're not hurting Cael..." Van said, his hand cupping my shoulder and his fingers digging into the muscle. "...By loving Logan, if that's what you need, what you want..." he added quietly, and before I could argue, Zoey barreled into the kitchen.

"Come dance!" She screamed at the two of us over the music and dragged us from the kitchen. Her tiny hand pulled me along, but all I could think about was Van's last words. Loving Logan. Did I? Was that what this was? Maybe I didn't argue because there was nothing to disagree about...

I had always thought I loved Cael, and maybe I did, for what our love could be; but it was never whatever this was. When Cael was out of sight, he was almost always out of mind. But without Josh here, by my side, it felt cold. Like I was exposed to the elements, to the rumors and gossip.

Cael loved me in the dark, where the shadows couldn't reach.

And at the time, that was what I needed, what I demanded of him, but eventually the darkness just became the shadows. The darkness became toxic, suffocating. It was a box of my own design, and I had nearly killed Cael by locking him inside with me.

Josh had taken a stand, he wasn't going to be pushed around. Not by me, not by anyone.

He loved me in the light.

Not caring about the shadows that bit into his skin as he stood by my side, protecting me with his own flesh and blood. The music was so loud, but somehow I could still hear my heartbeat in my ears as I thought about him. All the times he had stepped in front of me, taken care of me at the expense of himself.

What the hell was I doing?

"I'll be back," I yelled at the group over the music and darted from the house. I jogged all the way up the hill, my feet digging into the path and my muscles aching from the unexpected activity. I'd never run so fast, and my lungs begged for reprieve as I leapt up the backstairs into the nest.

"Josh!" I called out to him a few times as I searched the main floor. I barely made it up the stairs to our room, finding him with his headphones on sitting in our bed staring at his textbook with a concentrated look on his dumb, handsome face.

"Why the hell are you so out of breath?" He pulled off his headphones and gave me a dirty look as I dropped to my knees beside the bed. "Tuck, I have too much work to do for you to have one of your dramatic hissy fits."

"Not a hissy fit," I said, pressing my hands flat against the messy comforter inches from his leg. My fingers itched to feel him, but this would have to do. "Van said something to me tonight," I said, and Josh raised an eyebrow.

"He gets too much air to his brain being that tall. Whatever he said is either a lie or altitude sickness." Josh shut his textbook at his feet and gave me his full attention.

"He said I'm not hurting anyone by loving men, that..." I stumbled over my words, not sure if I wanted to confess everything. I clenched my fingers in the fabric, and his eyes darted down to them. "That I shouldn't feel guilty about who I am and... I just," I stopped again.

That time Josh reached out as I dropped my gaze from his, and I could feel him counting in his head as he wrapped his fingers into my hair and tugged my head back, our eyes meeting.

"Spit it out," he ordered, but it was encouraging and warm. *Wanting*.

"I like you, I like this... I like us."

Josh laughed, his eyebrow raising. "What the hell are you talking about?"

"I want this, I want...us." I waved my hand between the two of us, and Josh stared at me like I was an idiot.

"One make out and you're on your knees, Tuck?" He teased.

"Begging," I said without hesitation.

"Begging for what exactly?" Josh smiled, his sharp teeth exposed at the corners of his pretty mouth. When he smiled at me like that, it made me feel alive, like being struck by lightning.

"I want to be your boyfriend, you insufferable asshole!" I blurted out in the most unromantic way I could think of.

"Correction, one make out and you want monogamy," Josh hummed, his smile never budging.

"Can you stop teasing me for two minutes?" I pleaded with him.

"There's no fun in that, Tuck. I kind of enjoy you being the nervous one for once," Josh said. His dark curls licked at his tan neck, and I wanted to memorize the way each one twisted with the pad of my fingers.

"I just want a label," I practically whined. I had spent the better half of my teenage years until now just hiding, not wanting labels or to have the attention on me. But with Josh, I wanted it, I wanted everyone to know what he meant to me.

"You want a label?" He smiled, still perched so gently on the bed as he watched me with his sable eyes. "Tell me why?" He insisted.

"Because..." I stopped, inhaling as much air as I could to slow down my racing heart. "I don't want to hide us, to hide this."

"And what's this?" Josh waved his hand between us.

"You just want me to say it, to embarrass myself some more."

"Maybe," Josh smirked. "Maybe I like the look of Dean Tucker on his knees, begging me to be his."

"See!" I raised my voice. "You know what I want."

"Of course I do, you're not subtle, Tuck." He let go of a soft, quiet laugh that I wanted to chase around like a dog after a bone. "But what I want is to hear you say it. What do *you* want?"

"I want you to be my boyfriend, I want to hold your hand in public if you'll let me, and I want to tell the guys," I confessed. I wanted what Cael described that day at the cabin: I wanted someone to celebrate with, to come back to the Nest with. I wanted an Ella, a Clementine... "I want you to be mine."

"That's all?" Josh's eyebrow arched.

"That's all," I confirmed, and he nodded his head softly at me.

"If that's what you want," he said quietly. "It's what I want."

I wasn't expecting him to give in that way; so easily and without conditions.

"Will you kiss me?" I asked him. He blinked softly, almost as if he had missed it. "It's necessary," I added when he didn't move.

"Yeah, Tuck," Josh said, slipping from the bed and settling so our knees were touching the floor. "I'll kiss you."

I watched as he breathed in, pushing away every single nightmare and letting me surround him as our lips pressed together. I kept my hands back, hovering but never touching as the thudding of our combined heartbeat grew louder with every shared breath.

Josh's lips were soft, pillowy against mine and for a split second, just like every time before, it was just us. The way his hair tickled my forehead and the smell of his body wash filled my nose. My fingers itched for contact, and despite the way my body fought against it, I tensed as he lifted his hand and brushed into my hair. The curls tangled in his grip as he twisted to keep himself from losing control.

Everything about Joshua Logan had a dizzying effect that I couldn't shake.

He cleared his throat as he pulled away to look at me. "Feel better?" He asked me.

"I like that," I said gently, and raised my hand to hover over his as he untangled his fingers from my hair. "Feels good."

"You like having your hair pulled?" Josh chuckled, the feeling less overwhelming than every second of the conversation we had just had. It felt almost silly to be discussing my turn-ons.

"I guess so." I opened my eyes and sighed, still so out of breath but now for a different reason.

"You never answered me earlier. Why were you out of breath?" Josh asked me, falling back against the bed frame, his legs stretching out around mine.

"I ran here," I said.

I could hear the word roll off his tongue, *'dramatic.'*

"Where did you run from?" Josh scowled at me.

"Delta." I shrugged, drinking Josh in, his lips were red from our kiss and his pupils were massive.

"You ran all the way up that hill to tell me that?" He scoffed.

"I did."

"That's a steep hill."

"It is."

"That's your most impressive hissy fit to date," Josh teased and offered me a small smile.

"Why aren't you at Delta, anyway?" I asked. "Would have made this all a lot less sweaty if I didn't have to go for a jog," I slid back on the floor and stripped from the damp sweater and shirt. It stuck to my skin and made me feel suffocated.

Josh traced his eyes up from the floor as I stood, the soft expanse of my stomach hardened only with each breath I took. I turned away from him and shoved my hand into the closet, tossing the dirty fabric in the bin and grabbing a clean shirt.

"Walking into Delta is a death sentence, Tuck," Josh said as I pulled it over my head.

"How?" I asked.

Josh scowled. "You're handsome, but sometimes you're an idiot. They don't want me there, they still see the enemy," he said, running his hands through his hair just to give them something to do.

"Because you act like you're the enemy. You tell them constantly how much you don't want to be here," I reminded him.

"Well, it's true," he said.

I walked over to Josh and squatted down on the balls of my feet. "If you want the guys to see you as a teammate, you need to start acting like one."

"By attending frat parties?" Josh scoffed. "No."

"Is it a recovery thing? If it is, say it and I'll drop it," I asked, my fingers digging into the fabric of my jeans. I was resisting the urge to make contact, I just wanted to touch him all the time but was constantly waiting for his go ahead.

"It's not that. I can be around drunk people, Tuck." Josh made the mistake of looking away from me, and he grumbled something under his breath like a little kid. "There's just a lot of people...and not a lot of space."

I smiled at him.

"What, Tuck..." Josh sighed.

"Coach tells me all the time the reason I play first base is because I take up space," I said.

"Yeah, because you're the size of a Mack truck, it's unnatural." Josh rolled his eyes, but I watched as they raked over my form.

"Why don't you let me make the space? all you have to do is stay close." I held out my hand to him and he stared at it. "I used to love those parties, but I was going out of my mind down there without you. Don't make me go back alone."

He met my hopeful gaze while I quietly begged him not to say no to me.

"Fine," he said begrudgingly and pressed his hand into mine.

LOGAN

Everything about Delta made my skin crawl. Everyone was all over each other, and the deeper we went, the worse it got. Dean kept his promise—his large body parting the sea of people as everyone instinctively moved aside. I had tried to let go of his hand when we climbed the steps to the party, but he gave me the dirtiest look he was capable of and I surrendered to his grip.

It was weird being led through the sea of bodies because, despite what my previous assumptions of how tonight would have gone were, none of them even cared I was there. There was a group of them in the backyard playing beer pong. Cael and Clementine were clearly losing because Clementine's cheeks were flushed red as she dropped the second-to-last cup back on the table and made a face like she might be sick.

"It's okay, at least you're pretty," Cael teased, cupping her face as we rounded the table.

When Dean finally let go of my hand, I didn't expect to feel the loss in my bones—but it hit me like a shiver. Luckily he didn't notice, no one did, they were too busy cheering Ella on as she stepped back and bounced another ball across the sticky table top into the last cup on the other end. Dean stood close enough to

me that his shoulder crossed over my back but he gave me room to breathe.

"Nice of you to join us," Van said from across the table.

"He's relentless," I grumbled, not looking back at Dean, who was talking to someone else.

"You should have been down here anyway," Cael added as Clementine chugged the last cup. "Alright, Plum, that's uh..." he laughed and cleaned the beer that dripped down her chin with his shirt. He smiled at her like there was no one else in the world, and it was suddenly pretty clear why he was willing to go nuclear over her love. It was enough to make me want to gag. "No more beer pong..." he said to Ella between peals of laughter.

"Do you play?" Ella turned on me in her black tank top and jeans. Her hair was pulled up in a bun and in the hazy blue lights that shone off the surface of the pool her scar looked deeper, meaner than it had before.

I had never played, I had never been asked if I did.

Everyone stared at me, waiting for an answer.

I thought about lying, I could refuse to play if she asked next.

"I've never played," I said honestly and the truth coming out of my mouth felt weird and left me oddly exposed to their ridicule.

"Perfect, means I'll kick your ass easier," she said, nudging Zoey.

"I never agreed to play." I shook my head. "I don't drink." I shrugged.

"But he does." Zoey pointed to Dean behind me.

"Half of us don't drink anymore, it's why we pick partners," Ella added as Dean clued into the conversation. "Dean, will you drink for Josh?"

"Sure." He caved instantly, flashing her a dopey grin.

"Just like that?" I grumbled at him.

"Yeah, so…" Dean scratched the back of his neck and turned his face away from Ella so he was closer to my ear. "We don't really ever say no."

"What?" I laughed and looked over at Ella.

"Yeah, we don't say no to Ella." Dean swallowed hard and it was then I realized he was serious.

"Oh." I turned to look at her and she smiled at me. "Why don't we say no to you?" I asked the blonde and she started to laugh.

"You can say no to me." She furrowed her brows and scoffed. "These idiots are cowards."

"Hey!" A chorus of whines broke out among them, and Ella glared at them into silence.

"Now, of course, if you do say no, it just proves you are scared of me." She was challenging me, seeing how far she could push before I caved to her. I enjoyed the fire that she provided, it was refreshing. She didn't treat me like I was made of glass or like I was some irredeemable asshole.

"One punch," I said, stepping up to the table. "You caught me off guard—I deserved it. But I'm not scared of you."

"Prove it," she hummed and leaned over the table at me.

"One game." I nodded.

"One bet," she added.

"Fine," I said, and everyone groaned. I cursed and stared around at them. "What now?"

"Don't make bets with Ella," Dean muttered under his breath.

"You're such a coward," I said, sighing. "What's the bet?"

"If you win, I'll take your dinner chores for the next week," she offered, and I agreed. "If I win, we'll pull out *Somebody to Love by Queen*." A sick, proud smile spread across her face as Dean lunged at the table.

"No!" He warned, and she nodded. "Absolutely not!"

"Don't let him take that bet," Jensen whined with a bottle to his lips.

Van started to laugh, and before Cael could catch on to what was happening I was agreeing to the bet. I had no idea what I was agreeing to, but the reaction from the players that hovered around the table was worth playing to find out.

"You have to win," Dean warned. "You cannot let her pull out that CD."

"What are you so worked up about?" I asked him and he swallowed tightly.

"Just win, please." He looked over at Van, Jensen and Cael who also looked nervous.

I nodded my path to the other end of the table cleared as Dean walked in front of me and bodies moved out of his way. I cleared my throat. "What are the rules?" I asked Ella.

"No elbow over the table, bounce shots are two drinks but can be swatted, if you sink a ball, you get to throw again," she said simply.

"I think I can handle that."

The concept of it wasn't hard to wrap my head around, it was more the reason why they found so much entertainment in it. They genuinely got more riled up about a silly party game then they did our baseball games most of the time and I just didn't see the point.

"Virgins throw first." Zoey chucked me the ball with a smile on her face.

"You wound me, Novak." I offered her a smile back, one that wasn't laced with malice or discontent. It was genuine, and Dean noticed because he huffed playfully beside me. "Yeah, yeah," I grumbled under my breath. I lined up the cups in my sightline, gauging the weight of the ball in my hand and finding it held nothing. I arched my fingers and chucked the ball, sailing it into the front cup with ease.

Ella narrowed her eyes on me.

"Beginners' luck," I said as Dean threw and missed. Zoey chugged back whatever was in the cups like she didn't weigh a hundred pounds soaking wet and chucked the cup into the grass.

Ella also didn't miss when she threw back, and I wasn't fast enough to catch the bounce as it skipped into one of the back cups. "Pay attention, Tuck," I warned him.

He laughed, emptying one cup into the other and drinking it all down in one breath. I watched him in disgusted pride as he stomached the beer with a smile and set the cups at the base of the table.

"What?" he said, and I cursed the affectionate wave of warmth that threatened to carry me out to sea. The sight of him alone was enough to swallow down an unfamiliar urge, one that, surprisingly and for the first time in my entire life, wasn't weighed down by the shackles of my trauma.

"Nothing." I shook my head. "You're disgusting," I said instead and turned back to the game. Ella was competitive; that much was apparent, the way she played beer pong was like an Olympic athlete chasing the gold medal. Why? I couldn't figure out, but it made it abundantly clear how she had wrapped Arlo around her finger.

The game continued, and Ella and I went cup for cup the entire time until only two remained on the table. Everyone at the party seemed to be on the grass surrounding us, Dean remained a barrier and seemed to grow impossibly large to keep people from creeping too close. Thoughts of thanking him later crept into my mind, causing unusual but welcome heat to swell at my fingertips around the ball.

"This is insane," Cael scoffed, his arms slung around Clementine's shoulders and his chin resting on the top of her head.

"No one has ever beaten her," Jensen said, and Ella practically lunged at him.

"Games not over, shit for brains." Zoey pointed at him, her body swaying a little. Van laughed and pushed her hand down.

"How many Jensens' do you see right now?" He asked her, and she narrowed her eyes at him.

"At least three." She giggled and hiccupped all at once.

"End this game so I can bring my girl home, Miele," Van said, standing behind Zoey to keep her steady.

I threw first, the ball soaring through the air but I could tell the second it left my fingers that I had pushed too hard and the ball missed the cup by an inch. Ella smiled, whether or not she thought I threw the game she didn't care. She didn't wait to throw hers the second Dean missed his and her ball dropped into the cup with a satisfying pop.

"Record stands," Ella smiled at Cael, who just sighed. "It was a valiant effort," she wandered over to him and slapped his cheek before he could move away. He clipped his teeth at her as she passed and let go of Clementine. "Now…"

"No!" Van, Jensen, Cael and Dean all chimed up in protest.

"A bet was made!" She hollered with a bright smile on her face, raising her arms to hush them. "A bet must be fulfilled!"

"I'm not doing it, he didn't even know what he was betting!" Van argued, leaving Zoey's side but linking his hand into hers and pulling her through the rowdy crowd.

"The people want blood," Ella laughed as everyone around them cheered and screamed. It was like they had been possessed.

"What the hell is going on?" I asked, but Dean was glaring at Ella, his ears bright red.

"Over the summer ,we spent a lot of time up at the cabin," Ella said, she was speaking to me but staring at Dean with mischief twisted up in all her features. "One night the boys got *real* drunk and went full 'Magic Mike'," Ella started to laugh as she turned to me. "It's hilarious the things they'll do with a little whiskey and *Queen*."

"I'm starting to think I won this bet," I said, still a little confused, but her enjoyment of their embarrassment was enough to spark a lifetime of intrigue.

Ella pushed everyone back as Dean, Van, Cael, Jensen, and a few other guys huddled in a circle, bickering back and forth. What they were fighting over was a mystery as Ella patted the grass beside her. "Sit," she said.

I sat, leaving a good distance between us, and watched on as the rest of the crowd parted for them to line up in the grass. *Somebody to Love by Queen* flowed out of the speakers into the backyard and everyone started to cheer.

They were standing there like a really badly staged boy band, each of them either drunk or embarrassed beyond belief. All at once, they started to move in unison, dancing like they had rehearsed the movements for weeks. I watched on in horror as they sang the lyrics out of tune and took turns one-upping each other with ridiculous dance moves.

Cael dropped to the ground, and in a surprising turn of events, was insanely good at the worm as he ground his body into the grass, his hips surging forward slowly enough to make Clementine dog whistle at him from behind us.

"Wait, you said they were drunk?" I turned to Ella who was beaming with pride and laughing so hard her cheeks were red. "Cael hasn't had a drop of alcohol since the accident," I said.

"Oh he did it stone cold sober the first time, it was his idea!" Ella said, stopping mid sentence to scream as they fell into line again, shuffling their feet and swaying their hips.

"What the fuck?" I couldn't help but smile as the chorus dropped into the thrumming beat of the bridge and they all spun to put their backs to us. "How long did it take them to come up with this?" I asked her over the music.

"Nevermind that, this is the best part!" She hollered back and pointed. "Watch!"

"Find me somebody to love," the music echoed over the grass, and Jensen turned around on his heel, smoothly tearing his shirt over his head and throwing it into the crowd.

"Find me somebody to love," it swelled as the words repeated, each time one of the boys turning around and stripping from their shirts as if they weren't being watched by the entire baseball team and then some.

"Find me somebody to love," Cael dropped to his knees, tearing his shirt in half like an animal and chucking it at Clementine.

"Can anybody find me..." Dean was the last to turn, his eyes darting over to mine. At first it had looked like none of them wanted to be there, but it was clear that they were having way too much fun with the attention. *"Somebody to love..."*

The black shirt stretched over his shoulders, exposing every muscle in his body and the soft expanse of his stomach. Dean was big—but not all sharp lines and six-pack abs like some of the others. He was strong, sure, but soft in places too. Like someone who lifted heavy but still ate what he wanted and actually enjoyed life.. He was quite simply just large. His pants were dangerously low on his hips and my eyes were drawn down for a split second before he decided he was going to make the show of affection I never asked for and he chucked the shirt in my direction.

Ella looked down at the fabric in my lap and smirked.

"Welcome to the family," she said, smirking, before turning back to watch the chaos.

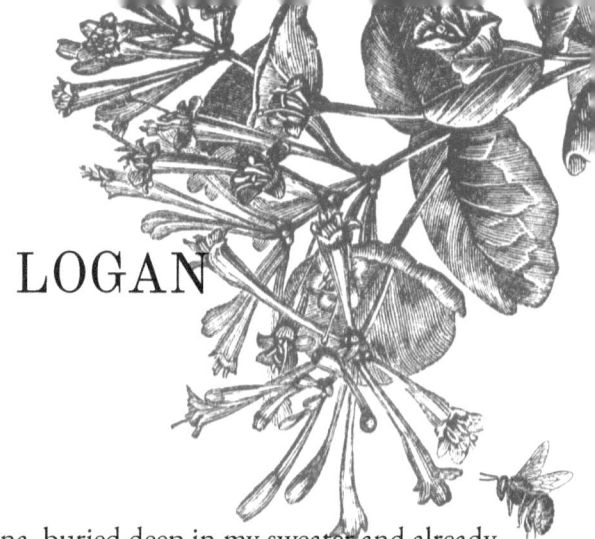

LOGAN

I sat across from Riona, buried deep in my sweater and already on the defensive. The flowers I brought her sat on her desk behind her and just like Dean had predicted it had softened her a little. We were doing okay until the back half of the appointment when she had asked me about my mother and whether she knew it or not, she had hit a sore spot.

"I don't know, it's my mom, she's always there. Like it or not," I shrugged and Riona stared at me like I had six heads. "Aren't you supposed to be like… impartial or something?"

"Who told you that?" She crossed her legs and the fabric of her brown dress pants stretched up enough to show a tattoo on her ankle of a moth.

"Why a moth?" I asked her and her blue eyes dragged down to her ankle with a scowl. "Why not a butterfly—something pretty?"

"Life isn't pretty, Josh. Moth's can symbolize a lot of things," she said, her eyes lifting to meet mine. "Cycle of life, rebirth. I got mine because I wanted to remember to chase the light, my life was dark for a long time, my head in the sand avoiding the hard truths of my failing marriage and my relationship with my daughter. I chase the light, like a moth."

I pressed my lips together and nodded. I hadn't wanted to admit that sometimes I lacked the ability to believe that happy people have hard lives. My brain couldn't wrap around the idea that someone could overcome hardship and just move on. I constantly felt like I was ankle-deep in setting concrete, jealous of the people walking past while I silently screamed for help.

"Your relationship with your mother is difficult?" She asked again.

"Yeah." I nodded, feeling at ease to explain more. "She's an addict," I said.

"You're Cael's sponsor, what was your vice?" She asked me and I narrowed my eyes on her. "You didn't think he kept that secret from everyone did you?" She smiled. "He's my nephew, therapy or not, I'm the one that knows all the things he can't tell his dad."

"It's still weird that you're Cael's therapist," I said.

"I'm not, he comes up here to spend time with me, not for therapy, not anymore," she said, her blonde hair brushed over her shoulders and she leaned back in her seat. "Who do you talk to? Outside of this room?"

I diverted my eyes to the massive windows that lined her office, the view of the diamond beautiful from this high. "Those must get broken a lot," I noted and she turned to see what I was looking at.

"Nope," she said simply. "They're out of reach from anyone, they've never even been touched by a ball. You're avoiding the question again," she said, so easily she swung the bat back to the harder conversations.

"Tucker." I swallowed. It felt weird saying his name out loud, like someone was going to pop out and point their finger at me with laughter. Like I was some joke or the team clown, there simply for entertainment purposes. "Why do you look surprised?"

"I just wasn't expecting it, Dean is…" she paused, looking for the words, but I had them, listed in permanent marker on the walls of my broken heart.

A sunshower, a golden retriever puppy, mango and sugar, he was electricity in the simplest form. He was mine.

"Too happy for me?" I finished her sentence.

"You are a little rough, Josh." Her eyebrow rose and she gave me a sympathetic smile. "What do you and Dean talk about?"

Everything.

"Nothing." I dismissed her. "School, baseball…"

"What about your mother, do you talk about her?" Riona asked.

"Sometimes." I chewed the inside of my cheek raw.

"Is it hard to be around her when she's using?" She stayed in her relaxed state and let me come to her with each question.

"Yeah." I nodded, just trying to keep some bolting from the office out of fear that Riona might see past everything and into the real issues.

"Do you remember when she started?" She asked, I knew what she was doing. She was all but writing it out on a white board for me to follow. She was digging into my mother's past to find out why my childhood was such a hang up. She wanted to know why I avoided the topic, I wasn't sure I was ready to explain the ins and outs but Riona didn't nudge when she asked, she shoved with all her strength until the levee broke.

"Nothing I say in here leaves right?" I asked her.

"It's a conversation between us, always. Unless I believe you're going to harm yourself, then I have a duty to you and the school to help whether or not you agree with it. Do you understand?" She asked me.

"Yeah." I swallowed the cotton ball in my throat and tried speaking again. "She started using after I was born, my... My biological father is a piece of work and she never believed that he abandoned us because of her. She blamed me for everything and what I think started as heartbreak turned into resentment. It festered and she got mean."

"Mean how?" Riona asked.

I rolled my shoulders back and she noticed the discomfort.

"I can't help if you don't talk about it, Josh. I can't force you to let go of the memories you have to do that on your own," she explained.

"Aren't you supposed to tell me how to feel or something?" I snapped, harsher than I meant to be.

"Therapy isn't a one way street, you don't get to have all the solutions without doing the work," her tone hardened, I was about to be mothered again. "You aren't here so I can tell you how to feel Josh, you're here to figure out how you *want* to feel."

"Sounds fucking stupid," I groaned, my feet bounced against the floor as I grew antsy.

"Doors right there." She pointed to it.

"You're kicking me out?" I scoffed.

"No, I'm telling you that if you want to leave you can, if you think this is a waste of your time, of mine. You don't have to be here," she said.

I took a deep breath and remembered what Dean said.

"She would bring guys over—boyfriends, strangers from bars—and she would..." I laughed, tears bubbling up over the anger out of nowhere. I looked up to meet Riona's gaze. "She would take money from them to spend an hour with me. It started when I was younger, it only stopped because I started fighting back and they didn't like when I struggled," I swallowed the bile that rose. "I was the reason she turned to drugs and the reason she had the money to keep doing them. I spent hours in that room, there were..." I picked at my nails and until the skin broke and I sucked it into my mouth as the blood welled.

"Josh," Riona said, making me look at her again, "there were, what?"

"Locks on the outside, sometimes days would pass before she'd let me out, or let them in," I confessed. "I can feel them on me, in me, their hands passing over my skin like sandpaper even though they stopped coming to my room."

"I'm sorry." The apology was genuine and softer than she normally spoke to me.

"You didn't rape me," I said with a bitter laugh, cursing under my breath when I heard how harsh it sounded. "I—" I ran my hands through my hair. "Sorry."

"It's alright," she said leaning forward in her chair finally. "That's the appropriate term and I've heard worse."

"You told me I could leave if I wanted to," I said, clearing my throat. "I don't want to," I felt like I was going to shred into nothing in front of her. The worst part is she didn't look at me any differently, her expression remained unchanged. "I can't touch him without...freaking out and I want to."

"Dean?" She asked. "You want to be able to touch him without a panic attack?" I nodded and she smiled at me. "Don't they warn you against attaching your recovery to another person?"

"Yeah," I huffed, she was right and it pissed me off. "But." I licked my bottom lip, my mouth felt so dry. "The last time I wanted something this badly I stopped drinking, cold turkey," I laughed. "I was enrolled at Lorette a month later," I said.

"Okay," Riona said, sounding a little confused.

"I can't quit this cold turkey," I confessed. "I've been trying to work through it but I can't do it myself, I don't know how..." I said. "You're sure you won't tell anyone about this?" I asked again and she nodded like I was being a lunatic. "I want this badly enough to try. And maybe that means I'm tying my recovery to him, but..."

"It's worth it," Riona smiled. "Let's try then," she pushed from her chair and set her folders down on her desk, digging around for something. "I have a few books on cognitive behavioral therapy that focus on touch and intimacy. I guess you won't be the only one studying this weekend."

"Are you sure any of that will work?" I stood from the couch.

"I'm not going to lie kid, you're pretty messed up," she laughed gently and looked up at me. "But speaking from experience, everyone can come back from the ledge if they find the path they need to take."

"Like a moth to a flame?"

"Exactly." She winked.

TUCKER

It felt good to be back on the field, nearly two weeks back from my suspension and winning felt even better. Everyone in the locker room was hollering and shoving as we flooded back inside and started to strip out of our sweaty clothes. Josh confined himself to a corner, but he was talking to Jensen, which was refreshing—and made me feel like maybe I was doing something right.

"I'm impressed, Tucker." Silas came up beside me with his arms crossed, his gaze on his brother. "I think he might have just laughed at whatever Jensen said."

"No." I shook my head. "That was a grimace." I laughed and Silas chuckled beside me. "He's doing okay though," I said. "He's been seeing Riona. Whatever they're doing is working."

"You aren't giving yourself enough credit," Silas added as Josh searched the room, stopping only when he found us standing together. His jaw tightened, but his eyes flicked to me as Jensen talked his ear off. "He seeks you out when he's uncomfortable, Tucker…" Silas clapped his hand on my back. "How are your meetings with Riona going?" He asked.

"Fine. We have lunch a couple times a week and it's helping with everything." I started to unbutton my jersey and shifted to my locker, Silas leaning against the side as we talked.

"She could talk a brick wall into confessing its darkest secrets." Silas nodded. "What about uh...your family?"

"What is this?" I looked up at him, confused. "It's weird..."

"What's weird?" Silas lowered his voice.

"You asking questions like you're my dad..." I stripped from my jersey and tossed it between my feet as I worked the buckle on my pants. "If this is some weird, *'if you hurt my brother I'll kill you'* thing I think you're about twenty four years too late to the party."

Silas stared at me with an unreadable expression that scared me a little. I shifted on my bench away from him a little and plastered a smile on my face. "Sorry that was mean," I laughed nervously. "You're doing a good job with him too," I said, trying to satiate my guilt.

"I'm just looking out for you, I know you've had it rough for a little bit and you never called pineapple," he said. That stupid safe word we used for press conferences was being brought up too much lately. I appreciated it every time he gave me the option but I hated that the situation kept arising for its need.

I shook my head and laughed. "I didn't need to but it's there in cases of emergencies," I said, looking over to catch Josh still watching us like a hawk. "You're making him nervous," I said.

You're making *me* nervous. I wanted to say.

"He probably thinks we're talking shit about him," I added.

"I've never met a guy that suspicious," Silas sighed.

"Do you blame him?" I said standing from my locker. "I stink...I need to shower, and to answer your question, my parents still aren't talking to me."

"Mmm." Silas nodded and looked over at Josh. "Good game today." He walked away from me without another word but I could tell he wanted to keep pushing the conversation.

I groaned as the water splashed over my dirty, sore skin. Stretching out my neck under the heat just chasing the relief that each rotation brought. The noise faded out around me, leaving me alone inside of my own head but the first time in weeks it wasn't filled with questions, or what ifs. It was quiet.

I inhaled slowly and pressed my hands against the tiles to keep myself upright through the exhaustion. We were winning games, the press had moved on to more important topics and Josh was finally starting to open up to the team. I laughed under my breath at myself, how scared I had been that day on the bus; unsure if I could manage it all.

And maybe I couldn't, not by myself anyways but I hadn't been alone in it from the beginning. I should have realized that sooner, that my family wasn't Sunday dinners and trust funds. It wasn't staying small to appease their wicked ideals and twisted morals. It was standing up for myself, for my *real* real family. The ones that'd would also have my back, rain or shine.

And Harbor often felt the effects of thunderstorms.

"Tuck," Josh's voice broke through my thoughts, and I hissed as I came back to reality, standing in an ice-cold shower and the locker room empty. "You alright?"

He's leaning against the wall at the door, watching me, waiting for an answer, but I was too distracted by his smile. It wasn't smug or forced, it wasn't one I'd seen before, but I liked it and it sent a shiver through my body.

"Yeah, I just lost track of time," I said. "You wanna go to Hilly's?" I asked, my stomach growling. Even my appetite had returned as the stress started to settle and I could breathe normally again.

"Yeah, they have a shirt and shoe policy, though," he smirked, and his eyes dragged down over my naked thighs.

My ears turned red at his adoration, completely forgetting that I was naked standing here. *Idiot*. "Guess I'll get dressed then," I turned off the shower and wandered over to the towels, Josh watching every move like a hawk.

"Shame," he whispered as I passed him, causing my breath to catch in my throat. Whatever he had been doing with Riona had made him braver, he still had a hard time with the physical aspect of our relationship. Everything was slow and one sided, but I didn't care, what mattered was the difference.

He was happier, and that wasn't to say he wasn't an absolute asshole most of the time but in quiet moments, between just the two of us, I could feel the ease within him. It radiated. Before it was suffocated, and used as a weapon. Now he was able to sit still for a second, he didn't need to be busy to keep the demons at bay and there was something so simply sweet in it.

I chucked my shirt at him, and he caught it against his face as I pulled on a pair of underwear and clean jeans. He wandered over and handed it to me, but didn't let go right away.

"You did really good out there today," he said in a low tone, his gaze locking on mine as they raked up over my chest. "The double in the fifth carried us home." He swallowed tightly.

The tension between was quiet but sparking like a wire. Josh's eyes were focusing carefully between my eyes and lips as I thanked him for the compliment. I laughed gently realizing what it was that he was doing.

"Do you want a kiss?" I asked him my voice low, practically begging him to say yes, knowing that he wouldn't ask himself. He rarely did, he usually just waited for me to ask for one.

"*Please.*" He licked his bottom lip and I obliged his need with deprived precision. Not that I had been counting but it had been three days since I asked last, maybe waiting him out to see if he would break before me but he never did. Until now. It was gentle and he hummed, his throat vibrating in nervous pleasure as we collided softly. His bottom lip brushed against mine, as our noses bumped together and static coursed through my body at his touch.

My free hand lifted and I felt him breathe through his nose sharply as my fingers pressed to his chin and tilted his head closer to mine. His fist curled into the fabric of my shirt held between us and I leaned into him for more when he showed signs of pulling back too soon. Like my touch was an open invitation, Josh's free hand curled into the band of my jeans. I swallowed and deepened the kiss as much as he would allow as he pulled on the fabric around my hips and urged me gently forward.

I couldn't even believe he had let it go on for so long that when he finally broke away I stayed there, leaning forward with my arm out suspended in time trying to catch my breath.

"Get dressed, Tuck. I'm starving," he said, pressing the shirt against my chest before grabbing his bag. He left me dumbfounded and scrambling into my shirt, chasing after him as his sneakers echoed down the hall toward the parking lot.

I tossed my bag in the back of my Jeep and watched as he silently mirrored my movements and climbed into his side. There were a few cars at Hilly's including Van's truck and Cael's stupid blue Subaru that should have been at the dump. Josh held the door open for me and wandered inside.

"Up." I pointed to the stairs when he paused at the size of the crowd inside. Usually after games the students would flood down the hill for drinks and either ended up here or Delta. But the loft was for the teams, it wouldn't be as busy and Josh wouldn't feel so caged.

He took the stairs and his shoulders relaxed a little when he saw that only two of the eight tables upstairs were crowded with the team. Van had Zoey in his lap as he argued with Jensen over comic book characters that I couldn't name even if I tried.

Cael rested against the side talking to Arlo with his arms crossed when we walked up to the table. "Where's Clem?" I asked him as he unfolded himself and smiled at me.

"She abandoned me for work." He pouted like a child.

Josh shook his head and pulled up a nearby chair, straddling it backward as I shoved Van deeper into the booth and leaned in on my elbows.

"Abandoned." Ella snorted. "You're so dramatic."

"It's part of the charm," Cael sighed in his massive hoodie and loose shorts. "Didn't expect to see Grumpy Bear make a Hilly's appearance." He reached out to tug on one of Josh's curls and was met with a snarl.

"Touch me and you'll lose that finger, Cody," he warned and Cael returned to his insufferable pouting when he realized he had no one to tease.

"Let's play pool." Cael bumped Arlo, and he shrugged, pushing from the table as Kelly came around with water and let us order some food. Josh stole their spot in the booth as more of them left to join the game, leaving us alone to wait for our orders.

I watched them all goof around, laughing and fighting as they played. I could be up against all the worst imaginable things and still feel like I could accomplish them if I could just remember how I felt in that moment. Watching them celebrate as a family, all of them happy and filled with so much love. I started to laugh when it hit me, I had it... I had what Cael was talking about.

I turned to Josh. "Will you be my date to the Gala?" I asked him.

"What?" he stopped, looking away from the pool table to meet my gaze.

"The Gala that the school hosts to raise money, it's hosted at the stadium...everyone gets dressed up and gets drunk. We let old ladies hit on us all night so they'll give the team money for shit," I explained turning on the booth so I was properly facing him.

"I know what a fundraiser is, Tuck, we did them at Lorette," Josh huffed and went still as Kelly put two plates on the table. "The Shores host that don't they?" He asked when she was out of earshot.

"No, well..." I swallowed tightly, he was going to say no to me. "Kind of, they're usually there."

"I don't think so. I—" he turned and focused on his food, his jaw set tightly. It was an entire two minutes before he spoke again and holding my breath was going to kill me. "We aren't going as friends," he said, not looking at me.

"What?" I asked, confused.

"It's a public event, and if you want to go, we aren't going as friends. We go as boyfriends or we don't go at all."

I smiled. "Is that all?"

Josh turned to look at me with shock twisted among his normally angry expressions.

"I can do it," I said. "If that's what you're worried about."

"You haven't even told Cael." He pointed to my best friend with his head, the anger seeping back in to take control

"I don't have to tell Cael!" I fought to control my tone. "He's known the second you stepped on the bus for camp. He's the reason we're in this mess," I said a little quieter. "You're only setting that stipulation because you thought I wouldn't do it," I challenged.

"I know you won't," he argued and shoved some fries in his mouth. "It's been two weeks since the party at Delta and you haven't said a word to any of them about *us*."

I laughed. "Half of campus has seen my dick, the other half saw my ass. I'm not scared to tell my friends."

He stared at me like I was insane but I could see the violent doubt swimming behind his eyes. "Are you seriously bent up about this?" I sighed, I understood his frustration but he wasn't seeing the truth. I stood from the bench onto the table as Josh slid his plate out of the way to protect it from my sneakers.

"What are you doing, Tucker?" Arlo was the first to notice me.

"I have an announcement," I said loudly over the music and crowd downstairs. Van leaned against the pool table, and Zoey pressed herself against him as Ella tucked against Cael, pinching his sides and making him squirm.

"Dean Tucker get your ass off that table," Josh spat.

"Full-named," I whispered at him in shock, a tiny laugh falling from me as I gently kicked his grabbing hand and turned back to the group.

"Fuck sakes." He pressed his hands through his hair.

"We're listening," Cael laughed, swatting Ella away.

Josh was a darker shade of red than my ears and I could feel the anxiety building from my toes to my throat as they all waited for me to speak again.

"Tucker!" Arlo barked, and I flinched into action.

"Josh is my boyfriend," I blurted proudly, arms out at my sides with a helpless little shrug.

They all stared at me for a moment and suddenly I felt like I shouldn't have said anything.

"I can't believe it…" Cael and Van dug into their pockets and tossed money toward Arlo on the table.

"You too, Novak," Arlo said, eyeing the tiny brunette.

Before Arlo could snag the money, Ella reached her hand across the table. "Sorry, that's mine," she said proudly and pocketed the money with a smile on her face.

"Blondie." Arlo leaned across the shabby green fabric of the table on his forearms, trying to look intimidating, his voice low and commanding, but Ella just laughed at him. "I said before the gala," he argued.

"And I told you it would be a spur-of-the-moment outburst." She pointed to me without looking at me, her eyes trained on Arlos'. Josh sighed deeply and rubbed the tension out from between his eyebrows. "It was a good outburst, Dean." She turned to look at me.

"What!" I hollered, stomping across the table and jumping down to the floor. "You guys were taking bets?"

"Cael collected them the day we got off the bus from camp," Jensen said.

"You too?" I grumbled.

"Oh no, I didn't think you had the guts," he shrugged, and Arlo slapped his arm out from under him on the table, sending Jensen stumbling.

"It was only a matter of time," Cael said, something unspoken passed between us that felt like someone cutting a wire. It snapped free and stung as it unraveled from our connected souls. I nodded, and he put a smile on his face that felt like a blessing even though we both knew I didn't need one.

"Guess that means you have no choice?" I turned to Josh.

"I hate to ruin this bizarre Brady Bunch moment, but I don't own a suit." Josh leaned back against the booth like he had won because he didn't have an outfit. Cael laughed loudly, and Zoey gave him a pathetic look of sympathy.

"Oh Josh," she sighed. He had no fucking idea what he had just done.

TUCKER

I hopped out of my jeep and waited for Josh to follow as Van and Cael climbed out of the backseat, groaning and stretching.

"It's a half-hour drive," I shook my head at their whining.

"I'm six-foot-five, Tucker. I was just crammed into a sardine can of death for thirty minutes. If I wanna complain, I'm gonna complain." Van rolled out his shoulders and pressed his hands to the sky in search of a good stretch.

"This is stupid," Josh said as he came around the front and stood next to me. "I can just wear my dress clothes."

"No, it's tradition," I said to him. "Everyone gets new clothes for the Gala, you don't get a choice."

"I don't have the money for this." Josh didn't mince his words; his voice was tight and low as Van and Cael started toward the small shop.

"How about you let me spoil you?" I turned, stepping backward into the quiet street and smiled at him. No favours, no deals, no exchanges. "Just once," I said.

Josh shoved his hands into his pockets and followed me out across the street to the sidewalk without saying anything. His sur-

render was enough of a yes for me and I opened the door to the shop for him.

"The shop owner is obsessed with Cael. It's hilarious." I moved past Josh and into the store, where it smelled like fabric and leather. It wasn't large inside, but the walls were lined with coats and shirts of every color. The dark walls were rich and made the entire place feel like a gentlemen's club without the smoke.

"Mr. Tucker." Mr. Malik came out from behind the store room curtain with lengths of dark purple fabric lying in his arms. The funny, small man was a ball of energy that only rivaled Cael's. He wore a dark dress shirt and suspenders, his smile stretching from ear to ear.

"He's been in the store for two minutes," I laughed, looking down at the tailor's arms.

"I picked these out for him two weeks ago." Mr. Malik winked. "He'll be the center of attention."

"He always is," Josh grumbled.

"Correct. This is our new pitcher?" Mr. Malik set the fabric down and gave Josh a small bow of welcome. I saw the surprise on his face when the tailor didn't offer him a handshake and smiled. Josh scowled at me as Van and Cael dropped something in the back of the store and took the attention away from us.

I turned to him. "Mr. Malik's store burned down a few years ago, you remember that massive fire, it took four trucks to get it out?" I asked and Josh nodded.

"That fire took out half the block," Josh said.

"They had to pull him out of it; most of his body is covered in burns, hands, neck... he doesn't really like contact, like you, but different," I explained. "He'll respect your space."

Josh's eyes drifted back from the commotion to mine. He took a deep breath, his hands flexing in his pockets. "So that's why we're here?" He finally asked.

"We always come here, they'll fit everything for you and send it over to the Nest the week before. Mr. Malik and you sharing trauma is just a coincidence." I shrugged and turned around to find Van holding up some suits for me to look at.

"No," Mr. Malik cried. "No, no!" He waved his arms. "They have to complement one another!"

Van scowled and put the suits back.

"Do you remember the sheer red shirt Mr. Cody wore at his first Gala?" Mr. Malik asked.

"Don't call me that," Cael hollered from somewhere in the store. "It's Cael, I'm not sixty!"

Mr. Malik rolled his eyes and waved his hand at me to remember.

"Uh yeah, I think so?" I said, I was so drunk that year I couldn't even remember what I was wearing, let alone Cael but it was better just to go with it.

"Good, I made you something." He clapped his hands together and ushered me to the back of the shop. Josh followed nervously, his eyes dragging over all the suits and racks as we walked. "Look!" He held up a sheer dark blue shirt with pride. "We can match it with a jacket," Mr. Malik nodded, and I reached out to rub the fabric between my fingers.

It was soft and thin under my touch and I could see my skin through it. "You think I can pull this off?," I laughed gently looking up to Mr. Malik and his frantic nodding. "Alright," I conceded and took the hanger from him.

"Now." He looked at Josh.

"I'd like a real shirt if possible," he chuckled nervously and Mr. Malik obliged, making Josh follow him through the back and away from me.

"I'm so excited to see your perky nipples all night," Cael teased in passing, his fingers reaching out to twist at my chest.

"Yeah, you and all the old ladies." I slapped his hand away and held the shirt up to the light. It was something I had never even thought about wearing before, and I wasn't even sure I could muster the confidence, but I was turning a new leaf. It was time to be a little louder.

"Sit, sit!" Mr. Malik returned after some time and shooed the three of us to the couch in the center of the shop. "He's very grouchy, Mr. Tucker," he commented. "Not in the least impressed that you called ahead," he laughed.

"He's all bark." I laughed as I settled onto the couch.

"What did you do?" Van asked.

"I asked Mr. Malik to put together some new dress clothes for him…" I said, looking over at them both staring at me like I was nuts. "He wears the same shirt every game, I'm sick of looking at it."

"Sure." Cael rolled his eyes and doubled back against the couch in laughter.

Before I could argue with Cael, Josh appeared from the back with Mr. Malik on his tail to push the pace. I could tell instantly that he hated every second of it.

"*Fuck*, he's handsome," Cael hummed under his breath. The low throaty sound of possessiveness left my chest before I could stop it, and Cael snorted. "Simmer down, big boy, it was just a compliment for our man."

Cael was out of pocket, but he wasn't wrong with his comment. Josh's sharp features were highlighted by a tight black dress shirt with gold embellishments around the collar. Corner pins that dragged the collar down and met in the middle with a long golden chain that buttoned into the top of his shirt like a bolo or a tie. He shifted in his dress pants, and Mr. Malik had even found him a pair of shoes to complete the look.

The dark fabric made the gold in his eyes glow against the dark browns, his lips pressed into a thin line that screamed unamused. "The collar is too tight," he grumbled.

"No, the collar is perfect," Mr. Malik hushed him and walked around to admire him from the front. "The beauty is here," he said, pointing to the fabric without touching Josh. All of us leaned forward to admire the way the shirt shone. When Josh shifted, the light caught it, and the faintest hint of deep blue reflective pinstripes appeared. "Navy, for the newest Hornet."

"Mm," Josh groaned.

"Navy to match." Mr. Malik looked at me before pointing at the sheer shirt. I smiled at him and nodded. "Now shoo, there's more to put on."

Josh glared at me, and I could feel the heat rising off him as Mr. Malik made him change outfits. Each one was fitted and much nicer than the shirt he had been wearing. A few dress shirts in dark colors, two new pairs of dress pants and two suit jackets and a grey knit sweater he could wear to dress everything down.

When Josh was finally set free it was Van's turn, it didn't take Mr. Malik long to tree the giant but we had to sit and wait for him to re-measure his gait four times. "You have grown since the last time you were here, it's unnatural." Mr. Malik grumbled as he worked.

"That's what I'm saying." Josh shook his head, sitting on the couch next to me with our knees almost touching. His hand was between us on the couch, and I nudged him gently before slipping our palms together. His jaw tightened slightly, but after a moment, he relaxed back into the couch with a sigh.

"Oh, hey." Cael sat forward on the couch. "Mr. Malik, do you still have the Christmas present I gave you last year?" He asked, and I instantly knew he was up to something by the sparkle in his mischievous blue eyes.

"Yes," he said without looking up from the hem of Van's pants. "Behind the counter, under the box of ties."

Cael leapt over the couch's back and hit the ground running before I could even stop him from ripping the Hornets calendar out from behind the counter. "Put it back," I tensed as he came toward us. "Cael, I swear—" I let go of Josh and pushed off the cushions to stand.

"It's only right he knows," Cael laughed, darting to the left out of my reach and around the couch toward the massive shelf of bow ties. "It's tradition!"

"I will burn every poster in your room!" I threatened, and Cael laughed.

"Worth it," he mouthed and decked me out again around the rack of dress pants and back toward Josh, who was watching on in annoyance. He flipped through the pages with precision and dropped the folded calendar in Josh's lap.

"Behold, Mr. November." Cael leaned over the back of the couch just behind Josh, whose eyes flickered down to the ratty page. The whole thing looked like it had suffered immense water damage, and it crinkled every time Josh moved even a little bit.

"Holy shit." Josh cracked a smile. "You guys still fucking do these things?" He looked back, and Cael shrugged.

"That was the last one before the school decided that it was morally wrong to issue school-sanctioned calendars that promoted using our bodies for fundraising purposes," Van said, his voice low and almost professional. "That was taken almost two years ago now." Van moved, and Mr. Malik threatened to stab him with a pin if he did it again.

"Look at this baby face," Josh laughed, his eyes roaming over the image. I hated it, those pants were too tight on purpose, the paint stung when it got in my eyes and they refused to let me wear a shirt even though it was the middle of February when we took those. "Did they grease you up?"

"With sunscreen," I grumbled, eyes shut in defeat.

"He smelt like a baby for a month," Cael said, laughing.

"It was like tar, it took four showers to get it out of my hair," I said with my eyes still closed, collecting my breath. I opened my eyes and Josh was still watching me, his gaze flickering to my bright red ears and embarrassed smile. I huffed, as he smiled and handed the calendar back to Cael over his shoulder without looking away.

"Please don't," I begged him.

Josh just pressed his lips together and shook his head. I knew I'd never hear the end of it later, but he wasn't going to let me have it here, not in public. Van got changed back into his sweats before Mr. Malik started ringing up the orders.

"Go across the street and order some pizza," I told Cael, and he looked over his shoulder with a shrug. "Go with him," I said to Van and Josh when they paused to wait for me. Once the bell over the door had silenced, I turned back to Mr. Malik. "You can put it on this," I said to him, handing Silas's black card over the counter.

If Josh knew that the shopping trip was on his brother's dime I would have never gotten him out of the house. Mr. Malik took the card and wrote down the numbers.

"He's a nice boy," he said, handing it back. I shoved the card into my wallet and shoved it into my pocket. "Very polite but very sad."

"Yeah, he's working on the last part," I sighed and watched the three of them disappear into the pizza place. Mr. Malik handed me the few boxes and bags of Josh's new game day wardrobe with a smile.

"Make sure you take lots of pictures for me," he said, nodding to the wall of photos behind him, a lot of them were us, especially the ones of us wearing the clothes he fitted for us. "Have fun Mr. Tucker, and don't spill anything on your shirt this year!"

I laughed. "I promise."

I climbed into the jeep after loading up the back, and it wasn't long before Josh was climbing in beside me.

"They're waiting for the pizza," he said. "Oh, hey also," he dug something out of his back pocket and unfolded something. "Will you sign this for me, Mr. November?"

"Fuck off!" I burst into laughter. "You ripped that out of his calendar! When did you even do that!?"

"That thing hadn't seen the light of day since Cael gave it to him, and man, what a shame," Josh practically purred as he shoved it in my face. "So?"

"You're not serious?" My smile dropped and he cocked his head to the side. "I'm not signing it, I don't even have a pen."

"I do." He handed me a pen with *Mr. Malik Tailoring* engraved on it.

"You stole his pen?" I snatched it from him, taking the torn calendar page.

"Dean," he warned. "Sign the page."

"Bossy," I grumbled and scribbled my name across it.

"What are you even going to do with this?" I laughed, handing it back to him. "...actually I don't want to know," I said with the shake of my head as Cael and Van climbed into the truck and Josh shoved the photo back into his pocket with a smug look on his face. Even when he teased me, all I wanted was to kiss him.

"Hey, Logan," I whispered, and he turned his face to mine for a split second, just long enough for me to reach over with my body, using the center console for support as I stole a kiss from his scowling lips.

Cael and Van cheered from the backseat like hooligans, and the entire jeep shook, still in park. "I'll fucking kill both of you," Josh snarled as I started the engine with a satisfied smile.

LOGAN

When Dean kissed me, I expected the feelings to bubble up—the anger, the panic. And it did, it was there but so was rationalized embarrassment and warmth. The feeling of his lips on mine causing my breath to hitch in my throat from the spontaneous moment.

It stung my lips in the best kind of way as I settled back against the seat.

When we pulled up to Dansby House there was a Range Rover out front that I've never seen before. Whoever was here had an exorbitant amount of money and parked like a douchebag in the middle of the driveway.

"Why is Mrs. Shore here?" Cael asked, leaning between the seats as Dean parked in his usual space.

"No clue," Dean popped his belt, and we all made our way into the house to find Coach, Silas, and Mrs. Shore standing in the living room, talking quietly. She was beautiful; tall like Silas and shared the same compassionate, pensive grey eyes. Her hair was pulled back into a sleek ponytail that pulled on her already smooth features.

"Josh." Silas turned and wiped his hands on his jeans. "Can we have a second?"

"Boys, scatter," Coach barked, making Van and Cael disappear with the pizza, but Dean didn't budge. "Tucker, this doesn't involve you," Coach said in a despondent tone.

"All due respect, Coach, I'm not leaving," he said before I could say he could stay, grateful for the conviction in his voice, my back gravitated toward his chest like a magnet.

"It's fine," Silas said, cutting off whatever Coach was going to say next. "He knows anyways," he sighed.

"Joshua, I'm Sylwia, Silas' mother." She held out her hand to me, and I felt Dean tense, waiting for my reaction.

"Mom," Silas shook his head, and she dropped her hand, stepping back next to Coach.

"It's nice to meet you." The words came out tense, but they came out. "What's going on?"

"Today the Shore company was raided and cleaned out for information on my father...our father..." Silas hissed. I had never seen him so uneasy. "It turns out that he was doing a lot of worse things than just sleeping with women and gambling," he said, and his mother flinched. "Sorry," Silas rubbed his thumb into his eye and took a deep breath.

"What does that have to do with me?" I asked.

"Everything," Silas sighed. "You know he didn't hide anything, Josh. Any transaction he made... they were all on those computers."

"So what he was paying some whore in Lorette monthly," I snapped, shoving the anger aside that tore up through all the boundaries I had built over the last few weeks. "Leave it at that, they don't need to know *why*. They can just believe she was sleeping with him."

"Her name is on the transfers, Josh," Silas countered. "They've called me three times today already asking about her, asking about *you*."

"That's bullshit. I shouldn't be involved at all. I never even spoke to the man before opening day!" I stepped forward, and Coach tensed behind Silas. "I'm not going to hit anyone, you can call off your guard dog," I grumbled at Silas and tried to relax a little as Dean followed my movements into the living room.

"You first," Silas nodded, his eyes flickering up to Dean's behind me.

Sylwia cleared her throat, and we both turned to look at her. "Josh, I know that all of this is very difficult and I'm acutely aware that you didn't ask for any of it to be thrust upon you like this, but it's here now. We've protected you from the press for as long as we can, the feds will go public with the case when the trial date is set and when that happens..."

"It'll be a free-for-all," I whispered.

"Yes." Sylwia was far too kind for someone who had been hurt as much as I had. She was a victim too, it was clear in her stance. "You have to understand that they'll twist the narrative, they'll use you as a weapon, and if you don't speak out about it, it will only give them reason to dig deeper," Sylwia lowered her voice and stared me directly in the eyes.

"We have to get ahead of it, Josh," Silas added. "And we need to do it fast, the longer we wait, the worse this will get."

"So I don't have a choice?" I said, looking around at the three of them. "Out myself as the bastard Shore son or have them tell the world about my sordid past?"

"That's a funny way to say painful childhood." Sylwia gave me a soft smile. "You have a choice, Joshua," she said, using my full name like a weapon. "If you choose to stay quiet, you have my promise that we'll do everything we can to protect you. You've suffered enough at the hands of," she paused, her breath short before she continued, "my husband. There's no need for you to suffer more."

There was something about the way she said it that made me turn to face her, our shoulders lined up. She was practically taller than me but there was nothing about her that was menacing. She just held her polite smile and waited for me to figure it out on my own clock.

"How long have you known?" I asked her, I expected her to turn to Silas for reassurance, but she held my gaze.

"Silas came to me the second he found out," she said, and I turned to him.

"You would be a momma's boy," I grumbled. We had fought about that more than once, and he'd told me that she didn't know. But Silas was a fucking loud mouth.

"She deserved to know, Josh, whether or not I had your consent," he argued.

"I don't disagree." I scowled. "What was your first reaction when he told you?"

Sylwia smiled at me still, her resolve unshakeable. "I was angry."

"At my mother? About me?" I asked.

"At myself," she said without hesitation. "I was too in love with a man who never had the intention of reciprocating that love, Josh. I was angry at myself for being a fool, angry that I never noticed the signs. Angry that he left you in that mess…" she trailed off.

"Oh, so you told her everything," I said, my voice breaking. "I guess that makes us kindred souls," I said to her. "Anger is all I feel."

Dean tensed beside.

"All I felt," I corrected myself, and he loosened the breath he was holding.

"Going to the press isn't about revenge or justice," Silas said. "It's about protecting the narrative and your future."

I turned away from his mother and ran my hands through my hair as I tossed my head back, trying to make sense of my panic. On the one hand, letting go of the information would feel great; I'd feel free. Released from the cage I'd be locked in. The Shore-shaped padlock was on the verge of being cut. On the other hand, it would disrupt everything I had built. Suddenly, my entire life would be in question. *Did he do anything himself? Or is he just another Nepo-baby thriving under the Shore family name?*

I swallowed tightly, the fear tipping the scales in favor of continuing on in silence.

"Josh," Dean's voice broke through the thoughts and I turned to look at him, still standing close with his arms crossed over his chest. His blue eyes were on fire and his jaw was tight from listening to the argument, holding his tongue and letting me get through it. He was too brave for his own good and it killed me.

"He doesn't deserve peace," Dean said, quiet but firm.

I cleared my throat and steadied my racing heart as I held his gaze.

No more words passed between us but I understood then that if Dean could find his courage to stand up to his parents, I could find the strength to stand up to mine. I nodded once and turned to Silas. "If we're doing this then the team needs to know first. No surprises."

"There's no time for that." Silas shook his head. "We have to sit down and put out a statement tonight." He argued.

"You smell that?" I asked, relaxing my shoulders as Silas sighed in defeat.

"Josh," Silas pushed, clearly losing his patience.

"It's pizza, Silas," I said. "I'm starving."

"I'll call the guys for dinner," Dean said, reading my mind; he left the living room without giving Silas a chance to fight back against the motion.

"*We're* telling the team before they find out from anyone else," I stared Silas down and stood my ground.

"You're doing a very brave thing, Josh," Sylwia said.

"It's not brave," I said. "It's necessary."

Everyone sat around the table eating, the chairs completely full except one that seemingly always remained empty. They chatted among themselves as Dean picked at his pepperoni, and I sat staring at Silas, waiting for him to start.

The room fell quiet when he stood from his chair. "I know it's unusual for us to have family dinners anymore, especially in the middle of the week, but..."

"Are you and Dad getting a divorce?" Cael asked, interrupting. The whole table groaned loudly.

"Cody, fuck off!" A crumpled paper towel soared across the table as people hollered at him. "Idiot!"

"Hey," Arlo barked across the table, and everyone fell silent instantly. "Shut up and listen," he warned, leaning against the door frame with pizza between his fingers.

"Some things are gonna hit the news in the next week or so about the Shores, and we wanted to get ahead of the rumors before you all get tangled up in it," Silas said.

"We?" Van instantly questioned the plural use and looked around.

"My mother, myself and..." Silas inhaled.

"Me." I stood at the other end of the table.

Everyone was silent with shock or amusement. Dean looked up at me from his seat, almost afraid to move. He was so still.

"Don't." I pointed to Cael. "I'm Silas's half-brother, his dad is..." I swallowed tightly as Dean pushed his foot against mine beneath the table. "My dad, I know that sounds insane, but I've been living with it most of my life, and Silas just found out recently. It's fresh, it's fucking weird but it's also now all of your problems."

Everyone remained quiet as they listened intently. Arlo had pushed off the wall, surprisingly out of the loop. He stepped closer to the table behind Van, suddenly a lot more interested in the conversation.

"The press is going to come down hard on the Nest," Silas explained. "Everyone is going to get questioned constantly for the next little while."

"Why do they care?" Jensen asked, pulling his hat off and letting his messy hair free. "It doesn't affect the game."

"I'm the bastard son of the richest man in Harbor who just transferred in after being kicked off Lorette for a fight I didn't start." I cut Silas off and took the brunt of the shame that followed the explanation.

"An incident the press believes *was* his fault, the problem is Josh was already a target in the eyes of the press. He came here under a cloud, and this is going to bring a storm down on our heads; we have to be ready." Everyone turned to Silas, some of them tapped their chests in understanding, some of them looked like they had more questions.

"Do you think they'll get that intense?" Arlo asked, his heavy brows pulling together.

"I do," Silas said, his tone exhausted. "They didn't pull a single punch with Dean, they never do. Our family is about to go through the ringer with this investigation, they're going to want to know every detail of how Josh ended up at Harbor, no matter how gruesome."

"And it's gruesome." I swallowed.

"Don't answer their questions—deflect to gameplay. We wanted to tell you so you weren't blindsided this week." Silas leaned over the table.

"I wanted to tell you because you're my teammates," I corrected Silas, who sighed and gave a defeated nod. Dean tapped his foot against mine as a few more of them tapped their chests. It wasn't a sentiment I shared, but I understood it a little more now. "And you don't deserve to take the heat for this no matter how it looks."

Cael's head flicked back and forth between us, eyes narrowed in suspicion. "What the fuck are you doing, Cody?" I finally asked.

"Trying to figure out how we all missed you being a Shore love child," he said, his words mincing at the end as the laughter took over.

Before anyone could say anything, Coach Cody reached out and slapped the back of Cael's head roughly. "Idiot," he sighed as the rest of the table erupted in laughter.

TUCKER

"You don't need to come today," Josh said, pulling on a clean dress shirt.

"I'm not letting you go alone..." I stepped forward and shook my head. "Not that one," I said, eyeing the deep red. "Wear the navy..."

Hornets colors.

He paused, looking down at it and conceded easier than expected. I watched as he buttoned it up with shaky hands while I resisted the urge to do it for him. Josh had decided to go forward with Silas and present the evidence of the assault to the NCAA committee and within days they had called a meeting with the two of them.

Josh said he would do it, and despite the resounding fear in his expression when he agreed, he tried to leave me behind.

"They won't let you in that room, Dean, and after your defiance the other day toward Coach and Silas, I don't think they'd allow it even if the committee did," Josh grumbled as he got the last button done.

"I know," I sighed. "I know... I just want to be there."

Josh looked up from tucking in the shirt and nodded. "Fine."

Silas was waiting at the bottom of the stairs for us when Josh finally found the courage to leave our room. His shoulders tight, his muscles straining against the shirt tensely. His entire body radiated stress with every step he took.

"Nope." Silas pointed at me. "Absolutely not."

"You aren't leaving him here." Unexpectedly, Josh was quick to argue in my defense. "He'll go insane and do something stupid if he's left alone. Just let him sit outside the room."

"You're starting to get on my nerves, Tucker," Silas grumbled.

"We're going to be late," Josh said, walking past him without another word.

Coach met us at the building, an annoyed expression on his face when he saw I was following close behind them.

"Who the hell let this happen?" He glared at me. "Sit," he barked to the flimsy chairs outside the conference room. I listened, planting myself firmly on the rickety plastic. "Logan," he turned to Josh, putting his hand up to stop him from entering right away. "Take it slow, keep your composure and let Silas present the case."

"I'm not a loose cannon," Josh said, his jaw clenching.

"No, you're a kid about to walk into a room of wolves. They don't want a scandal, and it means one of two things," Coach warned. "Either they believe you and deal with Ian, or they dismiss this entire case, and you keep the title of problem child in the NCAA. Do you understand?" Coach asked.

Josh swallowed, his throat bobbing roughly as he nodded.

"Good," Coach said, letting him turn the knob. "Don't move," he snapped at me before the door shut in my face. On top of everything, sitting outside a conference room with my head between my knees, out of breath and more anxious than I'd ever been wasn't on my list.

It felt like hours had passed, I wore out the tile in front of the room as I paced back and forth, just waiting and worrying. But when the door opened, I couldn't tell if it was for the better.

"What happened?" I asked.

Coach and Silas looked over at Josh, who was the last to exit with grim expressions on their faces. Josh shoved passed them and down the hall before I could stop him and get more answers. I whirled on Silas and waited.

"That was..." he rubbed the back of his neck, his complexion pale like he might be sick.

"Rough," Coach answered for him. "He did good, Tucker."

"Good enough for them to expel Ian?" I asked, my chest constricted tightly and it felt like the air had been sucked out of the cramped, beige brick hallway.

"He was honest and detailed," Silas croaked, clearly disturbed before he headed in the same direction as Josh.

"Josh is going to need you," Coach said, patting my arm. "Keep him close."

I watched as Coach left me standing in the hallway, still completely in the dark about what happened in that room. My skin itched like it was on fire as I headed toward the parking lot, finding Coach and Silas, but Josh was nowhere to be seen.

"He probably just needed some space, come on." Coach opened the door of the truck for me. "We have a game to get ready for."

"Fuck," I came off the field rolling my arm over my head. Ella was on me the second I stepped into the dugout. Her delicate fingers work the muscle around the rotator cuff with precision and caution.

I had been so distracted with everything surrounding Josh and the Shores that I had been slacking off in practice and missing appointments to follow him around like a puppy. I knew that I was being ridiculous, and I was aware that Josh also thought that, but I couldn't help myself.

Every game that week had been hell; we were all walking around on eggshells, waiting for the other shoe to drop. Nothing had been released on the Shore's, but it was only a matter of time.

"You're pushing too hard, Dean," Ella said quietly, her eyes tracing the round of my shoulder as she worked. "Your body is struggling because you are, it can't keep up with this grueling pace."

"El," I grimaced when her fingers found the knot in my muscle, and she grinned like a happy cat.

"Unless you want to add two appointments with me a week to your schedule, you'll slow down and take care of yourself," she warned me, and I groaned under the pressure of her hands, but the knot came loose, and instant relief flooded my shoulder.

"Alright," I conceded to her when she didn't let go of my sleeve. "I promise."

The conversation was short as we were funneled back out on the field for the last inning. Everything else was a blur as the game was called, with three losses we were officially on a streak and Coach was pissed.

"I am well aware that the noise buzzing in your ears is loud, its obnoxious and makes it hard to focus but you have *one* job when you step onto that field and it isn't to worry about the press or your families," he stood with his hat hanging at his side as he yelled at us. "They will scratch and dig until they take every ounce of your courage and your pride, do not let them take the game from you," he looked around the locker room.

"Yes, Coach," we said after a moment of silence, letting his words evaporate into our exhausted minds and hearts.

"Get cleaned up, get some rest," he ordered, and everyone started moving again.

Everything else around me became a haze of bodies and noise. I focused on getting out of my dirty gear, not bothering to shower because my body had the potential to fall asleep standing up. I climbed into the jeep on auto pilot not even remembering the drive back to the Nest but Josh walked step for step with me in silence as we went through the motions.

We showered and sat in bed, flipping through pages and binders of homework that I didn't want to do. I had dropped the class my father taught in favor of another with a professor who didn't care how far behind I was. Being stuck with six papers hadn't been in the plans, but I didn't have an option. It was that or be ostracized publicly by my father in front of a room of students that would very easily turn on me with a few well-placed dirty looks and off-handed comments that could snowball into rumors. It was simultaneously a good thing and a bad thing, but I had to suffer through my decision if I wanted to stay on track.

I chewed on the end of my pen, staring at him while he worked on his paper quietly. The way his hair curled around his ears and tickled the back of his neck was distracting and made the tips of my fingers itch for contact.

"Your eyes should be on your paper, Tuck," Josh grumbled without looking up from his own.

"Yeah, well, they're not," I argued gently. "How much work do you have to do?" I asked him, mindlessly flipping through my binder.

"Too much, but not as much as you," he snapped, finally looking up at me. "You need to focus," he said, tapping my papers with his finger.

"I don't want to focus. I want to win games and I want to spend the rest of my free time kissing you." I let my head fall back and groaned but Josh wasn't having my shit.

"Too bad you aren't winning games, you dropped two balls today, recorded four outs in the first half of the game and almost put your shoulder out," he replied without pulling his punches. "Do you want to go over the last five games? We can," he stared at me.

"We only lost three," I reminded him.

"We didn't win the first two with your help, *Captain*." He dropped his pen. "You think they don't notice when you start to buckle under the pressure? They do, you're failing them," he said, his voice was lower and mean, more mean than usual.

Guilt scattered through my nervous system, and I pushed my books aside. "I'm sorry."

His whole body tensed at the apology, like he had never heard the words before. I laid my hands on the bed, palms up and waited for him to process it. He stared down at my hands, his heavy brows coming together in confusion before he looked up at me again. There was a storm behind his brown eyes, one I couldn't calm but one I could help him brace for.

"Are you okay?" I asked him, shoving down my own anxiety to check in on him. His life was falling apart too. I was just quicker to admit it and even quicker to crumble beneath the pressure. The problem was Josh was made of diamonds, not a scratch on his confidence that anyone could see in passing.

Only when I slowed down could I see his crumbling walls.

"I'm fine," he deflected.

"No, you're not," I argued. "You're mean, tough guy, more often than not, but you're only *cruel* when you're lashing out."

He huffed, a tiny, defeated laugh that bubbled painfully from his chest.

"It feels like I'm walking on glass," he said after a moment of silence, he pushed from the bed and I sat back watching as he walked to the other side of the room. He was stretched tight like an elastic band, every movement looked painful. "Part of me wishes that they would just let the news break so that I can stop holding my breath. Every class, every game, I'm just constantly waiting for my phone to blow up."

"Give me it," I put my hand out and he narrowed his eyes on the motion but it interrupted his pacing long enough for him to give me the phone.

I looked down at it, the screen flashing on to show a picture of the lake at spring camp. I smiled down at it. "Do you wanna go for a drive?" I asked him before I turned the phone off and slipped it into my pocket.

"Right now?" He looked at the clock. "It's ten o'clock, Tuck," he scowled.

"So?" I slid from the bed to grab a hoodie. "Indulge me."

"Are you going to give me my phone back?" He asked me and I shook my head.

"Mine's on, if there's an emergency, someone will call," I said softly and pulled the hoodie over my head before opening the door.

He was apprehensive until we finally got on the road. The highway pushed back the defensive feelings and soon enough he had actually fallen asleep. Three hours later I pulled down into the gravel road, the shift in terrain waking Josh up. He shifted in his seat, looking around at the dense tree lines in the pitch black.

"Where the hell are we?" He asked, trying to regain his bearings.

"Camp," I said, pulling the Jeep into the empty parking lot.

"What the hell?" Josh scowled. "We have practice tomorrow, Tucker," he said, his voice deep and angry. "And there's no fucking service out here!"

"Exactly," I said. "Get out of the Jeep, we're going for a swim."

"This isn't a joke," Josh hollered as I hopped down to the ground and shut the door behind me. He could sit in there if he wanted, pout and whine but I brought the keys with me and I had his phone...

I stripped off the sweater and then my shirt, tossing them on the dock as I approached. I kicked off my shoes and nearly lost my balance getting out of my socks. I shucked from my jeans and underwear, and the silence of an empty camp was liberating. The water was warmer than when we were here for spring camp, and it engulfed me in an overwhelming static noise that drowned out all the worries as soon as I hit the surface.

I held my breath as long as I could before pushing to the top and falling back into the water on my back to stare up at the stars. The water lapped around my sides, muting the world as I lost myself in the serene feeling of being completely unbothered.

Josh's footsteps creaked against the dock, and I turned my head to see him standing there in his sweats. The moon, the only light around us, practically made him glow. Every scar on his torso, the bigger ones that maimed his chest and ribcage, all places that no one was ever supposed to find them.

"What the fuck is with you guys and this damn lake?" He growled, his eyes scanning the glossy surface.

"Are you going to stand there and stare at me or get in?" I asked him, standing up in the water. It rose to my chest as my feet sank to the bottom and dug into the soft, muddy lake floor. "You're halfway there," I smiled at him as he ran his shaky hands through his hair.

"I don't think so, Tuck," he said nervously, and it was such a strange tone coming from him. "What if there's someone around? We shouldn't be up here. Coach is gonna flip his lid if we're too exhausted to practice tomorrow and neither of us gets enough sleep to begin with. Let's just go back to Dansby..." He said.

"It's just us here," I said to him, pushing back toward the dock. I knew that the riverside of the camp that ran off the lake was more shallow, but Josh had been adamant that he could swim. "Forget Harbor. Just for an hour—it's you and me," I said, resting my arms on the dock. Hopeful that it would be enough to get him in the water.

Josh squatted down in front of me and sighed, his hand coming out and daring to push through the damp curls that stuck to my forehead. I caught his hand before he pulled away, pressing my lips to his wrist and mumbled. "Get in the water, Logan."

"Alright," he conceded. He stood up and pushed his thumbs into the band of his sweats, rolling them down over his hips and kicking off his shoes in the process. He left his boxers on, but they gripped his thighs as he slipped down into the water from the dock directly in front of me.

I waded back from the edge, giving him the space to adjust to the water but never taking my eyes off him as his arms moved in soft circles. The moon reflected off the ripping water between us, and there was a simple, calming silence that fell over the lake. He closed his eyes, and I could see every muscle in his body start to relax in the water. He was letting his mind go just for a moment, breathing in the silence and letting it fill in all the spaces that held anxiety and panic.

It was just him and the quiet.

Josh inhaled slowly, and I mirrored his breathing.

After some time, he opened his eyes, and they were lighter in color, softer.

"Feel better?" I asked him.

He nodded, keeping his lips in a tight line while his eyes flickered up to the sky. It'd been a gamble whether or not being out here would work. I knew how it made me feel when I was overwhelmed by everything, stepping off that bus every year and having the fresh air hit my face, the quiet rustle of animals unbothered by city traffic. The early morning and late nights, the crackling of a fire and the laughter of my friends.

The three-hour drive was almost always worth it.

Josh inhaled again, filling his lungs and letting them out just as slowly. The scars on his chest stretched and pulled with his muscles from the motion. I let myself reach out and touch the one on his collarbone. I traced it over the jagged line wondering what caused the damage, he shuttered gently under the contact.

"They wouldn't ask questions," I said to him, and he looked down at my hand, his own coming around it to hold it still.

"About the scars, if you wanted to change in the locker room, they wouldn't even bat an eye."

"It's not one or two, Tuck," he mumbled, his throat bobbing.

"Doesn't matter," I said. "We're all covered in scars." I turned in the water, showing him my back. I couldn't see it, but I knew it was there because Cael used to trace it as he fell asleep. "Just below my shoulder blade is a deep scar from my brother pushing me out of our tree house. I hit the wooden ladder, needed thirty-two stitches," I said.

"It's not the same," Josh said, but his thumb ran over the scar as he listened.

"No," I shrugged. "But it was stupid, like a lot of my scars... Like a lot of all our scars, bad decisions, drunken nights, fights, accidents," I said, turning back around to look at him. "Survival."

He huffed. "You see them as trophies, Dean...I see them as reminders."

I nodded, it was understandable, but it didn't mean it had to be normal forever.

"When Ella started at Harbor, I don't think I ever saw her with her hair up, in anything but a sweater. She hid the scars because she was ashamed of them, guilt-ridden for that accident that killed her family," I said.

Josh sighed.

"But she was healing from it, making her peace, and that's fine... I'm sure if she had wanted to hide for the rest of her life, she could have. But Arlo isn't the kind of man who just lets people cower away in corners. He never let any of us, so it only made sense that he pushed Ella to forgive herself for shit," I said, swimming back a little in the lake and letting my head duck beneath the water for a second.

"Tuck, is there a point to this story?" Josh asked when I broke the surface.

"I'm just trying to say that you have the team's support, they'll have your back, no matter what." I stared at him as he processed the statement.

"Half of them still think I'm an asshole," he said.

"I mean, you can be an asshole... but trust me, they have practice in dealing with that...half of them had to play with Nicholas King."

"Who's now been ostracized from *the cult*?" Josh sneered, sarcasm thick in his voice.

"Nick did that to himself. He went after one of his own. He made it clear that he was never a Hornet," I said. "I know that you don't believe in it, you think we're a cult or some crap...but we're a family. And when you made a stand to tell the guys who you were, they saw that, they took it to heart. It doesn't matter that you're covered in scars, or wading through years of trauma, you can be mean to them, you can be mean to me. But whatever happens next..."

"We deal with it." He nodded.

LOGAN

"Are you warm enough?" I asked as Dean tucked himself into his hoodie on the bunk. We'd decided to stay the night and drive back in the morning, but there wasn't much around to use as blankets except for a few old scratchy wool ones left behind. We'd spent longer in the water than expected, our skin cold and sensitive as we got dressed and tried to get warm.

"Yeah, I'll be fine," Dean said, settling against the wall, always leaving space for me without a second thought. I climbed into the bed with him, our faces inches apart and the air chilly around us.

"The quiet is nice," I admitted to him. My mind was still racing from what he had said about the team, about trusting that they'll have my back. There wasn't any reason for me not to believe him, but I had spent my entire life taking care of myself.

"Are you going to tell me what happened in that room?" He asked me and I tensed.

"You know what happened with Ian," I said.

"That's not what I asked," Dean said softly, his expression heartbreakingly hopeful..

I ran my tongue along my teeth trying to decide whether or not it was worth telling him. The meeting had gone basically exactly as

expected and at the end I could tell by the looks on their faces, it hadn't swung in my favor.

"I told them what happened," I said quietly. Dean held his breath. "Every single detail, I..." I swallowed the cotton balls that strangled me from within. "I told them everything so that there was no room for doubt that I was lying."

Tears pricked at the corners of my eyes, and I scrunched up my face to get rid of them. Dean watched on patiently while I got through the retelling one painful sentence at a time.

"At the end of all of it, one of them asked me if I had been leading Ian on, flirting with him inappropriately. I said no, and his follow-up question was whether or not I ever touched Ian without consent," I said, clenching my jaw tightly. "It didn't matter what I said to them in that room, they had made up their minds about the situation before even hearing my side."

"That's bullshit," Dean said in a dark tone.

"It's sports politics—you know that better than anyone. The scandal of a misguided player with anger issues is easier to navigate than sexual assault involving two men." I wet my bottom lip.

"Doesn't mean it isn't bullshit," Dean grumbled. "I'm sorry," he said quietly immediately after, as if what he said would hurt my feelings.

"Thank you," I said to him and tangled my fingers into the sheets between us on the mattress. I shifted the tone of the conversation, just wanting him to understand that even though the day had started horribly, I was grateful that he was still trying to turn it around. "For this, for today."

"Hold onto that gratitude for tomorrow when Coach is screaming at us," a quiet, sleepy laugh tumbled from him as his eyes closed over.

"Oh, you're taking all the blame for this," I teased as his hand slipped between mine and the bed. I inched closer, unsuspectingly needing to breathe him in to settle my racing heart, and he felt the shift because he smiled and pried one eye open.

"What are you doing?" He asked me, his voice husky and low.

"Putting all my time with Riona into practice," I said with a shaky, quick breath, and both of his eyes opened at the sound of it.

"Stay still for me?" I asked him and he nodded, always so patient and understanding. Something that in the beginning had been a sore spot for annoyance and rage was now something I searched for in his presence. He was no longer the wall I beat my fists against, but now the wall I used to lean on when I was too tired to fight. I was hesitant at first, unsure that if I started this time I'd be able to stop, but the way the moon painted his cheeks and glittered in his damp curls, I was willing to try.

Our lips brushed and Dean tilted his chin up into me as I sank into the feeling of him and I melting together. His grip tightened on my hand as I slipped my tongue into his mouth and two became one. His chest pressed forward into mine, warm and welcome. I lifted onto my elbow and angled my face down towards him.

I could feel his apprehension, his delicate hesitation as I kept control of the situation. His tongue lapped at mine, and I closed my eyes as our noses pressed together. The sounds of what felt like a teenager's first make-out filled the cabin. Heavy breathing and low groans, his hips pressed against my thigh, and my hand carefully slipped into his hair with a precise tug of his damp curls.

"Are you okay?" He asked as I broke the connection and rested my forehead on his. His hand brushed over my wrist and up my arm, stopping to grip my elbow gently when I didn't answer his question immediately.

"Yeah." It was the truth too, surprisingly. There were no dark thoughts or sudden panic. Just Dean and me, making out in a bunk bed in the middle of nowhere. "Riona and I have been practicing communication," I said.

"Okay," Dean said, his body still against mine. "You say stop, we stop. You say go, we go," he laughed but it was low, almost considerate and sweet in tone. "You have all the control, Josh. Just tell me what you need."

"You." I swallowed when the word came out so quickly, like I had been itching to say it for months. I smiled, Dean's eyes flickered down, and a similar smile appeared on his face before he slowly leaned in to collect another kiss.

The response was enough for Dean to take liberty with his touches, placing an open-mouth kiss on my jaw that tingled my skin in a strange, welcome way. My hips pressed against his involuntarily, and I could feel his need for more through his jeans against my thigh.

"Take it slow, Tuck," I warned, and he listened, slowing his hip movements to a gentle pace that shouldn't have made my chest tingle, but I dug my hands into his hair and pulled to direct his attention.

I could feel his growing erection beneath his jeans, straining tightly as our lips met again and he took my lips between his teeth in breathless huffs, waiting for me to take control again. His eyes were closed, but I needed to see him. "Open your eyes?" I asked him.

Dean's lashes fluttered open and his blue eyes twinkled like stars in the moonlight as he peered up at me. I pressed my knee between his legs, deepening the kiss and pulling him against my chest before anything darker could creep in and ruin the moment. His hips moved back and forth, the pressure building apparent as his stomach tightened under my touch.

"I feel like a horny teenager," Dean confessed, his breath warm on my neck as he grinded my thigh methodically losing himself in the sudden bliss.

"You sure do," I laughed, and he buried his face in my neck, cursing under his breath. He planted small, shameful kisses across my hot skin as his hips stuttered from the buildup in his jeans.

I counted to ten in my head, steadying the shake of my hand and pushed it between our bodies. My fingers found the button of his jeans. He trembled as I popped the buckle and slid my hand inside his boxers.

I'd seen Dean in most of his glory before—never really caring—but as my hand closed around his shaft, hard and ready, I couldn't help but smile.

"Are you laughing at my dick?" He gasped as I started to help him release the tension with gentle pumps down his length. I adjusted my body to get a little higher than him in the bed and tugged on his hair to bring his eyes to mine.

"No." I kissed his lips. "No," I said again, dragging my teeth over his bottom lip. I inhaled slowly, preparing for him to tease me at my next confession. "I'm nervous, Dean."

Dean's lips were red and swollen from making out, his hair messy and tangled in my fingers as he looked up at me, an intoxicated look in his eyes and smiled so softly I thought that I might… my breath hitched for a second and I shook away the feeling.

"Don't look at me like that," I said gruffly, pushing away the sentiment, and he huffed, going back to adorning my skin with sloppy, hot kisses. His body arched into my touch as I worked him closer to the edge, his breathing becoming short and shallow. I wished I were better at the talking part of it, stroking him to the point of breaking wasn't enough. He needed praise, but I just couldn't figure out how to get the words out. I let go of his hair and cupped his throat just below his strong jaw, angling his head back and squeezing just enough for his lips to fall open gently.

It was seconds before he spiraled down from the clouds, his whole body shuddered against mine as his erection rattled in my grip. Warmth spread across my fingers, palm and his jeans, sticky and wet as his eyes fluttered closed and he fought to control the shake of his thighs. I pulled my hand free and used one of the scratchy blankets from the floor to clean my fingers while Dean fell back against the bed. His chest was rapidly rising and falling as he gripped it with his hand and lay in silence.

He flinched, turned his head toward me and opened his mouth. "Jesus, I'm an idiot...did you want..."

"I'm not ready for that," I said, lying back down in bed next to him and quelling his intense guilt.

"You did really good," he said, still short of breath. "Like, *really* good..." He licked his bottom lip and adjusted in his pants. "I'm going to have to clean these in the lake." He started laughing and stripped off his jeans, still lying on his back.

"It's getting easier," I said, as he chucked the jeans across the cabin.

"How's your head?" Dean asked. I wasn't expecting that kind of question—not when he was lying next to me in his boxers, flushed from orgasm. I hadn't actually thought about it... which in itself was progress. Months ago, a moment like this would have never happened; I would have thrown myself into a week-long panic attack or found myself at the bottom of a bottle.

"Alright," I said, it wasn't perfect. The sounds, the touch... in the darkness most nights it still felt like too much but... "the bad isn't so loud anymore."

"That's progress, right?" he asked, his tone so patient with me.

"It is," I nodded, ready to tell him the truth. "I'm not scared of the news, or what they'll say about me or the Shores," I confessed, and his brows pinched together tightly in confusion. "I'm scared that I can't control how it affects all this progress. What if I end up back where I started because I shut down again? I can feel it starting," I rubbed my hands in my hands. "I'm going to get lost in that anger again because it's comfortable, Dean."

"It's different this time," Dean said, shaking his head and sitting up a little in the bed.

"It's the same anger," I argued.

"Only this time I won't let you get lost in it, we're tied together." His hand reached out, crossing the gap between us, and he pressed his fingers to my racing heart. "Wherever you go, I follow," Dean said, so matter-of-fact I felt a heat bloom across my chest—and for the first time, I believed it without doubt.

LOGAN

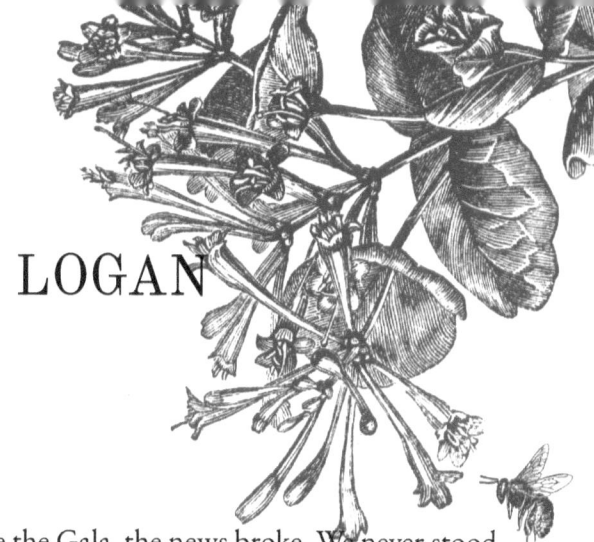

A few weeks before the Gala, the news broke. We never stood a chance once Charles was arrested—those reporters moved fast. The statement we wrote to deliver at Friday's game was sitting on Silas's desk in his office.

I sighed. *We were screwed.*

In the short time of living at Dansby I had never seen them close the gates to the driveway but as Jensen and Arlo pushed the large, black doors together and locked it I realized that everything had gone to shit.

Reporters weren't just harassing the players at the stadium anymore—they'd climbed the hill to the Hornets' sanctuary, desperate for any scrap they could find. The cameras flashed at all hours, and the yelling never stopped even as the sun went down.

Silas pulled up the morning after on his bike, he had been staying at his mother's place in the city more and more. He looked exhausted with dark circles heavy under his concerned grey eyes, and his jaw set tightly at all times. He stood in the driveway with Jensen and Arlo, the three of them watching the gate as they spoke.

"That can't be good," Cael muttered, leaning against the wall beside me as we watched from the upstairs hallway window. "They didn't even close those after the accident…" he said.

"Yeah, Cody, I know," I huffed, and he put his hand out to stop me as I started to walk away. I didn't have the emotional bandwidth to deal with Boy Wonder. The issue at hand was bigger than just some drugged-up baseball player crashing a car, I wanted to say, but kept my mouth shut. He didn't deserve that. He was just trying to be nice.

"How are you doing?" he asked me, crossing his arms over his chest when I stopped and squared up with him. If Cael was good at anything, it was getting under my skin at the exact wrong time.

"I'm fine," I said. Everyone seemed to want the answer to that question. Silas, Coach, Dean… Riona and her annoying nephew.

"Mmm, no," Cael hummed and shook his head. "Try again."

"I'll throw you down the stairs if you don't get out of my way," I threatened him.

"Empty threat when it would mean having Dougie as backup for the rest of the season," Cael called my bluff.

"Would feel really fucking good right about now though." I narrowed my eyes on him.

"Answer me honestly and I'll let you go." he smiled at me and I wanted to knock all the teeth out of his mouth.

"I'm stressed out, tired, overwhelmed and right now, really fucking pissed off," I snapped at him.

"Is it '*need a meeting*' overwhelmed?" He asked me, finally getting to his concern.

"No," I snapped. "Are you finished?"

"You love him, don't you?" Cael asked. It should have felt blurted out, rushed—spontaneous. But nothing Cael did was without thought. No matter how much people liked to believe him to be chaotic. It was just him, brutally honest to a fault and never one to cut corners.

"It's none of your business, Cody," I said, clenching my jaw. It was such a heavy question, one that if I answered it wrong, everything I was building towards would come crashing down around me. And with everything else going on, I couldn't afford for the one safe place I had left to become hostile territory.

"It is my business," he said, his tone dropping.

"It's really not," I argued. "If he wanted to talk to you about it, he would."

"I'm asking you." Cael stepped forward, that possessive little shit head reared his ugly head and I couldn't help but laugh in his face.

"You walked away from him, remember that," I snapped. I watched him wince, his jaw ticking in anger before he shoved it aside and nodded.

"Do you love him?" He asked again, but I couldn't figure out why he was pushing so hard. It was a hilarious notion, and I couldn't tell if he was jealous or just genuinely concerned about the whole thing.

"If this is a pissing contest over Tucker, you better be prepared to *lose*," I warned him and a stupid smile formed on his lips. "What the fuck are you smiling about?" I asked, my voice breaking into a snarl.

"You just answered my question." Cael looked me up and down as he backed away, his vague statement set me on edge as I started down the stairs to meet Silas as they entered through the front door. "And Josh," Cael leaned over the banister. "I'm not competition, I'm just the guard dog," he added, lifting his hands in surrender.

"What's he whining about now?" Arlo threw his hat on the table in the hallway and tried to catch a glimpse of Cael.

"Nothing, he's just being a brat." I stepped down from the last step. "You guys locked up?" I asked as Jensen tossed his keys away and excused himself into the house.

"We caught two more of them trying to come up here, I don't want them on the lawn. Harassing us from the street is bad enough." Arlo shook his head. "It's on an automatic lock, I'll have Dean get you an opener for your car..."

"Don't bother," I said, and Arlo scowled. "I'm always with him anyway. Honestly, my car might be better off sold for parts." I laughed awkwardly. Arlo just glared. I was trying to be personable, but the joke fell flat, and a tense silence fell over us.

"Yeah... I'm going to go find Blondie." Arlo looked between Silas and me before disappearing, leaving us to suffer in silence alone.

"You've been staying with your mom?" I asked him and he nodded, crossing his arms over his chest. The dark red long-sleeved shirt he wore stretched over his arms, and I could see how tense he was through the thin fabric.

"She's fine. It's just... a lot. She didn't expect her husband to wind up in jail, but she's been meeting with lawyers. Money is moving, news is talking... I didn't come up here to talk about my mother," he said, pulling his hat off and fixing his hair with his hand.

"Alright, what do you need me to do?" I asked, expecting him to need testimony or to meet with lawyers. I didn't want a cent of their money more than getting me through the rest of school. I just wanted everything over with.

"Nothing, I-" he sighed. "I came over here to talk to you about getting your mom into a facility, there's a bed for her if you think she'll take it."

"You want to put my mother in rehab..." I scowled, aware that I wasn't hiding the confusion or the resentment for his family in my expression.

"It's not a handout or an apology. It's something I wanted to offer, maybe in a desperate attempt to show you that I do care. That this isn't about the money or the news... I really am trying to be your brother, Josh."

I chuckled, the air leaving my lungs in a low huff.

"Dean told me that you aren't big on favors." Silas swallowed and I made a mental note to kick Tucker's ass for telling him anything. "Riona runs a program on the weekend in Lorette for underprivileged kids, it's a sports program that runs in hand with the child services committee in the city. They work with kids, teaching them how to manage their emotions through play," he said. "She wants you to come coach the baseball team."

"A trade." I chewed the inside of my cheek, still angry with Dean and his big mouth but also grateful for his stupid, soft heart. "Fine."

"Yeah?" Silas perked up, and a smile spread across his face. "They're middle school kids, rough and mean, but you have experience with that."

"There's really a bed for her? For my mom?" I swung the conversation back around.

"Yeah, we can bring her in today if you want, we can run by before practice," he said, his mood lifted from before. He must have been trying to figure out a way to ask me for days before he finally found the courage.

I nodded. "She's going to fight it."

"That's okay, do you need to bring anything..." he asked, staring toward the door.

I looked up the stairs, tempted to bring Dean, but I shook my head. "No, let's get this over with."

"I forgot how horrible this neighborhood was." Silas cut the engine on the fastback Arlo had reluctantly handed over the keys to. There was no way I was getting on the back of the bike and holding on to him all the way to Lorette.

"It's fine, just lock the doors." I shrugged. "If they break the windows, you're taking the blame, me and Arlo, I just became friends."

"I'm not, that's what I would define your relationship as, he doesn't want to strangle you anymore, and that's a start." Silas locked the car and followed me up the cracked pavement to the front entrance. The building reeked of mold, smoke, and stale beer as we climbed the stairs to her apartment.

I knocked once, but as predicted, she didn't answer. "You should probably stay here. If she sees you, it's only going to make this worse."

Silas's jaw tightened. "I told Tucker I wouldn't let you go inside alone," he said quietly.

"That idiot," I sighed and pushed the key into the lock. I popped the door open, and the smell of rotten fruit was the first thing to invade my senses. "Fuck sakes." I gagged, stepping inside to see the kitchen infested with fruit flies and trash.

Silas covered his nose with the collar of his shirt as we made our way through the apartment. I called out to Mom more than once without an answer, kicking the trash out of my way as I went to create a path.

"Maybe she's not here," Silas mumbled under his breath.

"She doesn't leave, Silas, *ever*." I chewed on my lip and pushed further into the apartment, my breath catching knowing that he would see the door.

"Shit, kid." His voice was low, practically breathless as he stood behind me, his eyes trained on the locks. "I'm sorry."

"You didn't lock me in there," I scoffed, ignoring how it made me feel to be back in the apartment. Even worse, without the backing comfort that Dean usually provided. I turned, pushing open the door to her room, and a blanket had been tossed over the window, making it dark inside and hard to see.

Silas flicked on the light beside my shoulder and swore under his breath as we both froze. I could feel him wanting to say something to me as I fought to control the panic that coursed beneath my skin as I stepped forward into the room.

Her messy hair was stuck to the yellow pillow case, and her shirt was pulled up around her pale blue back, exposing the decaying skin around her hip bones and the band of her pajama pants. My stomach churned, the walls built to keep out the sadness and grief already starting to crumble.

How long had she been like this?

I knelt beside the bed, where she lay face down in a puddle of vomit that looked days old. The bile ripped from my stomach at the smell of it, and I turned away from her, putting my face in a trash can that was shoved under the table across from the mattress.

"Josh." Silas grabbed me by the arm, and I nearly swung on him, but he moved back, putting his hands in the air. "Let me do it," he said, pointing to her again. "I'll check, go…" he gagged, pushing down the vomit and moving around me to block my view. "Call the police."

I stumbled backwards over some trash, hitting the wall hard and knocking the wind out of my chest before I turned and left the bedroom while Silas knelt to check her pulse.

I sank against my bedroom door, and as the shock wore off, I dug my phone out, dialling 9-1-1 and listening carefully to the operator's instructions. It was clear that she had overdosed on something, the signs of her distress strewn across her dirty sheets and floor.

Silas appeared from the bedroom with a grim expression. I looked up at him, and it was clear he wanted to say something, but he wasn't sure how. I shook my head, all that work, all that struggle... Every ounce of pain I suffered to get myself out of this shit hole because I didn't want to end up like her.

I never thought that I would feel guilty for leaving her behind.

I shoved whatever guilt I felt down, pushing it aside to leave room for logic.

"She's dead, isn't she?" I asked him.

"Yeah, she's uh... gone." Silas brushed his hand through his hair again, turning toward the bedroom and back to me. "I'm sorry..."

"At least it's over," I said and watched Silas flinch. I walked through the apartment, leaving through the front door and wandered down to the front to wait for the cops. The fresh air hit me like a ton of bricks and I stared out at the overcast just trying to micromanage the way I felt.

The hardest part was trying not to blame Silas for her death. But it wasn't his fault, he had nothing to do with this, and I knew that, but it was easy to hate someone standing in front of you. Especially when he looked so much like the man who was responsible. He hadn't put the drugs in her hand, he didn't fill the needle or tip the booze down her throat, but leaving her was the catalyst. She had been emotionally beaten down until the only solution was drugs and booze.

I just didn't think she'd ever cross the line; she had drunk herself to death and left me with even more mess. Sirens lit up the silence as the paramedics and cops arrived on the front lawn of the apartment. I inhaled slowly, knowing that all my pain had come to a crashing, tragic conclusion.

The freedom I'd been chasing my entire life, left at my feet in the form of my dead mother. I closed my eyes, just trying not to lose it entirely, a few tears streaking down my hot cheeks as I worked the emotions down and back away from the surface.

"Joshua Logan!" My name was called from my left. I turned to see a reporter cruising toward me from across the patchy dry grass with his recorder held out front. "I just have a few questions!" He yelled, but Silas was there, stepping in front of me like a wall out of nowhere.

"Fuck off," Silas barked the curse and I had never experienced such raw anger from him until now. Usually he was buttoned up, careful with his words and calculated with the press. "I said, fuck off!" He lifted his arm, and the reporter flinched like Silas was taking a swing, but he backed away and shoved the recorder into his pocket.

"Get inside." He turned to me and I listened without protest, letting the glass door slam behind me, just wishing that Dean and I had stayed out at camp.

TUCKER

"Franklin," a voice called.

I had been on campus for all of two minutes before my entire day was ruined by the sound of my name. I turned slowly, adjusting my bag to see my mother standing in the hallway. I'd stupidly taken a shortcut through a different building, forgetting that she taught a class on Thursdays.

"Hey, Mom." I swallowed roughly and watched as she approached me.

"You haven't been coming to dinner." She didn't bother softening the blow.

"Don't have much of an appetite lately." I nodded, just forcing a smile on my face so all the people passing by would see a pleasant chat between a professor and her student.

"You're avoiding a difficult conversation," she said.

My hand flexed around my backpack strap, and I fought to hold in all the anger I wanted to let go of, knowing that it wouldn't do any good to explode in front of a hall of students.

"We have to get your illness dealt with, Dean. It's not healthy to continue like this, it's harmful, and I don't want to see my baby

boy in pain." She reached out to touch my arm, and I stiffened, leaning away from her fingertips.

"I'm not in pain, Mom," I said through my teeth, even though it felt like I was in pain at that very moment, but not for the sick reasons she was trying to blame.

"You're sick, Franklin. Just let us help you," she said, moving forward again.

I opened my mouth to argue when a commotion came from the end of the hall and Cael appeared out of nowhere, flushed and out of breath. He jogged down the hall, stopping in front of me and looking over at my mother before putting himself between us with his back to her.

"Excuse me," she hissed, backing away from him.

"Mrs. Tucker, you're looking especially judgmental today!" He scowled at her. She stared at him like she was trying to kill him dead with her glare, but it only riled him up more. "Make sure when you speak to the Dean about my suspension, you tell him I called you a homophobic crone with bad breath and witch hands," Cael snapped at her before he turned back to me as she started to argue with his back, completely unbothered by her anger. "...You don't answer your phone anymore?" He said quickly, poking me in the chest.

"Why what..." I pulled it from my pocket to find a ton of missed messages from Silas.

"Josh's mom is dead," Cael said quietly. "We've been trying to get a hold of you!"

His mom was dead... my chest tightened around my chest at the news. It wasn't like she was a good person, but that was his only family... I shook my head. *Silas had said they were going over there this morning, but...how had I missed so much?*

"How did you even know I was here?" I asked, confused about all the wrong pieces of information, as he grabbed my arm to drag me away.

"I have your location, big boy, now let's move," Cael urged.

"We're not finished with this conversation, Franklin!" My mother said to me as Cael pushed on my arm to get me moving down the hall. "You are a part of this family and you have to start acting like it!"

"Mrs. Tucker, never a pleasure." Cael turned back to my mother, who was still ranting at him. She recoiled at his movement, and Cael laughed. "Gets me everytime that she's afraid of gay cooties." His laughter died into a baffled chuckle as she continued to turn red with anger. "Fuck sakes, please open a fucking book... maybe learn something about modern society?" Cael shook his head as she glared at me over his shoulder.

"I'll be speaking to the Dean about this!" She snapped at him.

"Yeah, I know, remember what I said," Cael smirked, backing up into me and pushing me to fall in line with his steps. "Homophobic crone..." he said slowly, pressing his hands together with each syllable.

"Cael," I grumbled, and he tripped over his own long legs, turning back around and restarting his jog at my warning.

"Come on," he shouted as he rounded the corner.

We made it to the Jeep without any more issues, my heart pounding in my chest as I climbed in and Cael followed suit. We drove out of Harbor and down the highway to Lorette, speeding the entire way until we reached the turn off. Arlo's fastback was parked in front of a cop car, and Silas was standing on the front lawn alone, speaking to the police when we arrived.

He stopped me before I could go inside, his hand planted firmly on my chest.

"Listen, he's..." Silas cleared his throat, "he's not sad."

"What do you mean he's not sad?" Cael asked, as he stood over my shoulder.

"We found her, she had been gone a few days. The ambulance came and got her body, took her to the morgue for an autopsy. But Josh... he's already cleaning the apartment... he's spoken to the landlord." Silas explained to us.

"Did Mark say anything?" I asked.

"He was sympathetic, apologized a bunch for not checking in on her. Josh didn't seem angry with him, just dissociated." Silas said.

"Him and Mark are close, he's the only person Josh has left." I knew that sounded silly because he obviously had me, had us but Mark was all Josh had left of his childhood. Shitty or not, Mark was his highlight. "Can you make sure anything he needs gets taken care of?" I asked Silas, and he nodded. "Josh hasn't flipped out at all?"

"He's eerily calm, and it's making me nervous," Silas said. "There's nothing, no anger, no sadness. He's just floating around up there cleaning and ignoring me."

I looked up at the building, turning to the two of them. "Let me go alone."

Cael surged forward, but Silas caught him.

"I know what he's going through." Cael fought against Silas.

"No, you don't," he corrected him. "The woman you lost would have moved heaven and earth for you, and she regularly did exactly that. Josh's mother was not that, she was cruel, abusive and sick. You have no idea what's going on in his head." Silas pushed him back.

"I can help." Cael surged forward again and again, but he was shut down. I was wasting time listening to the fight and started to move around them.

"Let him do it," Silas warned Cael, who stared at me with concerned blue eyes. "Go call Arlo, Van, Jensen... We're going to need help." I heard him say as I started inside, I took the stairs as quickly as I could, only to freeze in the apartment doorway.

I couldn't see him from where I was standing, but I could hear him rustling around inside. It immediately smelled of death and trash, the entire room was putrid enough to make my eyes water as I wandered inside.

"Josh," I called out to him. I looked around the disgusting living room and continued back down the hallway to the bathroom. His mother's bedroom door was shut but the hinges on his were blown off completely and the door was lying across the floor, splintered into pieces.

Not so calm.

"Hey, Logan," I called out again and heard a trash bag snap open from my left. He was squatting on the floor, shoving garbage from the bathroom floor into a bag, completely disassociated from everything around him. I called out to him one last time, but he didn't stop; he pushed off the floor and floated past me like I wasn't even there.

Silas was right; whatever was going through his head wasn't like what happened to Cael at all. There was just quiet rage and a lot less crying as Josh tied off the bag and started a new one. He moved around me like a ghost, never stopping to make eye contact with me as he went back to the bathroom to keep cleaning.

"Stop!" I shouted. Josh flinched. *Good*, I thought, it meant he knew I was here. "Stop for one second and look at me!"

"There's too much to do, man." Josh kept his back to me and started to throw more garbage away. The bathroom was a pile of old bottles, cans and magazines... used tissues and sticky laundry that crunched as Josh picked it up and chucked it away.

"We'll do it," I huffed, trying to reach out for him but knowing it would only cause him to shut me out more. "Just stop for a second." I stepped into the bathroom, blocking his path as he tried to leave again.

"Move," he said, eyes fixed on the floor. He was avoiding the confrontation, which was the least Josh thing he could have done and simply the most alarming.

"No," I argued. "Not until you look at me." My shoulders filled the door frame as I settled between the small sink and door in the cramped space.

"Tucker," Josh sighed. I hated that it was Tucker or man...It was Tuck now, or Dean. But never Tucker or weird things like man or dude, and the sound of it was grating against my skin.

"Don't call me that. Look at me," I snapped.

Josh looked up at me, and I watched the dam break inside of him. I reached out to him, meaning to pull him closer. "*It's necess-,*" I barely got the words out before he crashed into me, his fingers digging into my skin around my shoulders and neck.

The sounds of his cry broke my heart as my arms curled around him in protection and squeezed him so tightly that it became nothing but muffled sobs that soaked my shirt. I didn't ask permission or wait for his cues, I just held him as close as I could for as long as I could. I held most of his weight, keeping him grounded while he shook. It felt like his body was fighting against my hold, but *he* wasn't against me. Josh was struggling against himself. Warring with the guilt and rage that was coursing through his veins and threatening to explode from him.

He wasn't used to losing control, and he had never been further from having a grip on it than he was in that moment. I let my hand rake up into his hair and pressed him closer to my chest until he melted into it and his sobs slowly became softer, dissipating into sniffles.

"Okay," I said, but I didn't loosen my arms until he released me from his intense hold, the marks that his fingertips left behind stinging as he pulled his hands away. "We do this together," I said to him, my hand still holding onto the back of his neck firmly.

Josh nodded, his eyes bloodshot and his cheeks red from the crying, but he was listening. He swallowed tightly with a clenched jaw as he stared up at me. It was killing me how sad he was, and for a woman who would have used him until his last breath. But he had taken responsibility for her, and her death felt like a failure.

"This isn't your fault," I said to him, and he flinched in my grip. "No, don't do that, look at me," I warned when his gaze flickered away, and tightened my hand around the back of his neck. "You did everything you could. You were a better son than most would've been."

"I'm a horrible fucking person, Dean." His voice broke.

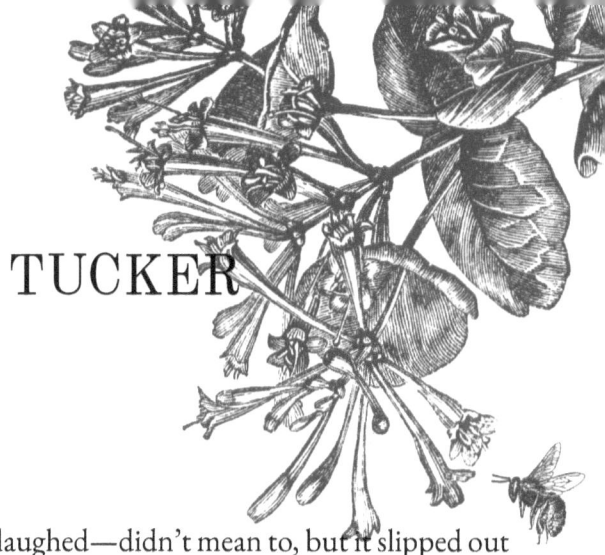

TUCKER

"Far from it." I laughed—didn't mean to, but it slipped out so easily I couldn't stop it, and Josh stared at me like I had lost my mind. "I held something back that day when I asked you if you would be mine, my boyfriend," I said to him. "Van said something else to me, and at the time I knew saying it would scare you, so I kept it to myself, but today… when I got the news about what happened, it was like my entire life had stopped. All I cared about was getting here to you," I explained, and Josh watched on in curious horror that only made me more nervous.

"Maybe now isn't the time…" I seized up.

"Out with it," Josh said, his voice gritty.

"I stopped myself from saying that I love you that day, that I'm not hurting anyone by loving you," I said, my chest feeling like someone had sucker punched me. Josh's head tilted sideways, confusion darkening his features in a way that terrified me. My heart was racing faster than it ever had on first base, and for a split second, I thought he might flip out, but he stayed eerily quiet.

"Okay so usually you're all talk, and I know today has been rough but uh…you not talking is freaking me out so if you could, like you know… talk?" I begged him in a rambled, breathy sen-

tence. His fingers tightened in my hair, and I winced from the pain. "Josh?"

"Say it again," he said after what felt like an eternity, his hand curled around my face and into the hair at the back of my head. The entanglement was rough, like he couldn't control himself from doing it.

I stared at him and I couldn't stop the smile that curled on my lips. "I'm not hurting anyone by loving *you*."

"Yeah, that's what I thought you said," he grumbled, his eyes never leaving mine.

"I fucked this up didn't I?" Fear gripped my muscles, and suddenly my knees felt like rubber. I wanted to sink into the floor and disappear out of his sight, but his grip on my hair was relentless; he was the only thing keeping me upright.

"Just shut up for a second, Dean." The begging sound in his voice was unfamiliar, but it ignited some hope that maybe I hadn't completely bombarded him with these feelings. Maybe he was feeling them too.

Each second felt like someone was tugging a cord around my heart—each moment of silence tightening it further, and the tighter it got, the more my heartbeat thudded in my chest. I wanted to open my mouth to say something to fill the quiet, but Josh had asked me so nicely that I had to obey his request.

It was just going to kill me.

My hand gripped his nape, careful not to hurt him, but my muscles were so taut that I had started to tremble.

"What do you mean?" Josh asked, and I could feel his nervousness. It rolled off him in waves alongside his confusion.

"I uh—" I cleared my throat. "I'm not ashamed to love you. I don't feel guilty doing it," I said. "It doesn't hurt anyone to do it, but it's killing me trying to pretend I don't."

Josh nodded, listening to everything I was saying and paused on the last bit. The muscle in his jaw ticked, and his eyebrows flickered up like he was having a conversation I couldn't hear.

"You're killing me," I said in a grumbly tone. "If you don't feel the same, it's fine, you don't have to love me back, Josh. You don't even have to like me, but I...after today, after feeling this scared. I needed you to know, I—"

"Slow down, Tuck," he said, his tongue darting out over his bottom lip. "I get it."

"But you don't feel the same," I groaned. I was an absolute idiot.

"Dean," he said in a short breath and let go of me finally. I lost my balance without his touch and stepped back into the doorframe.

"It's okay." I raised my hands to stop him from talking.

"Don't be dramatic. Let me finish," he warned, that sharp tone I knew so well returning to his voice.

I rubbed the back of my neck and sank into the distant ache of my scalp from his fingers. A foolish idiot who missed a man's painful touch, a man who didn't even love me back.

"I don't know how to love someone," Josh said and looked up at me with a foreign look in his eyes. It wasn't pain or anger. It was a neutral expression that felt so far away and disconnected.

"What?" I asked, leaning forward and moving back toward him in the bathroom, keeping the distance between us so the tension in his jaw would soften and he would stop flexing the muscles in his arms and shoulders. "You're born knowing how to love, Josh."

"I might have been born knowing how to love, but I had it stripped from me, Dean... beaten out of me," he said to me. "I'm not capable of loving someone, certainly not you."

"You're going to want to hit me," I said, squaring my shoulders and bracing for his rage, god knows he had a reason to be angry today. "But that's bullshit."

But it never came.

"It's not," he quietly said.

I shook my head at him in disagreement. The sweater I wore tugged tightly across my chest and showed off every ragged breath I took. "I was hiding behind what people expected me to be, the golden boy," I huffed. "You pushed me to be better. Called me out when I was wandering around with blinders on. You were the only person who called my bluff; well, I'm calling yours."

"It's the truth," Josh said.

"It's what you believe to protect yourself, I would know," my voice had fallen into a frustrated territory that came out of nowhere. "I believed that if I just kept those parts of me hidden, that I could make everyone happy and that eventually one day I could live with it. Forget how shitty it felt to be alone, to never have someone to celebrate with, to watch all my friends fall in love, get married and die old with their soul mates. I *believed* that all of that just wasn't in my cards, but I was playing with the wrong deck, Josh!"

"That has nothing to do with this," he argued, and I could see where he was coming from, understanding that one thing couldn't lead to another. We were standing in the middle of filth, surrounded by his dead mother's garbage, and I was pouring out my soul just to elicit a reaction out of him. I didn't blame him for pushing back. He believed that he didn't have the capacity to love me back, but he was wrong.

"You believe you aren't capable of loving me because it's difficult to *touch me*, but I don't care about that," I said with conviction, there was not a hint of hesitation or confusion in my voice. "You prove yourself wrong with every look, every laugh, every insult. Your love isn't conventional, Josh. It's barely recognizable. But I see it, I *feel* it." I pounded my hand against my chest. "You know how to love someone because you figured out how to love me against all odds."

"That's—" Josh shook his head.

"You said whatever comes next, *we* deal with it," I reminded him.

"Yeah, I meant about your parents, your career, hell even this mess but..." Josh shrugged. "I hadn't meant about *us,* our...relationship..."

"You said '*we*,'" I snapped. "That means you're not going anywhere. It means we do this together. And I'm holding you to that," I threatened. "I don't care if you don't think you can love me back, or if you never say it. I don't need to hear it, I don't need to feel your touch to know it's there."

"Dean, that's weak, it's pitiful," Josh clenched his jaw, hissing through his teeth. "You look like an idiot," he snapped.

"So what?" I shrugged, my muscles rolling out as my body started to relax. It was then that Josh knew he wasn't going to win the fight. That I'd already decided the outcome and Josh's fear, his anger, it wasn't a challenge I couldn't overcome. I sank down among the garbage, proving that he would always have the control, giving him the higher ground, hoping he'd take it. I was past caring about appearances; the only thing I wanted was him.

"I'm here on my knees telling you I don't care, I'm groveling at your feet to prove you wrong. I don't care how pathetic I look as long as you understand that I'll spend hours in this position if that's what it takes to convince you, days, months, years." I looked down at myself and put my arms out, gripping the door frame.

"I'll get on my knees every day for you, Josh—if that's what you need from me. I'll worship you from a distance, memorize the sharpness of your tongue from your words, and dream about the smell of your skin just to show you what love means."

He stared at me—my words seeping into the cracks of Josh's heart, shining light through all the pain to reveal the love that still lingered. Scraped against the lining of his barely beating heart, it still existed; it just needed to be found.

"I can't say it, Tuck," he said to me, and he knew how disappointing that would be.

"I don't expect you to," I responded just as quickly, the honesty didn't rattle me in the least.

"What if I can't ever say it?" Josh asked me, his disbelief still running rampant.

"You will," I said with a soft smile, my knees practically jello at that point.

"You're incessantly hopeful." He rolled his eyes.

"That's the power of love, tough guy." I rose from the floor and pressed my hand to his tense jaw.

"Fuck off, Tuck," Josh choked out, his hand catching my wrist roughly but his lip tugged upward into a pathetic smile. The struggle was apparent but he was trying, with each small unsteady breath he came back to me. "This place is a disaster..." he was clearly trying to avoid any more hard conversations, and I was willing to follow the conversation off the cliff with him.

"We don't have to deal with it right now..." I said, looking around, his thumb pressed against the inside of my wrist in response. "Or we can..." I stumbled over what to do next, what he needed. "Tell me what to do and I'll do it."

"I need it done, I need it all gone..." he said, his breathing still shallow and his eyes shifting around the space frantically. "I can't come back here," he said, the tone shifting to desperation as his eyes met mine again.

"Okay, done." I leaned in, not waiting for permission for the second time that day and stole a reassuring, tender kiss from his bottom lip. His tongue swiped out over it when I pulled away, but he didn't seem upset about the contact. "Let's get to work," I said, letting go of him.

We started with the bathroom, and at some point in time, Cael and Arlo started in the living room. Josh instructed that everything went to the dump, and when Silas tried to get him to look over the stuff in question, Josh nearly went toe to toe with his brother. Once we had them separated again, Van, Todd, and Jensen had shown up with trucks, and Reyes had managed to borrow his uncle's trailer.

We loaded it up in silence, no one talking or asking questions. Just hours of silence. At some point after a massive argument, Josh finally consented to Silas and I clearing out his bedroom. He didn't want anyone else inside and was willing to leave it locked up but Silas made a case for nosy reporters and Josh was broken by logic. The room was disgusting, not because it was dirty but because it was the cleanest room in the house. It broke my heart. It was clean because it had once had to take visitors and Josh had just formed a habit of keeping it that way. It barely looked lived in.

Like a conjugal cell. There was a real bed, with a mattress a size too small for Josh to fit in and a clean dresser that was spotless except for a lamp. Silas and I cleaned it out in silence but my skin was crawling and for a split second I was glad she was dead. For doing this to him all those years. When I was finished I went out beside the dumpster and emptied the contents of my stomach onto the asphalt.

By the time the sun fell in the sky the entire team was there following directions. Josh never spoke to anyone but Silas, Cael or me but I saw his eyes wandering around from time to time. He was observing the team with silent adoration; it was written all over his face.

Midnight came and went, Silas ran for pizza, stopping for ice cream by my request, and Cael found an old stereo that still had life. It only played one horrible Backstreet Boys CD—and skipped during the last tracks—but it made some of the guys laugh. Jensen nearly put out his shoulder carrying out the old furniture with Arlo and Dougie. While Cael complained that we should just toss it out the window from the seventh floor.

The apartment was completely bare by two am, and we all were lying around on the tile, stuffing our faces with pizza in silence. Josh sat beside me with a box of pizza at his feet, but he hadn't touched any of it. I cradled a tub of ice cream in my palm and held it out to him, but his eyes remained in the distance, somewhere far away that I couldn't reach him.

"You should eat." I nudged him gently, and he nodded but didn't move to touch the food. Instead, he pushed off the floor and stood up with his shoulders pinned back tightly and a dark look on his face.

Everyone watched as he worked up the courage to say something to them. It was extremely out of character to address them at all, but for the second time that month, Josh had reason to.

"You didn't have to come here tonight," Josh said, and the team listened, everyone setting down their food and drinks to give him their full attention. "And I know that I'm not always the easiest person to get along with, but I need to say thank you. For showing up and for having my back."

Josh shifted on his feet, clearly unsure of his next move, but then he lifted his fingers and tapped the space over his heart twice. I looked over at Silas, who was staring up at his younger brother with a set jaw, but there in his eyes was so much pride that it was seeping from his typically stoic features. My chest ached for him as the rest of the team followed in succession, each of them tapping their hearts in a show of unity.

Josh lowered back to the floor without another word and slumped against the wall. "Very cult leader of you," Cael whispered across the gap—and any other day, Josh might've smacked him for it, but a smile spread across his face, and he reached out for a piece of pizza.

TUCKER

"You look handsome," Cael said, leaning against the doorframe behind me.

I turned to look at him over my shoulder, buttoning up the sheer dress shirt with a smile on my face. I tugged at the collar, but it just didn't seem to wanna lay flat against my chest. He wandered over, still in his sweats and stupid *fuckboy* cropped t-shirt, but with a soft look in his big blue eyes.

"There's still time for us to be a throuple," he said quietly as he forced the collar into position with ease. "Clem wouldn't mind her boyfriend having a boyfriend."

"I'd mind my boyfriend having a girlfriend." I rolled my eyes at him as he backed away, and I turned to the mirror. Cael shifted away from me, crossing his arms over his chest and causing his shirt to ride up over his stomach.

"Offer will always be on the table." He cocked his head to the side, completely unbothered.

"How come you aren't dressed?" I asked him, turning to grab my belt from the bed. "We have to leave in twenty."

"It takes me five minutes to put on clothes." He rubbed his shaved head with a smile. *True*, I thought and did up my belt buck-

le with shaky hands. "You alright?" He asked me, his demeanor softening.

"Nervous." I inhaled a strangled breath and tried to convince my heart to stop beating so fast in my chest.

"About what?" Cael stepped forward again, swatting my hands away to help me with my belt. I hate being babied, but just for the second he was there, everything seemed a little less daunting. "Tonight or in the grander schemes of falling in love?" He smiled at me, and I found the balance I needed to stand on my own two feet again.

"Both," I said with a tiny huff. "I've never actually released a press statement, and my father will be there tonight, they're one of Harbor's biggest donors..."

"So we do what we do... well, you do what we always do, get drunk and have fun," Cael suggested.

"I can't. I have to do that speech. I'm captain now, I don't get to enjoy the gala," I said. "Do you ever wish we could go back to that first year?" I asked him.

"No." He shook his head. "That year was hell for both of us. Mostly because of me... I would never want to live through that again, no matter how fun some of it might have been." His gaze met mine over my shoulder in the mirror as I turned around to double-check my outfit. The sheer shirt left nothing to imagination, every muscle was pulled tightly and radiated with uncomfortable tension and anxiety.

Tonight was going to be a shit show.

"Dad wouldn't have given you the job unless he knew you could handle it, and Josh wouldn't have given you his heart for the exact same reason. So maybe you need to stop doubting your ability to step up to the plate." Cael watched me with a curious look on his face. "Maybe you just need to believe in yourself instead of letting the corrupt words of a family that never appreciated your heart turn you rotten."

I nodded, his words heavy on my chest.

"I wasted a lot of time, Cael," I said, chewing on the inside of my cheek. "Fighting against people that didn't deserve it, not pushing back against the people that did. I'm sorry," I said to him.

"Time can be created," he sounded so sure of himself. "Hey," Cael tapped my shoulder, and I looked over at him again. "Do you remember what Mama used to say to us when we fought?" He asked me, and I could hear the pain in his voice. His throat had the tendency to close over when he thought of her even to that day.

"If we can fight that hard against the people we love, imagine what we could do against the rest of the world," I repeated it with him, and I could hear her voice in the back of my head like a mantra. "I wish she were here."

"She is," Cael's voice was soft and sad, and tapped my chest gently before he started to walk away. He was running out of time to get dressed and if we were late Arlo would beat our asses.

"Cael," I called to him before he left the room, and he poked his head around the door to look at me. "I love you."

"I know, big boy." A goofy grin appeared on his face.

"Hey, I know that reference," I said to him with a smile, and he winked before disappearing again.

I stood in the quiet for a second, pushing my hair back off my face and really making sure that I was ready for tonight before leaving my room. The Nest was quiet, everyone having either left or been on their way out the door. I could hear Cael shuffling around his room and stared at the open door, my heart no longer hurting at the thought of him.

"You ready?" Josh's voice travelled up the stairs and I turned to see him with a hand shoved in the pocket of the well-fitted black dress pants.

"Holy shit," I inhaled, my chest rising slowly at the sight of him. His hair was combed back in slick waves that curled around his ears and nape. He was wearing a few rings, but the star of the show was the black dress shirt and all the gold embellishments that made him shine. They balanced out the darkness in his eyes, making them glow a beautiful shade of amber in the dim lighting.

"I look fucking good," he said, that smug smile I missed so much returning to his handsome face. It had been a rough few weeks dealing with his Mom's passing, but I'd never admired him more as he took everything in stride.

Silas and he had delivered a late statement on everything that happened, including the untimely death of his mother. The questions circled madly, but they had done an impeccable job of answering what they could without letting the press run them over.

"You look damn good," I said with a smile, descending the stairs. I reached the bottom, and his eyes trailed over me with a satisfied look on his handsome face. "We'll be lucky if I don't puke on this before the night's finished," I said nervously.

"I puked before I put mine on, like a responsible adult," he said, stepping forward and brushing his hand against a rogue curl that slipped out and fell against my forehead. "You clean up pretty good, Tuck," he whispered—a quiet moment just between us before the chaos started.

"I'm a wallflower next to you." I breathed him in as he stole a reassuring kiss from my lips. His bravery was inspiring, each kiss and every touch a testament to how hard he was working to feel better. "Can't believe I get to take '*the*' Joshua Logan tonight," I laughed. "Most hated man in Habor."

Months ago, that sentence would have been more unbelievable than me saying I was straight. Now, having him standing in front of me, neither of us weighed down by the suffocating pressure of our families, everything felt a little lighter.

"Yeah, yeah." He laughed gently, ready to get the public show over with. "Do you have your speech?" He asked me.

"It's on my phone," I said.

"Do you have your phone?" He laughed, and I patted down my pockets before swearing and darting back upstairs to grab it off the bed. When I returned to the main floor, Cael, Ella, and Arlo were standing with him.

"You ready, Tucker?" Arlo asked, looking more buttoned up than usual in a clean dark suit and dress shirt. Ella matched him in a long black dress, the ring she always wore around her neck and a pretty smile that instantly brought me a little comfort.

"Do I have a choice?" I asked and he shook his head.

"Guess I'm ready then," I said.

Everyone made their way out to the car, but before we took the stairs, Arlo stopped me.

"You never looked at it, did you?" He asked, and I looked down at him at the bottom of the stairs, confusion all over my face. What the hell was he talking about? "Open the binder, Tucker."

"We don't have—" I started, the last thing I wanted to know was read what he thought of me on that page, tonight would be hard enough without knowing.

"It'll take five minutes, they can wait," he said. "Go."

I scratched my neck and shrugged. Who was I to argue against Arlo? He waited, watching me as I turned back to the house. I took the stairs to my room and dug the binder out from the bottom of my duffle bag, cradling it in my hands and opening it to my tab.

Franklin Tucker.

I stared at the picture he had pinned in the folder and laughed, it was my rookie year photo. I still had a skinny face and a hopeful look in my eye. My hair was short, and there was no trace of exhaustion anywhere.

The file was normal, it had all my stats, my best plays scribbled down in bad handwriting, but taped behind the picture was a little faded yellow sticky note dated from that year.

Next captain.

My chest constricted my heart painfully, all the anxiety I had been feeling burned raw at the sight of the simple words. He had known, that season, all those years ago that eventually one day I would be here. How long he had been training me to fill his shoes, and I hadn't even been aware of it?

I pulled the sticky note out of the folder and rubbed it between my fingers.

He had so much faith in me, and I had never seen it.

I tucked the sticky note into my pants pocket and put the binder away to join the others. The car was still waiting out front of the Nest, and it took us down to the stadium like it always did. The music was loud coming from inside, the parking full as we climbed from the car and straightened ourselves out. Cael excused himself, no doubt to find Clementine, and for the first time since meeting him, I wasn't desperate for him to return to my side.

Josh bumped my shoulder and swiped his ID on the box to let us in the door. Ella and Arlo's voices echoed gently around the concrete hallway as the four of us made our way down through to the main entrance of the field. My heart was pounding in my chest and there wasn't a damn thing I could do to stop the feeling of it trying to run away. We stepped out into the concourse, the concrete sturdy beneath my feet, and I looked down over the party.

Everything looked amazing, twinkling lights and a massive dance floor that framed a large stage and a live band. There were tables of chatting people and waiters rushing around to make sure everyone was happy. My parents would be down there, waiting in the shadows like a pair of vipers. Toxic and ready to destroy every good thing I'd been working to create. My heart was running rampant beneath my chest and my head was dizzy with anxiety.

"Stop looking for them," Josh whispered from beside me.

"I can't," I breathed out and turned around on my heel to take a second before I stepped down onto the field, only to be met with the team. Cael stood, shoulder to shoulder with Arlo, Van and Silas, surrounded by the rest of the team, starters and second string alike. All there like a wall.

"You didn't think we'd let you do this alone, did you?" Cael's voice was sturdy and comforting as he asked with a smile on his face.

I didn't know what to say to them. But I felt stronger with them standing in a united front, supporting me without question and under extreme scrutiny. Arlo nodded, pride tucked into the quiet curve of his smile.

"Two steps at a time," he said, raising his hand to his heart.

Cael stepped forward, looking over at Josh for a split second and letting something unsaid pass between them before he reached out to the suit jacket I was wearing. "You forgot someone," he said, pinning a small lavender boutonniere to my chest with practiced ease. "And Clementine got one thing wrong in her article, don't tell her I said that," he whispered with a smirk as he got it in place. "But there's never been only one heart of the Hornets, our strength lies in numbers."

"It's perfect." I looked down at the little stalks of delicate purple flowers and smiled, my jaw quivering with raw emotions.

"She would be livid for missing such an insane outpouring of love," Silas said when I went quiet, trying to collect my emotions and to keep from crying. I cleared my throat and squared my shoulders to fight the grief and gratitude that tangled dangerously in my chest. "And for the record, she would have loved you like you were her own." He looked over at Josh. "She had a thing for grouchy asshole misfits," he added, laughing as Arlo shoved him.

"If it's any consolation, I would have been honored," Josh said, and I turned my head to look at him. All serious and stoic in his statement, the lights from the stadium backlit the sharp cut of his jaw and the long, harsh swoop of a nose broken more than once. The bright white lights created a halo around him, kissing each plaited curl and making him glow.

I'd never felt a rush of love like the wave that washed over me just admiring him.

"I'm ready," I said, the words sticking in my throat as I swallowed the fear. Josh looked over at me and nodded, his hand tangling into mine at our sides and the team cheering like a bunch of idiots at the top of their lungs. The music and chattering from the stadium, the anxiety in my chest and the fear in my heart were completely drowned out by their love.

LOGAN

An angel–that was Dean Tucker in all his glory. He wore tight-fitting dress pants that hugged his thighs and a sheer shirt that outlined every muscle in his arms and back like a work of art. His hand pulsed in mine as we turned back to the stairs, the team cheering behind as we started the terrifying descent to the field.

With each step, I felt him tense—his breath slow and methodical as he fought to control the panic. Nearly everyone on the field had stopped to watch the team enter the party, and while the support was loud, furious even at our backs. The quiet judgment was pounding in my ears, and I knew that Dean felt the same because his throat bobbed roughly as we stepped out onto the field with every eye on us.

"Breathe, Tuck." I squeezed his hand, and he let out a strangled breath before inhaling again and setting his jaw.

"Dean." Coach met us at the bottom and offered his hand to him. His dark blue suit jacket stretched as they shook hands. "Logan." he turned to look at me with a nod. Silas's mother was close behind, and she offered both of us a small, caring smile.

"You both look very handsome," she said. "It's nice to see the hair out of your eyes, Joshua." She complimented me before turning to Coach. "We should find our table," she said to him, and he cleared his throat, nodding to Silas and Arlo before leading her off in a different direction.

"You're sitting at that table," Silas leaned down over his shoulder. "Follow them..." he instructed, and Dean started moving again. It was like he had never done any of it before, even though he had more than one Gala under his belt.

When Dean went to follow I stopped, "I'm going to go get us some drinks, I'll be there in a minute." Dean's eyes widened, terrified to be on his own but I had something I needed to do before I keep good on that promise. "You need it," I said, my tone grumpy. Silas watched me carefully as I walked toward the bar but it wasn't for the drinks.

Mr. and Mrs. Tucker stood watching us and I could feel their eyes on me as I made my way carefully through the crowd. It was clear that they had come tonight with one objective, to speak to Dean in a place that he couldn't easily escape from without making a scene. I tapped the bar and ordered a drink for Dean before turned toward the two of them.

"He's accepting an award tonight, did you know?" I asked them when the silence dragged on.

Mr. Tucker's eyes found mine, "You did, good." I nodded, "tonight is a very important night for him."

"We know, Mr. Logan. You don't need to lecture us," Mr. Tucker sighed, a tight frown forming on his old face.

"I think I do," I corrected and that gave me his full attention. "I want you to know if you speak to him, if you make him uncomfortable in anyway, if you even think about ruining tonight for him. You will have to deal with me. I will not be as respectful and calm as I am right now and I will not call you sir or ma'am. I grew up on the other side of the tracks, where we don't have manners and deal with bullies the correct way, Mr. Tucker."

"Are you threatening a professor, Mr. Logan?" His body language turned rigid as the band started to quiet and everyone took their seats.

"I am," I confirmed, and from the shocked expression on his face he had expected me to be so bold.

"That's a serious offence," he started but I cut him off.

"I know what it is, and I meant every word." I took the drink in my hand and started back toward Silas.

"You can't keep me from my son," he warned, his voice like nails down my spine. I turned back to look at him, eyes narrowing on them both as my jaw ticked tightly in controlled anger.

"He's not your son," I said, "you made that very clear."

Mr. Tucker went to open his mouth but stopped as Silas appeared at my side, "I'll show you to your table," he said over my shoulder. His eyes glaring at the Tuckers. "You look lovely tonight Mrs. Tucker, enjoy dinner." He said politely before he led me to the table. I knew the chances of me getting to sit with Dean were low, but surprised to find my name at the table between him and Silas. "You're his date, kid," he huffed and pulled out his chair to sit.

Dean still looked on edge, but when he realized I wasn't leaving his side, the tension in his shoulders eased slightly. Everyone took their seats, and Coach made his way to the stage after a long, dry introduction from one of the committee members. He waited for Sylwia to accompany him, letting her take the stairs slowly until they were both at center stage looking out over us. Coach looked more uncomfortable than anyone, hating every second of being out of his gym shorts and t-shirts and into dress clothes and combed hair.

"We wanted to sincerely thank every member of the Harbor Organization for joining us today for the seventh annual Harbor Athletics Gala," Sylwia said, her voice like honey and the light catching the sequins of her navy dress as the crowd clapped. "The money raised from tonight's events goes to fund the many scholarships and programs that trickle down through the department here at Harbor University, and without your generosity, many students wouldn't have the opportunity to further their education. Your kindness has helped many Harbor athletes grow and flourish into incredible members of society."

Coach clapped from beside her as she stepped aside and let him take the mic. "Every year, the athletics department chooses one student who has displayed exemplary values on and off the field here at Harbor University. Last year, before graduating and being drafted into Harbor's beloved NHL team, Kenji Carter was awarded this honor for his kindness and his leadership of the Harbor NCAA team."

Dean stilled, his chest barely rising, his breath going silent. He was so nervous, and for no reason, the award they were giving him was an honor, it was holding him in the highest regard. And yet... he didn't want the accreditation.

"I have been a part of the selection process here at Harbor for eight years, and the decision is always difficult because we're blessed at the University to have so many wonderful athletes. For those of you who don't know, the coaches come together mid-way through the year with a folder full of nominees that we believe would make the best candidate for the award. It usually takes us a week of coffee, donuts and complaining before a decision is made. This year, Coach Allerson of the women's basketball team," Coach said, pausing to let them clap as the light shone on the coach, she waved and smiled at everyone awkwardly.

"Whiskey... and water." I nudged it toward Dean, and the command reached him on a minute-long delay before he reached out for it. I pressed my knee against his under the table and looked around, catching a glimpse of his parents at a table in the corner near the secondary bar.

Coach told Dean he was receiving it three days ago at practice. *"I think you earned the heads up, you've had to pull one too many surprise press conferences out of your ass."* He said it like it was going to comfort Dean, but it only riled him up more.

We spent hours writing the speech on his phone, and I wasn't even sure he was going to be able to get through it without puking. *If he makes it up the stairs at all...* I thought, feeling his leg shake against mine.

"Coach set a folder on the table with all the nominees and, like many times before, we opened it, but it was closed five minutes later, and a decision was made based on an incredible show of bravery and leadership. I wouldn't be up here if the chosen athlete weren't a Hornet—obviously," he grumbled, and a few of the audience laughed at his horrible, tense joke. "This player has gone through hell and looked down the barrel of a press video camera more than once this season, all while defending what it meant to be a Hornet and, more importantly, defending what it meant to be a man. I'm honored to present this award to Dean Tucker—captain and first baseman of the Harbor Hornets—for his unshakable morals and ability to endure struggles no young man should ever face."

Coach turned to look at Dean as the light panned to him at the table.

"Stand up," I cleared my throat and urged him upward. His knees buckled a little, but he stood as the cheers from the team rumbled through the party louder than ever. Screams and whistles echoing around swallowed up any doubt he was feeling. He looked down at me and our eyes met, his full of raw fear as I nodded, encouraging him to move toward the stage. "You can do this," I said.

Dean's eyes flickered shut—and if I hadn't been standing beside him, I might've missed it—but the fear dissolved, and he summoned that golden boy smile. His cheeks were flushed from the heat of the spotlight, but he waved, shaking hands with Silas quickly and putting on the best show he could for the clapping crowd.

"Bets on puking?" Cael appeared at my left, squatting in his suit as his massive blue eyes watched the stage.

"He won't," I said to him, not looking away. And I knew, without placing a single bet, that I was right. He wasn't going to be sick, he could get through this.

"Yeah, you're probably right," he whispered. "He's pretty determined when he wants to be."

"He sure fucking is," I said before holding my breath as Dean shook Coach's hand and kissed Sylwia on the cheek.

Dean reached out, adjusted the microphone with a sharp screech, then stepped back and cleared his throat. He had been handed a crystal plaque, no doubt engraved with his name, and he looked down at it like he might cry. His jaw quivered, and his hand wrapped around the wooden podium to brace himself as the silence dragged on.

"Show us that boyish charm, Tucker!" Van yelled, and Zoey's giggles could be heard, but the outburst helped, and Dean smiled, looking up and squinting into the lights shining on him.

I whirled around in my chair quietly and barked under my breath at Cael. "Tell them to turn that shit down."

Cael understood, darting off bent over to avoid blocking anyone's view and before long the lights dimmed a little on the stage. Dean looked around, finally able to see everyone and relaxed even more. he set his phone on the podium and took a quick second to find himself before starting.

"I've been playing baseball since I could run," Dean said. "I was always the biggest kid on the field, Elementary school was a riot when I was as tall as some of the teachers. Being that big, from a respected family... I had every opportunity I wanted when it came to sports. Coach Andrews has tried to get me to join the football team more than once," he laughed, and so did a few others. "But baseball was always where I belonged, the sunshine, the dirt, the camaraderie..." he sighed. "The family."

The team erupted again, and Dean laughed, a true smile forming on his lips.

"I've also been gay my whole life," he said, gripping the podium tighter. "Which apparently wasn't a surprise to the team but I definitely figured it out watching Saved by the Bell." Everyone was quiet, but a few of the guys hollered to encourage him through the silence.

"Fuck," Silas swore under his breath. "He's losing it."

"No," I said. "He's fine, just let him get through it." Dean's eyes found mine like he knew I was talking about him, and I nodded for him to keep going.

"Being gay shouldn't be as difficult as it is most days, but it's especially taxing on an athlete playing at a high level. I knew accepting the captain position would shake things up at Harbor, that I could handle the pressure of leading the team to victory." He licked his bottom lip, his throat no doubt dry. "What I wasn't confident in was my ability to be myself and be proud of who I am. When the majority of the league still finds comfort in slurs used in jest, directed at me unknowingly, it's difficult to navigate. Remaining quiet, letting the moments pass, pretending that I was just one of the guys just to get through the games."

Something crashed from behind us and the spot where Mr. Tucker was sitting was empty, leaving Dean's mother, the color of a tomato, staring up in anger at her son. Good.

"The beginning of the season was rough," he said, digging something out of his pocket. A small piece of yellow paper, along with a folded white one that looked like it had gone through the wash. "I've gotten pretty good at talking to the press. It was a team effort writing this press statement," he held it up, still folded. "But I never read it because I was scared. I didn't want to disturb the status quo."

I smiled up at the stage, proud of Dean for everything he was standing for.

"It sucks, keeping the peace," Dean shook the award in his other hand. "But I didn't get this for keeping the peace. I got this for being brave and unshakeable in my morals." He held it up higher. "But it was only because of a teammate, a friend..." he stared at me, those blue eyes burning through the darkness. "Someone I love and respect looked at me when I was at my lowest this season and told me that those people didn't deserve peace. That I had to step up because there are kids like me all over the country that need role models, the kind that I needed growing up. They don't need peace—they need a voice when the noise gets too loud. They need gay baseball players. Gay captains. Gay men. In the original statement, it was written that I will not apologize for my personal life. And that stands true. This award proves that the articles and gossip will not change who I am, or how good I am at baseball."

A smug smile formed on his face, and in that moment, Dean Tucker glowed the brightest shade of gold. A true beacon of disrupting the normal, stepping outside his comfort zone to be what so many of us needed.

The team stood, cheering and hollering for him in waves of unbreakable noise.

Dean smiled at the crowd. "So thank you to the athletics committee—but this award doesn't just belong to me. It belongs to the Hornets."

TUCKER

Standing on that stage felt like flying—after I pushed past the violent nausea in my gut and dug up the courage buried deep in my chest. My father locked eyes with me as I accepted the award, pride burning in my chest brighter than it ever had. He stormed off like a bull in a china shop, and it only made me stand taller and smile harder.

I was done hiding.

I thanked everyone again, climbing down from the stage back to my seat. Everyone was still clapping as I rounded the chairs and dropped the award to the table with a thunk. Josh stood, clapping the loudest—an arrogant smile on his face, pride blazing in his eyes.

"That was amazing," he yelled over the sound of the applause, and his hands separated to take my face between them.

The world dropped away, sound reduced to a muted roar as our eyes locked. His fingers curled into my hair as I leaned in, capturing his lips in a heated, confident kiss that turned my body to rubber.

My stomach was tingly with nervousness, and my head dizzy from adrenaline. I mirrored his movement, pressing my hands to his cheeks to prolong the greedy kiss that I never wanted to end. Silas's hand on my back was the only reason I pulled away. With

my confidence at an all-time high, willing to get lost against Josh for the entire night.

"You're in public, boys." Silas cleared his throat.

I pulled back from Josh but kept my hands around his face as I looked around. His forehead pressed against my jaw as I took in everyone staring at us. My cheeks flushed with embarrassment under their attention. Josh laughed, straightened out, and took his seat as I waved and offered one more thank you before sinking into mine.

Josh's hand found mine under the table, his touch gentle and familiar. I looked over at him one more time as the next award was handed out, everyone having turned their focus back to the stage. I watched out of the corner of my eye as he turned to look at me with a smile on his face. "I'm proud of you," Josh said after a moment of staring and only loud enough for me to hear.

I was proud of both of us, tonight had the potential to be a disaster. Proud that I had found the courage to sit here next to the man I loved, to show the world that love without hiding. I found my person, and Cael was right, all that time I just wanted someone to share these moments with. Now that I had it, it felt surreal.

But I was also proud of Josh, he had every reason to fall apart the last few months. He had gone through the ringer more than once, and instead of crumbling into dust and letting the wind take him. He grew harder, he was starting to understand himself, and all of the emotions that made him up.

The Joshua Logan that had climbed onto the bus for spring camp was angry, it had been all he knew and all he wanted to know, but... The Josh that sat in front of me, smiling like an idiot under the twinkling lights, was so much more.

I wanted to kiss him again so badly that my body was leaning toward him without conscious thought. I stayed there, as close as I could, while we ate and the band started back up. Josh never complained for more space or grumbled that I needed the contact; he just ate in silence while the table talked, the awards were handed out, and the music blared.

I turned in my chair as a swarm of players flooded the dance floor—already drunk, ready to party, grinning like idiots. Josh leaned into my back, head resting on my shoulder, eyes closed as his hand found the back of my hair.

We sat like that for a long, calm moment, watching our friends dance and enjoy the night. For the first time in my entire life I felt free. There was no judgement around us and everytime my mother attempted to cross the field and speak with me, she was intercepted by a player or Coach, shutting her down with conversation or directing her attention elsewhere.

Josh huffed with pleasure every single time it happened, and the sound of his content was like a warm blanket around me.

"I'm done here. I want ice cream," he said as slower music vibrated through the stadium. "Take me back to the Nest?"

I turned to look at him, our noses brushing from how close we were. A smile crept onto my face. "The Nest?" I raised an eyebrow.

"Take me home, Tuck."

His brown eyes were soft, and the smile on his face was lazily curled to the side as he admired me in the dim lighting.

"Alright, alright—you don't have to beg," I teased, rising from my chair. I looked down at the award and then over at Silas. "Put this in the display case, it doesn't belong to me." I chucked it at him and he barely caught it.

"You're finally starting to sound like a captain." Silas nodded, cradling it in his palm.

"Yeah, well, I'm starting to feel like one," I said, slipping my hand into Josh's as he stood.

I pushed open the back door of the Nest for him, and he brushed past me into the kitchen. I tossed my jacket on the counter and popped open the freezer with my foot before reaching inside for the tub of vanilla ice cream.

Josh undid the top buttons of his dress shirt, stretching his neck as I tossed the tub onto the counter.

"I got it," he said, nudging me out of the way as I reached for the junk cupboard. I grabbed two spoons as he dumped half the container of sprinkles straight into the ice cream. I laughed while handing him a spoon. "You deserved extra today," he said with a shrug.

"Yeah, so did you," I said, stuffing a massive spoonful into my mouth.

"You know, I don't think I told you how handsome you looked tonight," Josh said, his eyes on the ice cream.

"Kind of rude of you," I hummed, taking another spoon.

"I have a reputation to uphold, Tuck." He hid his amused smile with another bite.

"God forbid someone finds out you're a massive softie for complimenting your boyfriend," I teased.

"I don't think I can spare even one after I kissed you in front of a room of teammates and strangers." He swallowed, and the corners of his lips turned upward.

"Oh, you met your quota?" I laughed, dropping the spoon in the middle of the tub and leaning back against the counter with my arms crossed.

"Yeah, once a week… if that…" Josh looked up at me, pulling the tub closer to him while he rested on his elbows.

"I hate you," I hummed.

"Do you?" Josh asked, his tone light and playful as I turned back to his treat. "Or do you just need to be on your knees to admit you don't?"

"I mean, I don't mind doing it for you," I smirked, my stomach tightening in response.

"All that attention is going to your head," he purred, and I swear my temperature rose. I could feel my ears going red and instantly hated it. "But look at that, same old Tuck." He licked his bottom lip clean of the melted vanilla ice cream.

"Doesn't help when I didn't get attention from the one person I actually wanted it from," I tried to tease, though my brain was swimming and my heart was racing. Josh set the spoon down and straightened out, his chest coming to meet my shoulder. He was so close now I could count the freckles that painted the bridge of his nose and the few golden flecks in his sable eyes.

"Is that so?" he hummed. "Because from my point of view, my attention never wavered."

I wanted to kiss him so badly that the need itched at my fingertips.

But Josh enjoyed the game more than the outcome, he always had, and if this was his foreplay, I would resist cutting it short because seeing him wound up only made me hard.

"I caught you checking Van out," I teased. "Is it a height thing or…"

"Yeah, I'm unreasonably attracted to trees," Josh smirked.

"I knew it." I smiled back at him. "It's alright, I get it. We've both seen what Mitchell is hauling around."

"So compliant, not jealous at all?" Josh whispered. "You know, there was a guy there tonight—tall, blond…" His eyes flicked to my hair, his lashes so long I could still feel the way they tickled my skin when we kissed. "Annoyingly happy with a smart mouth, I enjoy kissing and an incessant need for attention twenty-four seven."

"He sounds horrible," I said, swallowing tightly as I turned so our chests were parallel.

"The worst," Josh said in amusement.

"Can we go back to the kissing part?" I asked quietly, and he laughed. "I'd really love to hear all the ways you enjoy kissing—maybe you can show me. Or not, that's fine too…" I rambled."I mean, if you want to find that guy from the party, he sounded handsome, and I wouldn't blame you—"

"Dean, would you just..." Josh huffed, completely exasperated with my shit—but still smiling like I was his favorite person in the world. His breath was warm against my lips. His hand moved to cup my jaw, his thumb tracing my bottom lip as he brought us closer together.

"Shut up and kiss you?" I asked more softly that time.

"Shut up and kiss me," he said, his voice low and sincere.

The kiss that followed was gentle as my hand came to his face, fingers curling into the sharp ridge of his jaw and tugging him forward into me. Josh groaned softly, his other arm wrapping around me to deepen the kiss. It was surprisingly passionate—slower than he usually kissed me—and I sank into the feeling, never wanting it to end.

After a while, Josh finally broke the kiss to rest his forehead against mine, his breath shaky and shallow. "Dean," he breathed out.

"Josh." I brushed my nose against his, tempted to steal another kiss.

His hands moved to frame my face, his baseball-worn fingertips brushing over my cheeks. "If you keep doing shit like that," he paused, his voice lowering and his breath hot against my skin. "I'm going to need you to..." He sighed.

"Only if that's what you want," I said quietly, and he leaned in, capturing my lips with more urgency this time.

"It's what I need," he said, pulling away.

"Are you sure?" I asked him.

"Are you?" he asked, his voice catching. "You seem…" I watched as the nervousness bubbled violently up inside of him, and I realized that he thought I didn't want it just because I was making sure he did.

TUCKER

J osh's gaze followed mine as I drew in a nervous breath, glancing down at him, then back up to his face. I could see how scared he was but how sure he was about it, and I wasn't going to question his courage. I thought for half a second before wrapping my arms around him and lifting him around my hips.

"Tucker," his voice was low with warning as he got comfortable in my arms.

"Yes, Josh?" I started toward the stairs, not giving him a chance to change his mind. A playful smirk spread across my face, despite how serious what we were about to do really was. "If you're about to tell me to put you down, don't waste your breath."

"What exactly *are* you doing?" He swallowed tightly, his grip sliding to my hair and tugging roughly in protest.

I reached the top of the stairs and started toward our room, not stopping even as Josh glared at me. I kicked open the door and brought him inside, setting him down on the bed.

"I'm making a point," I said.

"And what point is that?" He stared up at me from the bed, leaning back on his elbows. His shirt fell open from the few un-

done buttons, and the sight of his tanned, scarred skin made my breath catch in my throat.

I leaned over him, planting my hands on either side of his head—our faces just inches apart. "The point is..." I started softly, my gaze fixated on his intensely, "that I have never wanted anything more than I want you."

Josh swallowed roughly, his throat bobbing.

"There's got to be something you've wanted more," he started to deflect with a joke, and I shut him up with a tiny, needy kiss.

"No, tough guy." I shook my head, our noses brushing from the motion. "It's you. It's just you." I leaned in and pressed my lips to his in a firm, insistent kiss that felt scolding. I held him there, not giving him time to think—just feel. I needed him present, here with me.

"Okay," he whispered, breathless. "You're being ridiculous, though."

I smiled, the corners of my lips turning upward as I admired his hazy, blown pupils and flushed cheeks. "Maybe I am," I admitted, shifting my weight so I'm hovering over him. "But you know what?"

"What?" He asked, his fingers playing with the buttons on my shirt, popping them free one at a time.

I leaned over on my knee and sat back, tearing the buttons free and chucking the shirt away, I wanted his focus on me and not the stupid buttons. I looked back at him, affectionately adorning every inch of him. "I don't care." I reached out and brushed my fingers through his hair. "I would have waited, but now that you've asked, I'm going to make sure that it's perfect."

"Stop looking at me like that." Josh's hands splayed out over my stomach as I leaned in for more contact, a smirk on his face.

"Like what?" I chuckled, my abs contracting under his gentle touch.

I leaned down, pushing against his resistance and buried my face in his neck, pressing soft kisses to the skin. My lips lingered on his pulse; it raced like a horse beneath his skin, and it only made my own heartbeat more frantic.

"Like you—" he tensed, but his hips arched upward against mine as I climbed over him and straddled his legs.

I pulled back slightly, a knowing smirk on my lips. My fingers traced down his collarbone, pushing the shirt out of my way. "Like I what?" I asked again, more persistently that time. "Like I adore you?" I hummed.

"Yeah, that," he grumbled, his hips stuttering again as my lips found his skin just below his ear.

I leaned down and kissed him—soft and sure—my hand at his jaw, guiding his gaze back to mine. "I do," I whispered. "I fucking adore you, Joshua Logan," I said.

"You say that to all your boyfriends?" Josh joked, but his voice shook, and I could see the effect it had on him.

"Shut up," I said as I brushed my fingers through his hair.

He inhaled sharply from the simple gesture, looking up at me, no doubt searching my expression for any doubt or hesitation.

"Are you sure about this?" He asked, his voice shaky.

"I'm sure... if you are," I said gently.

Josh nodded, taking a moment to calm his nerves. He looked at me with love and adoration seeping from him, and I knew in that moment that even if he never said the words out loud, he would always show me. He leaned forward, our mouths colliding in a gentle, loving kiss that I felt all the way down to my toes.

"I'm sure," he whispered against my lips.

I smiled against his mouth, stealing another from his bottom lip before helping him out of his dress pants and shirt. I undid my own belt, shucking from my pants and staring down at him as my chest rose and fell rapidly.

I had seen him without clothes before, but everything about that moment was different. That time I could touch, I could taste, I could make him mine. A low growl slipped from me as he reached forward, fingers curling into the waistband of my boxers. His eyes darkened as he pushed them down over my hips and ass, letting them fall to the floor. The look in his eyes was intense, darker than I had ever seen them, and it was enough to make my stomach clench tightly under his gaze.

Something in Josh clicked into place, it was like he went from trying to convince himself he could do it to needing it so badly that nothing else mattered. I rose, his hands shaking as he reached for me, he grabbed my hip and guided me back toward the bed gently.

"Tell me what you need," I said, lying back on the mattress.

"Control," he whispered, his voice hoarse and tight.

Was that all? I thought, looking up at him, overwhelmed with emotion. I needed to feel every inch of him, needed him to feel just how much I wanted him.

"Take it," I said, giving him permission. Anything to make him feel comfortable.

Josh let out a soft growl as he settled over me. He spread my legs with his knees, his hands roaming possessively up my chest. He nipped at my jaw, my throat and collarbone. His teeth cool against my hot skin. He was more confident than usual, and it was impossible to contain the pathetic moan that left my lips.

He stopped, his head tilting back, and a smug look appeared on his face.

"Enjoying yourself, Tuck?" He whispered, and all I could do was nod in response.

He huffed darkly, the small nod clearly breaking him a little. I was completely at his mercy, and it was intoxicating. He chuckled against my neck, kissing and biting gently as he committed every inch to memory.

"You should hear yourself." Josh smiled, his chest rising and falling. His hands traced my side, fingers ghosting over every sensitive spot and drawing more tiny sounds from my lips. "Fuck, Tuck…"

Josh's breath hitched as he listened to the small noises. It was a relief to see him enjoying himself. His teeth found my neck again, biting harder this time as his hand slid up my thigh and wrapped around me with care. His grip was careful and precise, his strokes slow as he found my ear. "Louder," he whispered, his breath fanning over my neck.

I couldn't help the next stuttering moan as he spread my legs wider with his knees and his touch became more possessive, more demanding. He stroked harder, twisting his wrist at the top and eliciting the sharpest sensation of heat in the pit of my stomach.

I pushed my head back into the pillows, arching into his touch, moaning so pathetically I should have been embarrassed, but his touch was so perfect that I knew in that moment I'd never touch myself again without thinking of him.

"Josh," I breathed out, just trying to control myself.

My heart thundered in my chest. It was clear that he felt the same as he leaned down, his mouth finding mine in a needy, claiming kiss. His fingers kept their steady pace, this thumb pressing against my head.

"Say it for me?" Josh asked. "You're mine, Tuck, only mine."

"I'm yours," I whispered—no hesitation, no fear, just truth.

He groaned softly, his fingers curling around me possessively. I was getting closer, the pressure was building, turning my body tight under his touch. I was a live wire, splintering at the core and completely at his mercy, and all he had done was touch me.

"Look at me," he demanded gently. "I want to see your face when you fall apart."

I was teetering on the edge of a full-blown meltdown as my body tightened, trembling under his careful touch. My skin was on fire and my mind was hazy with pleasure as he started to move faster. It was moments of heaving breathing and soft coaxing before I came completely undone in his hand.

Josh caught it, his fingers still gently working me through the aftershocks.. His eyes flickered down to the mess with a proud, satisfied smirk. He adjusted, inhaling me as he positioned himself above me and kissed the sweat from my jaw.

"This was supposed to be about you," I murmured, fingers threading through his hair as he eased between my legs and notched himself at my entrance.

He looked down at me, his eyes softening, his voice barely audible when he whispered. "It's about *us*, Tuck, it's always about us."

"I love you," I said, my heart beating painfully in my chest at the sight of him. He was happy and proud, every scar highlighted on his tanned, sweaty skin; Just begging to be touched.

He leaned down, pressing his forehead against mine as he pushed inside with one slow and gentle thrust. My mouth fell open from the pressure as he sank deeper, his hand squeezing my hip and the other bracing against my bicep. His brows came together with a small stuttering breath as his shaft twitched inside of me.

"I know," he whispered, his voice cracking as he held himself still and both of us adjusted.

I squeezed my eyes shut as I fought to maintain myself. I felt too full, too complete, *too fucking loved*. Josh pressed his lips to mine in a soft, gentle kiss as he started to move, his thrusts deep and purposeful.

I was prepared for the kind of sex I always had. With Cael, it was fun, quick and almost always about him. I loved him for who he was and what he needed. He was a giver, but it was always just sex. I'd braced myself for rough and mean—for the anger to bleed into his lust—but I wasn't prepared for Josh to *make love to me*. It was soft and slow. Like he wasn't fighting with himself or just bearing the pain from the contact.

He was enjoying himself.

"Dean, you *have* to look at me," he said. "I need that," his voice was breaking and it demanded my attention because even through his strength he needed my help, and that was okay.

"I'm here," I whispered. Our eyes locked—and Josh finally exhaled. "It's me." I pressed my open hand to his lower back, guiding him deeper with a guttural moan, his hips instinctively responding by pushing harder as he bottomed out against me.

His gaze seared into mine, lit with a kind of heat I'd never seen from him before. Every twitch, every moan was echoed by the sound of our skin coming together. I watched as Josh became dizzy with lust, his thighs tightening and his breaths becoming shorter. His eyes glazed over as he hit that spot again. His lips found mine as he panted my name while his entire body shook around me from the force of his release.

I brushed his sweaty hair from his face as he slowed his pace and tried to catch his breath, his cock still fluttering from his release. My chest clenched as he nuzzled into the touch, his breathing slowly returning to normal. He finally looked up at me, his eyes softer and sated. He peppered soft kisses against my jaw, his skin glowing as he drew his hips out and rolled off of me into the mattress.

Josh pressed a kiss to my lips, his hand coming up to graze my jaw with a smile on his face. "Against the wall," he ordered under his breath, and I rolled my eyes, moving over so my back was against the cold bedroom wall.

"Are you okay?" I asked him as he got settled.

"Yeah, Tuck." He put his hand on the mattress between us like he always did, palm down and fingers spread, waiting. I tucked mine in his and he looked down at it. "For once, I'm really okay."

"Good." I smiled back. "'Cause that was fucking insane, and I'm going to need you to do that again..."

Josh surged forward, catching my lips in a quick, smiling kiss. "Shut the fuck up," he said, but all I heard was compliance, and as I fell asleep with him next to me, all I felt was love.

LOGAN

"Wow, you brought me up here just to rub my nose in your generational wealth?" I asked, staring up at the massive cabin. Silas sighed.

"*Our* generational wealth, asshole."

"I'm still a Logan." I followed him around the back of the cabin.

A few weeks after the Gala, the committee came back with a decision: Ian had been suspended pending further investigations. Turned out that I wasn't the only fellow student he had assaulted. On top of another former Lorette, two girls came forward with accusations. It was enough to make the school pay attention, and whether or not they believed me didn't matter anymore. As long as he was being punished for what he had done.

I started spending Sunday with Mark after Riona suggested that I figure out who was important to me. She hadn't liked my answer at the time when Dean's name was the only thing off my list. *That's not healthy*, she scolded me on the importance of having people outside our relationship that I could rely on.

So I started bringing dinner over to Mark's, and sometimes we'd go out, sometimes even Dean would join us. And I'll admit it to her, but she was right, making an effort to keep him in my life meant something. Aside from our troubles, communicating with Silas was getting easier... Thanks to Dean, who forced the friendship at every turn, we were starting to learn that we had more in common than expected.

"Just give him a chance, he'll surprise you," Dean said this morning when Silas called asking me to drive up here with him ahead of the team. It was the Hornets family weekend, and despite not fully understanding what that term meant just yet, I'd agreed to join him for the drive.

"In name, sure. But your bank account says otherwise," he added, carrying a cardboard box under his arm as he wandered down the path.

I followed close, avoiding the branches that threatened to whip me in the face. "Did I ever tell you guys how much I fucking hate the outdoors?" I cursed as one scratched my arm in passing. Silas laughed from ahead of me but kept walking, ignoring my struggle to follow him.

"Did you bring me out here to kill me?" I asked him.

"I'd pay someone to do that. These hands are too soft and smooth," he called over his shoulder as we reached a set of stairs.

"Like father, like son," I jabbed.

"I walked into that one," he laughed.

"This place is ridiculous," I said as we reached the bottom of the stairs. The stained wooden slats continued down off the store and over the lake. Bushes of lavender covered half the hill and made the air smell sweet.

Silas walked across the dock and set the box down, kicking off his shoes and settling down on the rocking wood. He rolled up his pants and stuck his feet into the water without an invitation for me to join, but I did anyway.

"This is where we laid Lorraine Cody to rest," Silas said after what felt like an hour of silence. The trees bristled in the wind, and the soft ripples of the lake tickled the shore as the sun grew lazy in the sky.

"Cael's mom?" I asked, and Silas nodded. "She meant a lot to you guys..."

"She's the reason most of us even made it to graduation," he said, eyes fixed on the horizon. "I just thought that maybe you'd want some closure." He picked up the box and handed it to me as I sat shoulder to shoulder with him.

It was heavy and unmarked, but inside was a bag of ashes. I stared down at it, realizing that he had collected them from the morgue. They had called every day the last two weeks, but I couldn't be bothered. I was done taking care of her, and there were just so many other important issues that took priority over a box of dust.

"They called you?" I tapped the side of the box with my fingers.

"Small towns... when you didn't answer, they went for the next best thing," he said. "You can lay her to rest here if you want."

"With Cael's mom?" I scowled. I couldn't do that. Lorraine Cody was a legend at Harbor, a ghost story they told when they spoke about unconditional love. Cael talked about her like she was the winning statement in every argument that involved parents being imperfect. They all did. My mother was nothing but dust.

I looked at the box, grinding my teeth together and trying to remember even one good moment about her.

Nothing surfaced.

I never faulted her for being sick, for having her soul shattered in such an intimate way that there was never a chance of putting it back together. Over the last weeks, I had lots of time to mull over the what-ifs. What if I had gotten to her sooner? What if I had never left her? But the reality was I was never enough to fix how broken she was, I would have never been the rush of her next high, the sting of her next bottle. I had to understand that, live with it, grieve with it.

But to bury her in a place like this, with a woman held in such high regard.

It left a pit in my stomach.

"She wasn't important to anyone, Silas."

"She was important to you," Silas said, meeting my gaze. "So if you want, she has a space here where you can come see her."

"You want me to drop my mom in the lake?" I asked, masking my gratitude with confusion.

"Ew, no," Silas laughed. In a passing flicker, I saw myself in the way his jaw tightened and his brows furrowed. "I'll get a shovel and we can bury her with the lavender bushes."

"Okay, well, you made it seem like that was the plan," I scoffed, setting the box down. I stared at it for a long moment. "Thank you," I said.

"It was no trouble." Silas leaned back on his hands, the fabric of his sweater stretching over his arms and chest.

"I meant..." I ran a hand through my hair. "For everything," I corrected.

For standing up for me, for going to bat for me. For showing up just when I thought everything was slipping through my fingers. *Thank you*, I thought a little more intensely, *for fighting for me even when I didn't deserve your kindness. Even when I couldn't return it.*

I watched the realization dawn on him as he pressed his lips together and nodded, his eyes on the lake. "I know that we haven't exactly been on the same page about everything," he said, turning back to me.

"Understatement," I grumbled.

"You're harder to talk to than Arlo, for fuck's sake," Silas said, sitting up. "Listen, we're not always going to get along, more often than not we're going to butt heads. But the day I found out about you was the day you never had to do anything on your own again." The conviction in his voice was loud, sturdy and unwavering in its truth. "I'm not trying to make up for the years I missed, I'd never be able to. I'm trying to be around for your future if you're okay with that."

"Are you asking if I'm okay with you being my brother?" I asked, my brows drawing together.

"The word brother spooks you," Silas said with a small smirk. "But I guess in not so many words, yeah, I'm asking if you're alright with having an older brother."

"You're not that much older than me." I shook my head. I stared at him for a second, breathing in the fresh air of the lake. Logically I knew no matter what I said to him here he'd keep banging his head against the wall until I gave into his whole guardian bullshit. "What about…"

Dad.

I couldn't call him that without the threat of vomit.

"He'll be in county until they collect all the evidence and take it to trial, you don't have to worry about him," Silas seemed sure.

"And the rest of the Shores?" I asked nervously.

"Mom keeps sending me paint swatches for the spare room, demanding input on your favorite color," he said.

"I'm not leaving the Nest," I said instantly, the thought of sleeping away from Dean causing a deep-rooted panic I wasn't expecting.

"Hey," Silas raised a hand, "no one's asking you to, I still live at the Nest too. She just wants to give you a space of your own at the house."

"Why would she do that? I'm not even her son," I said, with a suspicious tone to my voice.

"Because you're *my* brother and we're all victims of Dad's bullshit," he said plainly. He chuckled, his head falling back between his shoulders as his eyes closed. "Grandpa is hesitant, he's still not sure about everything, but he's the oldest living wretch in Harbor, and his paranoia is fueled by dementia."

"He sounds fun," I said to lighten the mood.

"You and him would get along, he's a nasty prick," Silas laughed, a smile forming on his face.

"I like him already," I said.

We sat quietly for a bit, mostly because I wasn't sure how to answer his question and I didn't want to accidentally give him the wrong one. It wasn't that I didn't want him as a brother in some capacity, I just didn't know how to accept the offer and be a brother in return.

I opened my mouth and shut it again, my jaw tense with concern for screwing everything up, when Silas spoke again.

"You don't have to answer me, Josh," he said. "I'm not the kind of person who needs definite answers. I have been best friends with Arlo since we could bully each other. He's never been a chatty guy, but I always know when he needs me and when to give him space. I'm seasoned in the emotionally unavailable teammate."

I chuckled under my breath.

"You call, I'll be there," Silas said. "Simple as that."

"I think I can handle that," I agreed, and Silas turned to look at me again.

"Good," he hummed. "Now let's dig a hole." He pushed off the dock and started toward the other end.

I turned back to the lake for a moment, letting the colors of the sun sink in. But it wasn't my mom I was saying goodbye to as my heart started to repair itself in my chest. It was me, the old, angry me, that couldn't fathom being loved by anyone, let alone myself.

He was gone.

I looked over my shoulder to see Silas waiting at the end of the dock for me. There was still so much work to be done, my mind was still at war with its memories, but for the first time in forever,

I felt like I could win the bloody battle that I'd never asked to be a part of.

Dean had been right from the start, I was born with the capacity to love. I just kept getting in my own way. And when I finally stopped arguing with myself, it flooded in like a tidal wave and filled every dark spot left inside of me with bright white light.

Capable of being loved, and capable of loving.

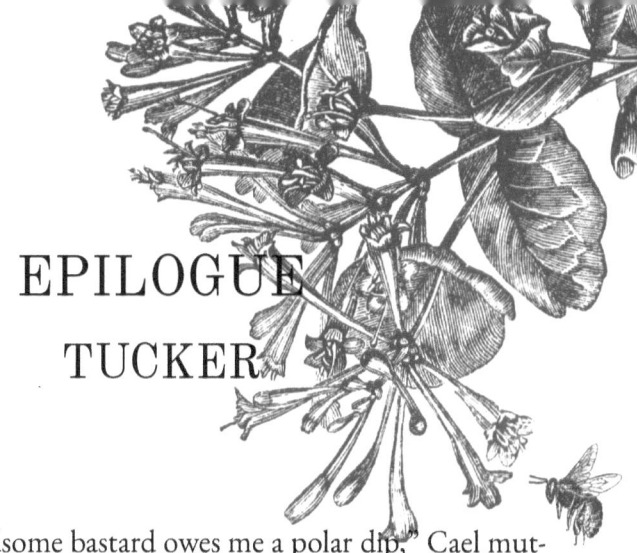

EPILOGUE
TUCKER

"That handsome bastard owes me a polar dip," Cael muttered, trailing Van down the stairs.

"He's going to flip out," I warned, looking at them.

"I'm counting on it." Cael grinned like an idiot and bolted the second his feet hit the ground.

"It's his nose that has broken." Van shrugged. "You know the rules."

"Really?" I backed away with my hands up in surrender. "Do we have to?"

"First in the lake, *Captain*." Arlo stepped off the bus in his sleeveless shirt with a wicked grin on his face.

I took another step back and he inched forward as Ella came down off the bus, watching everything transpire between us. It was a warm enough day out, and the temperature of the lake was what worried me. It was how much they let ride on the stupid superstition.

"You've been waiting a long time for this, haven't you?" I asked him, looking for my outs and backing straight into Van. His hands came down on my shoulders and gripped them tightly.

"Three. Fucking. Years," Arlo said, savoring each word like a kid on Christmas morning.

"Can't you wait just like—" I took off running in the opposite direction, but I wasn't fast enough, and Silas was waiting like they had seen my escape plan ahead of time and accounted for it.

"No running, Tucker," he warned.

"Oh come on, Doc," I lowered my voice. "I'm not above bribery?"

"Ah," Silas smirked, his eyebrow raising in amusement. "But I am, you better run..."

"You look like a terrified calf, Tucker!" Jensen laughed, standing with Todd on the deck, blocking my way into the cabin. I was being corralled like an animal.

"Oh, I see," I hollered out. "I'm too fuck big for any of you to pick up so I'm being wrangled!"

Arlo barked out a laugh. "Golden boy's not as dumb as he looks!"

"You're going in the lake, Tucker," Van said, blocking the path to the other side of the property, down by the field. "One way or another," he smiled, putting his arms over his chest.

"It'll take all five of you, and you're going to need Cael!" I challenged them.

"Three, and Cael's busy," Arlo said, coming up behind me by surprise, he hooked his arms under me and put me in a headlock. His biceps pressed against my jaw and kept me snug to his chest despite trying to muscle my way out of the hold. Arlo tutted as Van encroached and grabbed my legs, and Silas swooped in to help.

I fought them all the way down to the lake, and almost made it out of Arlo's grip, but he was too strong and fast for me to get free.

I hollered a hearty "fuck you" at all of them just before I plunged beneath the surface.

The water was colder than I expected as I pushed to the surface. My t-shirt and jeans made it hard to fight upwards, but when I broke into the sunshine, I could hear Cael and Josh arguing. Arlo was standing nearby on the dock as a bunch of the other players had jumped in to join me.

"It's the rules." Cael fought, surging forward into Josh's personal space.

That was going to end badly.

"Back the fuck up, Cody," Josh warned, his stance sturdy on the dock.

Cael shucked off his shirt, throwing it and in the motion of doing so, Josh sucker punched him in the face. Ella gasped as the sickening crunch rang out and a few of the players groaned loudly in response.

"Fuck," Cael yelled, shaking his head free of what was no doubt very loud ringing. He shoved forward, ignoring the pain and pushed Josh as hard as he could back off the dock and into the lake. "You!"

Josh resurfaced in a gasp, his dark curls sticking limp to his head and his hoodie soaked through, clinging to his muscles. Cael gasped for air, his eyes watering as he patted his nose, checking for blood.

"It's tradition," he coughed as Ella turned his face toward her, and he fought her grip for a split second. "You're a Hornet now," he barked at Josh, dripping wet and grinning.

"You broke his nose!" Ella called out.

"I've warned him before." Josh shrugged.

Cael didn't give a shit about the nose, he never had. It was just about getting Josh in the water. It was about tradition. He smiled at Ella, kissing her on the cheek. In the most dramatic fashion, he back-flipped off the dock and into the water directly in front of us.

Josh turned his face away from the splash, and I laughed.

"I hate this team," he sighed, but there was a small smile on his face that said otherwise.

"No, you don't." I squinted at him in the sun and kept treading water. "How was your drive?"

"Fine," Josh clipped. "I'm going to go change before Mark gets here, he's going to be overwhelmed by all this shit," he said before pushing to the shore as Cael broke the surface finally with a stupid grin on his face and a stream of diluted blood dripping from his nose. I didn't have a chance to argue that Mark was more excited to be included in family weekend than Josh was.

It didn't really matter, it wasn't about Mark anyway.

"One more broken nose and you'll be ugly," Josh said to him in passing, and Cael looked even more proud of himself.

"There's plenty of uses for a crooked nose," Cael called after him. "Clem doesn't mind!"

"That's disgusting," Ella laughed from the dock.

Arlo looked down at her with his arms crossed, a smile spreading across his face. "If I remember correctly, you made a new tradition last season," he said, bending down and scooping her up before she had a chance to scramble away. He held her against his chest, and she scowled back up at him.

He launched them off the dock, and before I knew it, everyone was in the water, having fun and letting loose after the hard first half of the season. I watched as Josh stopped to talk to Coach before climbing the hill to the cottage. I wish he had stayed, but for all his growth, he was still getting used to the crowd, and that was alright.

He got into the lake.

I smiled and started roughhousing with Cael as the sun hung high in the sky. That evening we all sat around the tables, eating too much food and laughing as our families started to arrive. At first, I thought that I would miss my own being there, but as seats started to fill and the rooms echoed with laughter, I realized I didn't even notice their absence.

Josh was pissed that he was losing at *Trouble* and Mark was having the time of his life strategizing with Ella.

"Isn't that cheating?" Josh scoffed, and Ella laughed with Mark.

"How exactly do you cheat at a children's game?" He asked Josh as he moved around the board.

"I don't know, but somehow you're both doing it," he grumbled.

"Someone's a poor sport," Ella giggled as Mark sent one of Josh's tokens back to the start of the game. He started to cough, bringing his handkerchief to his mouth to conceal it.

"I'll grab you some more water." I reached for his glass as I stood, narrowly missing running straight into Cosy as I turned toward the kitchen.

"Hey, golden boy." She smiled at me. "You're looking happy," she added in passing and raised her beer in my direction as she joined her brother and Zoey.

Coach stood at the counter with Mrs. Shore, who was giggling at something he said, as I approached to fill Mark's glass with more water. She took the glass from me and filled it with a bottle from the fridge as Coach stared at me.

"So who pulled the short straw and had to talk to my parents about this weekend?" I asked him as Mrs. Shore gave me the glass back.

"Oh, Silas." Coach scowled. "What I wanted to say to them was rude and without professionalism. I lack tact."

Mrs. Shore stifled another bout of laughter, and Coach looked at her over his shoulder with a smile. I watched them both interact, getting the weirdest of feelings from the situation.

"You'll need more than tact if Silas finds out whatever *this* is." I pointed between the two of them, and Coach glared at me like he might kill me if I didn't disappear faster. I put my hands in the air and started to back away slowly as Mrs. Shore turned her back to the counter with red cheeks and the hand towel against her mouth to cover her bright smile.

I was happy for Coach, I couldn't remember the last time I saw him smile. And for the first time, I understood the joy of just having someone around that made you feel like that. I hadn't skipped a meal in weeks. I still had lunch with Riona, and Josh watched my dinner schedule like a hawk. But I was feeling better and it showed.

I looked around the cabin, and a peace settled against my chest that I hadn't ever felt in my entire life because for once everything seemed to be falling into place. My eyes scanned over the room, taking in everything and letting myself be grateful for every single person.

They stopped at Cael. His hair was getting longer, and his head was propped up on Clementine's shoulder as she sat in his lap, chatting with Silas, who seemed to finally be getting back to normal despite everything going on with his dad.

Josh found me standing a few feet away from the table. "You okay?" he asked, taking the cup from me as his other hand wrapped around my waist to my back, beneath my shirt, just to feel my skin.

Cael must have felt me staring, because he looked over, smiled softly, and winked. He had been right, I'd never admit it to him because it would make him even more insufferable. But, I had gotten everything I ever wanted and didn't have to sacrifice a damn thing to get it.

"I've never been better."

Acknowledgements

This book means *so much* to me. I knew setting out that I wanted to write a book that wasn't afraid of any of the hard conversations. I wanted to create a space for Dean and Josh that made them feel safe and able to have those conversations, it was a lot of work but it was beyond worth it. This is by far the book I am the most proud of in our journey with the Hornets and I can only hope that everyone else feels the same.

The usual suspects are about to be listed so if your sick of me gushing over my perfect husband, you can skip this next part. To the man who is the first to preorder every book, who finishes his current read just to pick up my new book and who reads them all with the same passion he does every other book. Thank you. For believing in every word that I write. I literally get to follow my dreams every single fucking day because of you and you will never understand how grateful I am for you. I love you more than mario and sonic.

To my friends and family, that always have my back and prove to me that the world can be an extremely cool place. Thank you for following me through all this insane shit, for believing in me when I forget to believe in myself and for always being my number one cheerleaders. I couldn't do any of this without all your support in my day to day life.

To my sweet as sugar editor, Bec. Thank you for being my mom from across the pond, for always instilling confidence while helping me grow as writer. Each and every book is only made better because of your patience with me and my dyslexia. You never tell me I'm too much work, even when I know I am. You never get frustrated with me asking the same question over and over, even after you've giving me google docs on the subject. You just answer the question and pat me on the head for being brave enough to ask. The world needs more people like you teaching our youth because if I had a teacher like you growing up, I would literally never forget your kindness and love. Thank you, from the bottom of my heart. (You may collect your one free hug next time I see you.)

To my terror twins, MK and JJ (My Arlo and Ella.) This series has brought so many people into my life, but you two are by far some of the most supportive, encouraging, badass friends I've made. You constantly reminding me how much work I've put into this, giving me the ability to fight my imposter syndrome at every turn and reminding me that I can only get better. Your resounding faith in me literally gives me the ability to move mountains. You alpha read every book like it was your only job, you foster the best work environment and are always pushing me to be better, to keep secrets, to form characters, to write stories that connect with readers. You two are the heart and soul of these books. JJ, my sweet as sugar, *Sunday*. You have no idea what you mean to me. My sweet little anxiety dog, you're the best friend a girl could ask for even across the ocean. I am so proud of every fucking thing you do, you're so smart and brave, and so kind to everyone you meet. Everytime I turn on one direction, I get to think of you and it makes me feel a little closer. I love you so much. MK, *my Kaia*. Thank you for always being someone who recognizes exactly what I need when I need it. And for never judging my harsh attitudes or bad words. I'm so proud of your strength and your ability to be kind when all you've ever known is being strong. I didn't know I needed a friend like you until you bullied your way into my DMs on instagram and I'll be grateful everyday for you. I don't believe much in God, you know that, but if I did, I'd thank him everyday for bringing you to me.

To my Golden Girls, go listen to Back To You by DJO. I love you down to my last breath. Thank you for believing in me from day fucking one. I wouldn't be where I am, who I am and doing what I love without you.

To my beta readers, JJ, MK, Mattie, Jes, Sarah, Netty, Aiku, Hannah, Madi & Tiffani. Thank you for taking such good care of our boys. You truly were an incredible beta group to have this experience with and I hope the world loves the boys as much as you did.

To you the reader, for always picking up my books and trusting that I'll deliver. You are the backbone to my career. Thank you for all the faith you have in me.

And last but never least, to my *Twinkle Toes*, the Bucky to my Bob, the PB to my Jelly, the hesitation to my impulse, the Robin to my Steve, the Barry to my Rafe, the Mental to my breakdown.

HONEYSUCKLE

The Buck to my Bucky, the Matthew McConaughey to my Kate Hudson. The Vinnie to my Pauly D, the Reacher to my Neagly, the Heather to my Ray Hall, the sunflowers to my daisies, the ponyboy to my soda pop, the Stu to my Billy, the moon to my sun, the charlie to my dean, the Mario to my Luigi, the Keanu to my Sandra, the Mac to my cheese, The pop to my lock, the Drew to my CM, the punishment to my crime, the crime to my punishment, the Hobbs to my Shaw, The Jurassic to my Park, the orange to my apple, the gin to my juice, the Kane to my Undertaker, the Surf to my turf, the Bed to my breakfast. The salt to my pepper & finally the love to my you.

www.ingramcontent.com/pod-product-compliance
Lightning Source LLC
Chambersburg PA
CBHW020512080526
44583CB00013B/570